ROMAIN ROLLAND
AND THE POLITICS
OF INTELLECTUAL ENGAGEMENT

Romain Rolland

ROMAIN ROLLAND AND THE POLITICS OF INTELLECTUAL ENGAGEMENT

David James Fisher

University of California Press

Berkeley · Los Angeles · London

University of California Press
Berkeley and Los Angeles, California

University of California Press, Ltd.
London, England

Library of Congress Cataloging-in-Publication Data
Fisher, David James.
  Romain Rolland and the politics of intellectual
engagement / David James Fisher.
      p.   cm.
  Bibliography: p.
  Includes index.
ISBN 0-520-05787-2 (alk. paper)
    1. Rolland, Romain, 1866-1944—Political and social
views. 2. Politics in literature. 3. Politics and literature—
France. 4. France—Politics and government—20th century.
5. France—Intellectual life—20th century. I. Title.
PQ2635.05Z584 1987
848'.91209—dc19   87-24387

Printed in the United States of America
1   2   3   4   5   6   7   8   9

This book is dedicated to the memory
of my mother,
Bess Kaufman Fisher,
and to my father,
Martin Milton Fisher, M.D.

Contents

Preface

As I reflect back on this work's various incarnations, I realize that its basic thrust was toward building bridges. I was trained in modern European intellectual and cultural history at the University of Wisconsin in the middle and late 1960s and early 1970s. Madison pulsated to the politics of the American antiwar movement, the life-style experiments and rebelliousness of the counterculture, and the theoretical preoccupations of the New Left. If I never fit into any single category or grouping, perhaps a function of my nonconformism and my desire to resist excess, I was influenced deeply by all these trends. I attempted to find my own independent path and to integrate what seemed valid among all three. My studies were highlighted by an immersion in the writings of Marx, Nietzsche, Freud, and Sartre, including a study of their contemporary commentators and the movements generated in their names and against their names. My graduate education perhaps failed to professionalize me, and certainly ill-prepared me for the life of an academic historian in the "real world" of shrinking jobs, but it did teach me how to think. For that I am deeply grateful.

Cultural history appealed to me because it presented a powerful method of analysis and because it was so all-embracing. We read astounding books by incredible writers—novels, philosophical essays, poetry, and culture criticism—yet did not get bogged down in technical philosophical disputes, circular language games, and the formalism of certain schools of literary criticism. I learned to interpret texts contextually, to tease out the various meanings in terms of the time, place, and circumstances of their production. Historical consciousness was exciting in itself, working against the passionate current to be relevant, while keeping me aware of the legitimate parallels between the recent past and the present. Looking to Europe, above all to European thinkers and cultural movements, meant getting away from America and all that was shallow, conformist, mediocre, and corrupt in American politics and culture. I was self-consciously alienated and I permitted myself to follow my alienation to certain extremes.

I became fascinated with a form of cultural history that focused on intellectuals themselves. Intellectual history, conceived of as the vertical history of intellectuals, was not narrow at all, in that it touched horizontally on the convergence of cultural life with ideology, politics, and social movements. I learned from the social historians, especially those not intimidated by ideas, who did not need to posture against the so-called elitism of researching realms of high culture. I became obsessed with the problematic of the responsibility of the intellectual. I turned to French high culture because the world of the French intellectual was closely linked to sociopolitical change. Cultural creativity and innovation, I discovered, were tied to an ongoing commitment to renovate, even revolutionize, modern society, while resisting the forces of decadence and outmoded tradition. I was intrigued by the concept and contradictions of the intellectual serving as an avant-garde of a cultural revolution.

There was a subjective component to this process as well. I was searching for a figure who worked at the frontier between disciplines, between genres, between different civilizations, between writing and politics, and who reflected on the meaning of being an intellectual in the twentieth century. I found a soul mate in Romain Rolland. I subsequently discovered that I was searching for someone who epitomized integrity, an individual articulating and defending, in moments of crisis, an idealistic stance grounded in a sense of fundamental decency. This used to be called humanism, or radical humanism. I suppose I am still moved by it. Romain Rolland was simultaneously, or at least serially, a man of imagination, reason, and conscience who attempted to use his talents to create a new version of committed writing. No typology or sociology of the intellectual helped me to situate his life and work in his own day. This book contributes to the existing literature on committed intellectuals by discussing the origins, significance, and limitations of Romain Rolland's engagement.

It is a pleasure to acknowledge the climate at the University of Wisconsin in the period from 1965 to 1973. As an undergraduate and then a doctoral candidate I was first exposed to an educational atmosphere where politics and culture intersected. In Madison there was a genuine spirit of inquiry; students were encouraged to raise questions, to respect authentic learning and rigorous research. My professors were inspiring, and in studying with them I felt close to European ways of thinking. At moments they became Europe itself. In Madison a respect for theory went with a disrespect for authority; scholarly learning was valued, not as an end in itself, but only if it provided a foundation for critical thinking about oneself and the world.

This work began as a George L. Mosse doctoral thesis, and I would be delighted to have it identified with studies associated with his name. Professor Mosse is a man of vast learning, intuition, and historical probity. I first learned of Romain Rolland in his provocative lectures on modern European cultural history. Mosse focused on how persons, institutions, and cultural movements helped to shape attitudes, values, feelings, stereotypes, and myths that subsequently determined historical choices and events. His distrust of posturing and idealization went with a demythologizing form of analysis. He not only dared us to think historically and critically, but showed us how it was done. In working with Harvey Goldberg, I encountered an oratorical genius. Goldberg's history of revolution blended his photographic memory, his mastery of historical narrative and analysis, and his own admiration for courage and commitment within a left-wing heritage. Goldberg's lectures were undoubtedly the best show in town. With the History Department divided between the dominant personalities and points of view of Mosse and Goldberg, there was pressure to choose one or the other. I declined this choice and tried to incorporate the most salient features of both approaches into my own vision. It was not accidental that Goldberg's magisterial *Life of Jean Jaurès* (1962) opens with an epigraph by Romain Rolland; Romain Rolland also emerged as the "hero" of Mosse's iconoclastic *Culture of Western Europe* (1961). This Rolland book then was unconsciously and consciously conceived as a tribute to Mosse and Goldberg; it represents my own effort to bridge their distinct personalities and world views.

Working with Germaine Brée at the University of Wisconsin was a rare opportunity. Professor Brée both practiced and taught a disciplined, methodical approach to her subject, contemporary

French culture. Her perspective was marked by its balance and generosity. She was a Camusian presence for me in a Sartrean era, a presence I found refreshing and invaluable.

I should also like to mention the impact of a number of courses with Hans H. Gerth. Professor Gerth was a sociologist in the tradition of Weber and Karl Mannheim; in practice, his courses were idiosyncratic versions of cultural history, where insight mingled with compassion, encyclopedic knowledge with a zany joy of living. My one year at New York University brought me in contact with Leo Gershoy, who introduced me to the scholarship and passions generated by the French Revolution. I also attended the brilliant lectures of Frank Manuel, whose articulation of the history of ideas was enormously stimulating and artful. His attempts to integrate history and psychoanalysis still fire my imagination.

I spent two years in Paris following the completion of my thesis. I enrolled in a postdoctoral seminar at the Sixième Section of the Ecole Pratique des Hautes Etudes directed by Georges Haupt. It was called "The Geography of Marxism." Professor Haupt was a Romanian intellectual who had survived the concentration camps, been educated in the Soviet Union, and finally settled in Paris. He had lived, as well as reflected on, the history of the European midcentury. As a distinguished historian of European socialism and communism, his teaching was characterized by his intellectual curiosity, love of the archives, a capacity to ask pertinent questions, and a personal warmth and accessibility to students. Haupt loved a good discussion, appreciated ambiguity, and knew how to bring interesting people together. He died prematurely and is much missed.

Living in Paris was itself an education. Combining elements of the bohemian, left-wing intellectual, and post-1968 life-styles, those years of my life were a movable feast. How rich it was to live and work in Paris as a young man, full of hopes and dreams, despite the poverty and student status.

Over the years I have had fruitful conversations with friends and colleagues concerning the themes of this book. The following individuals were exceedingly empathic to me, especially in some of my more despairing moments. I want to thank by name Laurie Baron, Richard Levine, Robert Nye, John Cammett, and Walter Langlois. Robert Frykenberg, Joseph Elder, and Stanley Wolpert helped me with my chapter on Gandhi and India. I had a valuable correspondence with the historian of pacifism Peter Brock. William T. Starr, a Romain Rolland specialist from Northwestern University, granted an interview with me, shared his bibliography, and was receptive to my work. More recently I received astute and generous critiques of the manuscript from Sandi Cooper, David Schalk, and Robert Rosenstone. Peter Loewenberg read several seminal chapters and Robert Wohl assessed the entire text; I have profited from their suggestions, encouragement, and desire to have me submit the book to the University of California Press. Robert Wohl persuaded me that the process of writing a book was integrally connected to cutting and revising, even after the author thinks it is done. Rudolf Ekstein patiently transmitted to me the distinction between "learning for love" and the authentic "love of learning," which he possesses in large measure. Among his many virtues, he understands experientially the dilemmas of the committed European intellectual.

Alain Hénon from the University of California Press was a tactful and discerning editor, who believed in my manuscript, appreciated the importance of Romain Rolland, and urged me to make this book accessible to my readers. Uri Hertz assisted me in editing the text. Jill Sellers was a superb copyeditor. Irene Baldon was a most cooperative and competent typist. Mike Sigman, publisher of the *L.A. Weekly*, gave generously of his time and expertise to proofread the text. Mary Renaud, project editor at the University of California Press, saw the project through, and Andrew Joron prepared the index. The book is dedicated to my parents, who first took me to France in 1961, instilled a love of books in me, and taught me to treasure the liberating effects of learning and cultural activity. My wife, Karen Fund, provided me with the psychological and emotional atmosphere necessary to complete the work. Her understanding of the heart and ability to get along in the world have become a necessary balance to my own orientation toward intellectual analysis and critical dialogue. To see this book in print will make her proud, and making her proud gladdens me.

PART ONE

FIN DE SIÈCLE IDEALIST

1

The Languages of Engagement

> I shall say that a writer is engaged when he tries to achieve
> the most lucid and complete consciousness of being em-
> barked, that is, when he causes the engagement of immedi-
> ate spontaneity to advance, for himself and others, to the
> reflective.
>
> Jean-Paul Sartre, *What Is Literature?*

Nietzsche says somewhere that only that which has no history can be defined. I will offer no definition of the intellectual in this book.[1] Nor will a definition of commitment be forthcoming. Rather, I propose to investigate the evolution of intellectual engagement in the context of twentieth-century European history, focusing primarily on the period from 1919 to 1944.

Recent scholars of modern French intellectual life have emphasized its negative aspects or have categorized several aspects of the phenomenon. In *The French*, Theodore Zeldin ironically advised "how not to be intimidated by their intellectuals." Régis Debray identified three historical stages of French intellectual life marking shifts in the sociology of knowledge: university professor, modernist writer, and media celebrity. Raymond Aron focused on the alienation of French thinkers from their own social origins and political ideology. Michel Foucault designated two intellectual traditions: the "universal" and the "specific," the first incarnating a timeless, suprahistorical form of justice, mercy, and law, the second contesting power concretely, materially, and on an everyday level.[2]

In focusing on one pivotal figure, Romain Rolland (1866–1944), my study examines the ways in which he espoused and revised the notion of being a committed writer in Europe during the period between the two world wars. This intellectual portrait reflects three years of rewarding research in Paris, where I frequented libraries for sources that are not available in America. My research was highlighted by extensive visits to the Archives Romain Rolland, where I was presented, thanks to the generosity of Madame Marie Romain Rolland, with thousands of pages of unpublished letters, diary entries, manuscripts, and invaluable primary documents.

After working on this intellectual portrait for over a decade, I am convinced that one writes a biographical study out of either an intense idealization or an equally powerful need to denigrate the subject. My attitudes toward Romain Rolland have oscillated between overestimation and unfair criticism. Time, distance, self-analysis, and constructive criticisms from outsiders have helped me strike a complex balance that emphasizes tensions. My perspective clearly tilts toward a critical appreciation of Romain Rolland the man and of his dilemma in finding an engaged position pertinent to his era.

A historical and critical study of Romain Rolland's engagement should not only explore areas neglected by previous scholars but also clarify ways to make progressive intellectual commitment meaningful in society today. An analysis of Romain Rolland's itinerary of commitment may help to decipher the basic ambiguities, continuities, and discontinuities that still constitute the engaged stance.

Romain Rolland does not assume every conceivable committed stand, especially if one were to allow for a fascist form of engagement,[3] for left-wing Catholic forms,[4] for anarchist or libertarian Marxist forms,[5] or if one conceived of engagement as encompassing a broad spectrum.[6] Sartre is historically correct in relating commitment to the conflicts and strivings of the non–party-affiliated French left-wing intellectual since the time of Zola.[7] Romain Rolland was a nonconforming writer who comprehended the contradictions of bourgeois society in Europe before the Great War and who consciously worked to reshape that society in the period between the wars. He also attempted to salvage and rethink the humanist stance for the man of letters.[8] This familiar theme of the crisis of liberal Europe, particularly of its belief system and political philosophy, takes on fresh meaning if examined from the perspective of the engaged writer's role and responsibility.[9]

Methodologically, I have situated this book at the points of convergence of Romain Rolland's writings with his times, moving back and forth from text to context. The book is organized around a consecutive series of open debates, each touching on what it means to be an intellectual. To understand Romain Rolland's quarrels with his contemporaries is to penetrate the dynamics of French intellectual life. Public collisions were often accompanied by private rumination leading to new research, the modification of previous positions, and the reexamination of the intellectual's function. The polemic appears to be the crucial framework within which intellectual life takes shape. The style of French intellectual discourse is both more ideological and rhetorical than equivalent forms in English-speaking countries. In following Romain Rolland's engaged career, I have discovered that polemics have rules and parameters. There are a common idiom and common assumptions among disputants. There are established ways of disagreeing, even of excommunicating someone who errs egregiously or who commits intellectual treason.[10]

Romain Rolland wrote continuously, creating lengthy cycles of novels, plays, biographies, musical studies, and essays, while producing newspaper articles, prefaces, open appeals, protests, manifestos, and petitions. He penned one of the most consequential correspondences in modern European intellectual history, well over sixty volumes (of which twenty-five have already been published in selected editions). His letters are often eloquent and intimate. They are almost always oriented toward promoting intellectual dialogue. The public outpouring was matched by private autobiographical musings: for every four years of his life, he composed well over two thousand pages of an intimate diary, recording his impressions about people and events to use for his own projects and self-clarification.

My choice of the title *Romain Rolland and the Politics of Intellectual Engagement* implies that the writer's engagement takes place on the border between solitary, contemplative activity and sociopolitical activity. Commitment occurs at this interface, where intellectual activity impinges on the political structures and struggles of the day, and politicized action transforms the contours and choices of those living a life of the mind. Each of Romain Rolland's languages of engagement encompasses values, feelings, and metaphors that make it possible for the writer to criticize the present and the past, while affirming possibilities for the future. If the engaged stance is always on the frontier between politics and culture, if it is always ideological and utopian, it is also designed to promote deeper consciousness and reflectiveness on the part of the intellectual.

In Romain Rolland's search for a viable form of intellectual politics consistent with his world vision and yet pertinent to his times, he experimented with five discernible languages of engagement: the language of the oceanic sensibility, the language of the free mind, the language of pacifism, the language of antifascism, and the language of fellow traveling.

Chapter 2 will illustrate his oceanic sensibility. Romain Rolland's vision included a progressive, democratic political outlook and a mystical form of religious belief. The oceanic feeling turned on a metaphysical notion of the wholeness of human beings, their inherent capacity for heroism, and their ability to take an ethical stance and to establish amorous bonds with other people and the environment. He would not relinquish the oceanic feeling as circumstances changed or as he evolved new styles of commitment. Chapter 3 traces the parameters of Romain Rolland's antiwar stance from 1914 to 1919, distilled enigmatically in the slogan "Above the Battle." Chapters 4 and 5 describe his version of the free mind, a defense of critical thinking that was combined with militant internationalism, extreme individualism, a refusal to accept one unified philosophical system of thought, and a reluctance to join political parties or social movements. Chapter 6 depicts Romain Rolland's contribution as the European popularizer of Gandhi. Gandhism extended his role as antiwar dissenter during the Great War and sharpened the pacifist and anti-imperialist discourses in which he trafficked during the 1920s. Chapters 7 and 8 map out his formulation of an intellectual antifascism and his subsequent merger of antifascist resistance and an effective form of political action. Antifascism was the culmination of Romain Rolland's intellectual politics. It determined his commitments during the Popular Front era, his repudiation of pacifist theory and practice, and his growing sympathies for international communism. Chapters 9, 10, and 11 explore Romain Rolland's career as a fellow traveler, documenting his metamorphosis from critical to uncritical supporter of the Soviet Union in the 1930s.

In Romain Rolland's journey, there were no sudden, unmediated leaps forward in the articulation of the engaged stand, in the transformation of one form of engagement into another, or in the politicization of engagement. The relationship of writing to commitment was dialectical. He could be engaged and disengaged at the same time. At moments, he was almost totally disengaged. His various languages of engagement were inextricably linked to the circumstances of Europe and the world. He was committed while thinking critically about the problematic of commitment. To be engaged is not to be married to the politics of dogma or blind faith.[11] Nor does Romain Rolland's career support the theory that engaged writing debases art while offering only a superficial gain in the artist's moral stature. The politics of his intellectual life serve to raise questions about the function of culture and morality and its intersection with politics in the twentieth century.

Romain Rolland summed up his version of intellectual engagement in one brilliant dialectical phrase: "Pessimism of the intelligence, optimism of the will." My task will be to analyze and elucidate what he meant.

2

An Oceanic Sensibility

It is a feeling which he would like to call a sensation of
"eternity," a feeling of something limitless, unbounded—as
it were, "oceanic."

Freud, *Civilization and Its Discontents*

Sigmund Freud's *Civilization and Its Discontents* (1930) opens with a
comment about the role of the writer in society. In fact, Freud had
Romain Rolland specifically in mind when he reflected on the uneasiness of man in modern civilization:

> There are a few men from whom their contemporaries do not with-
> hold admiration, although their greatness rests on attributes and
> achievements which are completely foreign to the aims and ideals of
> the multitude. One might easily be inclined to suppose that it is after
> all only a minority which appreciates these great men, while the
> large majority cares nothing for them.[1]

Freud composed these lines at a midpoint in the period between
the two world wars. He presented Romain Rolland as someone
who used authentic standards of judgment and sought neither
power, position, nor money for himself. Freud pointed to the
Frenchman's unique cultural achievements as distinctly contrary to
the daily activities of the multitudes. Romain Rolland's "greatness"
consisted of mastering the process of cultural affirmation, in a context of miscomprehension, indifference, even hostility from large
sectors of the society. He participated in cultural production while
appreciating the widely divergent ideas and contrasting methods
of inquiry of others also involved in the work of civilization.[2]

For Freud, Romain Rolland's sensibility blended artistic intuition
with intellectual rigor and psychological probity with encyclopedic
erudition. His writings were pleasing and exalting to his readers.
His plays, novels, biographies, and essays were recurrent sources
of consolation. Freud recognized that Romain Rolland's idealism

was not sentimental, passive, or mystified. Nor did it spring from a naive faith in the omnipotence of ideas or in the soothing but illusory ideals of beauty. Rather, it was anchored in struggle and adversity. He had the courage of his convictions—an attribute that was especially telling when he was confronted directly or challenged in a crisis. He affirmed idealistically the possibility that love and good will could be extended to all of humanity.[3]

Freud did not customarily compose tributes to living European intellectuals. Romain Rolland received this homage precisely because he asked profound, if elusive, questions. Just as he understood the limits of available knowledge, so too did he recommend further research and reflection to expand what was knowable. Romain Rolland's living presence as a writer could not be ignored. His ideas escaped facile labels, simplistic categories, or mechanistic refutations. His audience lived with or against his perceptions, welcoming the invitation to enter into dialogue with him. To read his works was to confront one's own cultural assumptions, to rethink one's methods of analysis. Thus, Freud's deepest acknowledgment to Romain Rolland was in taking seriously his critical perspective. Many European intellectuals of the interwar period reacted as Freud did to Romain Rolland's writings, whether in the form of a public debate or in private forms of self-clarification.[4]

Freud had sent Romain Rolland a copy of *The Future of an Illusion* in 1927. Romain Rolland replied in a letter on 5 December 1927, coining the phrase "oceanic feeling" and describing it in evocative, vitalistic imagery:

> Your analysis of religions is fair. But I would have liked to see you analyze spontaneous *religious feeling* or, more exactly, religious *sensation*. . . .
> I understand by that—quite independently of all dogma, of all Credo, of every Church organization, of every Holy Book, of all hope in a personal survival, etc.—the simple and direct fact of the *sensation of the "eternal"* (which may very well not be eternal, but simply without perceptible limits, and in that way oceanic). The sensation is, as a matter of fact, subjective in character. . . .
> I, myself, am familiar with this sensation. Throughout my whole life I have never lacked it; and I have always found it a source of vital renewal. In this sense I can say that I am profoundly "religious"— without this constant state (like an underground bed of water which I feel surfacing under the bark) in any way harming my critical faculties and my freedom to exercise them—even if against the immediacy of

this internal experience. Thus I carry on simultaneously, freely and smoothly, a "religious" life (in the sense of this prolonged sensation) and a life of critical reason (which is without illusion). . . .

I add that this "oceanic" feeling has nothing to do with my personal aspirations. Personally, I aspire to eternal rest; survival has no attraction for me. But the sensation that I feel is thrust upon me as a fact. It is a *contact*.[5]

Spontaneous religious sensation, he told Freud, was a prolonged intuitive feeling of contact with immense forces. The oceanic feeling was connected with an energy that surpassed traditional categories of time, space, and causality. It transcended limits, empirical boundaries, and scientific definitions. It had nothing to do with organized religion or faith in personal salvation. It promised to be a spontaneous source of action and thought that might regenerate decadent Europe and the underdeveloped nations of the world.

The oceanic feeling was an intimate sensation of identity with one's surroundings, of sublime connection to other people, to one's entire self, to nature, and to the universe as an indivisible whole. It ended the separation of the self from the outside world and from others, and it allowed the individual to participate in higher spiritual realms. Romain Rolland attributed the sensation to a primeval force in all people, nothing less than the divine inner core of existence. It had the quality of perpetual birth; it was an idea-force that could mediate between human beings as they were and as they could become. Because the sensation fostered relatedness among individuals, it could break down the barriers of class, ethnicity, nationality, gender, culture, and generation and so lead to universal fraternity in the distant future. The oceanic sensation represented an indestructible moral aspect of humanity's spiritual nature. It was the basis of religious experience: spontaneous, innate, and omnipresent. It propelled the individual to make amorous bonds with other humans and the universe. Romain Rolland asserted that the oceanic sensation contained enormous imaginative possibilities, providing the artist with reservoirs of inspiration and unconscious sources of creativity. It unified the works of literature, music, and humanistic culture. Exploration of the oceanic feeling could lead to new forms of self-discovery and self-mastery, to the purification of ideas, and to insights about the nonrational foundations of being. Not simply a fantasy, this sort of mysticism was a form of knowledge that operated through the emotions.

Freud was thoroughly perplexed by Romain Rolland's description of the oceanic feeling. It did not neatly fit into the theoretical frame of his writings on religion. He confessed, "Your letter of December 5, 1927 containing your remarks about a feeling you describe as 'oceanic' has left me no peace."[6]

Freud nonetheless offered a compelling analysis of the oceanic sensation and a penetrating insight into Romain Rolland's sensibility. He denied the hypothesis that the oceanic feeling was at the root of religious beliefs. The oceanic sensation was rather related to a primitive, preverbal period of ego development. The sublime feeling of fusion with the universe reflected sensations of early childhood, when the infant distinguished imperfectly between the self and the external world. With the ego's boundaries blurred or incorrectly drawn, the infant experienced an indissoluble bond with his surroundings. "Our present ego-feeling is, therefore, only a shrunken residue of a much more inclusive—indeed, an all-embracing—feeling which corresponded to a more intimate bond between the ego and the world about it."[7]

Freud suggested that the oceanic sensation recurred in adult life as a wishful fantasy, reassuring the individual about such disagreeable features of existence as mortality, the harshness of everyday life, and the compromises and accommodations necessary for survival. Oceanic feelings were powerful forms of consolation for the precariousness of human existence.

In the final analysis, Freud viewed the oceanic sensation as largely a regression to a childlike state in which the subject had no conception of self as differentiated from individuals or from the environment and in which an ecstatic feeling of well-being was experienced. It was related to the function of the ego whereby the self could be extended to embrace all of the world and humanity—a "limitless narcissism." Freud rejected mystical and idealist positions as irrational retreats from external reality. From the point of view of Freud's psychology and his value system, mysticism was a mystification. He wrote to Romain Rolland:

> We seem to diverge rather far in the role we assign to intuition. Your mystics rely on it to teach them how to solve the riddle of the uni-

verse; we believe that it cannot reveal to us anything but primitive, instinctual impulses and attitudes—highly valuable for an embryology of the soul when correctly interpreted, but worthless for orientation in the alien, external world.[8]

For Romain Rolland, however, the oceanic feeling was above all a bond that had nothing to do with knowing, desiring, or even believing. The oceanic feeling expressed his deepest longing for wholeness and for visceral relationships. Harmony, synthesis, reconciliation, infinity, and unity were other words chosen to express the oceanic. He used water imagery to condense this jubilant state of well-being into one symbol. At the border between mental and emotional life, Romain Rolland's oceanic sensibility was marked by a preoccupation with the epic, the unbounded, the universal, the ethical, the life-affirming aspects of existence:

> I belong to a land of rivers. . . . Now of all rivers the most sacred is that which gushes out eternally from the depths of the soul and from its rocks and glaciers. Therein lies primeval Force and that is what I call religion. Everything belongs to this river of the Soul, flowing from the dark unplumbed reservoirs of our Being, the conscious, realized, and mastered Being. . . . From the source to the sea, from the sea to the source, everything consists of the same Energy, of the Being without beginning and without End.[9]

Romain Rolland certainly had an oceanic sensibility. Three major agencies of the oceanic sensation can be identified in his prewar writings: the populist and socialist collectivity (the people); the musical or literary genius (the hero); and the healing power of European cultural integration (Europe). Romain Rolland's earliest experiments with intellectual engagement were objectifications of the oceanic feeling.

Romain Rolland's background was Catholic, provincial, and petit bourgeois. Descended from a line of notaries, Romain Rolland was born in the small, sleepy village of Clamecy on 29 January 1866. Clamecy is in Burgundy, 150 miles southeast of Paris. The Nivernais section of the Côte d'Or is noted for gentle green rolling hills, fine vineyards and mustard fields, Romanesque cathedrals and ruins. The long history of this picturesque and sweet countryside is an endless source of local pride and tradition.[10]

Romain Rolland's provincial and lower-middle-class origins influenced his lifelong attitudes and cultural orientation. His parents were reliable and conscientious folk; like other notaries in small communities, they were respectable and conservative. Throughout his life, Romain Rolland maintained the traditional value of loyalty to family and intimate friends. He remained frugal and nonexperimental in his manner of living, considering such things as luxury, material comfort, and ostentatious display of wealth or social status superfluous. He had no use for fashion or fad. His domestic life was extremely orderly, simple, and unpretentious. Though intellectually curious, he had the French nineteenth-century reluctance to travel. From his provincial upbringing, Romain Rolland developed very mixed feelings about urban life and a deep suspicion of Paris. He preferred to live and to work in solitude, away from cities.[11] During the crucial years covered by this study—1914 to 1939—he lived primarily in French Switzerland among the mountains. Their majesty inspired wonder in him and made him aware of an alpine boundlessness, another variation on the oceanic sensation.

The German poet Rainer Maria Rilke described Romain Rolland's domestic life as "a little spinsterish (I exaggerate, but a shade in that direction) and discreetly quiet."[12] Romain Rolland remained conservative in life-style and dress (in his high white collar, dark tie, and dark suit he resembled a somber clergyman). Outwardly he radiated sobriety, earnestness, and austerity. Not a gregarious or frivolous man, he lived a reclusive existence. He was not a possessive individualist; besides his books and simple pieces of art, mostly gifts from friends or inexpensive objects he collected, he owned no elaborate furnishings. He avoided mindless amusements, trivial socializing, gossiping, pleasure seeking, and all forms of banal entertainments. He loathed café society and the salons. There was something stern, even disembodied, about Romain Rolland's mode of living, something excessive about his constant need to write and his strict puritanical morality. He had an early intensity about his mission in life, a monumental sense of personal responsibility. Creative endeavors, he insisted, required renunciation of pleasure. Character meant avoiding all forms of temptation. He developed a self-conscious and monitoring conscience that became central to his character and subsequently to his world vision.[13]

Romain Rolland's early school days at the Collège de Clamecy, from 1873 to 1880, were undistinguished. He was an emaciated and sickly looking boy, and he kept to himself. As an antidote to solitude, he fantasized and took flight from reality through reading; he was particularly drawn to Jules Verne, Gustave Armand, Chateaubriand, and Corneille.[14] He was his mother's favorite, even after the birth of his sister Madeleine in 1872. (An earlier child, also named Madeleine, was born in 1868 but died at the age of three.) Madeleine subordinated her entire life to her brother, serving him as a loyal confidant and collaborator. That service continued after his death in 1944, when Madeleine devoted herself to collecting the French writer's papers and to helping set up societies to honor his memory.[15]

Romain Rolland's mother believed in the natural genius of her son. To ensure that his gifts were properly nurtured, she concentrated on advancing his career. It would be through the French educational system that her son would make his mark, she thought. At her instigation the entire family uprooted itself from Burgundy and moved to Paris in October 1880 to allow Romain to pursue his higher education under optimal conditions and her supervision. He was fourteen years old. The move to Paris resulted in a loss of social status and income for the Rolland family. It was, moreover, disorienting psychologically to be suddenly wrenched from the security and much slower rhythm of life in the provinces.[16]

After the family settled into its Parisian apartment on the rue Monge on the Left Bank, Romain Rolland prepared for the entrance examinations to the Ecole Normale Supérieure (ENS). An omnivorous but unsystematic reader, he was more absorbed by the theater of Shakespeare and Victor Hugo and the operas of Wagner than by gaining admission to the prestigious ENS—the classical training ground for the Third Republic's intellectual and political elite. Romain Rolland failed his entrance examinations twice, in 1884 and again in 1885.[17]

From 1886 to 1889, Romain Rolland was secluded in the "cloister" of the rue d'Ulm—as he dubbed the ENS. Throughout his student days and for the duration of his life, he loathed the French university system. Professors, he once remarked, know everything but understand nothing.[18] After passing "victoriously" the *agrégation* in history, a comprehensive national examination entitling him to teach in the French secondary schools and universities, Romain Rolland's contempt brimmed over: "Oh, how I despise all these examinations!"[19]

The historical discipline required the mastery of scientific techniques of archival documentation and rigorous methods of textual criticism. Rolland learned how to place sources in their historical frameworks. From his masters at the ENS, he imbibed a conceptually precise use of language. Intellectual discipline curbed his leanings toward abstract speculation and his flights into cosmic realms. He proved to be a first-rate researcher, making important archival discoveries in the Vatican about the seventeenth-century composer Monteverdi. His principle thesis, "The Origins of Modern Lyrical Theater: History of the Opera Before Lully and Scarlatti" (1895),[20] was the first French state doctoral thesis in the area of musical history. Romain Rolland's Latin thesis was entitled "On the Decadence of Italian Painting in the Sixteenth Century."[21]

Romain Rolland regarded the six-hour defense of his doctoral thesis as a "formality." He was amused and angered by the antics of the professors on his jury: "So that's what the doctorate is! Six hours of empty chatter, of discussion which misses the point, to say nothing."[22] He developed a style of judging the judges. He regarded himself as an exception, never feeling bound to obey conformist rules and laws.

Romain Rolland was dissatisfied with his teaching career from 1895 to 1910, which he spent in Paris as a faculty member of, respectively, the ENS, the Ecole des Hautes Etudes Sociales, and the Sorbonne. Although respected by his students, he was disenchanted with professorial posturing and considered himself unsuited to the role playing, exhibitionism, theatrics, and oversimplification required of university lecturers. Pedagogy bored him. He interacted with his students in a kindly, remote, rather formal way. More important, preparing lectures and doing scholarly work were time consuming, a deflection from his grandiose literary projects. Once he was able to maintain himself as a free-lance writer, he resigned his university position and never taught again.[23] He never developed a taste for public speaking or oratory. Even at the height of his career as an engaged writer, he rarely made public appearances and he declined invitations to address rallies or large demonstrations.

Romain Rolland's fifteen-year teaching career coincided with a problematic Radical republican synthesis. He defined himself sharply in opposition to the hegemony of the Durkheimians, positivists, anticlerics, and false, sentimental idealists who pervaded the French university system in the decades before World War I. Bergson was the significant exception to these trends, and Romain Rolland, as a vitalist and a man of intuition, was always indebted to the Bergsonian tradition.[24] He distrusted the professionalization of the French academic, holding that it was self-serving and hypocritical. He always drew sharp distinctions between academics and intellectuals. If the French university served the French state as a center of ideological consensus and educational conformism, it was also marked by a conspicuous absence of critical and creative thinking. To have an authentic intellectual commitment, and certainly to be an artist, was fundamentally inconsistent with being a French academic.[25]

Despite his mordant criticism of the institution, the years at the ENS were ones of intellectual growth and self-discovery. If the *grandes écoles* were outdated and stifling, one nevertheless left them educated, able to write, to solve problems, to use logic, and to raise pertinent questions. While immersing himself in nineteenth-century Russian novels, particularly those of Dostoevsky, Turgenev, Goncharov, and above all Tolstoy, Romain Rolland conducted a probing self-analysis.[26] In 1882 he began his sixty-year habit of recording his thoughts in a personal notebook.

His earliest autobiographical renderings were of a young man "mystical and retired within himself." He suffered from recurrent bouts of "nervous and cerebral fatigue," precipitated by a constant fear of death. He was tormented by the notion that he would die prematurely, perhaps at the age of thirty-five. What Romain Rolland described as a "nihilistic crisis" was in fact a depression coinciding with his rupture with organized Catholicism. Disoriented by doubt, obsessed by feelings of his own fragility, desiring separation from and yet relationship to his parents, the adolescent Romain Rolland also experienced great pangs of conscience about breaking away from his mother's cherished beliefs. His need for distance from her may have seemed like a betrayal, generating great guilt and remorse.[27] In addition, he was haunted by a fear that a bloody war was inevitable between France and Germany, a prospect that reinforced his anxiety about death. He projected his fear onto the whole French generation born after France's defeat by Prussia in 1870. The survival of France, of Europe, of culture, all seemed bound up with Franco-German reconciliation.[28]

Romain Rolland's earliest literary creations were dramatic. From 1895 to 1904, he completed ten full-length dramas, including a trilogy called *The Tragedies of Faith*, and the first three volumes of a projected twelve-part dramatic cycle entitled *The Theater of the Revolution*. The plays inaugurated his involvement in the people's theater movement. They were also his first sustained campaign in creating an engaged form of literature, and his first experience and defeat as a committed intellectual.[29]

In May 1892, at the age of twenty-six, Romain Rolland jotted down some goals for his theater projects. He rejected the principle of art for art's sake and hoped to develop a life-affirming art that did not capitulate to the whims of the marketplace.[30] Twentieth-century art had to identify itself with, serve, and direct the people. Dramas with a popular form and content would mediate between the "imperishable" realms of art and a culture with democratic roots. The populist playwright was urged to speak in an idiom comprehensible to all classes.[31]

Romain Rolland's writings about popular theater oscillated between denunciations of anachronism in French theatrical genres and the desire to preserve what was valid in them. To an inquiry on the value of French dramatic criticism, he replied that its suppression would be useful to the public and to artists. He provocatively suggested that artistic innovation would be the result of a "social movement."[32] He sharpened his analysis of the cultural crisis of 1900 by polemicizing against the uncritical assimilation of German influences in France, particularly Wagnerian "neomysticism." A committed idealist was always more opposed to hypocritical idealism than to the reductionism of modern materialism. He condemned insincere idealistic thought, not on nationalist grounds, but rather for its rhetorical excesses and its sterile abstractions. False idealism was a poison that encouraged romantic illusions and enervated humanity. It prevented clear-sighted observation from "real facts, real feelings." Modern politics and art were linked, he proclaimed; the "sentimentalism" and "illusions" of such works as Rostand's immensely popular *Cyrano de Bergerac* benefited the same clientele—the "political and literary reaction."[33] When asked to comment on the contemporary role of the state-supported Comédie-Française Rolland stopped just short of calling for its closure.[34]

He always considered the divisions between art and society to be arbitrary. He became involved with the people's theater movement in order to combine creativity with action. As early as November 1897, he told Maurice Pottecher, the founder of the People's Theater of Bussang in the Vosges,[35] that he regretted having no influence in the literary world. If he were better known, his support of the people's theater would carry more weight. His writing would ultimately be inextricable from commitment: "I am waiting to have a more solid base to engage myself in struggle."[36] This may be the first explicit connection between intellectual activity and political commitment in modern French history. The assertive, even abrasive, style of the engaged writer was in its first utterance hesitating and ambiguous. Before struggling, he needed to construct a "solid base."

Long before he became attuned to ideological nuances, Romain Rolland was temperamentally a man of the left. However, to be a socialist with an oceanic sensitivity did not necessitate active participation in social or political struggles. When the Dreyfus Affair exploded in France with the news of another inquiry into the case in June 1897, Romain Rolland was thirty-one years old. He lived in Paris during the various stages of the crisis and he recorded these events as a continuous outburst of "frenzy" and "delirium."[37] He had inherited a genuine respect for historical continuity, the preservation of valid French republican institutions, and the democratic traditions of civil liberties. He had also inherited a petit-bourgeois fear of rapid social change and political disruption. Yet he was married to a French Jew, Clotilde Bréal, and was exposed to an articulate Dreyfusard viewpoint in his wife's family: the Bréals were prominent Parisian intellectuals and academics. Most of his literary and political friends were Dreyfusard or sympathetic to the Dreyfusards. Emotionally and ideologically, he appeared a natural recruit to the Dreyfusard cause.[38]

Nonetheless, he adopted a stance of silence and solitary distance from both camps. His detachment reinforced feelings of repulsion for both "parties." He alleged that Dreyfusards and anti-Dreyfusards were self-serving, manipulative, contemptuous of the truth, and extraordinarily violent. Withdrawal from a clear choice allowed him to maintain his "lucid reason," as he put it, an exceptional posture in a context that threatened civil war or, even worse, a "war of religion." Like many other literary figures of his generation, Romain Rolland had mixed feelings about the Jews. He recoiled against the Bréal family's insistence that he take a definite public stand on the Dreyfus case. His failure to do so exacerbated dissatisfactions in his marriage and prepared the ground for a divorce in early 1901. He indiscreetly told Lucien Herr that he refused to take a position for "Zola-Dreyfus" because of his "anti-Semitic feelings." This remark expressed a specific dissatisfaction with his wife and a temporary perception that the French Jewish community was exploiting the affair opportunistically, without a demonstrated commitment to fairness, justice, and democratic principles.[39]

He was disgusted by the virulent anti-Semitism of Drumont, the demagoguery of the right-wing press, and the militaristic excesses and authoritarianism of the anti-Dreyfusards. France, he felt, was being ripped apart by the confrontation of two forms of fanaticism. He felt threatened by the transformation of the "bestial and murderous instincts" of the multitudes into collective pathology and mass hysteria. Romain Rolland was clearly appalled by the anti-Semitic riots and violent demonstrations in the streets.[40]

He thought that the mobilization of French intellectuals on either side of the political spectrum vastly increased the climate of hatred. Writers on the left and right seemed oblivious to logic, evidence, and the complexity of the issues. They took refuge in invention or inflated verbiage; their slogans pandered to the worst prejudices of their partisans and thus intensified the confusion and spread the fear. Unable to provide direction or clarity to the masses, French intellectuals responded to the anarchic situation injudiciously, by obscuring profound principles and juggling language to the detriment of ideals. The mystique of social justice and of democratic rights for all French citizens had been twisted into vulgar politics. Romain Rolland would not let his name be exploited by either side. In an apocalyptic mood, he yearned for the intervention of a "great conscience," an impeccable man of honor, someone of the stature of Victor Hugo.[41] Yet he himself was unable to become that prophet at this historical conjunction.

Instead, he chose a position of detached neutrality and did not try to mediate between the two camps. He asserted that a disinterested critic (presumably himself) could not deny "the chaotic grandeur and benefit of the struggle." Moving from political to moral terrain, from the contemporaneous to the abstract, Romain Rolland retreated to an elevated defense of "Reason" and of "Love." He was not lured into a pragmatic political quarrel, preferring to remain remote, uninvolved, stubborn, and pure.[42]

These are sanctimonious rationalizations. Romain Rolland's perception of and reaction to the Dreyfus Affair represented a great evasion of its central issues, a failure of historical imagination. This was a regressive moment in his own emerging style of intellectual engagement. His refusal to take a position during the period 1897–1900 was a singular instance of nonengagement and retreat in a career of social and political responsibility. Neutrality contrasted vividly to his strong anti-Boulangist position during the 1880s, as a student, when he opposed the demagoguery and mass hysteria generated by that dubious military hero. In a judicious self-criticism written June 1940, Romain Rolland commented on his own political and intellectual immaturity during the Dreyfus crisis and reproved himself for having neglected a just cause.[43]

Romain Rolland's play *Les Loups* was first performed at the Théâtre de l'Oeuvre in Paris in May 1898, a climactic point in the Dreyfus Affair. The play failed to communicate his advocacy of an intermediate, conciliatory position. It reflected the ambiguous— and ultimately bankrupt—nature of his aloof stance. In a letter, he complained that "it is difficult to be independent in a milieu of fanatics."[44] That sentence condenses the dilemmas of an independent left-wing intellectual in the context of fin de siècle Paris. Standing self-consciously alone, his intention was to avoid sullying himself in the muck of mass politics and collective emotion.[45] The concept of critical support for the Dreyfusards did not pose itself as an alternative to the young idealist.

Romain Rolland's preoccupation with the French Revolution grew out of his historical training, the populism generated by the Dreyfus Affair and the international socialist movement, and his crusade to rejuvenate the French dramatic tradition. He once referred to the French Revolution as the "Iliad of the French people."[46] He aspired to become the Michelet, not the Homer, of the French theater.

To capture the panoramic sweep of the revolutionary decade, Romain Rolland conceived an epic cycle. This work, *The Theater of the Revolution*, reflected the potency of the revolutionary heritage among French intellectuals; the revolution could still raise, in a cultural framework, unresolved social and political questions unleashed a century before.[47]

Whereas important historians such as Aulard and Jaurès investigated the political and social aspects of the French Revolution in the same era, Romain Rolland focused on its cultural orientation and theory. In a daring stance for his period, he insisted that one could not dismiss the Terror as an aberrant period of revolutionary violence or unfettered tyranny. Rather, its cultural assumptions were positive and worthy of emulation.[48]

His interest in socialism arose from his fascination with history (particularly the French Revolution), collective psychology, populist aesthetics and ideology, and individual morality. As early as 1895, Romain Rolland recorded the imprint, often against his will, of socialist ideas on his consciousness. He described himself as a "Socialist of the heart" or, more paradoxically, as an "individual Socialist." Nonetheless, he was unwilling to compromise his artistic integrity and unable to accept the discipline, dogma, and political priorities of the organized socialist mass movement. This stance was complicated by his unequivocal sympathies with socialist goals and by the perception of himself as a man of the left.

Despite his knowledge of German culture, Romain Rolland, like most Frenchmen of his generation, had read neither Marx nor Engels nor the early French translations of Marxist works.[49] He had also fallen out with influential intellectual socialists, most notably with Lucien Herr, the librarian at the Ecole Normale. In a rhetorical formula that crystallized his pessimistic idealism, he prophesied that "Europe will be socialist in a hundred years, or it will not be." Typically, he considered French syndicalism a more profound expression of the popular will than parliamentary socialism. The semi-clandestine worker unions and cooperatives, with their hostility to bourgeois politics, were a "formidable subterranean movement."[50]

In the period 1900–1901, Romain Rolland aligned himself with the "extreme left" of the French Socialist Party. He attended sessions at the Chamber of Deputies both to observe and collect impressions of people's theater: "The Palais-Bourbon was then, in my sense, the first theater of Paris." His feelings toward the Socialist leader, Jean Jaurès, were highly ambivalent. The Socialist Party leadership furnished a direction and lent a "grandeur" to the cause that the rank and file lacked because of their inexperience and immaturity. Not least of all, he loathed the political enemies of the socialists in France, associating them with the obsolete tyrannies and mindless superstitions of the past.[51]

Never one to take his role lightly, he agonized over his relationship to socialism. During one of the most difficult personal crises of his life, the breakup of his marriage in 1901, Romain Rolland seriously considered affiliating with the French Socialist Party.[52] He resolved the political question by posing it in psychological and aesthetic terms and by placing the decision within a moral framework. Socialism might be a necessary ingredient in constructing a nonalienated and modern society, but the oceanic feeling was absolutely essential in maintaining a fundamental respect for individuals, artistic independence, and a personal sense of justice. His oceanic feeling made him a socialist, allowing him to feel bonded to the French working class. Most contemporary socialists resisted such a mystical construct. Detachment from mass parties allowed him to work for two parallel goals: the democratization of French culture and the ethical mission of keeping the "divine" alive in the social revolution. He would accomplish the first through the people's theater movement and the second through a voluntary collaboration with Charles Péguy's *Cahiers de la Quinzaine*.[53]

What distinguished intellectual sympathizers from socialists was merely the realm of the struggle, not the end: "We pursue an analogous task: they in politics and I in art." For Romain Rolland, Péguy's iconoclastic socialist position became both a model and an ideological alternative to membership in the Socialist Party. He assumed that he could serve as an unrelenting critic of capitalist society and bourgeois culture while simultaneously opposing Socialist abuses, sectarianism, and intolerance.

Romain Rolland's play *Le 14 juillet* expressed most comprehensively the social populism of the period. In terms of his collective portrait of the people and his insistence that the masses themselves were fully able to make their own history and forge their own destiny, it was far more advanced in conception than either *Les Loups* (1898) or *Danton* (1900).

The playwright situated the drama in Paris at the crucial moment leading to the assault on the Bastille, consciously subordinating the roles of the individual characters and spoken dialogue to the heroic actions of the masses. The people became the drama's key actors and the beneficiaries of the popular triumph at the conclusion.[54] Romain Rolland endowed the people with positive attributes in *Le 14 juillet*. They could be defiant, impetuous, enthusiastic, and fraternal. They were motivated by collective pride, self-defense, a sense of decency, and the awareness that they were participating in the first stage of a global drama of freedom. They were united in their opposition to the Old Regime. Certain members even articulated a primitive class consciousness concerning the future—specifically, a distrust of the bourgeoisie.

Romain Rolland demonstrated that the taking of the Bastille was a spontaneous outburst of moral indignation, that the people were capable of acting alone, rapidly and intelligently. The role of leaders was conspicuously small. Those who vilified the people (with such epithets as scum, rabble, trash, vermin) represented the forces of the past, who capitulated, in the end, to the people's superior idealism and force.[55]

Romain Rolland elevated the storming of the Bastille into a world-historical struggle against darkness, oppression, brute force, and centuries of inequality. The essence of the collective activity of *Le 14 juillet* was the "heroism and faith" of the masses, out of which was born modern republicanism. He significantly referred to the people as the "popular ocean"—a metaphor suggesting their fraternity, vitality, vastness, and above all their creative possibilities for making history and seizing control of their destiny. He depicted the revolutionaries of 14 July 1789 as mature activists united to fight for justice, risking disorder in their resistance to oppression. Fired by the idealism of this first act of collective emancipation, modern audiences would complete the social and political work that had been interrupted in 1794.[56]

The play concluded with a spontaneous people's festival. Revolutionary violence gave way to bacchanalian song, dance, and procession: "The general impression of the play must be that of a national popular festival where all classes feel united, and where they are not separated into this or that faction." For Romain Rolland the "conquest of freedom" in 1789 reflected the rationally purposeful and vitalistic mass behavior of the people.[57]

In the spring of 1902, after the closing of *Le 14 juillet,* Romain Rolland inaugurated a series of public lectures at the Ecole des Hautes Etudes Sociales on the history of music, including papers on popular music and music during the French Revolution.[58] The practical failures of the people's theater experiments suggested that his concept might be premature. As an idealist he worked for vast cultural undertakings without guarantee of success. If they failed, he struggled against despair, preferring to get on with his other creative endeavors. He astutely saw the philosophical and political limitations of his socially engaged experiment. Intellectuals, however déclassé, were not members of the working class, nor could they easily shed their middle-class backgrounds and ideologies.[59]

Romain Rolland emerged as the principal figure of the popular theater movement; he was its leading journalist, propagandist, drama critic, populist playwright, historian, and theoretician. His 1903 manifesto, *The People's Theater,* summed up the movement's theory and practice and proposed a strategy for qualitative forms of popular culture in France. It also demonstrated his considerable abilities as a writer of manifestos—one of the key genres of engaged literature. *The People's Theater* was the climax of populist theatrical innovation for the years 1895–1904. Subtitled an "Aesthetic Essay for a New Theater," its publication in Péguy's *Cahiers* coincided with the existence of seven apparently viable French ventures in popular theater and heightened expectations of state or municipal funding for a full-time Parisian popular theater.[60]

The essay was neither a comprehensive aesthetic system nor a blueprint for the people's theater, but it synthesized some of the significant concepts underlying the perspective of social populism. Without using Marxist vocabulary or referring to "alienation," Romain Rolland showed that the working classes were brutalized both by the appalling conditions in which they worked and by their lack of access to spiritually enriching forms of leisure and entertainment. His critique of bourgeois society emphasized the cultural fruits of economic oppression. He opposed the capitalist system for perpetuating a huge gap between the beneficiaries and nonbeneficiaries of a variegated culture.

In Romain Rolland's positive view of the popular masses, they were capable of acting reasonably and maturely, without leaders. They had often been defeated and betrayed, but they had also won important battles and were destined to be victorious in the distant future. Unlike Michelet's relatively static concept of the people as exemplars of good nature and devotion, Romain Rolland's emphasized their collective energies, virtues, and potential for intellectual and political development. He contended that the masses were corrupted by civilization, in particular by the mania for earning, consuming, and pleasure seeking in modern urban centers.[61]

The people's theater movement hoped to encourage mass participation by bringing the theater to working-class neighborhoods, drastically reducing admission prices, offering collective subscriptions, producing shows of high quality and wide variety—musical concerts as well as theater—and by converting the hall into a community center or house of culture. The people's theater, in contradistinction to the church, school, or town hall, would become the focal point of neighborhood activities. Romain Rolland urged his partisans to use modern propaganda techniques such as newspapers, posters, and public meetings to publicize the theater. He expected—but was unable to mobilize—wide-scale collective support for the people's theater from existing populist and working-class associations: unions, consumer cooperatives, socialist organizations, and the popular universities.[62]

In the distant future, Romain Rolland envisaged the people's theater as an international, secular, and humanistic art form that would contribute to the foundation of a "new Europe." However flexible its form or contemporary its content, he hoped that the people's theater would remain relatively steadfast in its educational objective—namely, to raise the consciousness of the people.[63] A disciplined effort was required to end the cultural annihilation of the people's class identity. A primitive level of class consciousness resulted from the absorption of the upwardly mobile by middle-class institutions and values and the pulverization of the lower sectors of the working class by overwork and extreme misery. Both developments were reinforced by the state's monopoly of cultural and educational life. Class pride and memory represented the people's only antidotes to collective assimilation or manipulation.

This notion of class consciousness operated outside socialist or political categories. Romain Rolland did not intend to aggravate existing social hostilities or to precipitate class revolt. On the contrary, he advocated a social-populist version of class identity that would unite the often sectarian and divided heterogeneous popular masses and simultaneously generate a healthy mental perspective among the people. Class consciousness was self-preservative, a double-edged defense against ignorance from within the laboring masses and external contamination by a corrupted bourgeois society.[64]

Romain Rolland once remarked that what interested him most profoundly about the theater was the "dramatic sense of the crowds."[65] The people's theater was merely a miniature form of collective activity. His ultimate goal was to surpass the narrow parameters of art, encompass the realm of social psychology, and create a modern collective consciousness—a new populist *mentalité*. Regular popular festivals would be the highest expression of joy, force, and intelligence. The festival would embrace all realms of civic life except commerce, narrow nationalism, and violence. The modern mass festival would approximate a new kind of communitarianism. There could be no higher tribute to the people's "sovereignty" than festivals that heightened the masses' "consciousness of their own personality."[66]

Yet there could be neither a network of people's theaters in France nor popular festivals unless there existed a highly self-conscious and revolutionary people. Sensing that the popular masses themselves had to win and experience equality, Romain Rolland placed the responsibility for the struggle for emancipation on the people. To democratize France's cultural realm, it would be necessary for the people to liberate themselves from ignorant biases and parochial dogmas as well as to radically renovate France's institutions and social values. Populism would never conquer cultural forms unless it were linked to a critical spirit.[67]

Although the people's theater movement proposed to create new forms of popular culture by and for the people, its deeper orientation was the formation of a modern cultural vanguard, consisting of artists and intellectuals who had partially transcended their middle-class origins and ideologies. In reaching out to the people and in rejecting much of what passed for bourgeois culture, these writers were acting as socially committed intellectuals. Consequently, their concept of popular culture was *engagé*, presupposing a posture of protest toward past and present forms of culture.

Romain Rolland as *engagé* social populist was caught in an ultimately tragic bind: he became a fellow traveler of socialist mass movements while refusing to make major concessions in his art, in his life-style, or in the theatrical fare offered to the people. He chose not to integrate the available entertainments and spiritual culture of the people into the artistic fabric of his plays or into his aesthetic theories. Instead, he invited the people to journey with him into the imaginary worlds of their heroic past and their dignified and festive future.

He plainly believed that populist artists and the working-class public could make this voyage together and that it would be mutually beneficial, but the travelers would not yet be equal partners. He implied that the cultural emancipation of the workers would ultimately be the work of the laboring classes themselves. But in the present, socially conscious intellectuals had to prepare the way, formulate the goals, and ignite the cultural transformation.

Throughout his life Romain Rolland searched for exemplary guides. He was an inveterate hero worshiper. He was drawn to male, non-French, artistic heroes of earlier ages. His faith in genius merged with his artistic romanticism and his oceanic religiosity. Great men were vast, uncharted continents. To explore their lives and works was to come into intimate contact with mysterious forces of energy, strength, and autonomy. To know an authentic hero, even vicariously, was to come into contact with a boundless source of vitality. Romain Rolland retained a sense of wonder while contemplating these great men and their masterpieces. If we remember that his own father had been relatively ineffectual in life, we can speculate that his idealization of heroes was a search for a surrogate father; it may have also been a protection against his own passivity, femininity, fragile and sickly nature, and powerful ties to his mother. Identification with a hero was a constructive way out of his frequent state of dejection. Reflecting on the pasts of great artists provided solace for his inferiority feelings and compensation for melancholia and social isolation. Meditation on the hero became a positive outlet to channel his social and psychological resentments. He mythologized great personalities into sources of spiritual nourishment, godlike presences, or archetypal forces of nature. As he wrote to Henrik Ibsen in 1894:

> Great men are trees with profound roots; around them the wind blows the rest of men like dead leaves. In the disarray of the human consciousness at present, in the dizziness of thought that oscillates from frivolous skepticism to insipid mysticism, it is a salutary spectacle that the view of a Man, of a powerful being who, equal to a force of nature, carries in himself his law and his necessity of being. That is a comfort.[68]

Geniuses radiated strength, will power, and single-mindedness. Their intransigence contrasted with the mediocrity of spirit and commercialism so noticeable in everyday life, including the compromises of cultural life. The feeling of contact with the artist-genius revitalized him. His identification with these figures fostered the fantasy that he was not alone in his "sorrow and grief."[69]

Romain Rolland composed five pre–World War I heroic biographies—*Millet* (1902), *Vie de Beethoven* (1903), *Vie de Michel-Ange* (1906), *Handel* (1910), and *Vie de Tolstoï* (1911). He attempted to make "these great souls" known to the general public. His aim: to allow the "common man" a glimpse of the "Eternal."[70] Through his biographical monographs, the young French writer hoped to transfer the psychic energies of the genius to the public. This transfer would have regenerative power, rescuing the educated masses from torpor, mediocrity, and spiritual impoverishment. In a world without security or the foundations of established religion, the artist symbolized humanity's divine possibilities and capacity to achieve human splendor. This "great man" theory of history posited that the creative genius had sacred value.

In the *Vie de Beethoven*, Romain Rolland perfected the genre of the popular biographical essay. It was part of a larger series of biographies entitled *Lives of Illustrious Men*. Intoxicated by his first literary success (he was thirty-seven years old when the book appeared), he imagined himself a "new Plutarch," who would produce unending cycles of modern life histories documenting courage.[71]

The *Vie de Beethoven* was a labor of love to repay a personal debt to the composer. Because the text was written during the rupture of his nine-year marriage, it had a strong subjective component, a transfer of amorous energy from his wife to the glory of Beethoven. Evocative portraiture and deftly selected biographical data were imaginatively woven into a historical setting. The text was unencumbered by academic scholarship or the technical jargon of musical treatises. To make artistic personalities and their oeuvres comprehensible to the population, Romain Rolland wrote accurate, linear, immensely readable historical narratives that resonated with the public without pandering to philistine taste and without sensationalizing the subject matter. By casting Beethoven as a neoromantic hero, and by constructing a "Beethovian religion," he made the German composer's integrity and achievement palpable to a French public that had developed an antipathy to all things German. The author had mastered the French genre of *haute vulgarisation* in a work that was neither high nor vulgar. He popularized without trivializing.[72]

Ultimately, Romain Rolland conceived of the hero's life as a perpetual combat against internal enemies. Since the essential terrain of struggle was psychological, the battles were waged in solitude. Beethoven's renunciation of society and physical pleasure was "for the good of universal humanity and dedicated to the unhappy."[73] By inference, the artist elevated and consoled the public, contributing to the social community and to posterity through his works. This meant, paradoxically, that his excessive self-absorption resembled true generosity of the spirit. Artistic heroism, however, was incomplete unless coupled with "goodness of heart" and a genuine commitment to the categorical imperative. Romain Rolland rejected the Nietzschean version of self-overcoming as contemptuous of the masses, glorifying power, and lacking in authentic empathy with the dominated in society. Beethoven's heroism was triumphant because of its resigned conquest of despair and its more democratic concept of joy. He accepted the tragic vision that there could be neither character, faith, nor beauty unless the artist suffered in life. Miserable, in ill health, painfully aware of his own martyrdom, Beethoven was vulnerable yet willing to fight against his "physical and

moral grief." Overcoming deafness became a metaphor for transforming physical deficiencies into lasting cultural achievement and
transcendence. The persistent antagonism between the individual
artist and his social existence, his heroism and his outcast situation,
gives rise to enduring art.[74]

Romain Rolland's *Vie de Tolstoï* was written on the occasion of
the Russian writer's death. In it he paid tribute to Tolstoy's seminal
influence as an artist, critic, and above all as an intellectual and
moral model.[75] Tolstoy was the key point of reference in his early
literary endeavors and his cultural-political interrogations. The Tolstoy monograph began a pattern of looking to the East for cultural
stimulation. Rolland felt linked to Tolstoy by temperament and by
shared common values: both implacably opposed the brutality,
shallowness, and hypocrisy that passed for civilized behavior; both
desired to have their art reach across class barriers and national
lines; both sought an art form that would entertain, enlighten, and
embrace all literate persons.[76]

Impelled to communicate directly with living cultural heroes,
young Romain Rolland had written Tolstoy inquiring about the
Russian's repudiation of modern art. In his letter of April 1887, the
twenty-one-year-old Frenchman wondered if Tolstoy had not exaggerated the intrinsic immorality of art, while overestimating the
cleansing power of manual labor and of living close to the earth.
"Don't you think," he asked Tolstoy, "that art could have an immense role to play, even in your doctrine, among those people
who die from the complexity of their feelings and from the excess
of their civilization?"[77]

Much to Romain Rolland's delight, Tolstoy answered his covert
plea for help with a letter in his own hand, in French, dated 4
October 1887. The substance of the letter was less important than
the fraternal tone of the response, and the fact that the elder writer
had taken the trouble to reply. "Dear brother! I received your first
letter. It touched my heart. I read it with tears in my eyes."[78]

Although he revered the Russian writer, Romain Rolland was
not uncritical. He found Tolstoy's advice "truthful and helpful" but
rejected his fuzzy conceptual framework and the moral austerity of
his propositions. Tolstoy, he felt, was inclined to impose his moral
gospel on his artistic works. Romain Rolland was learning that he

could not depend on others, heroes included, in the project of developing an authentic world vision and a personal voice.[79]

In discussing Tolstoy's writing style, Romain Rolland revealed his own concept of artistic creation. He called Tolstoy the "least literary of writers," who subordinated stylistic considerations to delineations of character and ideas, without forgetting the symphonic complexity of social existence.

Tolstoy's art brought together "absolute sincerity, pitiless insight, and independence of judgment."[80] For the remainder of his life, Romain Rolland deified critical and unfettered thinking, which he linked to individual liberty and the freedom to conduct research and to publish results without external censorship. The process of discovering and uttering the truth revealed that one system of thought, no matter how scientific or rigorous, could never fully encompass the truth. He remained an iconoclastic pluralist, bound by no single school or definitive method. He had no wish to be perceived as a master thinker with a cult of disciples.[81]

Romain Rolland connected Tolstoy's anti-institutional religiosity and his advocacy of the Golden Rule to his protest against warfare and his notion of a Christian nonresistance to evil. Tolstoy had set the precedent of a major writer's publicly declaring his opposition to war.[82] Romain Rolland's Tolstoyism was a crucial point of departure for his own brand of antiwar dissent, for his elaboration of a pacifist political philosophy after 1919, and for his receptivity to Gandhism in the early 1920s. He astutely assessed Tolstoy as a "revolutionary conservative," in that his concept of nonobedience to the state challenged established institutions such as the czarist state hierarchy, the army, and the church. Tolstoy's propaganda for conscientious objection and his renunciation of wealth were radical negations in the Russian context. He was conservative in his lack of sympathy for socialist revolutionaries or even for democratic radicals. Tolstoy rallied to Russian dissidents only when they were savagely repressed. Above all, Tolstoy claimed that economic materialism addressed itself to people's "lowest needs," thus neglecting their spiritual needs, conscience, and feeling for human fellowship. Tolstoy's preoccupation with the tension between moral revolution and social revolution was to pervade Romain Rolland's itinerary as an engaged intellectual.[83]

After Tolstoy's death, Romain Rolland imagined that the torch had been passed on to him, both as a writer and as a responsible intellectual with an international reputation. He appointed himself a European Tolstoy, attempting to destroy idols and to see reality with merciless insight while remaining a "dreamer and lover of mankind."[84] Romain Rolland modernized the Tolstoyan temperament, while maintaining Tolstoy's fundamental values, sense of mission, openness, and largeness of view.

Charles Péguy, in the Parisian context, was another prototype for the responsible intellectual, particularly during the years 1900–1905. In the young Péguy, Romain Rolland found a man of passionate and implacable idealism, an arresting blend of conscience and integrity. Péguy had character, a commitment to personal honor, in addition to a philosopher's concern for the truth. As early as 1900, Romain Rolland was drawn to Péguy's *Cahiers de la Quinzaine.* He associated Péguy's "cause" with a secular crusade against the intellectual terrorism of many Parisian cultural chapels. Writing for the *Cahiers* meant working for cultural renewal, and he dedicated himself to it fervently and without compromising his pessimistic idealism: "[Péguy] has undertaken to purify the public sense, to found a social Revolution on a reform of customs and of intelligence—like Mazzini and the great Revolutionaries."[85]

Romain Rolland contributed to the *Cahiers* because of the wide latitude and eclectic spirit with which Péguy infused his review. Affiliation meant neither joining a hermetically sealed coterie nor identifying with a narrow literary sect or evanescent but flashy movement so typical of Parisian avant-gardes. The *Cahiers* published original literary endeavors, opened its pages to young writers, and combined thought-provoking essays with muckraking journalism. The review cut across several disciplines and blurred the boundary between politics and culture. Its politics were left-wing but independent, and it eschewed all forms of dogma, including that of the left. It served as an outlet for many of Rolland's creations, including the cycle of French revolutionary plays, his early biographies, the first edition of the novel cycle *Jean-Christophe,* and his essay-manifesto *The People's Theater.* The *Cahiers* also protected the puritanical Romain Rolland from the whims of fashion, commercialism, irreverence, and the sectarian spirit so rampant in Parisian intellectual circles during the "Banquet Years." Most of the subscribers to the

Cahiers, estimated at about twelve hundred, were tolerant and independent in their thinking. Many were school teachers and members of the liberal professions. Writing for Péguy's *Cahiers* would never lead to co-optation or celebrity status. Editor Péguy did not interfere with his need for solitude. Although the two never developed an intimate friendship, Péguy had high esteem for Romain Rolland, who repaid his debt to Péguy late in life with a two-volume biography of his former collaborator, editor, and mentor. From Péguy, Romain Rolland gained an intuitive grasp of the frontier where politics and culture converged. He was destined to live on that frontier.[86]

Péguy was committed to preserving an integrated view of twentieth-century man. Romain Rolland admired the younger Péguy's courageous campaign in favor of Dreyfus and his audacious break with the opportunistic French Socialist Party, in which he retained his socialist faith. Romain Rolland depicted Péguy as a tough and stubborn man, an *original*, totally escaping classification. Péguy did not mute his idealism by abdicating personal responsibility or refusing to tackle controversial or elusive issues. For both Péguy and Romain Rolland, politics and mysticism were compatible: they could be fused. Romain Rolland fundamentally agreed with Péguy's motto for the *Cahiers*, a felicitous mélange of socialist politics and mysticism: "The social Revolution will be moral, or it will not be." He was proud to be affiliated with Péguy's review. "It is therefore an elite, less intellectual than moral, and an avant-garde of Society on the march toward new forms of civilization."[87]

Romain Rolland's prewar fictional masterpiece, *Jean-Christophe*, was written between 1903 and 1912. It was serialized in the *Cahiers de la Quinzaine* and concurrently released in ten volumes by the Parisian publishing house of Ollendorff. He wrote most of the novel while living alone, deeply isolated, in his Left Bank apartment at 162, boulevard du Montparnasse. The process of writing was his only deliverance in a joyless and friendless period. In the novel, he expressed his extreme ambivalence toward fin de siècle European culture. One of the longest bildungsromans in the corpus of European literature (the definitive French edition is 1,600 pages; the English translation 1,580), *Jean-Christophe* traced the birth, development, conflicts, creative resolution, maturation, and death of its composer hero.[88]

For the intellectual historian, *Jean-Christophe* can be considered the great European novel of the prewar epoch. Its thesis was that French-German reconciliation was crucial both for the survival and renewal of European culture and for the foundation of a stable European peace. Romain Rolland conceptualized France and Germany as two powerful forces living on opposite sides of a river. The problematic of the novel was how to wed the two sides. Music was to bridge the river, enabling each culture to complete the other. If Europeans realized they could choose to integrate, rather than to select one side and annihilate the other, the resulting cultural production might be abundant. France and Germany were two civilizations that mingled in the same stream. Union would permit each nation to maintain its balance and political equilibrium while absorbing foreign energies and perspectives. Cultural interpenetration was vastly preferable to military preparations and imperialistic rivalries. It was music, much more than literature, that broke down national barriers and restored health, joy, solace, strength, and hope to humanity.[89]

The hero Christophe composed music embracing the national characters of both France and Germany. Romain Rolland made Christophe a German, in order to explore French attitudes and values from an ostensibly non-French orientation. Christophe's music mediated between both civilizations by discounting the barriers to interpenetration as artificial and by emphasizing the basic similarities between the two cultures: common ideas, common tasks, and a common moral frontier. This blatantly idealistic novel of European harmony posed two frightening, realistic warnings: If the French and the Germans did not collaborate on the great projects of the present and the future, culture might be severely ruptured or even destroyed. If they failed to establish a rapprochement, world war might be unleashed.[90]

As an artist in the Beethovian lineage, Christophe expressed his world vision through the universal art form of music. Living in exile in Paris freed him from the oppressive nature of German family life and from Germany's hierarchical, authoritarian cultural and social life. In Paris, he remained distinctly German in appearance, accent, taste, and sensibility, always an outsider to the mainstream of French artistic life. He totally rejected the basic tenets and practices of modernism as cowardly, decadent, immoral, and overly aesthetic. He resisted the infighting, snobbishness, ideological polarities, and intellectual terrorism of the Parisian avant-garde. Romain Rolland depicted Christophe as a man of force and vitality. Yet he was no overman in the sense of the Nietzschean warrior. He was a gentle Nietzschean who struggled to overcome internal interferences in creative expression.[91]

Christophe's art transcended spatial, temporal, and institutional boundaries. He intuitively searched for the totality, motivated by an ethical imperative "to see, to know, to feel, to love, and to grasp everything." The highest freedom was the freedom to create, and to create he was obliged to spend most of his time in solitude. Foreshadowing the extended exile of the novelist, Christophe moved to Switzerland in order "to stand above Europe." In Switzerland, he breathed better, remained in contact with elemental forces, and experimented with a model for a potentially united Europe. The mature Christophe became an incarnation of a "moral force," his music "irradiated life" and set a lofty example for others to emulate. Christophe's art was truly universal: it aimed for communion with other men; its energies were all-embracing.[92]

Romain Rolland split his voice in the novel between two central characters: Christophe and Olivier Jeannin. Olivier not only became Christophe's loyal and devoted comrade but also represented the fin de siècle French idealist intellectual. Whereas Christophe was candid and unsophisticated, Olivier was cosmopolitan to the core and excessively complicated. The novel clearly helped to popularize the word "intellectual." It also evoked the internal ambiguities of French intellectual life. Olivier came to stand for authentic, as opposed to dilettantish, forms of intellectuality. Through Olivier, the novelist launched a comprehensive critique of the Parisian cultural marketplace (*La Foire sur la place*). What set the retiring and sensitive Olivier apart from his peers was his psychological understanding and his absorption of a vast European culture informed by non-French sources. His form of intellectual inquiry was sincerely internationalist. He was frequently "overwhelmed" by examples of injustice and suffered inordinately for the outcast and humiliated in society. Having known personal injury and having been victimized himself, he expressed "generous sympathy" for others less fortunate or less verbal than himself. Yet there was something desiccated, remote, and aristocratic about him. After years of study, Olivier's analytical detachment, his "lofty outlook," and his ability to judge people without illusions made him inaccessible. Like Christophe, he lived a solitary existence, removed from any viable form of collective association. Having acquired his individualism after great internal struggle, Olivier hated, perhaps feared, the "herd" mentality in intellectual groups or political movements.[93]

Because of his precarious mental stability, obsessive ruminations, skepticism, and self-doubt, Olivier never linked thought to practice. He became the paradigm for Romain Rolland's free spirit, the intellectual who liberated himself from religious, political, national, or artistic dogma. He emancipated himself from the parochial side of Parisian intellectual life but was still catalyzed by the passionate debates and the enthralling life of the mind in that great city. Olivier's strength and health were cerebral. He was a Parisian intellectual who "abhorred" Parisian intellectual coteries while speaking their idiom. He "dreaded" militant political action, yet ironically he died fighting for the French working class on the barricades in the streets of Paris. As an intellectual freed from the parochialism of political parties, academies, organized churches, and competing intellectual cliques, Olivier refused to sanction any expression of nationalist hatred, just as he opposed social, ethnic, or class injustice. He remained "just to his enemies," hoping to preserve "the clarity of his vision" in the midst of violence and chaos. Realizing that Europe hovered on the brink of social revolution or world war, Olivier was intransigent on basic moral questions. If world war were to be declared, he would have refused to participate in it or to legitimize it in any way. Anticipating the stance of the novelist himself, Olivier would call for "love and understanding" if hostilities were unleashed, while attempting to keep his "reason uncontaminated."[94]

Jean-Christophe celebrated the grandiose ethical and social possibilities of art. It argued that the idea of moral frontiers between nations was shallow and absurd. It attempted to fill the void left by the death of God and the decline of organized religion in the late nineteenth century. The Beethovian cult of heroism was offered as an alternative to the neurasthenia and doubt saturating European art and thought. The authentic culture hero could serve as an ideal. Truly epic literature had to be addressed to all people in their own languages. Romain Rolland contributed *Jean-Christophe* to the healing of European fragmentation and the gap opened by the decline in spirituality and loss of faith in human transcendence. *Jean-Christophe* was designed to be "a common book for all of Europe." The responsible artist did not address a tiny, privileged minority of refined sensibilities, but endeavored "to think and to write for all."[95]

The enormous popularity of *Jean-Christophe* decisively changed Romain Rolland's life. The novel developed an enthusiastic cult of readers, inspired by the characters, the story, and the thoughtful and effusive idealism. Perhaps up until 1945, a multitude of readers regarded *Jean-Christophe* as a trusted companion and source of spiritual nourishment. Parents passed the book on to their children. As the author of a classic recognized in his own day, Rolland was no longer an obscure teacher of the history of music at the Sorbonne or a reclusive Left Bank artist. The success of *Jean-Christophe*, both in France and in the many countries in which it was translated, made Romain Rolland financially independent for the remainder of his life. He could now write what he wanted and publish his writings almost where he pleased. He had been on leave from the Sorbonne since 1910; he officially resigned in July 1912. He won the prestigious Grand Prix de Littérature from the Académie Française on 9 June 1913. The French have a long tradition of honoring their novelists. Characteristically, Romain Rolland denigrated the literary award: "The hell with all these prizes!" He and his work became sources of discussion and controversy in the French literary community. His name and face became familiar to the French public. The entire novel was widely translated. For the most part, it was extensively and favorably reviewed, although literary modernists found it hopelessly anachronistic and nineteenth-century in form.[96] Romain Rolland's reputation was that of a Frenchman who had humanitarian sympathies, internationalist perspectives, and an empathic but critical understanding of Germany.

Having earned the solid base of authority and credibility lacking in his campaign for the French people's theater, he was now prepared to engage himself in intellectual and political battles.

3

Above the Battle

For Peace is not mere absence of war, but it is a virtue that
springs from force of character.
                                    Spinoza, *A Political Treatise*

Romain Rolland was disengaged during the Dreyfus Affair and
partially engaged during the campaign for a people's theater. His
activities during the Great War marked another stage of his entrance into the political arena.

Just before the declaration of war, Romain Rolland was in transition. He conceived of an alliance of international writers, clustered
around a review, that would lead a "crusade against worm-eaten
literary, moral, and social dogmas, against the lies of our nations."
Intellectual collaboration would also have a positive thrust: "These
small fraternal armies would struggle for a renewal of life and of
thought."[1] Against the racial and militaristic excesses of those with
fixed nationalist ideas, exemplified by Action Française writers
Bourget, Barrès, Maurras, Bazin, and Prévost, he called for a fusion
of idealistic thought and realistic action. His engagement was predicated on both a critical analysis of the present and a capacity to act.[2]

Romain Rolland increasingly disassociated himself from Péguy's
brand of nationalism and Catholic revival. Péguy could no longer
be counted on to give direction to an international journal. "I do
not have worse enemies than the new friends of Péguy." To recruit
intellectuals, the crucial criterion of the review must be that it enlarged freedom of the mind. One had to be strict about membership in such an association of free thinkers. Although he appreciated André Gide's talent, Romain Rolland would exclude him.
Gide was a great dilettante; his intelligence was primarily "critical,
contemplative, and static."[3]

Romain Rolland had brief ties with the Italian journal *La Voce*,
published in Florence under the direction of Giuseppe Prezzolini,

Gaetano Salvemini, and Giovanni Papini. Unlike most French writers of his generation, he was encouraged by the new developments in Italian cultural life. His two-year fellowship in Rome, 1889–1891, taught him to love the Italian people, landscape, language, and artistic and musical sensibility. *La Voce* articulated a courageous and vital pan-European vision that incisively addressed social questions and positioned itself at the interface of writing and politics.[4]

On the eve of World War I, Romain Rolland seriously entertained the idea of inaugurating an international review. He hoped to unite writers of distinction from all Europe around a cultural conception of European community. He was in direct contact with such figures as Léon Bazalgette, H. G. Wells, Rainer Maria Rilke, Stefan Zweig, Jean-Richard Bloch, and Emile Verhaeren.[5] The war temporarily postponed his dream of intellectual fraternity; it did not entirely shatter it. After the war, in 1919, and again in the 1930s, he returned to his project of recruiting an international elite of principled, non–party-affiliated thinkers who would stand for independence and mutual understanding between cultures. Romain Rolland's oceanic idea of intellectual fraternity—his belief that united voices swayed public opinion more than solitary voices—predated the war. It became a leitmotiv in his career as an engaged writer.

When the Great War was declared on 3 August 1914, Romain Rolland was forty-eight, too old to be conscripted. He remained in self-imposed exile in Switzerland throughout the war years. Though this is the most well-documented period of the French writer's life, it is still subject to a variety of interpretations. The meaning of his activities has been obscured by the ultimately ambiguous connotation of the words "Above the Battle" (Au-dessus de la mêlée), the title of Romain Rolland's best-known essay and subsequently of a collection of writings from the period 1914–1915. From the summer of 1914 until his death, his name and intellectual politics would be associated with that phrase.[6]

Above the Battle contained sixteen articles, primarily open letters, essays, appeals, manifestos, literary criticism, and political journalism. These pieces addressed the loss of good sense by all the participants in the mass slaughter of World War I. Despite the detachment, neutrality, superiority, and distance implied by the word "above," Romain Rolland was profoundly touched by all aspects of the war. The sources dispel any doubt about his thoughtful, subjective involvement. Nothing could be further from the oceanic feeling than the reality of total war. He lamented the destruction of reason and the abandonment of critical judgment, which were early and serious casualties. If Europe were to avoid further holocausts, reasoned judgment had to be restored. To begin that process a few isolated voices must be heard.[7]

For Romain Rolland, European war meant civil war, the unnecessary but deadly duel between misguided brothers, exacerbated by the deployment of new scientific and technological weaponry. In the international as well as the French context, where force confronted force on the most primitive level imaginable, his situation as a writer became anomalous. He departed from the almost universal capitulation of writers, philosophers, scientists, and academics to the war effort, regardless of their prewar ideological positions or of nationality, regionality, class, generation, or gender. Everyone wanted war and rallied to the war effort in the first months of mobilization. This bellicosity was strikingly evident among socialists, syndicalists, pacifists, and religious leaders, who had been vociferously antiwar in peacetime. During the war itself, very few were heard either to oppose it or to raise questions about it.[8]

Above the Battle was Romain Rolland's refusal to bend to the considerable pressures of the historical moment, including the mass uncritical support for the "Sacred Union." He challenged the sacredness of the Sacred Union, as well as the notion of unity in war. His call for the restoration of sanity on all sides of the trenches disrupted the unprecedented unanimity in favor of war. By lifting the veil of consensus, he provided Europeans with another perspective on these events besides nationalism—an example, if only moral at first, of how to oppose the war colossus. He argued that a mindless and pretentious collusion with the war effort intensified the catastrophe. The virulent intellectual counteroffensive clearly showed that his writings touched a sensitive nerve.[9]

Romain Rolland's war criticism derived not from socioeconomic analysis but from the vantage point of the indignant moralist. His writings unmasked the ways intellectuals enlisted their learning and their imaginations in the effort to legitimize the war. He spoke out against the war precisely because of the unexpected, near-total collapse of movements organized to prevent wars or at least to keep war circumscribed. He was not surprised by institutional Christianity's direct sponsorship of the military effort, but he was perplexed by the rapid and almost complete breakdown of the Socialist International. He was shaken by the assassination of Jean Jaurès, a monumental figure in the Second International, who might have become an antiwar leader and spokesman.[10] He refused to allow his intelligence and oceanic sensibility to be mobilized in 1914 or in the years thereafter.[11]

He was sensitive to the scope of destruction but did not forget the smaller tragedies in the lives of the soldiers fighting and dying on their respective fronts. The incantatory opening of "Above the Battle" conveyed a tender sorrow for the young shedding their blood generously but uselessly:

> Come let us make a stand! Can we not resist this contagion, whatever its nature and virulence be—whether moral epidemic or cosmic force? Do we not fight against the plague, and struggle even to repair the disaster caused by an earthquake? . . . No! Love of my country does not demand that I hate and kill those noble and faithful souls who also love theirs, but rather that I should honor them and seek to unite with them and for our common good.[12]

There was an apparent paradox in his calling for temperateness and compassion in the midst of the most furious and barbaric of passions. Romain Rolland's tactful moderation required that he control his own feelings of moral repugnance for the war. In a context marked by frenetic expressions of hatred, nationalistic diatribes, and racial excesses, his writings suggested that love, cooperation, and empathic understanding were possibilities unextinguished by the hostilities. His self-restraint and faith in the unity of mankind stood in stark contrast to the verbiage extolling the inherent superiority of one civilization over another. He appealed to intellectuals, whose learning and critical method should have made them immune to nationalism and militarism, but who had been the most easily swept away by xenophobia and primal imperialistic emotions. He had no illusions about his ability to convince others, break through the darkness of censorship, or calm the ubiquitous ferocity of murderous rage: "I know that such thoughts have little chance of being heard today."[13]

In attacking the unanimity of war support, Romain Rolland recognized World War I's modernity. A prolonged and savage war required a well-orchestrated ideological reinforcement; to maintain national unity, high morale, and the will to fight, techniques of mass persuasion and manipulation were employed. The cultural sector became an invaluable collaborator because of its special ability to juggle words and ideas. Language was denatured in the attempt to justify the immensity of the violence and sacrifice, all sanctified in the name of patriotic principles.[14]

Romain Rolland insisted that the manufacturers of warmongering rhetoric were hypocritical and nihilistic. He refused to recognize any metaphysical or metalinguistic legitimacy for war. He organized his protests around this key perception: that intellectuals, public officials, journalists, labor leaders, and clergy had deepened the murderous passions of the war and thus perpetuated the conflagration. They not only undermined the possibility of a compromise peace, but prepared the ground for future bloodshed.[15]

Intellectuals had betrayed their function as guardians of European culture, preservers of knowledge. The Great War, Romain Rolland predicted, would be remembered as the war of the intellectuals: "The intellectuals on both sides have been so much in evidence since the beginning of the war, they have, indeed, brought so much violence and passion to bear upon it that it might almost be called their war."[16] The responsible intellectual should meet the challenge of war by retaining his commitment to social justice and understanding of others, by refusing to circulate distortions and partial truths, and above all by rejecting any position grounded in hatred and cruelty. Generalizing from his own association with the International Red Cross, providing aid to prisoners of war, Romain Rolland demonstrated that meaningful humanitarian work was possible in the midst of combat. An idealist without illusions, he admitted that "we cannot stop the war, but we can make it less bitter."[17]

He exhorted intellectuals to use the liberating elements of their cultural and historical legacies, never subordinating themselves to legalistic, military, or governmental authorities. Against the frightening spectacle of the "militarization of the intellect," more pronounced in Germany but insidiously present in France, he urged intellectuals to practice antiwar protest, aimed at civilians behind the lines, who constituted public opinion. The apparent monolith of war enthusiasm was not universally solid. Though the governments monopolized the media, though articulate voices refused to speak out, Romain Rolland intended to make dissenting ideas accessible to the public.[18]

Romain Rolland's ideal intellectual served as a moral guide especially to untutored youth and to misguided intellectuals. The critical task was to see reality clearly and to maintain a humane perspective on all the combatants. War resistance might tax internal resources, but the antiwar thinker did not permit emotional biases, personal preoccupations, or political allegiances to distort reality. The intellectual liberated by contesting and dissolving all forms of cult worship. Idols such as patriotism and national honor were amalgams of the irrational and mediocre, served by conformism and the blind acceptance of authority. To prevent intellectuals from further fetishizing the nation, a few must illustrate that an opposition to such grotesque and disorienting forms of devotion could be mounted.[19]

World war demanded that thinkers demonstrate the fullness of their characters. Resistance to war, grounded in analytic understanding and the refusal of collective murder, became central in the modern intellectual's scale of values. Without it an insane chauvinism would prevail.[20]

The *Above the Battle* articles launched a career of heretical intercessions around the question of how to prevent war. The substance of these writings contradicted the regrettable associations of the word "above." Romain Rolland's message should not be misconstrued as objectivity, aloofness, insensitivity, or self-righteousness. *Above the Battle*, contextually, was an active form of engagement, directly addressing the all-pervasive atmosphere of massacre in Europe. Composed at the height of his popularity, these pieces transformed the public's perception of him. He became the proverbial intellectual traitor. His name was banished from the literary press. Many parents forbade their children to read his texts. In months, the darling of the French literary left and the cultivated public became a pariah. He was accused of the ultimate treason—the betrayal of France at the hour of its greatest trial. He opposed the war at great risk to his life, his reputation, and his future influence as a man of letters. After 1914 his works were misrepresented and slandered because of this opposition. For the remainder of his life, opponents would attack Romain Rolland ad hominem by invoking the slogan "above the battle."[21]

There was an eighteen-month interim between his last public statement in *Above the Battle* and his first journalistic piece in late 1916. After being actively engaged, he disengaged and entered a period of introspective meditation. The combined pressure of his isolation, vicious attacks from France and Germany, and the desertion of respected friends prompted him to reevaluate his position. On 9 November 1916, the Swedish Academy awarded him the Nobel Prize for Literature for 1915. The Nobel Prize symbolically legitimized his humanitarian antiwar stance and was widely regarded by Europeans as a surrogate Peace Prize. Romain Rolland's name reverberated internationally. He was irritated about being awarded the Nobel Prize, which might injure his claim of independence and interfere with his need for solitude.[22]

In 1914 and 1915, Romain Rolland had a prepolitical consciousness. If the war educated him, opposing the war gradually politicized him. His writings began to stir people, and from 1916 to 1919 he was a point of reference for antiwar opinion in Europe, America, and the world. After studying documents on the war, he asked searching questions about its causes and its consequences. Self-examination and the dictates of conscience gave way to more political and ideological considerations. He reluctantly realized that his own generous feelings had become dangerous and that acquiescence in a murderous atmosphere was impossible. He argued that the real responsibility for the war lay not with European leaders of state, but rather with the financial and industrial oligarchy who reaped huge profits from the hostilities. Eventually, his outrage at the continuation of the war fueled a major critique of European capitalism and its complicity with the political reaction. He connected these developments to the worldwide policies of imperialism. Romain Rolland abandoned his Eurocentric worldview during the war and became increasingly receptive to non-European civilizations and the emerging movements of national liberation in developing areas.[23]

During the early years of the Great War, it was difficult to distinguish his antiwar sentiments from the antimilitarism of minority Socialists and syndicalists in France. Romain Rolland's relations with certain Socialist and syndicalist journalists were more often precarious than comradely; he disagreed with their advocacy of

class struggle and desire to see a violent socialist revolution ema-
nate from the global war.[24]

Romain Rolland's relationship with Henri Guilbeaux illustrated
the tenuousness of his connection to the revolutionary-left Zimmer-
waldians and underscored the political limits of his antiwar dissent. To avoid having his name compromised or his thought an-
nexed by Guilbeaux, Romain Rolland separated his vision from
that of the revolutionary socialists. Separation was complicated by
the fact that he published in Guilbeaux's journal. He admired Guilbeaux's courage, talent, and loyalty but disapproved of his excessively polemical tone. Especially he deplored Guilbeaux's efforts to
transform *Demain*, the Geneva periodical he edited from 1916 to
1918, into a leading propaganda organ for the Bolshevik wing of
the Russian socialists exiled in Switzerland. Through Guilbeaux,
Romain Rolland became peripherally associated with the great revolutionary adventure soon to begin in Russia. Before returning to
Russia in his sealed car, Lenin telegrammed Guilbeaux to "bring
Romain Rolland if he agrees on principle." Obviously, Romain
Rolland disagreed with Bolshevik principles at that moment. Despite efforts to link him with the Russian revolutionaries, he remained unenlisted, a sympathetic but critical outsider.[25]

During the Great War, he tended to draw cultural and moral
conclusions from his own public positions. If there were implicit
politics in his message they were reformist and pacifist. Yet his
texts cogently criticized the social conditions of a decaying European society and were often accompanied by angry denunciations
of the political and educated elite. His writings echoed among the
tiny pockets of socialists and revolutionary syndicalists throughout Europe. Romain Rolland's themes made members of the *Vie ouvrière* group, in France, conscious that political action was possible. Inveterate European revolutionaries read him for spiritual as
well as political sustenance.[26] Rosa Luxemburg's letter to Luise
Kautsky, written while Luxemburg was imprisoned in Breslau
jail, is a poignant example:

> I too learned to love him (Romain Rolland) and suggested to Hannes
> that we either travel to Paris together to make R.R.'s acquaintance,
> or else invite him to come to Germany. After all, we live but once
> and good men of this caliber are few and far between; why should

we forgo the luxury of knowing them and seeking spiritual contact
with them? . . . Shall we not carry this idea out, "God willing?"[27]

Lenin, living in exile in Switzerland, expressed uneasiness that a
Bolshevik comrade had not received Romain Rolland's articles: he
volunteered to go to the library to make exact copies of the texts.
Even Bolsheviks, who disagreed with his antiwar position, found
Romain Rolland's writings illuminating on the massive upheavals
created by the war. During the entire postwar period, Romain
Rolland was invoked as a symbol of intellectual opposition to war
by communists, syndicalists, and revolutionary socialists of many
nations, not just France.[28]

The threat to individual conscience and intellectual responsibility kept Romain Rolland from accepting mass political movements
on the left as the exclusive agents of progressive social change. He
feared that a social revolution after the Great War would lead to
grave distortions. He withheld support from revolutionary movements in Western or central Europe because they lacked leadership, organization, discipline, and an appropriate sense of timing:
it would be premature to unleash a revolutionary offensive on an
exhausted Europe. Revolution would inevitably degenerate into a
failure, a *jacquerie*; it would trigger a violent repression. He struggled to articulate an autonomous antiwar vision based on the dictates of conscience. His thought was not to be expropriated by
those with a political or ideological ax to grind.[29]

Romain Rolland's stance was essentially humanitarian, charitable, Christian, and apolitical. He designed his writings to destroy
the fallacious justification of the war, to demystify all idealization
of military glory, and to signal his disapproval of the consensus
mentality. In doing so, he transformed the content and style of
intellectual commitment, popularized by Zola during the Dreyfus
Affair, into an instrument of antiwar education and resistance to
the warlike policies of the state. His perspective was militantly
international and cosmopolitan. His public statements were typified by a spirit of tolerance and fairness, a concern for accuracy and
documentation, and by the wish to diffuse the climate of fury and
paranoia on both sides of the trenches. In a climate of war psychosis, he spoke the language of sound judgment, unfettered intel-

lect, and compassion. His opposition to the dehumanizing and hypnotic mass effects of the Great War, he claimed, would be vindicated by history.[30]

Romain Rolland had no illusions about the practical efficacy of his stand or his power to alleviate suffering either at home or on the fronts. His words were religious acts that would not alter the shape of the war. He spoke out to be at peace with himself and his conscience and to be true to his own oceanic sensibility. After the war, he expected to be regarded by a minority of left-wing and progressive public opinion as an example of humble heroism, intellectual independence, and moral intransigence. His name might remind the young and idealistic that it was possible to refuse war.[31]

In the period 1917–1919, Romain Rolland again played with the idea of a fraternal organization of intellectuals, an "intellectual's international" of thinkers who had not capitulated to war propaganda, but had honored the commitment to free and open inquiry, pursuit of the truth, and rigorous logic. The intellectual of conscience was the herald of a humanitarian society in the future. Romain Rolland's honor role of potential members included Bertrand Russell, E. D. Morel, Norman Angell, Israel Zangwill, George Bernard Shaw, H. G. Wells, Henri Barbusse, Marcel Martinet, P.-J. Jouve, Maxim Gorky, Max Eastman, John Reed, G. F. Nicolai, August Forel, Albert Einstein, Hermann Hesse, and Gerhard Gran. These men upheld the idea of mutual cooperation between nations in their writings and in their personal lives. They withstood vituperative attacks, personal threats, and the prospect of trial and imprisonment. He endowed these intellectuals with Promethean power. They were life-affirming, creative, courageous, nonconformist, and unalterably opposed to the menace of modern warfare: "The register is, as it were, a picture of the untrammeled souls of the world wrestling with the unchained forces of fanaticism, violence, and falsehood."[32]

Romain Rolland exited from the war with oceanic sensibility intact. He was readying himself to reassemble an elite of world thinkers around his own pluralistic internationalist, pacifist, and humanitarian vision. As he had opposed the affiliation of intellectual forerunners with left-wing parties, so he urged them to remain separate from the institutional networks of the nation-state and its artificial borders, which obstructed the circulation of anti-war thought. His libertarian stance heroicized the powers of independent thinkers in their resistance to the state:

> The State is not our country. It is merely the administration of our country, sometimes a good administrator, sometimes a bad one, but always fallible. The State has power and uses power. But ever since man has been man, this power has invariably broken vainly against the threshold of the free Soul.[33]

Romain Rolland, the free Soul, emerged from the debacle of World War I emotionally and intellectually prepared for future battles.

PART TWO

THE POLITICAL AND IDEOLOGICAL AMBIGUITIES OF ROLLANDISM IN THE 1920s

4

The Intellectual's International

We are in one word—and let this be our word of honor—
good Europeans, the heirs of Europe, the rich, oversupplied,
but also overly obligated heirs of thousands of years of
European spirit.

Nietzsche, *The Gay Science*

Romain Rolland's immediate postwar dilemma was to discover a
means of struggle against future war that would preserve intact his
nineteenth-century conception of the responsibility of the intellectual. His engagement during the Great War did not permit him to
be swallowed by postwar ideologies or mass movements. Beginning in 1919 and continuing throughout the 1920s, he tried to salvage a purposeful role for the committed European writer.

Like Freud, Romain Rolland emerged from World War I with an
altered and more tragic sense of death.[1] His experience as an antiwar
writer reinforced his refusal to support postwar cynicism, violence,
or realpolitik. To prevent further war, he urged Europeans to work
actively for peace. He cited Spinoza to underscore his point: "For
Peace is not mere absence of war, but it is a virtue that springs from
force of character."[2] He tried to restore a sense of fellowship, mutual
comprehension, tolerance, and authenticity to the intellectual elite
of Europe and the world. He aimed his efforts at the literati and the
young members of the cultural sector.

The notion of an international of the mind was originally an
antidote to all that was retrograde about the war: nationalism, militarism, the uncritical consensus mentality, the mass delirium and
destructive frenzy.[3] With the prolongation of the hostilities, Romain Rolland feared that the fundamental fabric and existence of
European culture were in jeopardy. In early 1919, he began to
mobilize for his dream of an intellectual's international. He did so
without having a practical or administrative sense and without the

secretarial or economic resources of existing institutions. It was a one-man venture, expensive in terms of time, money, and energy.

The intellectual's international was to be a voluntary association of artists, scientists, and thinkers organized around universalist, supranational, progressive, and humanistic principles. Romain Rolland's vision presupposed an intelligentsia independent of national institutions or academies, the League of Nations, the Socialist International, or the Communist International inaugurated in March 1919. In crisis situations these free thinkers might retain a dissenting and nonconforming view.

He proposed that the intellectual's international hold regular congresses and conferences to provide stimulating scholarly dialogue. If it were established in conjunction with an international university, the international would create networks of student and educational organizations. He hoped also to link it to a publishing house and to issue a newspaper, a bulletin, and a multilingual journal mixing literature, biography, science, and scholarship. Europeans would extend their knowledge of other cultures through reading excellent translations of non-European classics and through the proliferation of popular biographies of seminal cultural figures.[4] Romain Rolland's proposal took direct aim at cultural nationalism and ethnocentrism, both of which were fostered by ignorance, the stereotyping of national characters, and xenophobia. The war had exacerbated such primitive forms of thought. Both the international publishing house and university, he argued, might better pursue their goals in Russia, Asia, or America—anywhere but Paris.[5] The French writer linked the intellectual's international to the dissemination of Esperanto, the international language for which he propagandized.[6] Moreover, he anticipated monumental collective enterprises, such as an Encyclopedia of the Twentieth Century.[7]

If Romain Rolland's idea of preserving and reinventing high culture was elitist, the elitism was muted by the proposal that writers should mediate between high and popular cultures. Cultural endeavors should be immediately accessible to the masses and not restricted to privileged groups. This international was apolitical in its organization and ideology. It could neither be tied to existing political parties, groups, programs, and electoral strategies nor to mass movements or politicized world views. He insisted that it be genuinely eclectic in the search for a new politics of truth, world peace, and cross-cultural dialogue. Internationalism was consistent with an intransigent individualism and a sentimental form of socialism. He saw himself as the prototype of the pacifist internationalist intellectual. He proclaimed that the valid role of the intellectual was to synthesize and unify, to set up bridges between peoples.[8]

Romain Rolland reacted ambivalently to the Russian Revolution. It caused him to reflect on modern social revolution and to reappraise his deepest cultural priorities. He was one of the first Western writers to be receptive to developments in the Soviet Union, but his career as a fellow-traveling intellectual remained uneasy. Over the interwar years, he agonized over and reevaluated his pro-Soviet stance.

Romain Rolland's enigmatic position on the Bolshevik Revolution was built on fragmentary and at times contradictory evidence. News was always filtered through the presuppositions of the reporter. Much of his information came from written accounts and from discussion with Russian intellectuals who spent the war in Switzerland. The most important of these were Anatole Lunacharsky, destined to become Soviet minister for enlightenment; Nicholas Rubakin, an encyclopedic scholar and philologist with pro-Kerensky tendencies; and Paul Birukof, a Tolstoyan.[9] Some of his confusions about the Russian Revolution reflect discrepancies in their accounts. He remained in close contact with the French militant trade unionist and radical journalist Henri Guilbeaux, editor of *Demain* and intermediary between the European Zimmerwaldian left, which was mounting an opposition to the war, and the Bolsheviks.[10] Many first visitors to the USSR (Alfred Rosmer, Jacques Mesnil, Victor Henry) visited Romain Rolland in Switzerland and shared their impressions of the early days of the revolution.[11]

Neither a zealous advocate nor an unyielding opponent of the Russian Revolution, he took the role of a friendly but critical sympathizer. Without enrolling in the Communist Party or its international organizations, he proclaimed an international solidarity with the events in Russia and welcomed some of its goals. One could offer an empathic understanding of the Russian Revolution without being a Bolshevik, without abandoning one's critical perspective. Throughout his career as an engaged writer, his writings on the Soviet Union remained personal and impressionistic.

Romain Rolland stressed what was universal and liberating about this world-historical development. Writing optimistic accounts primarily to a French and European audience, he quickly anticipated that the Russian Revolution might counter Western political stalemate and obsolete social structures. Revolution could become a viable alternative to decadence. The Russian Revolution could free human beings from the futile sense that history could not be made or understood. On the pessimistic side, he warned the Bolsheviks to avoid the distortions, isolation, and arrogance of their eighteenth-century French predecessors. He specifically counseled the Russian Communists and their European followers against gratuitous violence and internal factionalism. The Soviet mission transcended Russian borders: it was to bring the world peace, liberty, fraternity, and a heightened awareness of the historical possibilities for freedom. "Let your Revolution be that of a great, healthy, fraternal, human people, avoiding the excesses into which we fell!"[12]

Writing contemporary history was a risky undertaking; advising revolutionaries about revolution was no less so. His critical support for the revolution left him vulnerable to attacks from the communists, the center, and the right. Romain Rolland's writings stressed the process of perception, the proper spirit in which to receive information about the Soviet Revolution. He urged his audience to confront the social upheaval in Russia with an open and nonpartisan attitude, to put aside their received and pejorative notions about communist insurrectionaries. He distrusted interpretations of Russian events that were emotional, demagogic, and uninformed and that fueled the anticommunist hysteria from European right-wing and middle-class circles, including the press. He insisted on making distinctions among the various groupings and parties on the left.[13] Throughout the interwar years, he never embraced a one-dimensional anti-Soviet standpoint, but carefully differentiated himself from those unnuanced vilifiers of the Soviet Union who, he believed, always served reactionary interests.

He realized that the Soviet Union was surrounded by hostile enemies and needed distinguished defenders, individuals of conscience, who were clearly non-Bolshevik. In October 1919, Romain Rolland penned a dramatic piece of humanitarian propaganda, entitled "For Our Russian Brothers: Against the Starvation Blockade." He linked the war mentality to counterrevolutionary politics. He bitterly denounced the Allied invasion of Russian territory. The crusade by the bourgeois democracies of America and Europe against the Soviets was a "hideous crime." Above all, this invasion revealed the class interests of the revolution's opponents.[14] The Russian Revolution belonged to those "chaotic and grandiose ventures of renewing the old and corrupted order." He portrayed it as a symbol of human potentiality, representing the unextinguishable possibilities of liberation.

To posturing critics who equated the Soviet Union with bloody anarchism, Romain Rolland replied that it was premature to discuss the results of the recently initiated social experiment. No European could dismiss the Russian Revolution as destructive given Europe's dismal record in four and a half years of total war: twenty to thirty million people killed or maimed, economies wrecked, land and industry devastated. In contrast, the Soviet Revolution arose from the debacle of the war, posed itself as a corrective to empire and to militarism, and promised an era of vast industrial and agricultural planning. "Bolshevism is not disorganized; it has attempted to organize chaotic disorder; it has attempted to provide new social formulas in the midst of the moral and material ruin of Europe."[15]

However much he praised the Russian Revolution, he refused to accept the mechanical exportation of Bolshevik leadership, party discipline, political agitation, or social analysis to the West. Toward the Bolshevik leaders and the Marxist-Leninist ideology, he adopted a mixed but on balance negative attitude. Russian revolutionaries were different from the democratic socialists or socialist humanists he admired. He viewed Lenin and Trotsky as honest, driven, faithful, and energetic leaders and never doubted that they were highminded and self-effacing. Both were motivated by an ideal of a just social order. Both had well-articulated ideas about internationalism and had lived abroad. Yet he felt that Lenin and Trotsky had an unusual capacity for violent discourse and actions. Their tempers were fanatical and despotic; they acted out of political expediency; they repeatedly displayed doctrinal intransigence and personal authoritarianism. Class consciousness and class struggle, he predicted, would not inaugurate a peaceful world. He was alarmed that the Bolsheviks wanted to "revolutionize the world" and resorted to force to accomplish their goals. His initial impressions of Marxism-Leninism were equally negative. He saw Leninism as a vulgarization of socialism, an amoral ideology that systematically eliminated a spiritual or psychological component of human endeavor. Its iron law of economic development stemmed from a narrow view of productive relations and political economy. It cynically justified a provisional class dictatorship to legitimize new forms of tyranny. Its view of historical process appeared deterministic and reductionistic.[16]

Romain Rolland fundamentally disagreed with the Bolshevik ideas of a minority dictatorship, centralization, secrecy, and regimentation of intellectual and artistic life. He found Leninism too politicized, dogmatic, intolerant of opposing political views, and blind to alternative methods of critical analysis and intuition. Leninists, he learned from his friendship with Gorky, were suspicious of intellectuals, if not anti-intellectual. The vanguard party had no tolerance for other avant-gardes. Lenin, in wanting to transform world war into revolutionary class warfare, dismissed all antiwar positions during the war as simpleminded, dangerous, petit-bourgeois "bacilli."[17] Despite the revolution's successes, Romain Rolland would never condone the Bolsheviks' centralizing opinion and curtailing individual or democratic freedoms. He refused to sanction any limits imposed from above on political opposition from workers' unions, artists, or thinkers. These groups had to conduct their affairs without harassment or party discipline.[18]

Romain Rolland's idea of an intellectual's international in 1919 was diametrically opposed to Lenin's view of the Communist International. Yet he appreciated the grandeur of the Soviet experiment from its beginning. The Bolsheviks had organizational power and were initiating worthwhile economic, scientific, educational, and cultural endeavors. They faced considerable internal and external obstacles in the gigantic project of social reconstruction, including the hostility to their successes by the bourgeois countries of the world.[19]

The end of the First World War and the successful Russian Revolution sparked revolutionary activity in central European countries. The repression of the European revolutions left a profound impact on him.[20] Romain Rolland summarized his attitudes toward these abortive revolutions in a piece documenting the crushing of the Spartacist revolt. "Bloody January in Berlin" narrated and interpreted the events of the Spartacist uprising from 5 January to 11 January 1919, which culminated in the double assassinations of Karl Liebknecht and Rosa Luxemburg on 15 January. Once again contemporary Germany demonstrated its worship of naked force, the drunkenness of its ruling-class establishment, and the obsequious mentality of its people.[21]

Romain Rolland defended the revolutionary socialists against the savage repression. He wrote as an independent intellectual concerned with historical accuracy and disgusted by the monstrousness of the murders. He sensed that the suppression of this uprising would have calamitous consequences for both the German revolution and the cause of world peace. He dramatized these issues to alert progressive French opinion in general, French socialists in particular, to the moral and political danger of the situation.[22]

Romain Rolland viewed Liebknecht and Luxemburg as attractive, impeccably sincere champions of revolutionary and Marxist democratic socialism. They were thinkers of stature and activists who had condemned the Great War and worked for Franco-German reconciliation, beginning with the fraternal contacts between the working classes of both countries. He contrasted the kind, disinterested quality of their commitment to working people with the ruthless smashing of their movement.[23]

This bloody repression clarified the depth of the militaristic and conservative reaction in Germany, characterized by its nationalistic rage, visions of revenge against France, and the fiction of the stab in the back. The establishment of the Weimar Republic had not substantially changed the German people. German capitalists, with the bourgeois press, seized on such emergencies as the Spartacist uprising to defend their class interests and material possessions. The Spartacist revolt became an opportunity to eliminate revolutionary Socialists, while retarding "the progress of the Socialist idea."[24]

Right-wing Social Democrats thus established a dreadful historical precedent, which they legitimized in the name of democracy. A majority of German socialists had supported the German Sacred Union and allowed the war to domesticate and bureaucratize the structure of the Social Democratic Party (SPD). In 1919 socialist heads of government behaved no differently in crises from liberals or reactionaries. German socialists had no scruples against calling in the imperial army and the *Freikorps* to crush the revolution with force. Nor did the Socialists Scheidermann or Ebert show remorse for their murderous deeds: "The fratricidal victors rejoiced without shame."[25]

The organized working class, Romain Rolland concluded, would have to be educated by this catastrophic turn of events to unite around its own interests. Spontaneous revolution was a dead end that only facilitated political repression. More significant, worker movements had to be on guard against the divisive, treacherous, and opportunistic actions of their former leaders. Socialists in power would use the instruments of state violence against the organized working class. "But it was the first time that Socialism found itself on the side of power and against the proletariat."[26] He predicted that it would not be the last such incident.

Reacting to the betrayal and deception by socialists of socialists, Romain Rolland distanced his intellectual's international from the Socialist International. Throughout the interwar years, he maintained a skeptical, even distrustful, posture toward European socialist parties and politics. He supported neither the extreme left wing of socialism, which believed revolution was imminent, nor the right wing and center, which were reformist, legalistic, and double-dealing. Postwar socialism, including French socialism, lacked leadership, ideological direction, faith, and the ability to distinguish itself from the establishment.[27]

Romain Rolland's attitudes toward Woodrow Wilson shifted during the period from October 1914 to the spring of 1919. He first imagined Wilson to be a moderate and disinterested man of good will. He was captivated by the American president's language, which appeared generous and enlightened while it camouflaged his class interests. But Romain Rolland's hopes were dashed by Wilson's refusal to intervene to end the hostilities during the war and his inability to assert himself as an arbiter for a just peace. After the Armistice, Wilson did not curb the appetites of the Allies for revenge.[28] By the opening of the Peace Conference on 18 January 1919, Romain Rolland saw that Wilson was a fraud and that the treaty being negotiated would lay the foundation for a future world war.[29]

Romain Rolland never accepted the credibility of Wilsonian democratic ideologists. The Treaty of Versailles and the League of Nations represented the final apotheosis of liberal idealism, the collapse of the expectations raised by the Enlightenment and the French Revolution. Wilson's betrayal was unusually harsh because it trampled so many of Romain Rolland's immense hopes. He remained critical of such false prophets, distrusting parliamentary politicians, including the French Radicals, who preached Wilson's brand of legalistic internationalism and democratic humanitarianism. Just as the intellectual's international stood in neither the Bolshevik nor the socialist camp, so too it rejected any official allegiance with postwar liberalism:

> The moral abdication of President Wilson, abandoning his own principles without having the frankness to admit it, signals the ruin of that great bourgeois idealism that for a century and a half insured the ruling class of its prestige and its strength, in spite of its many errors. The consequences of such an act are incalculable.[30]

Clarté was initiated in 1916–1917 by four young French writers and journalists: Henri Barbusse, Victor Cyril, Raymond Lefebvre, and Paul Vaillant-Couturier. Barbusse and Lefebvre were inspired by Romain Rolland's antiwar position and were sympathetic to his form of pacifistic left-wing intellectualism. Their original conception of *Clarté* coincided with Romain Rolland's principles of intellectual independence and the regeneration of cultural life. Under its umbrella, *Clarté* attempted to assemble war veterans, antimilitarists, republicans, Radicals, protocommunists, socialists, pacifists, academics, and even nationalistic intellectuals.[31]

In 1919, Romain Rolland expressed deep misgivings about the recruits to the *Clarté* movement. Its members lacked literary and intellectual authority, were arrivists, and resembled "the fashionable world of Paris at a dress rehearsal."[32] A collection of journalists and theatrical celebrities, such as Colette and Edmond Rostand, might produce some glitter and some "facile camaraderie" in times of relative calm, but in a crisis they would prove unreliable. The Parisian tone of the *Clarté* movement disturbed him. Its parochialism suggested an evanescent commitment to peace and internationalism. Many of *Clarté*'s members (J. H. Rosyn, Paul Fort, Anatole France) had taken self-serving and plainly chauvinistic positions.

Many adherents were virulently anti-Soviet. Rather than turn the intellectual's international into a meaningless gathering of French literati, he suggested a more democratic, more international organization. Such associations were better located outside Paris, where "foreign thought and action" were received more openly.[33]

Romain Rolland found the organizational structure of *Clarté* to be misconceived, overly eclectic, and diffuse. "Above all, the present situation demands the constitution of a closed, solid, resistant nucleus of intransigent souls who carry the new faith."[34] He advocated a smaller, more carefully selected group of thinkers, earnestly prepared for permanent opposition to war. As apostles of peace and internationalism, they would be inflexible on key issues, personally honorable, and undeflected by practical considerations of career, reputation, or political affiliation. The experience of the Great War would have taught the value of refusal. The postwar context would confront intellectuals with sharp choices: "Prudent silence, the amiable neither yes nor no, must be interpreted 'No.' "[35]

He objected to *Clarté*'s equivocation on contemporary events in 1919. Not speaking out suggested either ideological confusion at *Clarté* or, worse still, a desire not to offend centrist or nationalistic members of the advisory board. This implied that *Clarté* lacked the resolve to emerge as an oppositional voice.[36] Privately, Romain Rolland feared that *Clarté* was too much under the moral patronage of Anatole France. He had condemned the French Voltairean for his xenophobic outbursts during the war and for his calculated silence about the unjust peace treaty.[37]

Before he resigned from the *Clarté* committee on 23 June 1919, Romain Rolland took sharp issue with its deceptive editorial structure, consisting of two parallel committees: an ornamental but impotent committee composed of recognizable international names (Anatole France, Thomas Hardy, Upton Sinclair, Stefan Zweig) and an invisible but powerful central committee dominated by the Parisian inner circle of *Clarté*. He felt it was antidemocratic and irresponsible to make decisions without consultation.[38] He was further alienated by the bungling bureaucratic mediocrity of Victor Cyril, the least talented of *Clarté*'s founders.[39]

Romain Rolland's refusal to stay with the *Clarté* group demonstrated the heretical and puristic nature of his ideals. His pursuit of the intellectual's international was without tactical finesse, flexibility, or the spirit of compromise. He was stubbornly prepared to risk becoming the "one against all." *Clarté* would not accept Romain Rolland's assumptions or his need for absolute moral decency.

Romain Rolland's intransigent individualism, his desire to complete ongoing cultural projects (novels, plays, biographies), and his efforts to reorient European cultural life to the sacred, all made his rupture with *Clarté* inevitable. Yet he could not tolerate total breaks. He remained friendly with Barbusse, Lefebvre, and Vaillant-Couturier, hoping still to collaborate with them on joint endeavors. In late 1919 and early 1920, such an opportunity presented itself. Along with Barbusse and the French writer Georges Duhamel, Romain Rolland attempted to prepare for the first in a series of International Congresses of Intellectuals. This congress was never held.[40]

About the same time, he wrote to E. D. Morel, secretary of the Union of Democratic Control, an English-based pacifist and internationalist organization, that he was unwilling to become an active member of that organization.[41] He could be at once committed and nonaligned; joining an association might be a full-time affair, distracting him from his art and his reflective solitude. His work for an intellectual's international went forward without the aid of political and ideological associations such as the Union of Democratic Control, even when he agreed with their goals and esteemed their leaders:

> I, too, have arrived at the stage of integral internationalism, and I believe in the necessity for human evolution of a radical transformation for the benefit of the world of Labor. But essentially I limit myself to my own task as "worker of the mind." That is considerable enough to demand all of my energies. I would like to introduce the great intellectuals of diverse nations who have conserved the independence of their thought, posing to them principles of an International of the Mind, which struggles against the disastrous work of intellectuals formed into regiments serving the enemy nationalisms.[42]

Romain Rolland opened his postwar career with a forceful, highly visible proclamation of intellectual autonomy and liberty, "The Declaration of Independence of the Mind." He unequivocally asserted the dignity of the intellectual's vocation. First published in Paris in the French Socialist newspaper *L'Humanité* on 26 June 1919, two days before the signing of the Treaty of Versailles; translated into the major languages of the day; read in the newspapers and journals of France, Switzerland, England, Italy, Germany, Austria, and America; cosigned by a select circle of the world's intellectual personalities, his manifesto received both attention and some measure of legitimacy.[43] The controversy triggered by the Declaration illustrated that he had touched a sensitive nerve in Europe.

The discourse affirmed his sense of the intellectual's "Rights of Man." Romain Rolland emphasized the intellectual's right and obligation to think, research, write, publish, and communicate honestly, without the shackles of censorship, nationalism, or political allegiances. After five years of conflict, he called for intellectuals to stand up against destitute moral relations and the silence, acquiescence, and embitterment among themselves. He asked them to clean up their own affairs, then make fraternal alliances with the democratic masses.

The final draft of the Declaration read:

Declaration of Independence of the Mind

Workers of the Mind, comrades scattered throughout the world, separated for five years by armies, censorship, and the hatred of nations at war, we address an Appeal to you at this hour when barriers are falling and frontiers are reopening, to revive our fraternal union, but as a new, more secure and reliable union than that which previously existed.

The War threw our ranks into confusion. The majority of intellectuals put their science, their art, their reason at the service of governments. We wish to accuse no one, to direct no reproach. We know the weakness of individual souls and the elemental force of great collective currents: the latter has swept aside the former in an instant, for nothing had been prepared to help in the work of resistance. Let this experience at least help us for the future!

And let us first of all acknowledge the disasters that have been brought about by the almost total abdication of the intelligence of the world and its voluntary enslavement to unchained forces. Thinkers and artists have added an incalculable sum of poisonous hatred to the plague that devours Europe's flesh and spirit; they sought in the arsenal of their knowledge, their memory, their imagination, old and new reasons, historical reasons, scientific, logical, and poetic reasons to hate; they worked to destroy comprehension and love between men. And thus they have disfigured, debased, lowered, degraded Thought, of which they were the representatives. They made Thought the instrument of passions and (without knowing it, perhaps) of the selfish interests of a political or social clan, a state, a country, or a class. At present, out of this savage battle from which all the involved countries, victorious or vanquished, emerge battered, ruined, and in the bottom of their heart (though they do not admit it) ashamed and humiliated by their excess of madness, Thought, compromised with them in their struggle, emerges with them, fallen.

Stand up! Let us disentangle the Mind from its compromises, its humiliating alliances, its hidden bondage. The Mind is the slave of no one. It is we who are the servants of the Mind. We have no other master. We exist to uphold, to defend its light, to rally around it all misguided men. Our duty is to maintain a fixed point, to point to the polar star, in the midst of the swirling passions in the night. Among these passions of pride and mutual destruction, we make no choice. We reject them all. We honor Truth alone, free, frontierless, limitless, without prejudices of nations or castes. Assuredly, we are not uninterested in Humanity. It is for Humanity that we work, but for it *as a whole*. We do not know peoples. We know the People—unique, universal—the People that suffers, that struggles, that fails, and that constantly rises to its feet again, and that always marches along a rough road drenched in its blood—the People of all men, all equally our brothers. And it is in order that they may, like us, become conscious of this fraternity, that we raise above their blind conflicts, the Arch of Alliance—the free Mind, one and manifold, eternal.[44]

The first paragraph emphasized fraternal unity between intellectuals and a reopening of the frontiers of the mind coinciding with the reopening of national borders. By referring to the intellectual as a "comrade" and a "worker of the Mind," he affirmed the principle of labor's fundamental significance, while raising the elusive issue of the link between workers and intellectuals. Intellectual solidarity might stem from negatives: opposition to the forces of militarism, nationalism, censorship, and hatred that had divided them during the Great War. Prewar cultural and scientific associations were anachronistic and insufficient; he pressed for a new model of intellectual dialogue.

In paragraph 2, he criticized Europe's intellectuals for allowing their intelligence and imagination to be manipulated by warring governments. He muted his censorious thrust, however, by a vague proposal for planned resistance to war in the future. To prevent a repetition of the catastrophe, he exhorted intellectuals to remember how subjective principles and expectations had been betrayed. Conscience was as crucial as consciousness and memory.

Romain Rolland's third paragraph indiscriminately attacked European intellectuals for contributing to the atmosphere of universal hatred during the war. Knowledge had been mobilized and twisted into an instrument of war. Thinkers had lost their perspective on events and on their own proper responsibilities in an emergency.

Intellectuals had shamelessly produced war propaganda and disseminated racist and chauvinistic slander. They colluded with the lies of ruling governments, Allied as much as Central Powers.

"Abdication of intelligence" meant the surrender of rational and ethical bearing in a moment of frenzy. European intellectuals had violated their authority. They had renounced their prerogative to defend culture, reason, and human values. The war had repeatedly negated the true foundations of creativity and critical inquiry; these freedoms extended to the right to resist warfare, oppression, and one-dimensional opinion. The mind, Romain Rolland insisted, had no master, no privileged hierarchy, no set of standards to which it must submit. The mind and the spirit were ends in themselves: pure, sacred, indivisible, inalienable.

If European intellectuals had degraded thought, they had degraded their own characters in the process. His repetition of scathing adjectives ("disfigured, debased, lowered, degraded") revealed the depth of his fury at the betrayal. Intellectual life would remain unhealthy unless intellectuals demonstrated their capacity for self-criticism and discovered effective, conscious ways to combat passion by reason and to struggle against murderous collective currents.

In the final paragraph, Romain Rolland triumphantly called for intellectuals to rise from the debris of a war in which there was no winner. To redeem their own bad faith and to revitalize cultural production, thinkers should refrain from any contributions to death and destruction. They should avoid all entangling alliances, including those of nation, state, party, group, or class.

Romain Rolland connected his totalizing notion of humanity to his oceanic conception both of the people and of the intellectual's mission to embrace the universe. This mystical idea worked against the nationalist, liberal democratic, socialist, and Bolshevik notions of popular and concrete historical struggle. The ideal intellectual worked fraternally for the miserable or exploited. Romain Rolland's idea of freedom was highly abstract, but it permitted him to link mental and manual labor. To reemphasize the necessity for intellectual autonomy, to overcome the taint of intellectual submission, his manifesto closed on a note of transcendence. Freedom, truth, and fraternity could only be attained if the thinker rose above the petty, blinding conflicts of everyday life. Still echoing the slogan "Above the Battle," he urged the writer to act as a detached, universalist, humanistic, morally uncorrupted individual.

The published manifesto was virtually identical to the first draft Romain Rolland penned on 16 March 1919.[45] Only one sentence, strategically located in the final paragraph, which affirmed the intellectual's mission, was changed. The original read: "We are engaged to serve only free Truth." (*Nous prenons l'engagement de ne servir jamais que la Vérité libre.*) The published version deleted the word *"engagement"*: "We honor Truth alone."[46] Romain Rolland implied that moralists could be *engagés*, but their overriding concerns, obligations, promises, pledges (all synonymous with the French term *engagement*) must be to discover deeper layers of meaning in human life and its relationship to the world.

Romain Rolland elaborated on the Declaration in August 1919 in E. D. Morel's English pacifist journal, *Foreign Affairs*.[47] To justify his initiating the dialogue between workers and intellectuals, he reminded his audience of his minority stance during the war. To advocate universal brotherhood, social justice, and mutual comprehension among the warring nations was necessary, but not sufficient. In addition, intellectuals must coordinate their efforts against conservative ideas and political forces, to struggle against the reassembled forces of tyranny. Romain Rolland hoped to use his prestige to mediate between the cultural sector and the working classes, or at least to prevent an increase in existing misunderstandings.

He urged the organized working class not to dismiss the intelligentsia out of hand. Just as he could not sanction intellectual contempt for the people, so Romain Rolland refused to countenance worker anti-intellectualism. He was particularly upset about developments in the Soviet Union, where intellectuals were distrusted and actively harassed, where latent Bolshevik paranoia about artists was coming into the open.[48]

Although he opposed intellectual censorship by the Soviets, Romain Rolland praised the Russian experiment in social reconstruction and the effort to eliminate material scarcity. The Bolshevik Revolution was a model of participatory social and economic development with enormous global significance.[49] To separate intellectuals from the working class at this juncture was to cut labor off from the natural creativity and critical perspective crucial to the construction of a durable society. Workers needed intellectual expertise and vision; intellectuals would grow enervated and anti-quated without meaningful contact with workers. Even more dangerous was the precedent of intellectuals' turning against socially conscious workers to become an ideological "tool of oppression in the hands of the exploiters."[50]

Romain Rolland predicated the proposed dialogue on two notions: first, that the goals of manual and mental workers were equally dignified, despite the division of labor; and second, that fraternity was best implemented outside of political parties or mass movements. For the moment, Romain Rolland worked to lay bare unexamined biases, including those stereotypes accepted by the working class and its representatives.[51]

For Romain Rolland the very future of the world depended on collaboration between workers and intellectuals. He concluded his commentary on the Declaration by echoing Marx's rousing *Communist Manifesto* of 1848:

> Manual and intellectual workers, let us unite. Let us unite all who believe in the possibility of a freer, dignified, and happier world, in which the forces of production and of creation would be harmoniously associated rather than working toward their mutual destruction, as they are doing now, in part through our mutual opposition, which is absurd and criminal. Let us not weary of hope and of action: let the intellectuals illuminate the road that the workers have to construct. There are different labor gangs. But the object of labor is the same.[52]

In an appendix to the Declaration published in *L'Humanité* in August 1919, Romain Rolland reiterated his critical support for the Soviet Union. He regretted that "our Russian friends" were prevented from signing his manifesto, condemned the Allied military intervention and the blockade of the Soviet Union, and proclaimed that "Russian thought is the avant-garde of the world's thought."[53] "Russian thought," in Romain Rolland's context, meant not Leninism but rather the Russian literary heritage or Soviet artistic developments.[54]

Romain Rolland composed an impassioned revolutionary dedication to a second volume of his antiwar essays, *Les Précurseurs*. He dated the dedication August 1919:

> In Memory
> of the Martyrs of the new Faith:
> the human International.

To Jean Jaurès, Karl Liebknecht, Rosa Luxemburg,
Kurt Eisner, Gustav Laundauer,
victims of ferocious stupidity
and of the murderous lie,
liberators of the men who killed them.[55]

In this dedication, Romain Rolland voiced his solidarity with
the assassinated martyrs of European socialism, communism, and
anarchism—particularly with revolutionary militants. The five celebrated persons he hailed in the dedication were devoted to revolution, internationalism, and socialist humanism. They were at once
revolutionaries and intellectuals of high caliber. In moving closer
to the proletariat, Romain Rolland seemed to imply that he saw
socialism as the only method of eradicating the material roots of
world war and social repression and establishing internationalism. Romain Rolland connected violence to ignorance, insincerity,
and class mystification. Socialism, on the contrary, appeared to be
the all-embracing ideology of "the human International"—and
thus the universal road to peace and to both collective and individual freedom.

This emotional identification with socialist revolutionaries was
incompatible with Romain Rolland's more moderate and apolitical
commitment to freedom of thought. Significantly, he opened *Les
Précurseurs* with this engaged dedication but closed with the idealist Declaration. In between were articles published between 1916
and 1919 that supported the ideals of an intellectual's international.
But the tension between the dedication and the Declaration remained unresolved. Whether the real forerunners of the future
were embattled working-class leaders or pacifist intellectuals was
undecided. The contradiction between outright allegiance to socialist revolution and the duty to exercise one's free spirit colored all of
Romain Rolland's committed writings in the 1920s. In offering unsolicited advice to workers while not being a worker, in praising
martyrs of the European socialist movement while remaining outside socialist organizations or revolutionary discipline, in urging an
end to the antagonisms between workers and intellectuals while
rejecting political struggle, he found himself entangled in a maze of
contradictions. To soften the paternalistic ring of his writings, he
formulated an image of the future harmonious mingling of all

forms of productive labor. He opted again for an ideal of totality and transcendence.

On 25 April 1919, Romain Rolland sent George Bernard Shaw a copy of the Declaration, requesting his signature.[56] This move was consistent with his original plan of securing signatures from a distinguished independent writer, artist, and scientist from every major country in the world.[57] The invitation triggered a private controversy that recapitulated his stormy relations with Shaw during the war.[58]

Romain Rolland told Shaw that the manifesto would not only help restore intellectual autonomy interrupted by the war, but also reverse the disillusionment of the young and silent members of the cultural sector. In an attempt to disarm Shaw's caustic wit, he confessed that such appeals were romantic attempts to take a stand against an apparent evil; their authors were Don Quixotes, attacking windmills. Instead of swords, idealist intellectuals employed their pens. Yet he wanted Shaw's support to reinforce the shaken confidence of an "intellectual youth which waits, disoriented, anguished, for its elders to rally it and render it confident in the power of the liberating Mind. . . . I have taken account of the Quixotism of this appeal. But once in his life Don Quixote did unhorse his adversary."[59]

Shaw replied in French on 7 May 1919, adamantly refusing to sign and returning paragraphs of the Declaration with unsolicited editorial corrections. He deflated Romain Rolland's unsubstantiated claims of virtue for the thinker while poking fun at his own linguistic deficiencies:

> We must have a confession rather than a reproach: without that we will have the air of being Pharisees, even snobs. To avoid this I have dared to correct your draft a little. What do you think of it? Naturally you will know how to edit my gibberish: I am a vile linguist.[60]

Shaw's revision stressed the necessity of national defense and the impossibility of detached neutrality in times of war. Survival took precedence over intellectual opposition or detachment: "Search as we might to soar above the battle. Useless: in war the first duty is to the home, to the neighbor, the supreme task is to divert death from them."[61]

Romain Rolland found that Shaw's changes distorted the spirit of the discourse. Shaw the entertainer, playing semantic games, simply caricatured his stance "above the battle." He, in turn, accused Shaw of offering an apology for the patriotic excesses of intellectuals during the war. Through his irascible sarcasm, Shaw justified the sacrifice of all forms of resistance to national defense and brute survival. Romain Rolland retorted: "I do not put the nation, the country, the home, before everything. Above all, I put the free conscience." Shaw guaranteed the future warmongers a "blank check." Romain Rolland's vigilance, however, would not politicize intellectual commitment: "I see no future in the efforts of free thought adapting itself to political necessities. . . . If it [thought] wants to save others, let it begin by saving itself. Let it make it its business to constitute, over and above nations, an International of thought, a world conscience."[62]

Shaw's reply ridiculed Romain Rolland's seriousness as an idealistic mystification of free thinking. Shaw bluntly reminded him of the material and biological needs of the ordinary man and soldier, as well as the imperative to "muddle through," especially in times of military emergency. He considered the advocacy of an intellectual's international excessively pompous and self-righteous, even hypocritical. With humorous self-deprecation, Shaw mocked Romain Rolland's ideas about the omnipotence of Thought. The man of thought was a linguistic construct, not a historical reality:

> You flatter war and man. "The man of thought" does not exist. I am not thought. I am Bernard Shaw. You are Romain Rolland. We eat, and eight hours after, we forget our philosophy, and only feel hungry. . . . All that you say of Thought is true. Therefore, let Thought sign your manifesto. But John Smith and Pierre Duval cannot sign. They have fought for us; and we at least paid the taxes. No man has been above the battle. Such a pretension would be repugnant to the world and would break our influence. Excuse my bluntness: in writing English I have enough tact; but in a foreign language one writes as one can.[63]

Romain Rolland rejected Shaw's dichotomies as false and cynical. Material necessity required neither the abandonment of vision nor the renunciation of rational conduct. He defended his antiwar position and affirmed charitable principles. Intellectuals ought to use their ideas and their ethical sensitivity to emphasize communion, not distinctions, between people and nations:

> It is not strictly necessary to forget ideas when one feels hunger. In all times there are men who die for their ideas. There are some who have died for them in this war. There will be some in this peace. . . . I am not above the battles—all battles. I have been, I am, I will always be "above the battle" of nations and countries. I am struggling against nations, countries, castes, against all barriers that separate men.[64]

Romain Rolland's next letter, in which he included a copy of his acerbic antiwar play *Liluli* (1919), was the turning point of this exchange. Shaw immediately appreciated the caustic irony of *Liluli*, lavishing praise on it with German adjectives: "*Liluli* is *kolossal, grossartig, wunderschön,* magnificent. I have tasted it enormously, boundlessly, with ecstasy."[65] Under Shaw's aegis, it was performed before the British public. Romain Rolland finally decided that Shaw's jabs were aimed at form, not content. Shaw's satire also worked to "brand the servile aberration of unregimented thought during the war."[66] But Shaw did not sign the manifesto; the debate ended as it began, deadlocked.

Romain Rolland's Declaration offended many postwar Marxist intellectuals, most of whom looked instead to the Communist International. He sent Max Eastman, the American bohemian and antiwar writer, a copy of the Declaration, extending the amicable exchange he had enjoyed with young American left-wing writers during the war. Eastman published the manifesto in the New York City periodical *The Liberator,* but he offered a Marxist critique in the very same number.[67]

Eastman considered Romain Rolland's view of intellectuals a grandiose self-deception, shrouded in Platonic rhetoric that blurred the real choice for intellectuals: to opt for or against the proletariat. "We must place ourselves and all our powers unreservedly upon the side of the working class in its conflict with the owners of capital. We must adapt—at least so far as we are engaged upon this social quest—a fighting mentality and we must engage in a conscious class struggle." Romain Rolland's notions were effusive and sentimental. Eastman doubted the real possibility of individual autonomy in a class society. The French writer overestimated intellectual activity, thereby giving his manifesto "the flavor of self-conscious superiority or importance." He lacked any sense of how to apply ideas in practical circumstances and failed to devise an instrumental view of human knowledge.[68]

Eastman argued that the current struggle for liberty and democracy was synonymous with the global mission of communism. Just as Marxism was the best scientific method for unraveling the complicated economic roots of social relations, so the international communist movement had become the key agency of social change. The truly committed intellectual joined with the proletariat to wage total class struggle against the bourgeoisie. Most intellectuals could not be counted on to participate in these revolutionary struggles. Eastman praised Romain Rolland's moral courage during the war, but he expected little from writers who proudly held themselves apart from the revolutionary venture. Eastman reaffirmed his general suspicion of intellectuals while repudiating the metaphor "Above the Battle" as a pretense of Olympian detachment and cosmic independence.[69]

Romain Rolland answered Eastman's public denunciation privately: "The disagreement between us is, in effect, complete. So complete that I will not try to discuss it here. I prefer to expose these two theses in a more objective fashion in a work that I am now writing." He denied that his idealism was a religion, insisting that it was an experimental, open-ended strategy of discovery, which stemmed from radical doubt: "I am not a believer in a faith, religious or Marxist. I am from Montaigne's country that doubts eternally but that searches eternally. I *search for* the truth. I will never reach it."[70] Against the injunction to intellectuals to work actively in proletarian social struggles or join communist organizations, he argued that happiness, social justice, and the general will of the people had never been served by minority dictatorships or dogmatic theories. "A social community that could only be saved by a renunciation of the free intelligence will not be saved in reality, but lost. For it would rest on corrupted bases." He ironically noted that Eastman wanted to subordinate free intellectual inquiry and individual conscience to the service of the "new science," Marxism. This was a naive form of intellectual arrogance.[71]

Eastman's attack was the first in a series of confrontations with Marxist intellectuals that would punctuate Romain Rolland's career as an engaged intellectual. It anticipated his celebrated debate with Henri Barbusse in 1921–1922. Romain Rolland welcomed dialogue with twentieth-century Marxist intellectuals. In the framework of these controversies, he always distinguished personalities from issues. He retained personal esteem for Eastman and respected his review despite their irreconcilable dispute.[72]

During the war, Romain Rolland's relations with Albert Einstein had been cordial.[73] In 1919, he fully expected Einstein to join his campaign for intellectual freedom and to help secure followers for his Declaration in Germany. On the fifth of June 1919, he recorded Einstein's "consent."[74]

Einstein's motives for supporting the Declaration were mixed. He viewed signing as the lesser of two evils, although collective appeals were risky at that moment. They might simply provoke counterappeals, or they might confuse the basic issues. Einstein suggested that quiet diplomacy through one's private connections might be more efficacious than open protests against the international climate of distrust and revenge. He urged the exploration of German war guilt:

> I was not among the authors who drafted the appeal [the Declaration]. Being only too well aware of the bitterness prevalent in the various countries, I do not believe that such efforts toward international reconciliation hold out much promise of success at present. I gave my signature because it would have been worse to withhold it; but I was convinced that the appeal would not produce much of a response.[75]

Romain Rolland had been generally sympathetic to Heinrich Mann's efforts during the war to promote Franco-German reconciliation, and to his controversy with his brother, Thomas Mann. In 1919, Heinrich Mann was one of Germany's most celebrated men of letters. Although he signed the Declaration, he carped at the phrase "We know nothing of peoples. We know the People." Romain Rolland regarded Mann's suggested revision as too great a concession to nationalism.[76]

Georg Frederick Nicolai, professor of biology at the University of Berlin and pacifist author of *The Biology of War* (1917), emerged as the earliest and most energetic supporter of the Declaration. Romain Rolland had praised Nicolai's "great Europeanism" during the war, and in 1919 Nicolai catalyzed the French writer's idea of composing his manifesto.[77] Nicolai circulated the appeal all over central Europe in 1919, partly to popularize Romain Rolland's point of view and partly to document the "German answer" to it. He published both the former and the latter in his brochure *Romain Rolland's Manifest und die deutschen Antworten* (1919). Nicolai lobbied to have the Declaration appear in several German newspapers, reviews, and even in theater programs in 1919, including *Demokratie, Forum, Freiheit, Berliner Tageblatt, Deutsche allgemeine Zeitung, Vorwarts,* and *Germania.*[78]

Karl Kraus, the eminent Viennese satirist, social critic, and poet, refused to sign Romain Rolland's Declaration and gave his reasons. Kraus was unprepared to forgive German intellectuals for their sordid behavior during the war. Nor could he express solidarity with other names already on the list. Kraus's opposition to the war was based on a conservative desire to preserve culture and traditions. He neither shared the assumptions of European pacifists or left-wing intellectuals about the war nor agreed with their methods for posing complicated moral questions.[79]

Romain Rolland and the Italian idealist philosopher Benedetto Croce had not corresponded during the war but knew of each other's activities through intermediaries. Croce signed the appeal in terms that underscored his ambiguous relationship to Romain Rolland's antiwar thought.[80] Croce pedantically referred the French writer to a text that summarized his own writings on the Great War:

> It is very willingly that I fix my signature under your noble appeal. But I wish, so that you may understand the sense and the limit of my approval, that you read the book [*L'Italia dal 1914 al 1918*] I am sending you, which is the record of all that I have written during the War. You will find your name sometimes, and thus the reason for our divergences. *I believe that war is sacred,* but that truth is equally sacred, and that it must not be employed as an instrument of war. The instruments of war are made of other materials.[81]

Romain Rolland admitted to Croce that the two had distinct social and ideological preferences. In exchange for the book he had sent, Croce should consult Romain Rolland's anthology of antinationalist and anti-imperialist writings, *Les Précurseurs.* Despite their differences, as idealists they could concur on intellectual liberty, which was implicit in their sacralization of the mind.[82]

Romain Rolland encountered unexpected refusals from four distinguished members of the French intellectual and scientific community. The French economist and pacifist Charles Gide objected to the Declaration on the grounds that it "neglected the nation's right of existence in order to recognize only the unity of the universal proletariat, which will become the doctrine of the International."[83] Likewise, Charles Richet, a Nobelist in physiology and member of the French Academy of Sciences, refused to endorse the text.[84] Marie Curie, Nobelist in physics and in chemistry, declined to sign, perhaps out of "timidity or nationalist obstinacy," wrote a disappointed Romain Rolland. He had reluctantly solicited Anatole France's signature, even after expressing his reservations about including France on *Clarté's* board. He angrily remarked that the elderly skeptic had "shut himself up smugly in a discreet and padded silence."[85]

There were many favorable reactions to his appeal, several of which opened new intellectual relationships in his life. The cordiality and emotional intensity of these letters reassured the French writer.[86]

Romain Rolland was both delighted and irked at the response of the British philosopher Bertrand Russell. Russell wrote warmly: "I do not know how to express to you how I rejoiced at receiving your letter and the Declaration which accompanied it. It marks the end of the isolation of war time."[87] Russell sympathized with Romain Rolland's efforts to reconcile intellectuals in all countries. Nevertheless, he had reservations about the third paragraph of the text, which he found too accusatorial and self-righteous, and which contradicted the manifesto's claim of fellowship:

> I do not desire to impose on them the task of saying publicly: *Peccavi* [I have sinned]. I would prefer to make the reconciliation as easy as possible. I would not want to proclaim that we are their total superiors from a moral point of view. I would like to do everything that is possible to diminish rancors within nations, as well as international rancors. For my part, I would prefer a constructive paragraph rather than a criticism, a paragraph attending to the future and the great tasks which now remain for intellectuals.[88]

Romain Rolland interpreted Russell's answer as encouraging and generally approving. Though disinclined to embrace those thinkers "who betrayed once and who will betray a second time,"[89] he urged Russell to petition for English signatories to the Declaration.

> In England, Bertrand Russell, who signs with enthusiasm, asks that one cut out of the Declaration all disavowals of past misdeeds. And certainly the sentiment which inspires this demand is noble and pure: it is fine to be modest; but we must know how to guard a just pride, in the interests of a great cause, and not rush to wipe away the treasons of yesterday, for they will give way to the treasons of tomorrow.[90]

Toward the end of the campaign to circulate the Declaration, Romain Rolland was disillusioned by its immediate reception:

> It is not even possible to unite the small handful of free intellectuals of Europe around a text, however mild and attenuated. One could say that certain of those who struggled most energetically during the five years of war are at present exhausted and doubt themselves. . . . My Declaration has received so many demands for modifications or attenuations from different sides, that in realizing them, nothing would remain other than the title.[91]

The principal objections concerned the Declaration's explicitly internationalist outlook and its demand that intellectuals criticize misbehavior and recant beliefs held during the war. Moreover, in an open appeal, it was considered inappropriate to treat nationalists and consensus intellectuals impartially. Compassion, it seemed, could be expressed in a moral history or in a psychological novel, "but not in a Declaration, which is an action, a rallying cry, an appeal to indecisive and disheartened youth who wait for a direction, a guide, in the disarray of souls."[92]

Intellectuals must be held accountable for their actions, inaction, bad judgment, and lack of moral fiber. Thinkers had served death and confusion by promoting a hatred that, Romain Rolland charged, "devastated, devastates, and will devastate Europe for a long time to come."[93] The same unrepentant men would prepare Europe for its next war, which seemed increasingly inevitable. He nearly abandoned the project of collecting signatures for the appeal. As a last resort, he might turn to younger intellectuals or enlightened war veterans. If they failed him, he would launch the Declaration under his own name, despite the personal risk, "because one must never stifle the cry of conscience, whether one is or is not understood."[94]

Romain Rolland explained his intransigence toward European pacifists in a letter to Russell. Many prewar pacifists—liberal internationalists, Christians, and antimilitaristic socialists—had become chauvinistic and warmongering during the hostilities. Their antiwar rhetoric had evaporated when the Sacred Union commenced. Their peacetime pacifism had to be regarded cautiously unless they could candidly confront their opportunistic reversal during the war. He would doubt their good faith until they proved their commitments to peace with action. He predicted that these "elements of moral compromise" would manifest themselves again as soon as a national emergency occurred.[95]

Romain Rolland lamented his failure to establish a center for intellectual internationalism in a neutral country. The free minds of Europe remained isolated in their own countries, "hermetically closed off" from one another. Common struggle was more efficacious than individual combat. While speaking out against "the corrupting lie . . . which infected all of European thought," he articulated his private conflicts about being engaged and disengaged at the same time:

> I speak in any case against my own inclinations. For I am from taste a solitary person who loves nothing more than living far from cities and from action, in art and in nature. Circumstances have constrained me, and I am not grateful to them for that. But I would at least like to be engaged to aid the young "workers of the mind" of Europe and of America (indeed of some other countries) to multiply the occasions to assemble, to discuss together, to cooperate if possible on common works and projects, so that they can prepare for or cope with the new hurricanes, which we see amassing on the horizon.[96]

In 1919 Romain Rolland's engagement was clearly more cultural than political. He began his postwar career with a notion that action and spirit, politics and morality, collective and individual struggle, could be fused. His writings glorified human fraternity, panhumanistic ideals, and the moral tenacity of those historical actors and witnesses with an identifiable ethical consciousness. He wrote to inspire his readers with the goals he deemed transcendent and eternal. In this he adhered to an older tradition of the French moralist. Despite disclaimers, Romain Rolland tended to attribute to the intellectual priestly qualities and divine functions.

Romain Rolland's writings in 1919 were oppositional. He urged intellectuals to protest the ill-conceived and vengeful Versailles Peace Treaty, to repudiate all forms of imperialism and latent and manifest forms of nationalism, to insist on his version of unofficial, nonlegalistic internationalism, and especially to reopen dialogue with one another, taking the first steps toward an international of the mind. Last, he linked a rudimentary pacifist outlook with a Western, secular, idealist and individualist position. Above all else, he wanted to demonstrate that the antiwar vision could not be domesticated by the Allied victory and that it could be differentiated from a Bolshevik, socialist, or liberal position.

Thus, many aspects of Romain Rolland's engagement with his contemporary sociopolitical reality veered toward the concrete, whereas much of the idiom remained abstract and aloof. To his poetic wartime confidant and subsequent biographer, Pierre-Jean Jouve, he wrote: "The only fecund action that we can take at this moment must be slow, tenacious, deliberate."[97] Creative action and quiet meditation presupposed mental readiness and understanding of process to yield lasting cultural results. Political intercession was evanescent and of doubtful efficacy.

Romain Rolland recognized that there were urgent, immediate abuses that required the committed intellectual's concern, if not active intervention. The end of the war did not erase glaring instances of social injustice, political oppression, economic exploitation, and cultural exclusion. Battles remained to be fought.

In 1919 Romain Rolland was engaged and disengaged at the same time. If he continued to address present-centered causes, it was always in the name of higher humanistic values. He was moving from the position of "Good European" toward a planetary vision. Romain Rolland's oceanic feeling enabled him to take public positions, often radical and militant ones, frequently uncompromising and impractical ones, while transcending time, space, causality, and particularity. His oceanic mysticism showed him how the part merged with the whole and prevented him from giving way to a persistent sense of futility. He continued to struggle without expecting a favorable outcome, always keeping humanity itself at the center of his engaged outlook:

> What preserves me from lasting despair is that I can always escape the present; whether by habit, or by nature, my mind embraces great

spaces—centuries and the entire earth. Inspiration requires a calm, large, equal rhythm—a suitable rhythm—which overcomes fevers. I believe that we must accustom ourselves to this great breadth; the enormous world crisis, in which we are now engaged, does not admit of speed; there is a century, perhaps more, for addressing it; we will not see the end of it; but let us mark it with the rhythm of our pulses; let our secular thoughts make something of it. . . . Let each of us be the whole Man.[98]

5

The Rolland-Barbusse Debate

When one has no character one *has* to apply a method.
Albert Camus, *The Fall*

Inasmuch as the unsurpassable framework of Knowledge is
Marxism; and inasmuch as this Marxism clarifies our individual and collective *praxis*, it therefore determines us in
our existence.
Jean-Paul Sartre, *Search for a Method*

Every decade or so the French intelligentsia produces a public
quarrel dramatizing an internal conflict of major importance. The
Romain Rolland–Henri Barbusse debate was one of these "great"
controversies.[1]

After the failure of European revolutions from 1918 to 1920,
Europe entered a period of political, economic, and social stabilization, marked by attempts to exclude socialists and communists
from any decisive influence on the state. The modernization of the
European economy along corporatist lines coincided with a reasser-
tion of the forces of consensus. Raymond Poincaré dominated
French politics for the period 1920–1924. He was harsh toward
Germany and pushed for full reparations. Domestically, Poincaré
was conservative, socially repressive, and nationalistic. France, preoccupied with its security, tried to keep Germany in an inferior
military and diplomatic position and hoped to achieve its own
economic recovery from the First World War without exacerbating
class struggle.[2]

Historians have conventionally dated the Bolshevization of the
French Communist Party (PCF) from 1923 to 1925.[3] If we examine
the PCF's perception of intellectuals, we can see that this hardening of line occurred earlier. Except for the brief interlude of the
French Popular Front, the PCF's approach to intellectuals in the
early 1920s foreshadowed the main features of its policy through-

out the interwar period, specifically, its intolerance of democracy within Communist organizations and its avoidance of critical dialogue with workers, trade unions, leftist organizations, and anarchist militants.

The PCF was formed after the acrimonious Congress of Tours in December 1920. Having split from the SFIO (Section Française de l'Internationale ouvrière), the French Communists accepted Lenin's twenty-one conditions for joining the Third International and adopted an antagonistic policy toward Socialist and Social Democratic parties.[4]

The situation of the PCF in early 1922 was precarious. The prospects for postwar revolution in the industrial West fizzled out by 1920, and with the absence of dynamic, competent leadership, the PCF found its membership and influence declining. The one successful upheaval, the Soviet Revolution, left a profound imprint on the French Communists, who accepted Bolshevik tactics and the Leninist emphasis on organization, discipline, and centralization. A simpleminded form of Leninist theory also prevailed.

After 1920 the Communist Party's press became more centralized. Organs such as *L'Humanité* evolved from the spirit and content of Jaurèsian socialism. As Marxist dogma triumphed, the French communists out-Bolshevized the Bolsheviks and adopted a position of loyalty to the official line of the Communist International. The party offered its followers a fundamental choice: expulsion or capitulation to Moscow. No independent path was acceptable. By 1924 the left workers' opposition had been expelled; dissidents had been condemned and eliminated. Following these purges, the PCF developed a bureaucratic leadership on the model of the Russian Central Committee. With Trotsky the leading Soviet architect of Comintern policy toward France, heterodox fellow travelers and heretics were exposed and discredited to the masses and party militants.[5]

French communism was action oriented, antiparliamentary, antimilitaristic and nontheoretical. It built itself into a coherent, strategically flexible, and tightly disciplined political movement, whose membership accepted the necessity of a monolithic, hierarchical organization. To tighten its links with the industrial workers of France, the party embraced both legal and illegal tactics, such as elections and subversion of the army. The tacit, unconditional loyalty of its leadership to the Soviet Union often led to tragic policies in France. By the end of Bolshevization in 1926–1927, the PCF had become an identifiable mass movement whose goals were subordinated to the priorities of Soviet foreign policy.

French communism developed a paradoxical relationship to French society and politics, which led to the ghettoization of the PCF. It remained ideologically primed for a revolution that never materialized. Party representatives had a puerile and vulgarized grasp of Marxist theory. The PCF, proclaiming its intolerance of democracy, disassociated itself from the French socialist traditions of free discussion and participation by the membership in decision making.[6]

Romain Rolland had a lifelong commitment to harmony and reconciliation. He considered the split in 1920 between the French communists and the socialists disastrous. This schism made it easier for the right to maintain its economic, cultural, and political hegemony by weakening the proletarian movement, confusing the working class, and deflecting it from its own interests. When he contributed to the French left-wing press, he adamantly refused to lend his name to one party as an instrument of authority against the rival. Thus he wrote: "I will not mingle in the unholy struggles that have divided and weakened the two halves of Socialism."[7] For him there were no enemies on the left. The real opponents were those who inhibited progressive sociopolitical and cultural change. He resisted fratricidal warfare, trying instead "to promote inside France the confederation of all forces of the revolutionary Left against reaction."[8]

Whereas activists had to limit their aims and narrow their focus to be effective, intellectual and creative activity had an absolute and timeless character. As his orientation shifted, Romain Rolland abandoned a short political biography of Karl Liebknecht. He exhorted younger writers to emulate him and concentrate on projects that would restore confidence in individualism and prevent them from "getting involved in social and political activity." He never underestimated revolutionary action or the educational possibilities in propaganda, but he considered such projects unsuitable for intellectuals. Intellectuals had to be disposed to "stronger, more vast and profound action."[9]

Coinciding with the signing of the peace treaties, Romain Rolland published three experimental works, a play, a novella, and a novel, that integrated a coherent antiwar stance and an aesthetic vision.

The play *Liluli* (1919) was Romain Rolland's fiercest critique of the wishful fantasies and conformist thinking of the war years.[10] He paraded an entire society before his audience, a civilization marching frenetically to war. The farcical technique unveiled the ways in which war twisted people, institutions, and ideas into one-dimensional forms. In the end, no individual or collectivity could oppose the pilgrimage to annihilation. "*Liluli* is the revolt of a French Jean-Christophe against the French lie."[11] The "lie" was the capitulation to a hypocritical idealism, specifically nationalism.

Liluli depicted how technology and propaganda intensified the momentum of mass aggression. Violence reproduced itself, as the intellectuals of Europe indulged an uncanny taste for death, glory, and nostalgia for their lost youth. Ideologues of the slaughter, they sang a monotonous hymn to war. Romain Rolland made them the chorus of the play, portraying them collectively as silly geese— solemn, stupid, self-satisfied, conformist, and manipulated.[12]

Liluli, the enchantress of illusion, cared for nothing and belonged to everyone and no one in turn. Her elusive amorality turned men's brains inside out, preparing them to kill or to be killed. Romain Rolland showed no way out of collective murder. The play was written to "shake the stupid assurance of the reader."[13] Its last laugh was a lethal one.

In the novella *Pierre and Luce* (1920), Romain Rolland revealed the universality of war through the experiences of innocent, amorous adolescents at home. Set in 1918, and climaxing with the bombing of the church of Saint Gervais in Paris on Good Friday, *Pierre and Luce* showed that no one was spared in total war. The author characterized the Great War as an immense, meaningless massacre that trivialized death and made people insensitive to loss. The war eroded such secure prewar institutions as religion, country, and family. When certainty, calm, and memory were eradicated, there was no escape from the present, even in romantic love.[14] The deaths of the attractive but doomed adolescents made a single point about the war: namely, that they died for nothing.[15]

Romain Rolland wrote the meditative novel *Clérambault* (1920) between 1916 and 1920. It summed up his philosophical position during this period. The novel is flawed by didactic passages and by the hero's virtual canonization. In experimenting with the genre of antiwar literature, Romain Rolland articulated metaphors that were to pervade pacifist discourse in the 1920s and 1930s. He offered two theses: that the Great War was criminal and that the idea of country was a fetish.[16]

The novel offered more than an indictment of chauvinism, pride, human cruelty, and militarism. In *Clérambault*, Romain Rolland advanced the integral or absolute pacifist position, which condemned all forms of violence, including the use of force by revolutionaries. Subtitled "The History of a Free Conscience During the War," the book addressed the postwar dilemma of pacifist intellectuals. "Free conscience" was independence of the mind, the intellectual's inherent capacity to be autonomous, to "stand alone and to think alone for all."[17] The free thinker thinks with his heart, understands all sides, and defends "eternal values," even if he is perceived by contemporaries as a public enemy. Thus the hero, Clérambault, could address his readers in a manner "inoffensive, fraternal to all, comprehending to all sides."[18]

Yet Clérambault's unlearned, spontaneous intelligence of the heart was not devoid of contradictions and self-doubts. It included feelings of deep loneliness and personal inadequacy. Conscience was freed through guilt and penance. As he evolved from a man captured by patriotic enthusiasm to one guided by compassion, Clérambault experienced the alienation of the unpopular dissenter from wife, family, friends, colleagues, and country. The war provoked a crisis of conscience in Clérambault, calling into question many of his nineteenth-century values. The key to his transformation was the death of his son, Maxime, in the trenches. Grief destroyed his uncritical idealism and made him confront his own responsibility for his son's death. He universalized the responsibility of parents for the deaths of European youth.

Clérambault discovered that ideas were as murderous as cannon. The war had domesticated European men of letters, robbed their independence and critical intelligence. The Great War revised the view of history as continuous progress toward harmony. Total war underscored the role of treachery and force in history. Clérambault indicted intellectuals for their collective bad faith, their collusion with murder: "The death of European youth, in all countries, lies at the door of European thought. It has been everywhere a servant to the hangman."[19]

Clérambault's pacifist stand during the war stirred up social tensions and political animosities: "For all true pacifism . . . is a condemnation of the present."[20] He soon ran into the realities of censorship and the confusions generated by partial information, misinformation, and rumor. Because there were few outlets for dissenting views in wartime, he published in journals of the extreme left. Thus he came into contact with worker militants and socialist revolutionaries. Clérambault accepted neither their analysis of the war nor their solutions. His own writings explicitly condemned capitalism and imperialism, but always in the context of a critique of the state, of nationalism, and of Western civilization. Clérambault spoke a class vocabulary, but it was neo-Jacobin and populist, not marked by a Marxist conception of history or class struggle.[21]

While admitting he was a prisoner of his own individualism, Clérambault remained outside the revolutionary social movement and refused to subordinate his free spirit to the directives of the proletarian leaders. Action for the sake of action was mindless, self-destructive, and contrary to the work of building a new society. Faith in direct action actually disguised a profound worker anti-intellectualism. He contested all political philosophies that rested on the premise that the end justifies the means. Clérambault defended sacred values and saw the revolutionaries as young Saint-Justs—hot-headed, dictatorial, simplistic, and scornful of the opposition. In political practice as well as in theory, means were far more significant than ends.[22]

Clérambault remained a solitary war resister, alone with his free conscience and internationalism. He was called a traitor for his pacifist writings: death threats multiplied, and he was tried for circulating pacifist propaganda among the working class. The nationalist press encouraged violent attacks on Clérambault, fearing that his seditious ideas might weaken morale. Finally, Clérambault was murdered by a nationalist in much the same manner as the French socialist Jean Jaurès.[23]

The pacifism outlined in *Clérambault* was idealistic, psychological, and decidedly tragic. Individuals must prepare to resist, be persecuted, and die to oppose social brutality and the menace of world war. Postwar pacifists must be moral without being sanctimonious, religious without being intolerant. A noncoercive, harmonious world did not require the pacifist intellectual to adopt short-term, practical solutions. The major struggle would be against personal impatience and weakness and the conflicts of a divided self.

Clérambault furnished Romain Rolland with a temporary ideological justification for the individual autonomy he craved. It articulated his personal sense of mission, illustrating his receptivity to nonviolent political strategies. *Clérambault*'s absolute pacifism, internationalism, individualism, and defense of moral freedoms remained above direct political involvements, which were polluting by definition. He made no effort to link his pacifism to existing organizations, to propose principles of leadership or a national or international program of organization or action. Romain Rolland's pacifism did not draw on the pre-1914 French peasant tradition of antimilitarism and resistance to conscription.[24] It lacked a systematic social and economic analysis of the roots of war or of the historical origins and political limitations of pacifism. It did not appeal to the longing for revolt that communists and fascists alike were able to tap after World War I. Most important, his pacifism did not seem destined to grip a larger secular public.[25]

"Integral pacifism" was merged with non-Eurocentrism and antinationalism. Romain Rolland's opposition to imperialism stressed the cultural implications rather than the economic and strategic dimensions of the Leninist view. It was difficult to distinguish integral pacifism from contemporary European liberalism or legalistic internationalism, as embodied by supporters of Wilson and the League of Nations. He did not adequately address crisis situations. What would pacifists do in case of foreign invasion, a new world war, or the fascist threats that by 1922 became increasingly real?

Romain Rolland, at fifty-seven, found his intellectual situation in France unique. He no longer had reliable allies in the French university system, an old center of intellectual influence. He was not associated with a Paris review, nor had he established a school of thought. He wrote episodically for the left-wing daily press. He was stigmatized as "anti-French" by right-wing and liberal opinion, which blurred distinctions between pacifist internationalism and communism.[26] Yet his writings were popular throughout France and his books sold extremely well at home and abroad. The novel *Colas Breugnon, bonhomme vit encore,* published in the spring of 1919, ran through fifty-two printings in that year. By 1920, several volumes of *Jean-Christophe* had been republished in 125 French printings. He earned a comfortable living as a free-lance writer. His works were almost immediately translated into the major European languages.

At the same time, the prize-winning novelist discovered that his name had almost disappeared from the French literary press and newspapers. He believed there was an intentional boycott of his works, motivated by political resentments or the vindictiveness of official intellectual circles in Paris.[27] He did not take into consideration developments in aesthetic or literary taste after the war.

Romain Rolland's literary reputation was damaged by the fact that André Gide and important editors of the *Nouvelle Revue fran-çaise* (*NRF*) disliked him, his style, and his views on art. Gide once remarked nastily that *Jean-Christophe* was the only French novel that read better in German translation.[28] The *NRF* exercised a decisive influence on cultural attitudes in Paris. Romain Rolland never wrote for the *NRF* and the *NRF* seldom reviewed his works. Reviews that appeared were overwhelmingly negative.[29]

Romain Rolland, for his part, had enormous contempt for the *NRF*. He considered its stable of writers to have been excessively nationalistic during the war and their aestheticism to be morally bankrupt, narrow-minded, and impotent. They might have taste and talent:

> But what great antipathy I have for this *N. Revue f.* [*NRF*]. They are people for whom theory is the whole of life! Since they can create nothing (or so little) by themselves, they manufacture boxes, boxes with the manic determination of confused wasps who build cells without ever putting anything into them. And how proud they are of their boxes! . . . They are very distinguished minds. France is well guarded. Oh! How glad I am to be outside it all![30]

Nevertheless, Romain Rolland was not completely isolated. In the immediate postwar context he had influence and articulate disciples. Although his *engagement* was too diffuse to be a coherent doctrine, Rollandists existed who were prepared to popularize the message. His activity during the First World War inspired a series of critical studies and biographies published between 1919 and 1921 by close friends and associates: Paul Colin, the editor of the

Brussels review, *L'Art libre;* Stefan Zweig, the popular Austrian writer, translator, and biographer; Pierre-Jean Jouve, the French poet and novelist; Jean Bonnerot, French literary critic; and Marcel Martinet, communist poet, playwright, and theoretician of proletarian culture.[31] Jouve's biography, introduced "as a poem and an act of faith," exemplified the reverential nature of these studies. They were labors of love, written to repay a personal debt to Romain Rolland, viewing his life as a work of art and a model of heroism, good Europeanism, and moral wisdom. Zweig's dedication to his intellectual portrait verged on hagiography.[32]

In the early 1920s, Romain Rolland's relation with intellectuals sympathetic to communism was rich but exceedingly contradictory. His exchanges with these writers revealed their differences, reenacted the dilemmas sketched in the novel *Clérambault,* and set the stage for his major collision with Henri Barbusse.

The novelist and essayist Jean-Richard Bloch opted for Bolshevism in December 1920 at the Congress of Tours. He was deeply disillusioned by nationalism and by the behavior of the socialist majority during the Great War.[33] Yet Bloch had signed Romain Rolland's Declaration and he remained receptive to particular features of Romain Rolland's populist, anti-imperialist, and humanistic vision. Internationalism could be sharpened, Bloch insisted, if it were linked to an unequivocal protest against capitalism.[34]

Romain Rolland reiterated that the authentic intellectual opposed any political, religious, or class dictatorship and resisted all forms of intellectual repression. The International of the Mind remained uncontaminated by Leninist and other politicized views of an international association.

> I will always maintain the International of the Mind outside of the 2nd, 3rd, or the 4th International of Action. These worlds are not juxtaposable. An International of Action is always relative: it aims exclusively, narrowly, toward a goal that will be and must always be surpassed; and it aims with one eye in closing the other. The International of the Mind has an absolute and eternal character: not to lie, either in word, or in thought; never to tolerate a shackling of the free search for and public verification of the truth. And consequently, it admits free groupings, but it refuses all official unitarianism, commanded by State, by Church, or by Party.[35]

In a review of Raymond Lefebvre's novel *Le Sacrifice d'Abraham* (1920), Romain Rolland penned one of his most memorable phrases, exemplifying the task of the committed intellectual: "Pessimism of the intelligence, optimism of the will." Lefebvre was one of French communism's most talented writers. He preserved what was valid in the past without diminishing his inventiveness; his intellect, probity, skepticism, and faith were combined with the determination to act, to dream, and to take audacious risks. His trials became the source of his resilient strength.

> But what I especially love in Raymond Lefebvre is this intimate alliance—which for me makes the true man—of pessimism of the intelligence, which penetrates every illusion, and optimism of the will. It is this natural bravery that is the flower of a good people, which "does not need to hope to undertake and to succeed to persevere," but which lives in struggle over and above suffering, doubt, the blasts of nothingness because his fiery life is the negation of death. And because his doubt itself, the French "What do I know?" becomes the weapon of hope, barring the road to discouragement and saying to his dreams of action and revolution: "Why not?"[36]

Lefebvre's review of *Les Précurseurs* typified the organized French left's perception of Romain Rolland in this period. Socialists and communists esteemed him for his impeccable internationalism and courage during the war. Sketching his transition from prewar writer of genius into one who "sounded the rally of the International," Lefebvre found Romain Rolland's judgments consistently generous: "He who never had a red card in his portfolio became the leader of an International of which he was not a member."[37]

Henri Barbusse had also been inspired by Romain Rolland's antiwar stance, regarding him as someone who had preserved the honor of the intelligentsia.[38] Romain Rolland had applauded Barbusse's impressionistic antiwar masterpiece, *Le Feu* (1916), as one of the most powerful works of literature generated by the war.[39]

Romain Rolland resigned definitively from the *Clarté* committee on 23 June 1919. The subsequent evolution of *Clarté* confirmed his initial fears. From pacifist internationalism in 1919 to Third International communism in 1920, *Clarté* resolved its ideological ambiguities by hardening its line. Excessive eclecticism had given way to dogma. Barbusse's denunciation of prewar pacifism, accompanied by an increasing number of unbalanced articles on the Soviet revolution, vindicated Romain Rolland's decision to stand apart from the review. He found the tone of *Clarté* increasingly strident: the review did not transform the consciousness of its readers but addressed only the convinced. *Clarté*'s sectarianism would alienate French and German intellectuals and prevent communism from being properly studied and from taking root in the cultural sector. Independent figures such as Einstein would recoil from "the extremism of opinions, tone, and followers of the group."[40]

Romain Rolland's initial impressions of Barbusse were mixed: "Very nice, amiable, but a bit too flattering."[41] Barbusse ingratiated himself; he yearned for public acclaim. In their social goals and orientation they shared "the same tireless constancy and wholehearted devotion," but Romain Rolland envisaged alternative means to achieve those goals. Barbusse seemed more oriented to journalism and mass manipulation.[42]

Romain Rolland resented Barbusse's desire for "ready-made success." He invidiously compared his own years of solitude and work discipline while writing *Jean-Christophe* to Barbusse's instantaneous fame with *Le Feu*, which failed to prepare him for the crucial work of the present. By April 1920, Romain Rolland considered Barbusse a failure who had squandered his moral authority by preferring the "role of orator at literary meetings."[43] Barbusse was just another French celebrity, a man of letters momentarily in fashion. He would not have a lasting imprint on his public. Barbusse had a "weakness of character": he was flighty, not well grounded in basic values, easily seduced by fame and by circumstances.[44]

From 1919 to 1922, Henri Barbusse tried to win leftist war veterans (the Association Républicaine des Anciens Combattants) and intellectuals (the *Clarté* group) to the cause of the Third International, while taking pains to publicize his political independence. He did not join the French Communist Party until 1923. In the short tract *The Knife Between the Teeth: To the Intellectuals* (1921), Barbusse equated communism with reason and the eternal truths of conscience.[45] Communist doctrine was "at the summit of the history of ideas." Workers of the mind not in solidarity with this movement were judged incapable of assuming their social responsibilities. Barbusse addressed the French intellectuals' lack of realism and congenital distrust of politics, by which they upheld the status quo. Intellectuals failed to see the necessary relationship between political action and social thought, to see that "politics is life."

Barbusse discounted the difference between political inactivity and conservatism: "Those who are not with us are against us."[46]

Barbusse's brochure bore out its title by aggressively attacking such competing ideological stands as liberalism, pacifism, humanitarianism, anarchism, and moralism as outmoded and socioeconomically ungrounded. Intellectuals had to accept the doctrine of the Communist International as well as indicate their fraternal sympathy for the Soviet Revolution, "the beginning of the second phase of humanity." Barbusse's advocacy of violence to achieve social progress ("Today violence is the reality of justice") was consistent with his support for a Leninist dictatorship of the proletariat. Violence and class dictatorship were temporary, justifiable means to the end of socialism.

Barbusse blunted the edge of his knife by making two concessions. The first reassured writers that an alliance with the Communist Party phalanx would not mean the total subordination of their work to politics or sociology. Nor would they be required to join communist organizations or obey party discipline strictly. The second was a gesture of conciliation toward Romain Rolland, "splendid incarnation of conscience and incensed perspicacity."[47] Such praise was curious after Barbusse had defamed pacifists for confusing the fantasy of peace with the reality. It underlined his reluctance to excommunicate Romain Rolland and his prestige from communist front organizations.

From December 1921 to the spring of 1922, Henri Barbusse and Romain Rolland carried on a heated exchange of open letters over the political and social responsibilities of the intellectual. The debate was triggered by Barbusse's polemical *Clarté* article "The Other Half of Duty: Concerning Rollandism."[48] Romain Rolland replied in the Brussels journal *L'Art libre*, and his rejoinders were reprinted in the Italian *Rassegna internazionale* and the Parisian dissident Communist newspaper, *Journal du peuple*.

Ostensibly, Barbusse aimed his attack at the "numerous and vague disciples" of Romain Rolland, who remained unaware of the impotence, social hazards, and "intellectual error" of Rollandism. The only "Rollandists" actually named by Barbusse were the Ger-

man pacifist intellectual Georg Nicolai and the English pacifist
E. D. Morel. Barbusse leveled three serious charges against this
nonreactionary "intellectual left": that they demonstrated an infantile antipathy to politics; that they had an ahistorical phobia about
violence; and that they trafficked in moralistic and nonapplicable
ideas. Barbusse condemned the Rollandists for their self-imposed
distance from events and their faulty analysis of the social causes of
war and misery.[49]

Intransigence on the issue of intellectual autonomy clouded the
actual commitments of the Rollandists. Although they posed as
representatives of advanced thought, their critiques of the existing
social order were always partial, insufficient, and after the fact.
"The role of the pure moralists is negative." Barbusse insisted that
protest and refutation were only half the intellectual's responsibility. Barbusse discovered the detachment and sentimental ivory-
tower humanitarianism of the Rollandists beneath the trappings of
modernism or libertarianism. Their domain was that of pure ideas.
Without organization, collective regulation, and scientific analysis
of social problems, they were unable to react effectively to the
present. Barbusse argued that their pacifist and liberal ideologies
were dated and irrelevant.[50]

In an elliptical reference to the novel *Clérambault,* Barbusse condemned the attitude of the "alone against all" as inadequate in the
struggle against a powerful enemy. Rollandist posturing was merely
"moral ceremony." Because the Rollandists' critique of society was
fragmentary, it could easily be turned in a reformist direction. Gradual changes and ineffective protests obstructed the total revolutionary emancipation of the workers by enticing them with temporary
rewards and false promises. The Rollandists remained pessimistic
because they were unable to enlist completely in the social revolution: they lacked a unified doctrine, a coherent method of inquiry,
and a viable program to replace what they condemned. "The revolutionary mind is the complement of the spirit of revolt."[51]

Barbusse advanced the model of *Clarté,* an implicit revolutionary commitment to the Third International and to Leninist socialism. Socialism was synonymous with scientific infallibility, realism, reason, advanced republicanism, and true internationalism.
The strength of *Clarté*'s commitment to socialism derived from its
capacity to unite philosophy and action, "idea and will." No other

stance could mediate between the oppressive present and the liberating future. Barbusse's socialist science operated by applicable laws, whereas the Rollandist view was imprecise, ornamental, and impressionistic. Independence for the sake of independence was circular and historically antiquated. Intellectuals needed communism to actualize their dreams.[52]

Barbusse's agency of social change was the popular multitudes, mobilized by their collective awareness of the inequities of the capitalist system. The producers (workers) implemented a "revolutionary social geometry" through violence and constraint. Violence remained a provisional, but neutral instrument in the work of socialist reconstruction. Rollandists exaggerated the role of force in class struggles, forgetting that "the imperialist, militarist regime" rested on social crimes. Barbusse urged his audience, presumably younger French intellectuals and students, to judge violence situationally, according to its historical utility. Violence was necessary to disarm the capitalist profiteers and parliamentarians and to begin the process of erecting a more rational and just order. "Violence is in the totality of the revolutionary social conception only a detail and only a provisional detail."[53]

Romain Rolland entered the controversy by attacking Barbusse's "neo-Marxist Communist" theory for claiming "the infallibility of its fundamental laws."[54] Such absolute certainty was unwarranted by the evidence: it reflected communism's arrogance and its intention to universalize the Soviet model to include non-Russian societies. He found the postulation of a "revolutionary social geometry" to be both absurdly rationalistic and reductive.[55]

Romain Rolland refused to justify Soviet errors by pointing to the historical context. Certainly, the period of the civil war and of war communism, including the villainous intervention by the governments of Europe and America, had contributed to internal Soviet difficulties. But Bolsheviks—and their Western supporters—must bear responsibility for the current repression and the rigidification of the political line. He had observed their secrecy, intolerance of any organized opposition, and tendency toward centralization. They had made the noble aspirations of the Russian people into vehicles of political expediency: "I do not struggle against one reason of State in favor of another. And militarism, police terror, or brutal force are not in my eyes sanctified because they are the instrument of a Communist dictatorship instead of being an instrument of a plutocracy." He found Soviet communist practice too pragmatic, too responsive to lies, and too political to suit his vision of what the Revolution could be. He refused the Manichean choice posed by Barbusse as intellectual blackmail. He simultaneously opposed Western democratic and Soviet forms of oppression.[56]

Romain Rolland particularly disliked the party spirit among the Bolsheviks. He distrusted the automatic attribution of truth, justice, and progress to the Soviet Communist Party. The claims of absolute correctness and scientific validity for Marxism remained unproved and unprovable. Lenin remained the only free communist, because he was permitted to criticize and exercise his capacity for judgment. All other Bolsheviks were epigones mouthing a political hymn. Even Lenin's freedom was limited by the doctrinaire parameters of his ideology and by his isolation in the Kremlin.[57]

On the issue of the communist justification of violence, Romain Rolland extended the argument first expressed in *Clérambault*. The communist legitimization of violence upset him more than the cruelty of the past. He was unable to differentiate the communist mentality from the labels and collective psychology of right-wing and nationalist groups after the Great War. The ideologies of both left and right only intensified aggression and bloodshed. His refusal to sanction violence even as a temporary expedient stemmed partly from his divergence from Bolsheviks about the possibility of revolution in Western Europe. His reading was that the era of revolution had passed. Europe was on the verge of "a long crisis . . . of an era of upheavals, during which the nations will have to suffer a great many more attacks than those they have just experienced. We are arming ourselves for this age of iron."[58]

He completely rejected Barbusse's proposition that violence was a "provisional detail." He advanced a theory of the self-perpetuating nature of human aggression. The experience of violence was traumatic; it left "indelible traces" in the human mind and memory, scars that endured for a lifetime. Thus the experience of violence—as victim or victimizer—was never temporary or trivial. Repeated acts of aggression predisposed individuals to act violently to protect themselves and their territory if threatened by an assault. Contemporary communists did not seem interested in ending human aggression but promised to escalate class warfare. No matter how rationalized the use of violence, past experience determined that the human psyche would answer coercion with further forms of coercion.[59]

Romain Rolland reasserted the integral pacifist position of *Clérambault*. The question of means was more crucial in revolutionary than in "normal" times. Although he accepted the necessity for radical social change, he hoped to minimize the disparity between brutal techniques and the society that was the goal. Because people were molded by participation in daily struggles and because the final goal was rarely reached, the emphasis was on the free, voluntary, and moral nature of conflict. Distorted by the excessiveness and arbitrariness of violence, the means might overwhelm the goal. "The means, however, shape the minds of men according to the rhythms of justice or to the rhythms of violence. And if it is according to the latter, no form of government will ever prevent the oppression of the weak by the strong."[60]

Communist intellectuals made a fetish of ends and overvalued direct action. Thus they were unwilling to promote debates within their ranks or exchange ideas with the progressive members of the European intelligentsia. Their propagandists belittled opponents with mindless name-calling and abuse. Rather than lift the discussion to the level of ideas or strategies, they dismissed the defenders of conscience and love as "anarchistic" or "sentimental." Romain Rolland predicted that communist intolerance would separate the intellectual left from the revolution; more important, it would polarize political lines.[61]

Romain Rolland knew that earlier revolutions had grown authoritarian, if not despotic, once in power. The victorious Bolshevik Revolution might also deteriorate into a new form of domination and injustice. He retained his independence and a firm resolve to oppose all despotic forms of government:

> With you and the Revolutionaries against the tyrannies of the past!
> With the oppressed of tomorrow against the tyrannies of tomorrow!
> Schiller's phrase: (it has always been my motto) *In tyrannos!* (Against *all* tyrants)[62]

Barbusse's second open letter alleged that Romain Rolland himself lacked generosity for revolutionary activists. Concepts like "harmony" and "wisdom," derivatives of metaphysical wordplay, postponed active participation in struggle. Barbusse criticized his world vision for the "absence of a viable, practical real solution, which it brings to human unhappiness." Romain Rolland's critique of communism, with its obsessive fixation on "violence," paralleled those "of the anarchists and the bourgeois." Those profoundly troubled by violence should denounce the policies of Western imperialist countries who were plundering the entire globe and holding the Soviet experiment in check. The disenchantment of men such as Romain Rolland hindered the revolution, retarding the communist efforts in social reconstruction.[63]

Romain Rolland's second letter to Barbusse spoke directly to the latter's "convenient and oratorical" placement of Rollandists in the ranks of the bourgeoisie.[64] He ironically noted that communists mouthed their class-conscious rhetoric to the detriment of their opponents, forgetting that members of the bourgeoisie were also to be found in the Communist Party—an oblique reference to Barbusse's own middle-class social origins. He offered an expansive view of the Russian Revolution as an alternative to the Communist Party view. He universalized the revolution's creative possibilities and hope for a "better and happier humanity," while Barbusse narrowed it to the exclusive property of a professional vanguard: "The Revolution is not the property of a party." Rolland stressed the coexistence of the revolution with liberty; Barbusse fused the revolution with equality.[65]

Total freedom of thought ought to complement revolutionary activism. Intellectuals were obliged to protest against all sloganizing, whether of a party, church, or caste. Flag-waving of any sort was anathema, no matter what color the flag or how attractive its symbols. Intellectuals must be unceasingly vigilant against all authority. Romain Rolland called for protest to be practiced during and after the making of a revolution, to question power permanently, and to take public stands against injustice and the usurpation of rights. He asserted that philosophically inclined writers not only prepared the revolution but also were crucial in constructing the just society after the upheaval. Against the Bolshevik denigration of the intelligentsia, he evoked the tradition of the eighteenth-century *philosophe* to buttress his idea of the intellectual's responsibility:

[the responsibility] to ridicule, to castigate, to fling stones at abuses, in emulation of the mordant criticism, the embittered irony of Voltaire and the Encyclopedists who did more for the downfall of the monarchy than the handful of rash men who took the Bastille.[66]

Romain Rolland's assessment of the potential for radical change in Western Europe clashed with Barbusse's. The war had left the working class apathetic and exhausted. The communist analysis lacked psychological realism if it felt that these "profound masses" could implement a program of massive social change. He was not reassured by the caliber of existing French Communist Party leadership. Time was needed to heal the injuries of the First World War and to accomplish the immense job of social reconstruction. Such a task required generations. Barbusse's remedy was precipitate and destructive. The unleashing of revolutionary forces in Europe in 1922 would be disastrous, triggering a painful repression, reopening the wounds of the war, and sapping the last resources of the progressive forces.[67] In relegating socialist victory to the distant future, Rolland suggested that his perspective was actually an evolutionary one.

Switching from rejoinder to affirmation, Romain Rolland introduced a novel element into the controversy—Gandhian nonacceptance of the state. He sketched Gandhi's contribution as a spiritual quest, a political philosophy, and a powerful tactic. Gandhi's life and work were little known in continental Europe, but the viability and adaptability of the doctrine had been proved by the work of "thousands of Anglo-Saxon Conscientious Objectors" and by Gandhi's efforts to undermine English colonial domination of India. Romain Rolland presented Gandhism as a strategic and ethical alternative to Bolshevism. It contradicted the Bolshevik overvaluation of collective forces by demonstrating the efficacy of individual resistance to the state. It refuted the communist insistence on the necessity of violence by revealing the practical option of nonviolence in struggles of national liberation, struggles against conscription, and labor battles.[68]

He introduced Gandhi's theory and practice to disprove the accusation that his vision was partial and disconnected from political practice. Gandhism promised to break the cycle of violence begetting violence. Neither passive nor negative, it required enormous willpower and self-discipline of the individual resisters, heroic moral refusal to collaborate with the "criminal State." The political and religious aspects of Romain Rolland's Gandhism intermingled. Implacable rejection of the state threatened existing power relations, while the individual's willingness to make sacrifices represented a return to the sacred, a release of moral forces, "the fire of conscience, the quasi-mystical sense of the divine that is in every being."[69]

Gandhism creatively extricated Romain Rolland from his political impasse and enabled him to integrate the processes of individual and collective emancipation. The work of constructing a revitalized and just society would tap the moral resources of the individuals but allow resisters relative autonomy. Individuals would be accountable to themselves, not to a party or a coterie.[70]

In a postscript Romain Rolland offered Barbusse an object lesson in modern science. He dissected the epistemology of Barbusse's "social geometry" to show that it was simply another form of faith. Barbusse confused scientific facts with irrefutable laws. A law required an abstract conception expressing relations between facts. Laws did not exist in nature, but in people's minds. There were no laws that did not eliminate certain facts, that did not take into account the mind of the scientist. Science, like all other human disciplines, had a self-reflexive component, was relative, as Einstein had established, and only approximated an exact view of nature. To think that one could arrive at precise laws was to indulge in metaphysics.[71]

Barbusse's communist methodology shifted abruptly from the pure to the applied sciences. An unmediated leap from mathematics to sociology stemmed from abstract reasoning, which failed to consider the living complexity of the human organism as well as the role of psychology in all social interactions. At its best modern sociology offered a "calculus of probabilities," "rough approximations" of existing reality, hardly Barbusse's geometric clarity and rigor.[72]

In his third and final letter, Barbusse again insisted that Rollandism was utopian.[73] Good will, faith, and honesty were excellent virtues, but insufficient to restructure society. Intellectual protest, too, was admirable but limited. Rollandists lent prestige to the forces of reformism, diffusing the militancy of competing groups who called for radical change. Steeped in self-contradiction, these

"half-liberals" and "half-pacifists" took refuge in the poetic exalta-
tion of individual freedom and conscience while omitting all reference to the privileged nature of that liberty.[74]

Barbusse revived Romain Rolland's distinction between liberty
and equality, but turned it against his opponent. That Romain
Rolland chose liberty was perfectly consistent with his position:
liberty was a vague notion readily modifiable by external circumstances. Equality, in contrast, was scientifically exact and attainable.
Nor would Barbusse retract the pejorative epithets "bourgeois" and
"anarchist" to describe Romain Rolland's thought: they were justified by the fragmentary and inapplicable nature of his theory and his
deductive approach to social problems. To glorify individualist solutions and to characterize all collective behavior as masking hidden
forms of tyranny was to indulge an infantile antiauthoritarianism.
Romain Rolland's arguments could be lifted by the Western ruling
class to "discredit the Russian revolutionary experiment." Rollandists refused to take risks. Rather than accept revolutionary practice,
they would choose noninvolvement in the daily political tasks required to implement their humanitarian dreams.[75]

As for Romain Rolland's reflections on violence, Barbusse found
them "confused, arbitrary, lost in verbalism." He conceded that the
word "constraint" was preferable, being less emotionally charged.
Constraint was an essential element not only of social struggle but
also of the cohesion and discipline of a functioning collective movement. Romain Rolland misinterpreted communist realism as bloodthirstiness or a desire for reprisals.[76]

Barbusse's reaction to Gandhi's political philosophy and methods was contradictory. He granted the efficacy of nonacceptance in
specific circumstances, seeing "this heroic passivity" as closely related to the weapon of the political strike. A "peaceful revolution"
might also be possible in certain historical frameworks. The success
of the nonviolent tactic depended on the nearly unanimous consent
of its participants. Unless the vast majority resisted, violence would
be multiplied. If only a few conscientious objectors refused to mobilize for war in France, their actions would backfire; they would be
jailed and summarily executed. Individualism in the absence of a
collective and international organization could not stand against the
deadly force of repressive agencies. Consequently, Gandhian resistance was beside the point in France.[77]

Notwithstanding the Soviet Union's "faults" and its waverings of doctrine, Barbusse compared contemporary socialist reality favorably to modern capitalist society, dominated by "imperialism, the rapacity of the metallurgical and military oligarchy, the oppression of the rich with all the pretexts of nationalism." Barbusse preferred communism, with its scientific predictability and practical attempts to build a better, more egalitarian, future. He regretted that Romain Rolland did not choose the same path; the former master must be surpassed to meet the pressing demands of the times: "What you have said—what you have done—will always remain sacred and precious to us, and in spite of you, we will use them to go further than you."[78]

The immediate backdrop for Romain Rolland's last letter was a polemical article by Amédée Dunois and several ill-tempered journalistic pieces by Marcel Martinet, literary editor of *L'Humanité* and a close associate of his. The rhetorical violence of these pieces coincided with the announcement of an open trial in Russia of the Social Revolutionaries, a party in opposition to the Bolsheviks. The trial was scheduled to begin in March 1922, at the same time as the Genoa Conference. This news suggested further ideological intolerance and a general tightening of the political dictatorship in Russia. Most Western observers were unaware that the trial was orchestrated by general secretary Stalin while Lenin was ill. Afterward, the Social Revolutionaries and all other organized political opposition in the Soviet Union were banned.[79]

Romain Rolland's last open letter focused on the distortions in Leninist theory and practice, rather than "prolonging to eternity" the Barbusse debate.[80] His letter was pervaded by "anxiety" and "doubt" about the open trial of the Social Revolutionaries.[81] Such events were easily exploited by the anti-Bolshevik forces of Western Europe. A progressive Western intellectual, he insisted, could criticize both the credo and the policies of the USSR without being denigrated as a bourgeois or a reactionary.[82]

He linked communist materialism to recent developments in capitalist industrial technology. Communists accepted most of the political and economic assumptions of modern industrialism but were ignorant of the advances in philosophy and psychology. They debunked and persecuted people of faith and spirit. Drawn from a "single book" (presumably *Capital*), Marxism was ill-equipped to explain the diversity of human nature. Nor were the legalistic and mechanistic formulas of Soviet Marxism supple enough to grasp the complexity of lived experience. Marxist rationalism tried to encompass all of human behavior under a "unitarian" political and economic system, forgetting those aspects of motivation that sprang from culture, education, or the psyche.[83]

He advised his "Communist friends" to be more humble, self-critical, and above all willing to make alliances with potential supporters. The Bolshevik "brutalization of European liberal opinion" was both unrealistic and self-defeating. Alienating such writers as Bertrand Russell, Georg Brandes, and Anatole France might sever the social revolution from "moral forces" who influenced public opinion. Anatole France, despite his allegiance to *Clarté* and self-proclaimed advocacy of communism, had publicly protested the trial of the Social Revolutionaries. Bolshevik denunciations of the intelligentsia for "petit-bourgeois sentimentality" ruptured a link with those attempting to reconcile the "exigencies of the socioeconomic Revolution and the no less legitimate demands of spiritual liberty." The intellectuals vilified by the communist press were in closer touch with the emotional pulse of Western society than were the sectarian communists.[84]

The communists were ignorant of the history of revolutions. Duplicating the fatal mistakes of the French Revolution, they lauded organized coercion, rationalized their conspicuous errors, deliberately rebuffed distinguished foreign partisans, and negated the humanistic principles that had originally motivated the social upheaval. Above all, they were unable to forestall an authoritarian dictatorship. In Russia and in France, communism was blind to the power of emotion and imagination:

> The politics of violence and above all the clumsy efforts to extol that policy have had the inevitable consequences of estranging from the Russian Revolution the elite liberal thinkers of Europe . . . ; just as the massacres of the French Revolution definitely alienated it from the Wordsworths, the Coleridges, and the Schillers. . . . In my opinion that was one of the causes of the ruin of the French Revolution. Let the Russian Revolutionaries be advised. Woe to those who scorn the forces of the heart![85]

Romain Rolland pitted his concept of the complexity of the human organism and of society against the Marxist materialism that reduced this multidimensionality to a dogma. Marxist horizons were "far too narrowly circumscribed by economic materialism." Implicitly retreating from Gandhism, he was now unable to conceive an alternative route to communism. Nevertheless, he would patiently wait for a strategy to extricate him from his dilemma. The article ended with an idealist glorification of "Mind" as an autonomous universe, a force of nature. He remained apart from all mass movements, attempting to harmonize insurrectionary forces with those of the heart in his effort to find the "revolutionary formula of the future."[86]

Romain Rolland was concerned that Barbusse, by initiating this quarrel, not only placed Rollandists on the defensive but also divided the left and weakened the forces for internationalism. The only beneficiary was political and intellectual reaction.[87] More seriously, he was appalled by *Clarté*'s refusal to publish the entire debate in its pages as the affair unfolded. This intolerant attitude mirrored communist views on intellectual liberty and freedom of the press, anticipating the kind of repressive society that communists might construct. His replies were published in the Brussels periodical, *L'Art libre*, directed by Paul Colin.[88]

The French Communists jumped into the midst of the polemic by publishing an article by Amédée Dunois in *L'Humanité* called "Concerning the *Communist Manifesto*." Dunois offered some rudimentary class analysis, relying on the Marxist distinction between infrastructure and superstructure. Marx had resolved this debate by pointing toward practical solidarity with the modern proletariat. Identifying capitalist society with decadence, war, and legalized exploitation, Dunois held that class reconciliation was impossible between the proletariat and the bourgeoisie. Bourgeois ideology and sentimentality were parasitical; intellectuals should side with the workers, whose historical mission it was to make the revolution and achieve socialism, despite "the convulsion of dictatorship and terror."[89]

Romain Rolland stated his position unequivocally in a letter dated 10 March 1922: "I am with the proletariat when they respect truth and humanity. I am against the proletariat every time they violate truth and humanity. There are no class privileges, neither high nor low, in the face of supreme human values."[90]

Dunois replied vigorously in the same issue of *L'Humanité*, in an article entitled "Neutrality Is Impossible." Communist intellectuals alone were committed in a realistic way; Romain Rolland had regressed back to his idealistic 1914 stance "above the battle." Circumstances forced one to decide between the organized working class and the middle class. Against the abstract devotion to freedom and justice, he posed the "pitiless realism" of Machiavelli and Marx to attain these sublime goals. Class struggle, not individual greatness, lay at the base of historical progress. Because an exploited class had to seize situations as they developed, it could not always exercise complete control over its actions or its means.[91]

Marcel Martinet climaxed his role in the polemic in an angry piece entitled "The Intellectuals and the Revolution." He announced his final break with his former mentor, whose disillusion with the reality of the Russian Revolution proved that he had not changed since the war. Defenders of "Independence of the Mind" had been repetitious and far too generous toward "imbecilic and cruel social regimes" in the West, while brimming over with complaints about proletarian demagoguery. During the war, Romain Rolland had raised global issues on which revolutionaries had meditated, despite their disagreements with him on methods and solutions. But that time had long since passed, and his views had to be superseded. The "vain retreat" of the intelligentsia from the workers' struggle showed their lack of vision and reluctance to dirty their hands in a bloody revolution.[92]

A by-product of this debate was a fervent exchange between Romain Rolland and the celebrated Marxist historian of the French Revolution, Albert Mathiez, author of *Robespierre terroriste* (1921). Mathiez questioned the nature of intellectual disengagement from the great Revolution of 1789. Apparently written to correct Romain Rolland's Dantonist misinterpretation, the book's hidden purpose was to establish precedents for intellectual allegiance to revolutionary upheavals. Contemporary intellectuals could logically and in good faith rally to the Soviet Revolution. He referred to the "fact" that most European writers had continued to sympathize with the French Revolution despite the Terror.

> There were without doubt then, as today, some Romain Rollands to take refuge above the social battle in a superior puritanism, but there were also the Henri Barbusses to understand the profound reasons for an unprecedented crisis and to maintain their sympathies and

their cooperation with the men of action who led the struggle with intrepid hearts.[93]

Romain Rolland contested Mathiez's evidence for Wordsworth's allegiance to the French Revolution. A three-line passage from *The Prelude* was hardly sufficient. Mathiez glossed over Wordsworth's horror of the revolutionary Terror, self-servingly misrepresenting the poet's historical disillusionment with these excesses. The distortions of the Terror pushed Wordsworth forever away from political commitments, toward an exclusive absorption in poetry and the imaginary process. Thereafter the revolution became a symbol of youthful illusions and self-deceptions. Romain Rolland, in fact, linked his own critical view on Bolshevik violence with the philosophy of Wordsworth. "He finally discovered that true freedom is inner freedom, that of the creative mind." Yet Romain Rolland also admired Robespierre as a historical personality and a leader with vision and political acumen. Mathiez's fine scholarship merely disguised his apology for the "dictatorship of violence at the time of the Convention." Romain Rolland's appreciation of the "incorruptible" changed neither his identification with the martyred poets of the Terror nor his opposition to any justification for dictatorships: "If tomorrow Robespierre became master in France again, I would go to die with [André] Chénier and not with Robespierre."[94]

Convinced that the substantive issue of the Barbusse debate was "a great subject," Romain Rolland encouraged *L'Art libre* to solicit responses from intellectuals all over Europe. Widening the forum, however, did not mean trivializing the ideas or dealing in personalities: no injurious remarks about Barbusse or *Clarté* were to be included. The debate must maintain a serious level of discourse and address divergent ideas to resonate with writers.[95] He appended a provocative appeal to intellectuals:

Do you think that it is the present duty of the artist, the scholar, the man of thought to be engaged in 1922 in the army of the Revolution, as they were engaged in 1914 in the Army of Right? Or rather does it seem to you that the best way of serving the cause of humanity and even the Revolution is to protect the integrity of your free thought— even if against the Revolution, if the latter does not understand the vital need for liberty? For not understanding this need, the Revolution would no longer be a source of renewal, but would become a new form of monster with a hundred faces: Reaction.[96]

The Romain Rolland–Henri Barbusse debate expanded in March 1922, when an entire number of *L'Art libre* was devoted to the discussion of "Independence of the Mind: Responses to Romain Rolland's Appeal." Twenty-seven intellectuals replied; the debate spilled over to the April issue.[97] Only three of the twenty-seven participants supported Barbusse.[98] Two intellectuals took middle positions between Romain Rolland and Barbusse.[99] The remaining articles were all strong statements on behalf of Romain Rolland's point of view, reflecting consensus on the importance of the World War I experience, an almost unanimous opposition to violence, and impatience with attempts to legitimize coercive methods and temporary dictatorships. The Rollandists appeared vehemently committed to a pluralistic society. Believing in personal transformations and a shared concept of internationalism that transcended class and party, they stressed the right of individual privacy and autonomy. Many invoked the idea of cultural revolution in contrast to the communist view of social and political upheaval.[100] There were significant omissions: only one reference was made to Marx's writings, which suggests the ancillary role of Marxist theory in the controversy. Gandhian theory and practice did not fare much better.

Edouard Dujardin's Paris journal *Cahiers idéalistes* provided an additional forum for the Rolland-Barbusse debate by publishing thirteen reactions from French, Swiss, and Italian intellectuals. Two of the thirteen sided with Barbusse.[101]

French anarchists and libertarian communists took a lively interest in the debate, partly because of the inherent magnitude of the issues and partly in response to Barbusse's defamation of anarchism. Articles appeared in *Le Libertaire, Revue anarchiste,* and *Journal du peuple* in the spring and summer of 1922. The French extreme left was alarmed by the persecutions of Russian anarchists and Social Revolutionaries. They protested repressive Soviet policies and criticized the Bolshevik worldview from a libertarian perspective.[102]

Romain Rolland especially admired the responses of Duhamel, Durtain, Vildrac, van de Velde, and Zweig. Writers on both sides of the issue were not always tactful or germane. He was satisfied with the private expressions of solidarity he had received from Albert Einstein and Maxim Gorky. The pacifist intellectuals Norman Angell, Frederick van Eeden, E. D. Morel, and Bertrand Russell agreed with Rolland's principles of intellectual independence but did not intercede because they were traveling or in ill health.[103]

Feeling that it was necessary to establish a forum for advanced thought free from partisan politics, Romain Rolland urged his colleagues to inaugurate a new Paris-based international review. It should contain "no politics" and should be "as individualist as possible." Besides ending the cultural isolation of intellectuals in Western Europe and the Soviet Union, he wanted it to offer an alternative to *Clarté*'s Marxist parochialism and to the *NRF*'s aestheticism and formalism. The review should promote a cultural taste for the foreign, a task best accomplished by translating non-French classics and by actively seeking the collaboration of Asian intellectuals.[104] The first number of the journal *Europe* appeared on 15 January 1923.

Romain Rolland deeply distrusted the prevailing politics on both the left and the right. He departed for Switzerland on 30 April 1922, never again to live permanently in the French capital. He explained his self-imposed exile in these words:

> I am leaving Paris, definitively this time, morally more isolated than I have ever been. . . . Political and intellectual reaction is ruling in France. I am leaving Paris at the time of the Conference of Genoa, at which the French delegation is the only one to obstruct the pacification of Europe. The people are indifferent. The nation is ready for another war, whenever it should please Poincaré. I foresee a second Waterloo, sooner or later. And it is sad to say that when it comes it will be but just.[105]

Once installed in Villeneuve, Switzerland, a town exquisitely perched in the mountains overlooking Lake Leman, Romain Rolland returned to creative activities. The first volume of his novelistic cycle *L'Ame enchantée, Annette et Sylvie*, appeared in August 1922.[106] Believing that the Barbusse debate was over, he expressed his feelings of respect for Barbusse "in spite of the errors of his thoughts." The public controversy had reinforced Romain Rolland's esteem for the younger French writer. Privately faulting his self-deceptions and unnuanced thinking, Romain Rolland praised Barbusse's sincerity, noble character, courteousness, faith in humanity, and "chivalric generosity."[107] He left open the possibility of fraternal collaboration.

During the summer of 1922 the pages of *L'Humanité* were open to Romain Rolland's attack on American capitalism for its "execrable persecutions" of radical labor groups such as the Industrial Workers of the World.[108] But they were swiftly shut when he interceded on behalf of Henri Fabre, director of *Journal du peuple*, who had been purged from the PCF, and protested the current trials of the Social Revolutionaries in the Soviet Union. Trials should not be coverups, he wrote in his journal; progressives in the West had to be kept informed in order to assess such confusing and disturbing events.[109]

Romain Rolland was enraged by *L'Humanité*'s refusal to publish his articles.

> There is no longer justice or truth in the French Communist press, only Communist justice and truth. This will lead to shipwreck, not for freedom, which does not concern the Communists, but for the Revolution. If the Revolution does not retain religious respect for truth and moral values, it will fatally break up into *combinazioni*—or otherwise become cunning and violent like Fouché or Bonaparte.[110]

He tried to restore mutual tolerance among the people and movements on the left. Communist intellectuals misconstrued his stance as "anti-Bolshevik," but the "anti-Bolshevism of the left" was actually a communist construction, revealing communist fanaticism and ignorance of the cultural sphere. "As I have said earlier: not 'anti-Bolshevik'—but 'aBolshevik.' For in the depths of my soul, none of this interests me."[111]

Leon Trotsky contributed a fitting epilogue to the Romain Rolland–Henri Barbusse debate in October 1922. Combining irreproachable revolutionary credentials and penetrating literary insights, Trotsky articulated the official Soviet view and relegated Rollandist humanism to the dustheap of history. In a review of Martinet's drama *La Nuit*, Trotsky unleashed an attack on Romain Rolland's philosophy: his narrow humanitarian egoism pertained only to artists; he lacked a program of mass action for the people. When the issues of war and peace and intellectual collaboration shifted to social revolution, Romain Rolland faltered and remained stationed "above the battle." The French moralist's blanket condemnation of violence and dictatorship stemmed from individualist moral and aesthetic notions—not from an understanding of history. Revolutionary violence was the sole means by which workers could reverse the exploitative regimes of their oppressors.

> As long as the people suffer the dictatorship of capital, Romain Rolland poetically and aesthetically condemns the bourgeoisie; but should the working class endeavor to burst the yoke of their exploiters by the only means in their power, by the force of revolution, they in turn encounter the ethical and aesthetic condemnation of Romain Rolland. And thus human history is in sum only material for artistic interpretation or for moral judgment. Romain Rolland, the pretentious individualist, belongs to the past.

Obliquely referring to Gandhian ideas, Trotsky argued that pacifism was not a revolutionary strategy. It raised expectations while fulfilling them with passivity and halfway measures. "Poisoned by skepticism, he soared high in contemplation, but in his decisive moments was always hostile to the insurgent proletariat."[112]

Romain Rolland recorded this going-over at the hands of the "Czar of all Russians, more powerful than Napoleon."[113] The comments of "Generalissimo" Trotsky were "not without justice" from the perspective of a Marxist revolutionary activist. Though Trotsky failed to understand his character or his faith, he was a far more interesting opponent than the bourgeois literary critics: "Trotsky's sabre dipped in red ink is better than the razor of Souday or Thibaudet." It was futile to reply to Trotsky's scathing remarks. He was convinced that the Bolsheviks had arrived at a conspicuous "point of aberration,"[114] namely, concentrating their energies on pockets of left-wing intellectuals, pacifists, anarchists, socialists, and antimilitarists rather than on the entrenched adversary—finance capitalism and the upper bourgeoisie.

The Rolland-Barbusse confrontation raised rather than resolved complicated questions. Its relatively wide-scale reverberation in intellectual and political circles testified to the relevance of the issues under discussion and to the tragic seriousness of the intellectual's search for a meaningful path after World War I. For a brief moment, European and French men of letters were asked to formulate their views publicly about their role in society. Posing such a question was itself a political act, and it raised the enigmatic question of the intellectual's political affiliation. The expansion of the debate into a public investigation, featured in special numbers of *L'Art libre* and *Cahiers idéalistes* and spilling over into the communist and anarchist press, testified to its resonance throughout the cultural sector. It documented how intellectuals saw themselves in 1922 and how they contested issues at the intersection of politics and culture.

As Romain Rolland aptly observed, the antimonies of the quarrel opposed liberty to authority, freedom to equality, but also the ideology of integral pacifism—*Clérambault*'s "one against all"—to the Marxist ideology of historically determined collective forces. The relationship of means to ends was posed, and the proposition that Gandhian noncooperation might be an alternative to revolutionary violence. Romain Rolland's stress on the intellectual's continuous search for truth collided head-on with Barbusse's communist view of class consciousness, itself a derivative of class conflict.[115]

The confrontation climaxed Barbusse's break with Romain Rolland's internationalism, pacifism, and intellectual independence. Barbusse was now aligned with Third International communism, and he held that all intellectuals with faith in the future would affiliate with such movements. Postwar Europe was almost completely politicized, and intellectuals could no longer deceive themselves that their relationship to exploitative society was apolitical. Partial politicization and aloofness were unacceptable; the only option was total commitment to both Marxist ideology and communist organizational structures. Following this debate, Barbusse marked out a successful career as orator, journalist, organizer, and spokesman for communist front operations. He never again wrote a great literary work. Until his death in 1935 he was a tireless servant of the Communist International.

Barbusse called for the fusing of class struggle and political struggle. His perception of the methodological value of Marxism as an instrument of social analysis was rudimentary. If anything, Barbusse's Marxism lived up to the title of his journal, *Clarté:* it was dedicated to enlightening its readers. Many of his key points were crude extrapolations of Lenin's writings. Barbusse bridged the gap between criticism and action by joining a mass communist party at least rhetorically devoted to proletarian emancipation and to the realization of socialism. The contours of Barbusse's later uncritical attachment to Stalinism are foreshadowed here. Romain Rolland would never reach some of his opponent's conclusions or embrace communist organizational structures. His journey as a fellow traveler was far more agonizing.

Barbusse's doctrine of the intellectual's responsibility was mechanistic and undialectical. Its primitiveness reflected the slow and fragmentary penetration of Marxism into France, an almost caricaturish grafting of the Bolshevik ideology onto Jacobinism and post-Enlightenment thinking. Barbusse's Marxism was the vulgar Marxism of the untutored worker and party militant of the period. His thought precluded even a preliminary sketch of socioeconomic or sociocultural analysis. Barbusse had assimilated an overlay of Leninist propaganda before the conceptual apparatus of Marx. His sectarian presentation of the communist case clearly represented the world vision of the PCF at this moment.

Barbusse dedicated himself to politicizing both the masses and the intellectuals and to wresting political control away from the dominant classes in French society. Romain Rolland backed off from overt power considerations, worked to depoliticize at least the intellectual sector of society, and refused to polarize the class struggle.

In Romain Rolland's outlook, intellectuals defended the cultural legacy of the past, worked to reinvent culture in the present, and helped to expand the consciousness of their public. Yet he had a healthy skepticism about the precise goal or meaning of intellectual labor. Intellectuals could not change the world but could only interpret it, perhaps contribute an element of transcendence and consolation. He took refuge in nineteenth-century idealist abstractions: thinkers should aim for truth, justice, humanity, the elucidation of ethical concerns. They should be heretics, reject all false dichotomies, and strive toward returning modern humanity to the sacred. Since Barbusse believed in the historic mission of the European proletariat, he viewed Romain Rolland's notion of the intellectual to be another elitist obfuscation, covering over old forms of class privilege, maintaining the separation of mental workers from manual workers.

Romain Rolland stumbled in explaining how his noncommunist intellectual politics could involve daily struggle, vigilance, exemplary activity, and significant social change rather than the token espousal of unrealizable positions. The reality of the Russian Revolution exacerbated his difficulties. It made him seem utopian and romantic and Barbusse realistic and scientific.

Romain Rolland tried to close the chasm between engagement and allegiance to critical inquiry and imaginative endeavors. To bridge the gap between freedom and social revolution, he defended traditional civil liberties. He stressed pluralism, unity on the left, and libertarian values as necessary antidotes to Bolshevik political expediency, centralization, purity of doctrine, and divisiveness. His plea for open criticism between communists and noncommunists, and for self-criticism within communist circles, had a prophetic ring. Anticipating the distortions if research conformed to ideological boundaries, or access to information were prohibited, he accepted no rationalization for policies that suppressed elementary human rights. He opposed all policies that circumscribed cultural freedom.

What ultimately separated him from his communist opponents was his view of the Soviet Revolution. Barbusse and his allies perceived Marxism and the Russian Revolution on a political level. For Romain Rolland, the revolution posed a moral problem. He accented potentials unachieved, ideals debased, power internally abused, and ideology hardened into formula. Part of his disappointment with the Soviet Revolution derived from his grandiose expectations of this world-historic event. He was convinced that revolutionary spokesmen dismissed the psychological and spiritual features of human existence. In offering critical support of the Russian Revolution, he tried to determine both its faults and its merits.

Despite his firm decision not to join the PCF, it would be a mistake to see his divergences with communist intellectuals as an indication of anticommunism. He remained a noncommunist intellectual who believed that dialogue among sincere and well-informed members of the left would be enlightening to all sides. The persistent adversary was the political, institutional and cultural hegemony of the reaction. The debate with Barbusse did not terminate in total rupture of relations or in long-term acrimony. If they differed on liberty and equality, they could still remain fraternal. Romain Rolland left the door open for their subsequent antifascist efforts in 1927–1928 and for their initiation of the Amsterdam-Pleyel movement ten years after their controversy.

Barbusse's attack on the political implications of Rollandism forced him to crystallize his critique of the Russian Revolution, to restate his philosophical orientation, and to advance a strategy that extricated him from his ambiguous position between revolutionary Leninism and the progressive and pacifist bourgeoisie. At this juncture, he ingeniously introduced Gandhi's political philosophy and tactics, foreshadowing the major line of his political evolution throughout the remainder of the 1920s. In 1922, Romain Rolland's knowledge of Gandhi's life and writings was fragmentary. Opening the issue in a debate with a communist intellectual set a precedent for future discussions of nonviolent resistance. Gradually, he elaborated the parameters of Gandhian noncooperation for Europe. Having passed through the stages of antiwar dissent, integral pacifism, and propaganda for an intellectual's international, Romain Rolland was now ready to study the Mahatma's writings and the history of his movements in South Africa and India. By 1923 he emerged as the European popularizer of Gandhi.

6

Gandhian

> Gandhi was still present throughout India, in his achievements, his example, his image. For Europe, he was simply a liberator with clean hands; a symbol of saintliness, with the quaintness that goes with many saints: an obstinate nun with a big toothless smile, dressed in a humble plebian garment worn like the uniform of freedom.
>
> André Malraux, *Anti-Memoirs*

To comprehend Romain Rolland's intellectual politics in the period 1923–1932, we must treat the ambiguities of his engagement as a Gandhian. Since the publication of his biography of Gandhi in 1924, over four hundred books about Gandhi have been released. Today, Gandhi's name and face are so familiar that it is hard to envision a time when he was not part of our consciousness. But before the French writer popularized his image—fusing anti-imperialism, the nonviolent political philosophy, and the holiness of his life—Gandhi was an obscure Indian lawyer, unknown in continental Europe or America.

Romain Rolland's critique of imperialism emphasized that Europe's destructive tendencies, so visible during the Great War, were active in the colonized regions of Asia and Africa.[1] The civilizing rhetoric of imperialism veiled nationalistic and expansionistic aims, the will to amass wealth and to subjugate weaker societies. "Under the mask of civilization, or of a brutal national idealism, the politics of the great States methodically practice fraud and violence, theft and degradation (rather, extermination) of the so-called inferior peoples."[2] Throughout the interwar period, he protested European imperialism and predicted that the awakening nations would turn this violence against the Europeans themselves. Imperialistic aggressors would inevitably be confronted with anti-imperialistic aggression, which might finally engulf Europe. If this happened, Europeans were ultimately responsible.[3] Romain Rolland sought some intermediary between the imperialistic and anti-imperialistic forces, between East and West. Progressive intellectuals of Europe and developing countries might be able to "use their hearts and geniuses" to work toward nonviolent solutions to imperialistic injustices. Because struggles for national liberation might unchain cataclysmic forces, he urged intellectuals to preserve an "Island of Calm," to not be swept away by the destructive passions.[4]

Opposition to war was meaningless unless buttressed by opposition to imperialism. The Great War and the Treaty of Versailles convinced Romain Rolland that imperialist rivalries were creating the conditions for another world war. In one issue of *Clarté* he signed a public indictment of the French suppression of the Riff rebellion in Morocco and condemned all wars unequivocally.[5] The oppressive reality of "brutal and greedy imperialism" would provoke a counterattack, unleashing insurrectionary movements in Asia and Africa. The revolutionary dynamic of decolonization would not necessarily follow a Bolshevik model. Anti-imperialist movements might turn against the Soviet communists, perhaps to follow another path of historical development.[6]

All critical inquiry into imperialism should rely on accurate, firsthand information. Most crucial, it should grasp the totality of the situation by considering the perspectives of "both the conquerors and the conquered." The historical destinies of colonizer and colonized played decisive roles in struggles for self-determination and in the construction of independent societies. For Romain Rolland, imperialism derived from the expansionistic policies of military elites and venal capitalists: the "imperialism of armies and of money."[7] He understood that French involvement in Morocco and Syria was strategically designed to protect French interests in Algeria. That was no longer a legitimate aim:

> [Algeria's] conquest was the fruit of an extortion, and to defend that conquest, it is necessary to commit in turn other extortions, other crimes against the independence of native peoples. If the conqueror stops on the road and wavers, all his conquests totter; all Islam rises in insurrection. And who can calculate the ensuing ruins, not only for France but for Europe?[8]

Gandhi's political philosophy offered one humane solution to the multiplication of imperialist and anti-imperialist aggression.

Gandhi's democratic and conciliatory methods were preferable to the Soviet model as a way out of the "iron net" of imperialist domination and privilege: "It would be necessary as certain great-hearted men have discussed—such as Gandhi and some magnanimous Englishmen—that both antagonists should consent to make mutual sacrifices and to treat together in a spirit of kindness and abnegation this terrible question on which depend the life and death of both." The Gandhian path moved toward international cooperation, redress of the grievances of colonized nations, and a negotiating mechanism to satisfy the mutual needs of the imperialist powers and the countries seeking independence. Romain Rolland advocated the Gandhian route but had few illusions about the reception of these nations by Western governing elites. He knew "the blindness and obstinate pride of the great States."[9]

Anti-imperialism included a defense of civil liberties. His 1926 appeal in favor of a jailed Vietnamese writer supported the absolute right of the colonized to freedom of speech. He also denounced the French presence in Indochina, and he advocated national independence. If "loyal collaboration" between the French and the Indochinese occurred, intelligence and mutual resources might be shared. Independence should not mean a total rift. Vietnamese students and workers in Paris ought not to imitate Western violence and insensitivity. Movements of national liberation should repudiate all forms of racial pride and nationalistic prejudice. Europeans could struggle with the Indochinese in their fight for self-determination, if both sides accepted an "equality of rights and duties."[10]

Romain Rolland's anti-imperialism was fundamentally Gandhian. His denunciation of imperialism was often harsh and violent, but his remedies left the door open for dialogue between East and West. His intention was to circumvent the massive dislocations and random violence of struggles of national liberation and the efforts to repress them. The real work of creating a durable society could begin only after the struggles ended. Romain Rolland's anti-imperialism was also accompanied by an uncompromising opposition to pan-European ideas, such as a United States of Europe,[11] and by recurring pressure for revision of the Treaty of Versailles.[12]

In the interwar period, the isolated pockets of French and European pacifists bestowed enormous prestige on Romain Rolland, calling him "the conscience of Europe" because of his antiwar

Portrait of Romain Rolland at about
the age of forty.

Romain Rolland on the balcony of his Left Bank
apartment in Paris during the time he was
writing *Jean-Christophe*.

Romain Rolland with Rabindranath Tagore
in Villeneuve, Switzerland, 1926.

Romain Rolland with Stefan Zweig,
his Viennese biographer and friend,
Villeneuve, Switzerland, 1933.

Photograph of Romain Rolland
with Mohandas Gandhi,
Villeneuve, Switzerland, December 1931.

Romain Rolland with Maxim Gorky,
in the vicinity of Moscow,
July 1935.

Romain Rolland with Nikolai Bukharin
and Otto Schmidt during his visit
to the Soviet Union, summer 1935.

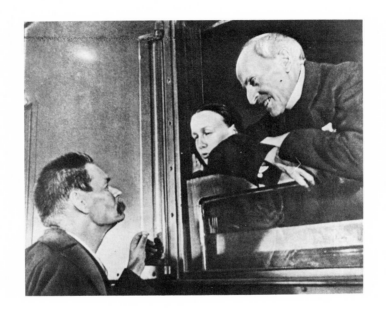

Romain Rolland and Madame Marie Romain Rolland
with Maxim Gorky at the Moscow
railroad station, July 1935.

stance during the First World War.[13] His introduction of Gandhi
and his dissemination of the nonviolent political philosophy further reinforced his stature. He was a paternal figure and pioneer
with unassailable pacifist credentials, an authority within the antiwar movement. Pacifists regarded him with affection, even if they
were unaware of his latest position. They repeatedly asked him to
clarify internal disputes and external dilemmas; to write interventions, petitions, declarations, manifestos, prefaces; and now and
then to contribute money to rescue a failing antiwar periodical.[14]
Romain Rolland debated continuously in the interwar era with
pacifist intellectuals along the entire spectrum of pacifist sentiment and ideology—educators, mothers, scholars, Tolstoyans, anarchists, Christians, and advocates of disarmament and conscientious objection.[15]

Romain Rolland seldom missed an opportunity for a symbolic
gesture to oppose war or to deflate the arrogance of the militarists.
When the Chamber of Deputies passed a conscription law in the
spring of 1927, and French right-wing Socialists such as Joseph
Paul-Boncour collaborated in supporting the bill, he published a
blunt oath of conscientious objection. The worst oppression of all
was the militarization of intelligence by the state:

> The monstrous project of military law, audaciously camouflaged by
> the warmongering pacifist verbiage of several Socialists, and voted
> by sleight of hand at the French Chamber, last March 7 [1927], claims
> to realize what no imperial or Fascist dictatorship has yet dared to
> accomplish in Europe: the entire slavery of a people from the cradle
> to the tomb.
>   I swear in advance never to obey this tyrannical law.[16]

In "The Duty of Intellectuals Against War," he again advocated
intellectual independence from institutions and parties. Intellectuals were exhorted to be "look-out men" for the eventuality of
war. Thinkers were enjoined to go beyond impartiality, beyond the
"laborious and scrupulous exercise of intelligence." Protest was
linked to action.[17]

Romain Rolland was not the first French writer to look to the East
for inspiration or consolation or the first to compare the Orient

with a materialistic, declining Occident.[18] He was, however, one of the first French intellectuals to conceive of modern India as a challenge to European political reality and global hegemony. He was drawn to the East because it differed from the violence and cultural stalemate of the postwar West. His meditation on India renewed the spiritual inquiry that had been interrupted by the world war and immediate postwar issues. Romain Rolland's Gandhian phase was, in part, a flight from sociopolitical preoccupations into oceanic metaphysics.

The Orient offered attractive regenerative possibilities for Europe; Indian thought might give receptive Europeans ontological as well as political options, introduce them to an alternative ethical system, encourage them to rethink their discredited values. The otherness of India could assist demoralized Europeans in rediscovering and tolerating their own otherness, thus initiating inner growth without precipitating anxiety or the need to dominate on the part of the Westerner. Romain Rolland's discourse on India emphasized similarities between East and West as well as the traditional contrasts. He discovered an exemplary personality to represent the East: a man of purity and self-sacrifice, a "great-souled" individual who was himself engaged in an epic political experiment. Romain Rolland mythologized Mohandas Gandhi into "the Mahatma."[19]

Unlike earlier Orientalists, Romain Rolland was convinced that European imperialistic domination of India must end. Empire building led to expansionism, imperialist rivalries, bloody suppression of native populations, and ultimately to war. The colonizers imposed their language, educational system, and cultural values on other civilizations. It is difficult to disentangle Romain Rolland's moral and political critiques of imperialism.[20] He recognized that European empires were crumbling and that movements of national liberation would eventually triumph. He hoped that decolonization would not reenact the violence of the colonizing impulse but would contain an explicitly internationalist dimension, rejecting the ethnocentrism of imperialist domination.

Gandhi provided Romain Rolland with a tentative solution to his dilemma as a committed intellectual in the 1920s, an ideological alternative to Bolshevism, and a corrective to postwar European pacifism. No matter that his political orientation was not pragmatic, or that his cultural writings crossed the boundaries of fiction. Romain Rolland became a self-appointed citizen of the world, mediating between East and West from his exile in neutral Switzerland. In the process he contributed the first documented study of Gandhi and modern India, using largely Indian and British sources.[21]

Romain Rolland's writings on India in the 1920s were not received in a total vacuum. A spate of books by Orientalists had appeared in France.[22] Between February and March 1925 the Parisian periodical *Cahiers du mois* sponsored an exchange entitled "The Appeals of the East." Twenty-two celebrated writers commented on the interpenetrability of Eastern and Western ideas, taking a position on the "grave peril" or value of Eastern influences on the West.[23]

Although writers such as Henri Barbusse and André Breton argued that interpenetration would be beneficial,[24] most participants adopted the stance of Paul Valéry, a lucid spokesman for the French conservative intellectual establishment:

> From the cultural point of view, I do not think that we have much to fear *now* from the Oriental influence. It is not unknown to us. We owe to the Orient all the beginnings of our arts and of a great deal of our knowledge. We can very well welcome what now comes out of the Orient, if something new is coming out of there—which I very much doubt. This doubt is precisely our guarantee and our European weapon.
>
> Besides, the real question in such matters is to *digest*. . . . The Mediterranean basin seems to me to be like a closed vessel where the essences of the vast Orient have always come in order to be condensed.[25]

Action Française writer Henri Massis remained hostile to Eastern influences and preoccupied with defending the West against foreign contaminants. His integral nationalistic stand favored the restoration of French will and grandeur, the preservation of its mental, religious, and geographical purity. He alleged that Romain Rolland's interest in Gandhi and Indian culture was politically motivated. Asian idealogues only weakened France, created disorder, and consequently played into the hands of hostile political forces such as Japan, Germany, and the Soviet Union. Receptivity to Eastern culture was nothing less than intellectual treason.[26] In a transparent display of cultural nationalism and contempt for the foreign, most of the writers argued that the East had far more to gain from exposure to the West, that East-West barriers were unmodifiable, and that limited exchanges ought to be guided by academics or Oriental specialists, not amateurs or propagandists.[27]

Romain Rolland replied, limpidly, "Where Henri Massis is, Romain Rolland cannot be."[28]

To Romain Rolland, the assertions of most participants in the debate were tinged with superiority and Eurocentrism, proving that French thinkers were rigidly closed to dialogue. They desperately needed an infusion of Eastern sources, and he was prepared to stand alone to promote substantive East-West exchange.[29] He used his connections to publish works by Tagore and to keep abreast of Indian affairs; he opened his home to prominent Indian visitors. He welcomed the works of Hermann Hesse, whose novels (particularly *Siddhartha,* the first part of which was dedicated to Rolland) irrefutably proved that Europeans could fathom Hindu thought.[30]

In humanitarian appeals during the same period, Romain Rolland attacked French nationalism and promoted Franco-German reconciliation. He responded to developments in Weimar Germany by writing from the perspectives of those suffering, the victims of runaway inflation, hunger, the military occupation of the Ruhr, political arrest, and indiscriminate hatred of Germans. If the French, from their postwar position of strength, failed to redress German grievances resulting from the unjust peace treaty and other punitive policies—failed to be sensitive to the desperate plight of the Germans—they would sow the seeds of German revenge, preparing to reap the next war.[31]

Romain Rolland was introduced to Indian thought in February 1915 in a series of letters from the Hindu writer Ananda K. Coomaraswamy. In becoming the European spokesman for Indian culture, he hoped both to regenerate postwar Europe and to avoid a fatal East-West clash resulting from mutual ignorance and stereotypes.[32]

As early as October 1916, he supported the work of the Nobel Prize–winning poet Rabindranath Tagore, whose 1916 "Message from India to Japan," a denunciation of European imperialism and the exclusively political and material foundations of European civilization, Romain Rolland addressed hyperbolically as a turning point in world history.[33]

The theme of Asian-European cross-fertilization permeated his thinking on India. In correspondence and discussions with Tagore, Romain Rolland stressed cultural exchange and advised against the imposition of either civilization on the other.[34] He was more concerned with cultural revitalization than with concrete problems of power relations.[35]

Gandhi's heroism contrasted with the absence of visionary leaders in Europe:

> That Gandhi's action of twenty years in South Africa has not had more reverberation in Europe is a proof of the incredible narrowness of view of our political men, historians, and men of faith: for his efforts constitute a soul's epic unequaled in our times, not only by the power and constancy of sacrifice, but by the final victory.[36]

An infusion of Eastern ideas might rekindle the old humanist torch. Romain Rolland did not propose to adopt Oriental forms of thought indiscriminately, however; they should be assessed impartially. He entertained high hopes that *Europe*, the review ostensibly founded under his patronage, would publish such assessments and propagate the ideas, but his hopes were dashed by the editors' refusal to publish Tagore's novel *A Quatre Voix*. This incident led to a temporary falling-out with *Europe*, though the "charming novel" was subsequently published by the *Revue européenne* in 1925.[37]

Romain Rolland first learned of Gandhi through conversations with Dilip Kumar Roy in August 1920.[38] The tentative nature of his defense of nonviolent noncooperation in the second open letter of the Rolland–Barbusse debate, in February 1922, mirrored his tentative knowledge of Gandhi and the Indian struggle for liberation. When asked in August 1922 to write an introduction to the French edition of Gandhi's *Young India*, he wanted initially to decline. Gandhi's spiritualized nationalism lacked the breadth of his own internationalism. Such important subject matter required more than a superficial treatment. He therefore postponed any writings on Gandhi in order to read about and reflect on Gandhi's mode of thought and action.[39]

With the assistance of his sister, Madeleine Rolland, Romain

Rolland (who neither spoke nor read English) spent the latter half of December and all of January 1923 reading Gandhi's texts. These included *Indian Home Rule,* articles in *Young India,* and writings from Gandhi's South African struggles. He was aided by the Indian academic Kalidas Nag, an intimate of both Gandhi and Tagore. Nag, Tagore, and others encouraged him to visit India.[40]

Gandhi and his French biographer had significant affinities. They were of the same generation—Gandhi was born in 1869; Romain Rolland in 1866. Both were influenced by and had corresponded with Tolstoy. Both emerged from their experiences in the Great War with an aversion to violence and warfare.[41]

If Romain Rolland was enchanted with Gandhi's blend of individualism, activism, and morality, he was equally troubled by Gandhi's distrust of science, his nationalism, and his nostalgia for preindustrial times.[42] Fascination far outweighed hesitation, however, and Romain Rolland planned a biographical portrait of the Indian leader modeled on his immensely successful *Beethoven* (1903). He wrote a short, easily digestible narrative essay centering on Gandhi's life and message, designed to acquaint as many readers as possible with the Gandhian movement. It was first published in three installments in the new Parisian monthly *Europe,* from March to May 1923, before it was released in book form in 1924.[43]

Gandhi's staunch opposition to oppression, particularly the British colonial variety that Gandhi had encountered both in South Africa and in India, became the connecting thread in the essay. His often indiscriminate attack on Western civilization derived from the brutality of British colonial rule, "written in the blood of the oppressed races, robbed and stained in the name of lying principles." Gandhi associated modernity and progress with domination and simplistically pitted the spiritual East against the acquisitive, technological West.[44]

Romain Rolland found the religious foundations of Gandhism reassuring. He drew on traditional Christian vocabulary to describe Gandhi and his movement, pointing to the similarities between Gandhi and Christ, St. Francis, and St. Paul to reinforce any religious associations the European reader might make. Since the nonmolestation of all forms of life had the standing of a categorical imperative, those who engaged in Gandhian resistance were acting spiritually. "Real noncooperation is a religious act of purification."[45]

Gandhi's methods demonstrated a capacity for tactical flexibility. His political philosophy contained a gradual theory of stages. In his campaigns there was first a concerted effort to work through legal means, employing negotiation and compromise to redress grievances. Only after exhausting legal resources, petitions, newspaper propaganda, and agitation by students, farmers, and the working class did Gandhi permit more disruptive, illegal tactics. Noncooperation moved from one level of resistance to another, increasing the degree of militancy at each level. Its campaigns were highly selective and cautious. Gandhi considered civil disobedience a legitimate but extreme form of noncooperation that should be focused on specific laws. Because personal risk was great and self-control was required of the resister, civil disobedience was applicable only when all other alternatives had been explored and was feasible only for the reliable elite.[46]

The concept of noncooperation was powerful and timely: Gandhi understood that "noncooperation can and must be a mass movement." His refusal to yield to the forces of the criminal state was not an infantile negation but an assertion of India's pride in herself. As Romain Rolland observed: "India had too much lost the faculty of saying 'No.' Gandhi returned it to her."[47] Gandhi appreciated the necessity for political organization and leadership; his strategy was a sophisticated staged program of cultural action employing meetings, demonstrations, fasts, and prayers, as well as music, national symbolism, and traditional Hindu imagery to guarantee maximum political efficacy.[48] Moreover, Gandhi demonstrated a shrewd sense of timing and propaganda and was adept in winning sympathy for his movement, both in India and among progressives in England.

Absolute sincerity of commitment was proved by the persecutions Gandhians suffered in all their campaigns. Gandhi himself had been imprisoned three times by 1923. Gandhism could be distinguished from other political ideologies by the moral restraint built into its doctrine, by the tendency of Gandhian resisters to circumvent power clashes whenever possible. Gandhians viewed their opponents as potential converts, if not allies, and tried to persuade the enemy by demonstrating the "irresistible" moral rightness of their positions.[49]

The most striking example of Gandhi's rejection of political expediency came in February 1922, after the riots at Chauri Chaura. In this small village eight hundred miles from Bardoli province, where Gandhi prepared to launch his mass civil disobedience campaign, a violent confrontation took place on 5 February between his followers and the local police. After provocation by the constables, the crowd retaliated by burning the police headquarters and murdering twenty-two policemen. Learning of the episode on 8 February, Gandhi immediately suspended the Bardoli campaign of civil disobedience. He made this choice against the advice of other Indian political leaders and despite the willingness of the rank and file to carry on with its more assertive action. The English government initially considered Gandhi's judgment an act of folly. It arrested him on 10 March 1922.

Romain Rolland contrasted Gandhi's tactical choice with repressive policies in Europe, including current Bolshevik practices. He stressed the purity, self-mastery, and silent suffering required of the Gandhian resister:

> To create the new India, it is necessary to create new souls, souls strong and pure, which are truly Indian and wrought out of Indian elements. And in order to create them it is necessary to form a sacred legion of apostles who like those of Christ are the salt of the earth. Gandhi is not, like our European revolutionaries, a maker of laws and decrees. He is the molder of a new humanity.[50]

Gandhi had generated a powerful momentum within the ranks of his movement. It is unclear how far this movement could have gone in 1922. As a contemporary commentator, Romain Rolland understood that the initiation and abrupt halt of the Bardoli campaign crystallized the ambiguities at the core of the Gandhian movement.[51] Nevertheless, he congratulated the Mahatma on his choice, thereby underlining the precedence of the spiritual over the political in his mission: "The history of the human conscience can point to few pages as noble as these. The moral value of such an act is exceptional. But as a political move it was disconcerting."[52] If Gandhi's acceptance of personal responsibility for the Chauri Chaura episode was naive, his penitential fast was a magnanimous gesture of legendary proportions.

The balance sheet of the biography was mixed. Though conceived in the genre of *haute vulgarisation*, it was not simply hagiography or propaganda. Gandhi's opposition to science and technology and his exaggerated hope in cottage industries were historically regressive, a feature of Gandhi's messianic approach to immediate conflicts. Other policies recalled the cloister of medieval monks, most particularly his xenophobic attitude toward other cultures. Romain Rolland had not visited India or learned its languages. But his writing on Gandhi proved that civilizations could interpenetrate.[53]

He also disapproved of Gandhi's puritanical outlook. The severe restrictions on sensual gratification and abstention from sexual intercourse were reminiscent of St. Paul's hostility toward the body.[54] Gandhi's personal saintliness did not obliterate the erotic and aggressive urges of less disciplined men and women. Because of his own freedom from "the animal passions that lie dormant in man," or perhaps because of his overcompensation for them, Gandhi denied the human potential for violence, including violence to self.[55] His answer to perennial reliance on cruelty was an exceptionally high standard of behavior. Conspicuously lacking the redeeming features of their master, many of Gandhi's disciples had vulgarized the doctrine, substituting discipline for idealism, dogma for principles, and above all narrowness for Gandhi's emphasis on the attainment of truth through experimentation.[56] Romain Rolland noted the aggression in much of the discourse of nonviolence: "Tagore is alarmed and not without reason at the violence of the apostles of nonviolence (and Gandhi himself is not exempt from it)."[57]

Not without disclaimers, his portrait underscored that Gandhi's message to the world was as urgent as it was great. Whether that message was peace, noncooperation, nonviolence, or voluntary self-sacrifice, Gandhi recaptured the full potential of Indian liberation. If his successes were studied and his techniques emulated in other battles against oppression, India's special message might be extended to the peoples of the world. His political instrument was equally the most humane technique known to history: nonviolence. For the biographer, Gandhism symbolized a universal hope and a political alternative to the pervasiveness of force in the West. It could give to the demoralized pacifists a vigorous faith and an experimental tactic for change. Taken by the immense power of the doctrine, Romain Rolland announced his own conversion to the principles of Gandhian nonacceptance. Anticipating scorn from the left and right, he asserted that Gandhi's methods had proved their value for the social battles to come. The real enemy in the nonviolent struggle was the resister's personal weakness and lack of conviction:

> The *Realpolitikers* of violence (whether revolutionary or reactionary) ridicule this faith; and they thereby reveal their ignorance of deep realities. Let them jeer! I have this faith. I see it flouted and perse-cuted in Europe; and, in my own country, are we a handful? . . . (Are we even a handful? . . .) But if I alone were to believe, what difference would it make for me? The true characteristic of faith is—far from denying the hostility of the world—to see and believe in spite of it! For faith is a battle. And our nonviolence is the toughest struggle. The way to peace is not through weakness. We are less enemies of violence than of weakness. . . . Nothing is worthwhile without strength: neither evil nor good. Absolute evil is better than emasculated goodness. Whining pacifism is fatal for peace: it is cow-ardly and a lack of faith. Let those who do not believe, or who fear, withdraw! The road to peace is self-sacrifice.[58]

In "Gandhi Since His Liberation," Romain Rolland stressed the strengths of Gandhi as an adversary of British imperialism and of nonviolence as a political weapon. This piece informed European readers of Gandhi's two-year imprisonment, the rupture of his direct influence on Indian politics, and his subsequent release on 2 February 1924. Gandhi had elaborated a four-part program for na-tional independence and social reform, the objectives of which were (1) work toward Indian home rule through the unity of Hindu and Moslem factions; (2) spinning as a remedy to Indian pauperism and as a pragmatic way to extricate India from economic depen-dence on Britain; (3) the disappearance of Untouchability; and (4) the methodical application of nonviolence in both propaganda and deed, including civil disobedience as a last resort. Gandhi opposed the British government and struggled against imperialism, while distinguishing between the English people and their administra-tors. He also realized that while colonization had ruined India's economy, decolonization would cause hardships on British indus-trial workers in Manchester: "A Gandhi is one of the very rare men capable of rising above the interests of individual parties in strug-gle and of wanting to seek the welfare of both."[59]

Romain Rolland's "Introduction to *Young India*" revised the point of view of the biography. The Gandhi presented here is decidedly more Mazzinian, complex, tragic, and ultimately more revolution-ary than in the earlier portrait. "Nonviolence . . . in other words the political nonviolence of the Non-cooperator [is] a reasoned method of peaceful and progressive revolution, leading to *Swaraj*, Indian Home Rule." He underlined the interlocking role of experimentation and direct action in Gandhi's politics. However, those who opted for class struggle and violence were also engaged in an experiment. Without judging which experiment was more viable for India or applicable to Europe, the French writer urged the partisans of violence to be "honorable" and "unhypocritical" in elaborating their strategy and tactics. Feeling an affinity between communists and Gandhians, he refused to dismiss the courage and idealism of violent revolutionaries: "Between the Mahatma's nonviolence and the weapons of revolutionary violence there was less separation than between heroic noncooperation and the sterile ataraxia of the eternal acceptors."[60] Satyagraha, insistence on truth, was based on the laws of active love and voluntary renunciation. Gandhi was different from passive, sentimental, "nerveless" European pacifists. Romain Rolland now emphasized the rational and accessible nature of the Mahatma's message, as well as the mystical side. The doctrine was also experimental: "But we must dare. Gandhi dares. His audacity goes very far."[61] Gandhism was characterized as an open-ended struggle, full of dangers for the half-believer, unsuitable for the individual who could not endure extended periods of self-discipline. "Nonviolence, then, is a battle, and as in all battles—however great the general—the issue remains in doubt. The experiment which Gandhi is attempting is terrible, terrifyingly dangerous, and he knows it."[62]

Romain Rolland's essays on Gandhi illustrated the positive attributes of the Mahatma's character and the wide possibilities of organized nonviolence. The point of view is best understood as noncommunist; Bolshevik and Gandhian methods were compared in just three brief allusions in the biography.[63]

As with his other biographies, he spent approximately six to eight months researching Gandhi's life and only three weeks composing the text. His small volume on Mahatma Gandhi sold extremely well in France (thirty-one printings in three months, at least 100,000 copies in the first year) and was translated into Russian, German, English, Spanish, and three Indian dialects by 1924 and into Portuguese, Polish, and Japanese by 1925. The critical reception in Paris was apathetic.[64] By 1926, nevertheless, a fiftieth printing was published. The biography was clearly a best-seller.

The French communist reaction to his introduction of Gandhi was politically inconsistent. In the midst of the Romain Rolland–Barbusse debate, the communist author Ram-Prasad Dube focused on the social aspects of Gandhi's movement in India, drawing a parallel between Gandhism and the European anarchosyndicalist movements. He praised Gandhi's expertise in propaganda and agitation and his willingness to engage the mass movement in illegal tactics but predicted that Gandhi's politics of concession to authority and the perfection of the individual would ultimately fail. Gandhi would be remembered chiefly as the initiator of the first stage in India's social revolution.[65] One year later, *L'Humanité* published a far more critical article by the Indian Marxist revolutionary and representative to the Comintern, M. N. Roy. Roy held that the Gandhian movement was socially suspect, composed of members of the "reactionary petite bourgeoisie." It was neither anti-imperialist nor committed to complete Indian independence. To harness the energy of the "revolutionary spontaneity of the masses," an indigenous Communist Party was necessary. Roy looked to the Indian leader C. R. Das to provide the Indian left with leadership and a radical direction. The country simply could not afford to become captive to Gandhi's moralism and theology.[66] Later, in March 1923, *L'Humanité* published an editorial signed by the executive committee of the Communist International. While condemning British imperialism and their fierce reprisals against the Indians for the Chauri Chaura incident, the statement carefully excluded criticism of Gandhi or his movement.[67]

Romain Rolland's portrait of Gandhi triggered a clever, if inaccurate, rejoinder by Henri Barbusse that blurred the political and ideological antagonism between Gandhism and Bolshevism. Following the pattern of the earlier polemic, Barbusse's article "Eastern and Western Revolutionaries: Concerning Gandhi" praised the spirit in which Romain Rolland wrote his essay. Although it opened communications between Europe and Asia, his "magisterial and lyrical study" of Gandhi nevertheless misrepresented the formal opposition between Gandhi's doctrine and that of Western revolutionaries. Barbusse asserted that Gandhi belonged on the side of the Third International. His intransigence, utilitarianism, and practicality indicated that "Gandhi [was] a true revolutionary."[68] As a pragmatic idealist with a realistic understanding of Indian political constellations, Gandhi, without being aware of it, was "very close to the Bolsheviks."[69] His verbal vilification of communism resulted from his unfamiliarity with Marxist doctrine and misinformation about communism in the Soviet Union.

In Gandhi's activities as a popular leader and his defense of the working and agricultural masses of India, Barbusse found a form of class struggle.[70] Noncooperation was irrefutable revolutionary activism, not passivity. Gandhi's ability to suspend his movement at a crucial moment after the violence of Chauri Chaura only dramatized the immense authority of the Mahatma over 300 million Indians.[71]

Barbusse emphasized that nonviolence was merely a provisional tactic.[72] If Lenin had been in India, he too would have spoken and acted as Gandhi did: the two "are men of the same species, prodigious characters, who know how to measure for and against."[73] The spectacle of the Indian masses agitating for their sovereignty shared many similarities with the Russian experience. Gandhi's goals were identical to those of Lenin's, namely, a society in which privileges would be eliminated, where people could live a peaceful, egalitarian life. Their methods were alike: "Lenin is for constraint— and Gandhi also."[74]

Gandhi would evolve closer to the Communist International's concept of a professional, socialist revolutionary. His grasp of the value of organization, leadership, and discipline added to his intimacy with the Indian popular multitudes did not contradict contemporary communist teachings. The only significant contrast between communism and Gandhism was Gandhi's patriarchal attitude towards labor, a residue of his repudiation of industrialization.[75]

Barbusse's article ended with a critique of Romain Rolland and Tagore. These "marvelous and admirable artists" telescoped social issues into individual categories. They overemphasized "moral values." The idealist hand Romain Rolland had extended to the East had to be politicized, by bringing the Eastern and Western revolutionary movements into closer contact. Gandhi himself was invited to participate in the "Left International" to guarantee the proliferation of his thought.[76]

On reading the first communist articles on Gandhi, Romain Rolland was moved to laughter. The slogan "petit bourgeois" was abusive enough with reference to the Gandhian movement, but this *"tarte à la crème* of Communist language" took on a thoroughly ridiculous savor when applied to India. Because India's social structure was fundamentally agricultural, Marxist phraseology obscured more than it explained. There could be no "possible analogy" between the politics and class structures of Europe and Asia. Communist polemicists used "sleight of hand" to debunk Gandhi while overestimating the significance of the Indian communist movement.[77]

The second series of communist articles by Barbusse and the Indian Bolsheviks devalued the "true and holy grandeur of Gandhi." Unable to arrive at a consistent line on Gandhi, the communists presented contradictory theses that would only confuse the European audience. On the one hand, the communists characterized Gandhi as a religious utopian, a "chimerical being without practical intelligence." On the other hand, they portrayed him as "a prudent Bolshevik who use[d] nonviolence as a provisional expediency."[78]

Romain Rolland was equally disturbed by information he received from Russian friends about Soviet overtures to Gandhi, directed by M. N. Roy and other Indians of Bolshevik persuasion. If Gandhi were sufficiently informed, he would perceive the underlying opportunism that motivated these gestures. Under no circumstances should Gandhi be deceived and manipulated by the Bolsheviks. There was a fundamental antagonism between nonviolent and communist tactics as well as between the basic philosophies of the two doctrines. He alleged that the Bolsheviks desired a political alliance with the Gandhians to prop up their own power base in India. In the end, the communists had contempt for nonviolence and would either attempt to subvert it or crush it entirely.

Romain Rolland's intention was to introduce and transmit Gandhi as an independent thinker, without linking him to an existing social movement or political party.

> I admire the intelligence and energy of the Bolshevik government; but I feel a profound antipathy for its means of action; they totally lack frankness. Its politics is to utilize, in its struggle to destroy the present European system, all the great forces opposed to European imperialism, even if these forces are also opposed to the system of Bolshevik oppression and violence. . . . Certainly I prefer Moscow

to Washington, and Russian Marxism to American-European imperialism. But I claim to remain independent of one as of the other. "Above the Battle!" The Civitas Dei, the city of nonviolence and of human Fraternity, must refuse every alliance, every compromise with the violent partisans of all classes and all parties.[79]

Romain Rolland was alarmed by the deliberate communist distortions of the spirit, internal dynamics, and goals of the Gandhian movement. They interfered with his own efforts to disseminate the Mahatma's message from a spiritual perspective consistent with the central foundations of the nonviolent movement. He urged C. F. Andrews, a British missionary and friend of Gandhi, to warn Gandhi about self-serving communist efforts to make procommunist propaganda within the Gandhian movement. Indian communists would infiltrate the nonviolent rank and file. Gandhi might also be invited to visit the Soviet Union and Germany. Above all else, he urged Gandhi to distinguish clearly his movement's motivations and aims from those of the Communist International.[80]

Gandhi acted directly on Romain Rolland's warning, delivered through Andrews. In his article entitled "My Path," published in *Young India* on 11 December 1924, he implicitly endorsed Romain Rolland's "Western" assessment of his doctrine and dissociated himself from communist interpretations. "It is my good fortune and misfortune to receive attention in Europe and America at the present moment." The good fortune was that his doctrine was made more accessible. But "a kind European friend has sent me a warning . . . that I am being willfully or accidentally misunderstood in Russia." The friend discreetly left unnamed was Romain Rolland. The biographer was now playing advisor, urging the subject of his biography not to be duped by the communist Machiavellians. Gandhi denied that he planned to visit the "great countries" of Germany or Russia. India was the main stage of his social experiment and "any foreign adventure" would be premature until his movement had succeeded in his native country. The Mahatma added that he was unsure of the precise nature of Bolshevism. "But I do know that insofar as it is based on violence and denial of God, it repels me. . . . There is, therefore, really no meeting ground between the school of violence and myself."[81]

Romain Rolland breathed a sigh of relief when he learned of Gandhi's categorical repudiation of Bolshevism in *Young India*.

That article ended the equivocation about the real nature of the nonviolent movement and terminated the hypocritical game of the pro-Soviet communists. Yet Romain Rolland regretted one aftereffect of Gandhi's statement—its manipulative use by the reactionary European press. The Parisian daily *Le Matin* exploited Gandhi's article as yet another weapon in their anticommunist crusade.[82]

Gandhi had made a powerful impact on Romain Rolland by the summer of 1924. Still strongly attached to his intellectual independence, the French writer felt obliged to make public statements not only to "relieve his conscience" but also to defend noncooperation, which he identified with a politics transcending party, class, nation, and force. He wrote: "It is clear that Gandhian noncooperation as an example will lead its apostles in Europe to sacrifice without any practical result—and perhaps for a rather long time. It is not less true and good in an absolute fashion; and it is the sole means of salvation for human civilization."[83]

During the period from February 1924 to September 1925, two significant events considerably affected Romain Rolland's relationship to Gandhi. The first was a postcard he sent to Gandhi excusing himself for inadvertent errors in his short biography.[84] This gesture initiated a unique epistolary friendship between the two that lasted until 30 December 1937. Second, he wrote a letter of introduction for a young Englishwoman, Madeleine Slade, asking Gandhi to accept her into his ashram. After reading his biography of Gandhi, she was converted to the Mahatma's philosophy, thereby discovering her life's mission. Slade not only became Gandhi's close disciple, but also remained the intermediary between Romain Rolland and Gandhi throughout the entire interwar period.[85]

Gandhi praised Romain Rolland's essay both for containing so few factual errors and for having "truthfully interpret[ed] my message."[86] Gandhi again expressed his satisfaction with the biography: "Tell M. Romain Rolland that I will try to live up to the high interpretation that he has given my humble life."[87]

Romain Rolland's idealization of Gandhi was bound to lead to disillusion. For ten years the personal contacts between Gandhi and his French biographer were marked by geographical distance, cordiality, and mutual respect, but also by consistently different conceptions of the world and their historic missions. Gandhi and Romain Rolland met only once. In truth, they had little in common.

Madeleine Slade mediated between Romain Rolland and Gandhi (the Mahatma neither read nor spoke French). Gandhi wrote letters of introduction to Romain Rolland for many of his colleagues and disciples traveling in Europe. They exchanged letters on birthdays. Romain Rolland often wrote before and after Gandhi participated in fasts, prayers, and marches or entered life-threatening periods of imprisonment.

Throughout this time, there were serious tensions between the two. Romain Rolland vehemently clung to his vocation of free-spirited intellectual. Gandhi did not see himself as a theoretician but rather as a popular Indian guru, devoted to his own brand of political and religious action. Gandhi's contribution to a festschrift for Romain Rolland's sixtieth birthday in 1926 stressed his own difference from his biographer. He wrote that he was not a man of letters and did not know a great deal about the French Nobel laureate. He also referred to Romain Rolland as "my self-chosen advertiser"—a distancing and slightly denigrating term.[88]

Romain Rolland emphasized his separation from the Mahatma's movement. He refused to become an official spokesman for Gandhi in Europe: "I am not a Christian, I am not a Gandhian, I am not a believer in a revealed religion. I am a man of the West who, in all love and in all sincerity, searches for the truth."[89] His motives in writing about Gandhi were personal; he felt called on to "relieve his heart." He wrote out of love, to present the Gandhian message to Europeans, alerting them to the possibility of a free and joyous choice. Wounded by the offhand remark Gandhi made about his biography (he supposedly said that it was "literature"), Romain Rolland countered that it was "not written for 'literature' (The *littérateurs* scarcely consider me as one of them)."[90]

In his private diary, the converted Romain Rolland entertained doubts about the realistic possibility for Gandhian nonacceptance being applied in Europe as early as November 1926. Nonacceptance could only be practiced by an elite corps of "apostles and martyrs." The faith required a well-trained, tightly disciplined band of self-abnegators. Nonacceptance might subvert the modern state if practiced over a long period of time, but in Europe only a minority of conscientious objectors possessed this faith, with the courage to sacrifice their lives, families, professions, and personal welfare for principles. To practice war resistance in an era of fascism and rearmament was to risk persecution. Conscientious objectors would be harassed and punished. He observed that even Gandhi practiced his doctrine inconsistently, lacking the spiritual hardiness attributed to the early Christians.[91]

Europe could not survive without peace. But European pacifists were obliged to connect their antiwar activity to a larger effort to "revise the values of life." Gandhism represented a cultural revolution that might assist them to reevaluate politics, morality, and social attitudes by beginning with the self. Romain Rolland's pacifism, although it contained critical components, was essentially positive and character building. That is why he so deeply appreciated the sentiments of Spinoza's *Political Treatise*.[92] By the middle and late 1920s he recognized that the religious and political climate of Europe was "unsuited" for Gandhi's heroic experiment.[93] Nonviolence promised salvation, but it had no roots in the industrial, secular, materialist West—especially in Latin Europe.

Their correspondence often debated Gandhi's views on war resistance. They had a brief controversy about two French peasants who resisted World War I and retreated into the mountains for thirteen years. The Mahatma refused to discuss the case in *Young India*. Romain Rolland, for his part, judged Gandhi's response to their action harsh and puristic.[94] This, in turn, gave rise to a more acrimonious exchange about Gandhi's role during the Great War, both his support of the British Empire and his active participation in the war. The French writer was dissatisfied with Gandhi's rejoinder in his *Autobiography*.[95] There were instances of "doctrinal narrowness" in Gandhi's message and a growing number of personal inconsistencies. Gandhi's justification of his activities during the Great War was not convincing; the Mahatma should have adhered to the strategy of individual civil disobedience.[96]

Romain Rolland urged Gandhi to visit Europe in the late 1920s to tell the anti-imperialist version of the struggle (Europeans usually heard only the viewpoint of the British Empire) and to enter into direct contact with other oppressed peoples.[97] On Gandhi's sixty-first birthday in 1930, he referred to Gandhism as a unifying "revolution of the spirit, . . . the refusal hurled by the proud soul against injustice and violence. . . . This revolution does not breed opposition between races, classes, nations, and religions; it brings them together."[98]

By 1931, Romain Rolland was writing more stinging indictments of European imperialism, largely in response to the social crisis engendered by the world depression. The language of pacifist engagement in the 1920s gave way to the revolutionary language of the 1930s. Europe's only hope, he exclaimed, was for a "complete reversal of the social order." Capitalist imperialism had to be toppled and replaced. Since Gandhism contained a revolutionary potential, he issued calls for a nonviolent revolution with Gandhi as leader.[99]

The warmth of their relationship peaked during Gandhi's five-day visit to the French writer's villa in Villeneuve from 6 December to 11 December 1931.

Historians have trivialized their conversations at this time by dwelling on the circus atmosphere that followed Gandhi's entourage (even Romain Rolland viewed ironically the incongruous assortment of nudists, vegetarians, crazies, lottery-card holders, and peasants bringing milk to the "King of India," who converged on his villa).[100] Most accounts mention the music and the metaphysics.[101] In fact, they discussed the political and economic crisis of Europe and the urgent necessity for Gandhi to clarify his views on social questions. Romain Rolland viewed Europe's malaise as deriving historically from the rivalries and expansionism of international capitalism. He asked Gandhi what options nonviolence posed for Europeans in the face of this crisis.[102] Rolland observed that nonviolence could work only if the resisters shared a common religious belief system. Nonviolence also required visionary leadership and a broad base of followers. For nonviolence to succeed in Europe, the organized workers in factories and arsenals would have to be mobilized. Workers, he alerted Gandhi, were already politicized, and many were inspired by events and the example of the Soviet Union. Most organized French workers were class conscious and prepared for class struggle, which might include violent confrontations. He pressed Gandhi for clarification of his perspectives on Italian fascism (Gandhi had chosen to visit Italy after leaving Switzerland), but above all on the clash between capitalism and the labor movement.[103]

Gandhi did not consider the antagonisms of labor and capital essential. If a collision occurred, he favored organized labor. The methods of satyagraha could be employed against capitalists, as he had demonstrated in India. Gandhi appeared insensitive to the plight of unemployed workers in England and in industrialized countries: "In *England's case* the unemployed have not many reasons to complain of the capitalist." He seemed ignorant about developments in Russia. Without having studied the facts, he stated that he was distrustful of the USSR; that he associated communism with violence, arbitrariness, intolerance, and terrorism; and that he was unequivocally opposed to the dictatorship of the proletariat.[104]

In summary, Gandhi's visit had a mixed impact on Romain Rolland. He still revered Gandhi as a man, admired his sense of humor, stamina, leadership qualities, and self-control, but he felt removed from him. At times it seemed that they had nothing to discuss, that the formidable differences in their sensibilities, lifestyles, and cultural politics were unbridgeable. He was dissatisfied with Gandhi's faulty knowledge of pacifist and left-wing politics in Europe and deeply disturbed by the Mahatma's planned trip to fascist Italy. Most significant, he reluctantly endorsed Gandhi's positions on labor and class struggle.[105]

Italian fascism was a controversy, an embarrassment, and finally an impasse in Romain Rolland's relations with Gandhi. After being Romain Rolland's guest in Switzerland, Gandhi visited Italy for four days from 11 December to 15 December 1931. Gandhi's trip to fascist Italy repeated Tagore's Italian fiasco of 1926, with its elements of farce and tragedy. The French writer tried to persuade the Mahatma not to risk traveling in Italy. If he were foolish enough to go, he should take precautions against being "swindled" by the unscrupulous regime. He was entirely unsuccessful in explaining to Gandhi the symbolic dangers of visiting a fascist dictatorship in Europe, but it was contrary to his style to veto Gandhi's trip. Gandhi made only one concession to Romain Rolland: he resided with the independent General Moris, declining shelter from the official fascist establishment.[106]

Gandhi had been invited to Italy by the Italian consul to India. The Indian leader delivered a short address at the Institute of Culture in Rome. Ostensibly, Gandhi was motivated to visit Italy by his unabashed curiosity, his empirical desire to test out and observe Italy's political and social context for himself. Gandhi also asserted, somewhat self-righteously, that as a messenger of peace his presence in Italy would ultimately have a constructive effect on the Italians. In Gandhi's words: "The distant effect of a good thing must be good." Before entering Italian territory, he requested that no secret meetings be held and that he be permitted to speak his mind freely in public. Gandhi's contact with Mussolini's Italy may have signaled to the British his bitterness after the collapse of the Round Table Conference designed to discuss Indian independence and the safeguarding of minorities in India. The prospect of India establishing friendly relations with Italy may have given pause to the ruling echelons in England. In reality, Gandhi's four-day trip to Italy involved a number of incongruous activities. He toured the Vatican museums but was denied an audience with the Pope. He met with Maria Montessori and visited two of her experimental schools. He had an appointment with Tolstoy's granddaughter. He also had an interview with the new secretary of the Fascist Party of Italy, Achille Starace. And last, he was received by Mussolini for twenty minutes in the duce's office.[107]

Although Gandhi's historical reputation was not irreparably damaged by the visit to Italy, it had immediately disastrous repercussions for the triple causes of world peace, anti-imperialism, and resistance to social injustice. Romain Rolland accurately predicted that the fascist press would misrepresent or suppress the content of Gandhi's public statements. The newspaper *Giornale d'Italia* quoted Gandhi as sympathetic to fascist opinions, alleging that he sanctioned the use of violence. Fascist press reports of his speeches simply deleted the "non" from the word "nonviolence." With the peaceful and loving components of his statements removed, Gandhi's critique of the British Empire seemed more menacing than he intended. The trip to fascist Italy tarnished his prestige among pacifists and leftists in France and Great Britain. Far more insidious was the effect of Gandhi's presence on thousands of oppressed antifascist Italians, both in and out of Italy: "Anything of this nature in Italy would be harmful to the Italians. People would say: 'The great saint is with the oppressors against the oppressed.' " The antifascist emigrés clustered around *La Libertà* in Paris reported that Gandhi's trip to Italy was marked by "ingenuousness."[108] Gandhi's misinformation about the degrading policies of the Italian government angered his French biographer. He began to reappraise the incisiveness and efficacy of Gandhism in the face of international fascism.

Unable to convince Gandhi that the "true face of Fascism" was murder and repression, Romain Rolland predicted that nothing worthwhile would result from Gandhi's trip. "I should have said to him: Well, then, you will not go. At no price ought you to shake hands with the assassin of Matteoti and Amendola."[109]

Gandhi, in fact, had been favorably if somewhat ambivalently impressed by Mussolini. Europeans should suspend judgment on Mussolini's "reforms," he thought, until an "impartial study" could be carried out. Although Italy was repressive, its coerciveness paralleled other European societies that were also "based on violence." There was merit, Gandhi held, in Mussolini's programs against poverty, his opposition to "superurbanization," and his corporate efforts to harmonize the interests of capital and labor. Moreover, behind Mussolini's implacable facade and his oratorical flourishes, Gandhi detected an "inflamed sincerity and love for his people," as well as a disinterested desire to serve his country. The Italian people were inspired by the duce—this accounted for Mussolini's vast popularity.[110] Gandhi subsequently told several Indians leaving for a European trip that there were two Europeans worth knowing: Mussolini and Romain Rolland—a distinction his antifascist French biographer ironically recorded but hardly appreciated.[111]

Romain Rolland was incensed by Gandhi's impressions of fascist Italy; they were "hasty," "erroneous," and "careless." He challenged Gandhi's capacity to assess the popularity of the fascist regime, given his short stay; his ignorance of the Italian language, history, and culture; and his failure to meet opponents of the government. Gandhi was astute at reading progressive British opinion and politics, but he seemed oblivious to the dynamics of fascism and to the abuses of organized state violence. The hidden Italy was a wounded country, best represented by the enemies and victims of fascism, that is, by those men and women silenced by lies, mystified by "bread and circuses," and brutalized by police terror. Gandhi knew nothing of deported Italians doing forced labor on volcanic islands off the coast of southern Italy. He had no idea of Matteotti's widow, hounded by the fascist secret police. Gandhi's insensitivity to the "moral sufferings" of the majority of the Italian people was shocking. Romain Rolland refuted Gandhi's rationalizations for Mussolini's policies by differentiating between Western countries. To say that all Western democracies were coercive was sophistic and ahistorical.[112]

Gandhi misunderstood that fascist violence had a bureaucratic apparatus and ideological legitimacy not to be found in the Western democracies. The various "crimes" of the duce's regime included state-ordered executions. Mussolini suppressed civil liberties. He systematically destroyed the Italian Labor Confederation, popular libraries, and the socialist municipal councils. He decimated the Italian Socialist Party, an act of vindictive revenge, for Mussolini had served as the second-ranking official of that party. He brutalized the Italian peasantry, exacerbating the divisions between north and south. Gandhi was mistaken to see Mussolini as a protector of the Italian people; he should not have swallowed the duce's self-aggrandizing rhetoric at face value. There was no self-abnegation, no ascetic ideal, among the Italian Fascist Party leadership. Rather, they were *arrivistes* committed to amassing personal wealth, impostors who craved domination. Mussolini's regime consisted of a "band" that "pillaged the State treasury and gorged [themselves] with millions." Romain Rolland pointed out that the symbiotic connection between fascist leadership and big business was explicitly expansionist and imperialistic. It would eventually push Italy into wars and into efforts to suppress underdeveloped countries.[113] A responsible political personality was obliged to support the anti-fascist cause.

Romain Rolland's preoccupation with Gandhi became the point of departure for another line of inquiry—Hindu mysticism. His biography of Gandhi was subtitled "The Man Who Became One with the Being of the Universe." By the late 1920s, he entered a period of scholarly researches on intuition, musical genius, and the nature of oceanic religiosity. The products of Romain Rolland's "journey within" were his autobiographical *Le Voyage intérieur: Le Périple* (1946); his multivolume biography of Beethoven, *Beethoven: Les Grandes Epoques créatrices de l'Héroïque à l'Appassionata* (1928) and *Goethe et Beethoven* (1930); and his three-volume study of Indian spirituality, *Essay on Mysticism and Action in Living India: The Life of Ramakrishna* (1929) and *The Life of Vivekananda and the Universal Gospel* (two volumes, 1930).[114]

Romain Rolland's immersion in mysticism plunged him once more into the oceanic current underlying his artistic sensibility. His period of intellectual disengagement culminated with the biographies of Ramakrishna and Vivekananda. There could be no greater flight from social and political reality than these introspective auto-biographical works, nothing more meditative than these volumes on Hindu mysticism. But even these works were designed to over-come the contemporary European ignorance of Eastern religious thought by paralleling common experiences of the divine. He com-bated the unbridled rationalism and scientism to which the twentieth-century mind was heir, claiming "the sovereign right of the religious spirit—in the true sense—even and especially outside of religious institutions, in every profound and impassioned move-ment of the mind."[115] While working on Hindu mysticism, Romain Rolland engaged Sigmund Freud in a controversy over the origins and meaning of the oceanic sensation.[116]

For Romain Rolland, the connections between Indian mysticism and the music of Bach and Beethoven, German idealism, the princi-ples of the French Revolution, and the metaphysics of Spinoza irrefutably demonstrated the unity of human nature. The oceanic sensation allowed him to think himself into the minds of people and cultures different from his own. The oceanic feeling was the imaginative source and the deep structure of access to others and the world. It allowed him to grasp intuitively the larger connec-tions the individual experienced in relationship to culture.[117]

After returning to India, Gandhi was arrested, led an unsuccess-ful campaign against Untouchability, and conducted fasts and marches. Romain Rolland kept the French reading public informed of these events by writing a total of nine reports, a serialized "Letter from India," published in *Europe*.[118] The British repression of the noncooperation movement made Gandhi seem to him a revolution-ary martyr, a partisan of labor against capital.[119] He argued that a social revolution was imperative in Europe, and he predicted that such a revolution would follow either the Leninist or the Gandhian model. He held that violence and nonviolence, communism and Gandhism, were not necessarily incompatible—at least among sin-cere practitioners and in terms of the desired goal. He saw himself as the mediator between the pro-Soviet and pro-Indian camps in the period 1931 to 1934:

> In the eyes of thousands of men who at the present moment con-sider it intolerable to maintain the present capitalist and imperialist society and who have resolved to change it, the great and ambitious Indian experiment with *Satyagraha* is *the only chance* open to the

world of achieving this transformation of humanity without having recourse to violence. If it fails, there will be no other outlet for human history than violence. It's either Gandhi or Lenin! *In any case, social justice must be achieved.*[120]

In April 1934, Romain Rolland definitively broke with nonviolent noncooperation as a tactic for revolution or resistance in contemporary Europe. The reason for the change was the historical ascendancy of fascism. Satyagraha having no realistic chance for victory in a Europe saturated by fascist movements, he switched his loyalties to the struggles of organized labor. Workers, at least, would actively resist fascism and right-wing extremism.[121]

By 1935, Romain Rolland revised his views on Gandhi's leadership of the Indian movement. For social reconstruction in India, the French writer preferred the younger leaders Nehru and Subhas Chandra Bose, who were more coherently socialist and who belonged to the left wing of the Indian Congress Party. Gandhi's sentimental and religious approach to politics no longer corresponded to realities in his own country. Nonviolence was not the "central pivot of all social action." He was particularly upset by the Mahatma's refusal to adapt the principles of socialism for his country. Gandhi's prejudices, his obstinate clinging to received ideas, meant that he was ill equipped to lead India, once it gained its independence, into the modern world.[122] Although he no longer advocated Gandhi's political philosophy and tactics, Romain Rolland always retained enormous respect for Gandhi the man; there was no personal rupture in relations, just distance. Nor did he waver in his judgment of Gandhi's prominence in modern Indian history. His last public statement on Gandhi condensed the ambivalence of his admiration for the man and his refusal to cling to nonviolence "in the face of the growing ferocity of the new regimes of totalitarian dictatorships. . . . We cannot, in this circumstance, advocate and practice Gandhi's doctrine, however much we respect it."[123]

To assess Romain Rolland's engagement as a Gandhian, we should note that his essays accomplished their immediate goals: they disseminated information about Gandhi's struggle in India and they familiarized the European public with the concepts of nonviolence and noncooperation.

From 1923 to 1932, he had harnessed his international prestige and his gifts as a writer to serve as the European popularizer of Gandhi. His articles, introductions, anthology of Gandhi's thought, and above all his biography transmitted the Mahatma's message in Europe. Romain Rolland presented nonviolent resistance as a concrete third way between Leninism and Wilsonism. By 1923, he was convinced that the revolutionary conjunctures of postwar Europe had passed, that the European reaction had consolidated its gains. He presented Gandhism as a potentially powerful political philosophy, a vision of politics and morality, that allowed both for individual refusal and for collective disobedience. In the European setting, it might provide postwar pacifists a viable model for the organization and structure of a movement, a paradigm for leadership and action. By the late 1920s he considered Gandhism a revolutionary movement of the spirit or soul. By the early 1930s he linked it to the revolutionary strategy and tactics of syndicalism. Civil disobedience and radical trade unionism could work together.

His World War I experience, coupled with his reaction to events in the immediate postwar period, made Romain Rolland psychologically and ideologically receptive to Gandhi's ideas. Motivated by his intellectual curiosity about India, he seized on Gandhism in part to extricate himself from his political bind: isolation, a posture of criticism without the proposal of a constructive program, and, above all, reliance on vague, metaphysical formulas in place of concrete notions of strategy and tactics. He assumed the task of expanding the consciousness of the European intellectual community by introducing Gandhism as a new area of study, a collateral branch of Indian spiritual thought, without compromising his intellectual integrity, and without having to join an established political party. Accepting the precept that no form of knowledge was foreign to the mind, he initiated a process of European acquaintance with Indian culture, personalities, and political conflicts and strategies. His campaign confronted European and particularly French xenophobia. Romain Rolland must be seen as a great challenger of French ethnocentrism.

If Romain Rolland's essays prepared the European public for Gandhi's message and methods, they failed to ask how Gandhism would ground itself in the materialist West. In his enthusiastic effort to demythologize standard East-West stereotypes and to stress unity, he blurred distinctions. He made a leap of faith to

Gandhism, but he did not consider the sources of Gandhian resistance in Europe or the training ground for its leadership.

Gandhi's methods might indicate to European pacifist intellectuals a way out of their impasse. He was painfully aware that members of the French and European peace movements had capitulated to the war in 1914 and after. Pacifists had been weak, contradictory, and unable to transform their theories into antiwar practice in the face of the grave crisis of World War I. Gandhism might provide European pacifists, especially religious ones, with principles requiring self-sacrifice, imprisonment, and even death. Nonacceptance of the state might allow European war resisters to move from isolated acts of conscientious objection to a massive civil disobedience that might ultimately subvert the state. With the Indian model in mind, one could not separate issues of social injustice from the foreign policies of major European powers.

Despite the genuine affection between Romain Rolland and Gandhi, the two were working at cross-purposes, even at the most cordial stages of their relationship. Gandhi's main platform was India: his movement would prove its viability there within the context of the independence struggle. The propagandistic edge of Romain Rolland's essays undoubtedly supplied the Gandhian struggle with an additional lever of prestige and authority. For his part, Romain Rolland seized on the universal aspects of the Mahatma's theory and practice. Though he sympathized with the Indian national liberation movement, he was committed to generating a French and European Gandhian movement—he wanted to internationalize the nonviolent cause. If Europeans did not accept Gandhi as a new spiritual and political guide, his ideas would at least stimulate dialogue among partisans of progressive social change.

Because he never considered systematic thinking a virtue, Romain Rolland was not perplexed by the internal contradictions within Gandhism itself. There was no critique, for instance, of Gandhi's policies when they were patently unreasonable, puristic, or even inconsistent with the dictates of conscience. Romain Rolland subsequently called into question Gandhi's support of the British Empire, as he did his voluntary participation in the Boer War and especially World War I. That the Mahatma had accepted—but transformed for his own purposes—the elementary Hindu allegiance to caste (with the exception of the barbaric tradition of Untouchability), cow protection, idol worship, and other aspects of traditional Hindu doctrine demonstrated that his political philosophy was inextricably tied to ancient Indian customs. Romain Rolland did not realize that Gandhi's failure to reconsider his attachment to Hinduism would leave India hopelessly backward looking or that Indian religiosity would obstruct the movement's acceptance by Westerners. Moreover, Gandhi's capacity to tap India's spiritual heritage illustrated a tighter grasp of political expediency in India than the idealistic biographer wanted to grant.

Romain Rolland pursued his flight from time by meditating on eternity. Gandhism pushed him toward depoliticization: his trilogy on Indian mystics represented his most disengaged stance in the interwar period. He tended to overlook the limitations of the satyagraha doctrine, which was anti-industrial, nationalistic, and entangled in a mystifying metaphysical web. His failure to visit India prevented him from seeing the stark and overwhelming reality of India's poverty and the ignorance of its populace. Only in the mid-1930s did he sense that Gandhism would never provide India with a complete tool by which to liberate itself from this misery. He never saw noncooperation in practice, hence he never ascertained its finite limits. In his mind it remained a beautiful ideal, something to be striven for and perfected in the future.

Like so many students and advocates of Gandhi after him, Romain Rolland saw in Gandhism what he wanted to see.[124]

He made broad, unsubstantiated claims about nonviolence, especially given the very limited nature of its victory in South Africa and its precarious state in India from 1923 to 1932. By refusing to extract the secular content and political appeal of the nonviolent message, his writings might have unwittingly retarded a mass European acceptance of Gandhi's novel political weapon. He did not initially try to politicize either the doctrine or the audience. At first he had not carefully examined whether the movement was inherently reformist or revolutionary, whether it could be stretched to encompass socialist goals. More important, he blunted the differences between national independence struggles and those involving war resistance and class conflicts in more advanced societies. Although some of the propaganda for nonviolence contained unwarranted rhetorical violence, he never developed a psychological critique of absolute nonviolence that questioned whether nonviolent resisters did emotional violence to themselves through their radical prohibition of the expression of anger.

In Romain Rolland's biography, the Mahatma is deified as a messiah for India and for the world. Gandhian noncooperation with the state became the gospel updated, alternatively described as a new Christianity and a religion of humanity. Gandhi answered his need not only for a splendid spiritual leader but also for a martyr. The British persecution of Gandhi and the violent repression of his movement suggested that he might die violently and soon. History bore out that dreadful premonition. Gandhi was assassinated in 1948, four years after Romain Rolland's death.

The Gandhian stage culminated Romain Rolland's evolution from antiwar dissenter to popularizer of nonviolent resistance. Gandhism was compatible with Romain Rolland's dialectical formula for intellectual commitment: "Pessimism of the intelligence, optimism of the will." Nonviolent resistance fused audacious action with critical analysis. There was no great gap between Gandhian nonviolent resisters and the violent social revolutionaries. He was most pro-Gandhi while disenchanted with the Russian Revolution, and he became most critical of Gandhi when he moved closer to the fellow-traveler position. For several years, he tried to be an international intermediary between the two camps.

If his introduction of Gandhism resolved a personal and spiritual problem for him, it simultaneously created major problems for pacifists throughout the twenties and thirties. Romain Rolland's Gandhism stressed character building, virtue, and integrity; it was oriented toward fortifying the individual's autonomy, healing inner existential splits. He wanted pacifists to be incorruptible and visionary, to stand above parties, classes, and coteries. They were not to dirty their hands. Rollandist pacifism was ambivalent toward the Communist International and toward the issue of social revolution. That ambivalence would plague pacifists during the period between the wars.

Gandhism did not provide a social, economic, or cultural analysis of the roots of war or a persuasive ideology for the masses. It was not readily absorbed in the postwar European atmosphere of speed, machines, automobiles, airplanes, jazz, and adventure. It did not appeal to the longing of youth for revolt or the yearnings of war veterans for camaraderie. Gandhism in Europe did not give rise to a surrogate Gandhi. Romain Rolland was not enough of an activist or professional politician to step into that role.

Gandhism served as a key transition in the history of commitment of French intellectuals between pre–World War I liberal humanitarianism and the socialist humanism of the 1930s fellow-traveling position. Gandhism allowed Romain Rolland to pass from the nineteenth century to the twentieth. It represented a noble wager to find a pragmatic political stance that elevated individualism and ethical concerns, rather than the primacy of force or the historical destiny of the collective. Romain Rolland's Gandhism permitted him to absorb the immediate postwar trauma without despair, cynicism, crackpot realism, or irony and to search for a nonviolent alternative. This quest and the discourse that established the myth of the great-souled Gandhi and disseminated the nonviolent political philosophy remain creative contributions. Romain Rolland's creativity was that of the mediator. Gandhian engagement symbolized the intellectual's refusal to sanction violent solutions to political problems. It epitomized a moral vision that insisted on struggle for progressive, even revolutionary, sociopolitical change through peaceful means.

PART THREE

LEFT-WING CULTURAL POLITICS
OF THE 1930s

7

Intellectual Antifascism and the Amsterdam-Pleyel Movement

We proclaimed ourselves the enemies of Fascism, but actually Fascism had its effect on us, as on almost all Italians, alienating us and making us superficial, passive, and cynical.

Primo Levi, *The Periodic Table*

In the 1930s antifascism fused a powerful emotional and intellectual approach to contemporary history. Romain Rolland occupied a prominent place in elaborating and popularizing this negative passion, situated at the border of politics and culture. Perceiving fascism as a potent threat, he attempted to organize and to create ideological legitimacy for a broad-based interclass coalition to oppose it. He deployed his talents and risked his international reputation as a moral force and pacifist spokesman, while transforming in the process the style of the committed writer. Antifascist politics also suffused his literary works in the era. His epic novel *L'Ame enchantée*, the successor of *Jean-Christophe*, made resistance to fascism central in its narrative, characters, and unifying vision.

Before Mussolini's March on Rome and the Fascist Party's seizure of power on 30 October 1922, Romain Rolland considered fascist theory and practice to be repugnant precisely because it contradicted the cultural legacy of Italy.[1] Fascism was a new form of barbarism, another deformation of the Great War, not simply a reversion to dictatorial politics. He quickly recognized fascism's dynamic strength, its capacity to tap thwarted Italian historical and military pride. He predicted that "Fascism will either burst open like an abcess or be reabsorbed into itself."[2] He saw the attraction fascism held for intellectuals such as Pierre Drieu la Rochelle and Henry de Montherlant, and he also realized its potential to take root in France as a mass movement.[3]

Mussolini was the incarnation of post–World War I Caesarism. Romain Rolland compared the fascist regime with the decadent years of the French Bonapartist tradition. He was appalled by the leadership cult around the duce. Mussolini lacked Napoleon Bonaparte's intelligence, strategic skills, and world vision. The duce was a mock hero who stood for conquest and adored destruction for its own sake. Romain Rolland distanced himself from left- or rightwing social movements that were intoxicated with notions of violence and domination. "I have indeed no sympathy for Mussolini and Fascism. . . . Between Bolsheviks and Fascists there are differences of ideas, but not of methods."[4]

He anticipated that Italian antifascist intellectuals might oppose Giovanni Gentile's edict requiring all state functionaries to swear oaths of loyalty to the fascist regime. His hopes were quickly disappointed. Modern Italy needed a Victor Hugo "to throw a glove in the face of a tyrant." Benedetto Croce was unable to play such a leadership role, despite his opposition to fascism. Croce limited his protest to "the absurdities of Fascist 'intellectual imperialism.' " The origins of fascism, Romain Rolland saw, were the north-south division in Italy, the disappointments after the World War I experience, and above all the backlash against the threat of socialist revolution in 1919 and 1920. Fascist movements emerged when industrializing societies entered chaotic periods of transition.[5]

The kidnapping and assassination of Giacomo Matteotti, the reformist deputy of the Partito Socialista Unitario (SPU), in June 1924 and the *squadristi* assault on Giovanni Amendola on 21 July 1925 provided the reference points for Romain Rolland's subsequent thoughts on Italian fascism. He was despondent over "the egotistical cowardice" of the majority of Italian intellectuals who supported the government. He was offended by philosophers who abused the dialectical method by "justifying all crimes and complacencies to reward force." He was outraged by the Jesuitical twists of Catholic writers who rationalized "the atrocities and shames of Fascism by quoting the Gospels." French intellectuals needed to be alerted that Italian fascism represented "a danger of the foremost kind." He urged *Clarté* to publish articles documenting and analyzing the Italian regime. All "healthy" forces would have to be mobilized to combat the spreading pestilence.[6]

Romain Rolland's first public antifascist statement came on the occasion of Mussolini's warlike provocations in Tripoli in 1926. Italian fascism's existence obliterated all hope for disarmament. Mussolini's regime demonstrated a nihilistic contempt for diplomacy and world peace, as evidenced by its belligerent rhetoric and its preoccupation with territorial annexations. Romain Rolland counseled pacifists and internationalists to oppose fascism. He called for vigilance against the threat in France, where internal fascist agitation was mounting. Fascists behaved like agents provocateurs. They appeared to be a stabilizing force while deceptively inciting their frenetic followers to violence and war. Fascists were criminals without a sense of guilt. Fascism negated the cosmopolitan spirit, violated civil rights, and perverted all civilized values.[7]

On the occasion of a Parisian street brawl between rightists and communists in the spring of 1926, he argued that fascism was incompatible with the French tradition of republican government and democratic process. It contradicted the legacy of the French Revolution—the rights of man and the struggle for human dignity. Fascism undermined individual creativity, critical thinking, freedom of conscience, and the right to resist oppression.

> Every regime founded on the principles of Italian fascism is degrading for the human conscience. It rules by contempt for the most sacred freedoms, by imposed lies, and by fear.
>
> Every attempt to introduce it in France is a crime. A crime against the France of free reason. A crime against the free people who made the Revolution. A crime against the free Soul.[8]

Romain Rolland endorsed antifascist activities in a letter to Filippo Turati, saluting the founding of his oppositional newspaper in Paris, *La Libertà*. He attacked Mussolini for enslaving the Italian countryside through the establishment of a tyrannical dictatorship. He voiced his solidarity with Italy's "most loyal and persecuted representatives," its antifascist refugees. He identified their struggle to emancipate Italy from Mussolini's yoke with the universal struggle against social injustice, cruelty, cynicism, and unreason: "The fight you wage is not only for the liberation of a great oppressed, humiliated, outraged people—it is for the freedom of the entire world."[9]

Amendola's death on 1 April 1926 personally affected him, for the two had collaborated before the Great War in the context of the intellectual movement, *La Voce*. Amendola was one of the Italian luminaries to contribute to Romain Rolland's sixtieth birthday fest-schrift in 1926, just a few months prior to his assassination.[10] In a letter of bereavement, Romain Rolland expressed his grief to the Amendola family and indicted the fascist regime for orchestrating the homicide. He elevated Amendola's death into a moral symbol for all antifascists. He began to sacralize the antifascist cause. There could be no antifascist resistance without historical memory:

> I have no need to tell you, sir, of our indignation at this hideous and disgraceful crime that made your father the sacred victim. Nothing will obliterate the stigma from the brow of the assassin. He will remain branded by it for the future. . . . The long suffering of this great, silent, and stoical martyr has reverberated in the hearts of the free men of France. As in the catacombs under the Compagna, near your home, where the eternal lamp of remembrance burned before the image of the persecuted, we consecrate an altar, in our memory, to the noble image of the wise and gentle Amendola.[11]

In 1926, Rabindranath Tagore was given a brilliantly orchestrated grand tour of the modern sights and cities of Italy, which showed him only the glories of the fascist regime. Tagore's visit in June culminated with two interviews with Mussolini. The duce disarmed the politically naive Tagore with courteous flattery. Throughout his stay, Tagore met only two antifascists. Tagore's speeches were distorted in the fascist press, making him sound like a fervent admirer of Italian fascism and insinuating that he attributed the renewal of Italy's grandeur to Mussolini's inspirational qualities.[12]

To make Tagore aware of internal realities in Italy, Romain Rolland placed him in contact with spokesmen for the refugee antifascist opposition. Tagore had been systematically misled by meetings with individuals who "apologized" for fascism or "adulated the Master."[13] Italian fascism was based on the "politics of crime and hypocrisy."[14] Romain Rolland emphasized the destructive side of Italian fascism, the repression of political parties, the jailing and wounding of five or six hundred innocent victims. Only fools mistook its militarism, annexationism, and primitive nationalism for grandeur. It was appalling that a man of Tagore's sensibility could enter into dialogue with this dictator, the "assassin of Amendola and Matteotti." Tagore's trip would demoralize progressive public opinion in Europe, especially young people, students and "antifascist personalities."[15] Antifascist refugees represented a free and authentic, but currently martyred, Italy. To rectify the situation, he urged Tagore to investigate the "moral misery and nameless suffering"[16] of the antifascists.

In 1927, Romain Rolland began thinking about an antifascist strategy for Europe. Because of their primary experience with fascism, antifascist emigrés should lead the campaign against Mussolini by publicizing the "unheard-of violence and political deportations," documenting the widespread atmosphere of domestic repression, and exposing the presence of Mussolini's spies in France. He exhorted the exiled Italian antifascists to contradict Mussolini's official lie that his regime was unanimously supported and to present evidence that "Fascist politics are the gravest peril to international peace."[17]

Romain Rolland preferred making public antifascist statements as an independent voice. Just as he remained outside pacifist and Gandhian organizations, so too would he refuse to make a permanent alliance with established centers of the antifascist struggle. He declined the invitation by the distinguished historian and liberal antifascist Gaetano Salvemini to join the central committee of the International Democratic League to Reconquer Italian Freedom, even though he was totally opposed to fascism's "crimes, lies, and stifling of all freedoms." He participated in charitable programs designed to aid the victims of fascist tyranny. He reserved the right to issue protests only in situations of real crisis. If he were to release one at each request, it would diffuse his moral efficacy. Currently, his cultural writing had a higher priority than his strictly political engagements. He disliked the ideological disposition of Salvemini's movement, specifically its liberal-democratic parliamentarism and its "simplistic" anticlericalism, which would divide and limit left-wing groups in France. He doubted that the antifascist struggle could be led by a "third force"; rather, it should reflect a political coalition of leftist and progressive forces. Salvemini's group placed hostility to communism at the center of its political philosophy, but one could be antifascist without being equally anticommunist. More crucial, Romain Rolland predicted that communism "could be one of the most vigorous battalions of the attack against Fascism." Communist intellectuals such as Henri Barbusse could heighten the public awareness of fascism.[18]

In November 1926, Romain Rolland joined forces with Barbusse to inaugurate an International Committee Against Fascism. Barbusse and he were aware that movements outside Italy would not necessarily replicate the Italian model. In February 1927, they issued an appeal "To the Free Minds, Against Fascism," which denounced the persecutions and savage terror in both Mussolini's Italy and Coudreanu's Romania. Romain Rolland became one of three honorary presidents (along with Barbusse and Albert Einstein) of the first huge French antifascist meeting, held in Paris at the Salle Bullier on 23 February 1927. Paul Langevin, the eminent scientist and vice president of the League of the Rights of Man, presided over the assembly.[19] Such symbolic gestures allowed Romain Rolland to justify his antifascist orientation without jeopardizing his distance from political parties or social movements.[20]

In letters to Barbusse, he criticized the communist perspective on antifascism for being no less parochial than the liberal approach. As a free thinker and a Gandhian, he urged Barbusse to extricate the antifascist committees from Moscow's tutelage. His antifascism was that of the mediator, bridging the ideologies and tactics of left-wing opinion in Europe. Because there were similarities of method between fascists and Bolsheviks, communists lacked the moral authority to contest fascist ideas and politics.[21] Communist antifascist propaganda was dogmatic and expediently served the foreign policy needs of the Comintern, cynically publicizing the misery of fascist victims to make a case for the superiority of communism over Western capitalism. The facts of fascist excesses should be presented to European public opinion so that intelligent readers could draw their own conclusions. By focusing only on the repression of Italian communists and by omitting Mussolini's reprisals against "bourgeois, preachers, Socialist or Radical republicans,"[22] the communists distorted the full picture of the fascist horror. Fascism threatened all progressive political parties, all cultural and leisure life, not just Marxists. Before associating with him in an all-out struggle against the extreme right in Europe and France, Barbusse should declare his own commitment to "democratic rights." If he protested the curtailment of civil liberties and political opposition in the Soviet Union, his universalism would be proved. "It is precisely because I belong to the army of proletarian progress that I demand of its leaders an exemplary moral discipline and a religious respect for freedom."[23]

Romain Rolland simultaneously opposed the red-baiting tendencies of liberal antifascists and the doctrinal posturings of communist antifascists. It was morally correct for unaffiliated intellectuals such as H. G. Wells, Shaw, Russell, Nansen, Unamuno, and himself to participate in public forums where fascist ideologies were dismantled. It was still possible to work against "fascist ideas" in the late 1920s without engaging in political action.

Two major shifts in the late 1920s and early 1930s prompted Romain Rolland to reassess his intellectual politics: the increasing expansionism of Japan and the rise of National Socialism in Germany. As these fascist powers ascended, he began to jettison some of his Gandhian and humanitarian formulas for world peace. Anti-imperialism preceded antifascism both as an ethical position and as a political commitment. He did not yet sharply distinguish between fascist and communist forms of violence.

When the revolutionary communists of the Parisian *Clarté* group provoked him to take a position on Western imperialism, he pointed out that the extreme left was partisan in its diatribes against right-wing violence but silent about the cruelties of the left, including communism: "For a very long time I maintained a position against all assassins—Fascist or revolutionary. . . . I spare no one. I make alliances with no one. I do not whimper over my solitude, but find that solitude is healthy in an epoch of herds."[24]

Fascism represented an extreme, undisguised form of imperialism. Fascists offered an ideological justification for aggression and conquest. The reality of secret treaties, capitalist coalitions, the armaments industry, the buying and selling of peoples in underdeveloped countries caused Romain Rolland to reject the soft thinking of pacifists who placed their hopes in international legal treaties, the League of Nations, or unilateral declarations of peace. If France disarmed in the late 1920s, it would remain isolated, permitting belligerent nations like fascist Italy to invade, occupy its territory, and plunder it. Despite its ideological connection to the Soviet Union and despite the absence of moderate elements in it, he welcomed the educational efforts of the Anti-Imperialist League, particularly its internationalism, antimilitarism, and defense of the victims of colonization.[25]

In a tribute to the American pacifist John Haynes Holmes, Romain Rolland leveled serious charges against American imperialism. Following Europe's decline after the Great War, America's prominent but abusive place in world affairs had to be recognized. He unmasked the ideological component of American foreign policy, especially the self-righteous legitimization of United States imperialism, the privileged position of the dollar, and the shallow, conformist nature of the American values imposed on the lands they dominated. American corporate imperialism fused arrogance and innocence:

> The Anglo-Saxon temperament of America is proud and strong, wholehearted in its likes and its ideas, self-assured and obstinate. It has a singular ineptitude—which strikes all of us, Europeans—to understand the mentality of other peoples, to enter into their psychology (and their physiology), to "size up" their spirit, their passions, their peculiar needs. It tends to believe that what is true for itself, that whatever is the Good for it, should be so for all other nations in the world. And if the latter do not judge the matter the same way, it is they who are mistaken, and America has the right to impose it on them, in their own interest and in the interests of the world. Such a conception leads to the will to conquer the world, under the cover of a narrow moralism, wedded (without its knowledge) to natural instincts of greed and domination.[26]

If the rigid and insensitive policies of the United States were not opposed by responsible American citizens, then America was preparing itself for the eventual rebellion of oppressed nations.

Like most opponents of twentieth-century colonialism, Romain Rolland saw the progressive edge of the imperialistic impulse. Underdeveloped countries now dominated by Europe had benefited from improvements in health and hygiene, administration, transportation, communication, technology, and the utilization of natural resources. However, these benefits were almost always forced on native populations without adequate cultural or psychological preparation.[27]

He warned anti-imperialists to be distrustful of the "pan-European" and idealist pacifists, who, despite their internationalist rhetoric, were wedded to increasing their profit margins and accelerating the process of "the exploitation of the rest of the globe." Nor would big business hesitate to collude with European fascist powers. Anti-imperialists had to decode the self-serving language of imperialism, unveiling the sinister interests at play.[28]

As a Gandhian internationalist, Romain Rolland contested the

British presence in India, but he also interceded on behalf of peoples colonized by the French, developing a mordant critique of French empire building. When French authorities forcefully deported a young Annamite student who joined the Communist Party, Romain Rolland collaborated with the Anti-Imperialist League. He articulated the human rights of a foreigner living and studying in France, angrily protesting the political savagery of the colonial bureaucracy:

> I join myself to the protest of the Anti-Imperialist League against the massacres in Indochina. And I spit my contempt in the face of the executioner's servants who have just delivered Tao to the associated French Indochinese assassins.[29]

Founded in 1927, the Anti-Imperialist League was a communist front organization. Romain Rolland was asked in March 1931 to become the "honorary president" of the League. He declined the presidency because he disagreed with the League's opposition to the Gandhian movement and because of the Comintern's hostility to pacifist ideology and peace movement activism.[30] Yet he sympathized with many principles of the Anti-Imperialist League. At an anticolonial meeting held in Paris at the Salle Bullier, sponsored by the French Communist Party, he denounced French imperialism for its political economy of larceny and for its extermination of native populations. "Colonial politics" contained the metaphors of his moral critique of imperialism, which spilled over into his writings against fascism:

> Dear comrades,
> I associate myself with your anti-imperialist action against the crimes of French politics in Indochina. Modern democracies are a compound of hypocrisies. Among all the hypocrisies one is particularly insolent and repugnant at the present hour: that of civilizing colonialism. It has been exactly a half century since Jules Ferry, representing the most intelligent and crafty part of the dominant bourgeoisie, tried to substitute conquest, after agreement and sharing of the rest of the earth, for the old traditional politics of nationalist rivalries on Europe's soil. They have clearly covered themselves with the flags of European Peace, or with that of civilization, in which these sharks call themselves missionaries. Undoubtedly, this politics has led Europe to an afflux of riches enabling an entire class to get fat off of it. But this peace and ease are paid for liberally by the price of oppression, theft, when it did not lead to the extermination of the races of Asia and Africa. And the petit-bourgeois egoism of Europe accommodates itself to it perfectly. It ungratefully acknowl-

edges that it wallows on the spoils of these peoples delivered over to the great European bandits.

Upright consciences can no longer tolerate this duplicity. Let us tear away the mask! Let us force these Tartuffes and cowards to see their face in the mirror! Let their mirror cry to them: "Liars! Thieves!" And let us not tolerate what is currently produced under the cover of idealism, a cunning pan-Europeanism, which is an association of the capitalisms of France, Germany, and the great business democracies, yesterday at war, today reconciled, so as to better ransom the world! We defend the rights of all men of the earth. All the oppressed are our brothers. We do not work for a nation or for Europe. We work for the workers of the universe![31]

By late 1931, Romain Rolland held that social revolution was the only effective instrument to smash European and American imperialism. The sentimental homilies and puerile tactics of the peace movement were insufficient in the face of a "murderous and brutal" coalition of imperialists bleeding the countries of China and Japan. To aid the process of self-determination, he urged the peoples of China and Japan to form a "fecund unity." This step would not only help get the "great bandits" off their backs but might also point the way to a general coalition of the working classes of Europe and America. He now fully justified the need for social—rather than national—revolution in order to extricate colonized people from the yoke of the colonizer and to ensure the possibility of a lasting peace: "He who wants peace wants the elimination of the eternal makers of war. He who wants international peace, wants revolution."[32] In attacking Japanese incursions into China in the autumn of 1931 for "beheading the revolution," he called for a worldwide union of European consciences and class-conscious workers to resist "the Fascist systems of plutocracy and militarism."[33]

Romain Rolland's most stinging denunciations of imperialism were triggered by political repression in India and Indochina. He protested events not widely publicized in Western Europe, unmasking breaches of the legal system, deportations, forced labor, and incarceration of the native populations. His interventions criticized the widespread abuses of both justice and the democratic process in colonial situations. He penned an impassioned appeal for the Meerut prisoners of India, thirty of whom had been held illegally for four years awaiting trial for sedition. Their crime: attempting to organize a trade union. Most of the Meerut prisoners were sympathetic with the Indian Congress Party; a minority were Indian communists. He demanded an immediate retrial and denounced systematic British repression. Imperialism was a system "based on the atrocious, degrading, and murderous exploitation of nine-tenths of the world's peoples." The captivity and eventual deportation of the Meerut prisoners stripped the British colonial rule of all pretense of legality and protection of human rights. Here was imperialism "that established and maintained itself by terror." The oppressed colonized would eventually develop awareness of their oppression, precipitating revolt to eject the imperialist dominators.[34]

After cataloguing the impact of imperialist "terror" by the Dutch in the East Indies and the French in Indochina, as well as the colonial penetration into China and Korea, he added some choice words about the American "diabolical" variety of open-door imperialism,

> compounded of hypocrisy and cruelty, which makes the churches the bagmen of the Standard Oil Company, which turns itself into the ally of the rotten Kuomintang generals, and the supporter of the massacres in Cuba; which grants the Philippines their independence in order to subjugate them better by economic means; and which lights up in South America the fire of wars and of bloody dictatorships.[35]

Romain Rolland predicted that the organized international of labor would ultimately "break the yoke of imperialism."

In a declaration in support of political prisoners in French Indochina, he deployed sarcasm to blast the Daladier government. It was cynical to invoke the rights of man to legitimize the imprisonment and forced labor of ten thousand Annamites. Any imperialist government that forfeited the rights of its colonized populations must be held accountable. It was "absurd" for Daladier to justify these policies in the name of "freedom." "And it is that sort of government that dares to speak, in the name of human conscience, against the butchers of liberty, against fascism. We deny moral authority to it." Against Daladier's deceptions and repressive actions, Romain Rolland linked antifascist politics and sentiments to the struggles against corporate capitalist and colonial exploitation: "Let France at least have the honesty to recognize the same right and duty for the citizens of the countries that the France of the great companies has conquered and that she is exploiting!"[36]

❖

The Amsterdam-Pleyel movement marked a gradual break with Romain Rolland's antiwar, idealistic, and Gandhian *engagements*. Fascism jeopardized the precarious peace and revealed the limitations of Gandhian theory and practice. He was stepping less obliquely into the political arena. He could no longer justify remaining intransigently independent or marginal in the face of obvious economic, political, and cultural crises. Amsterdam-Pleyel propelled Romain Rolland into the 1930s, changed his way of looking at the world and at the role and responsibility of the intellectual, politicized his language, and oriented it toward action. His engagement with the Amsterdam-Pleyel movement turned him away from abstract, universalistic forms of social and historical analysis. Because the dangers of imperialism, war, and fascism were transparent, his style of intellectual politics changed. Amsterdam-Pleyel provided one last opportunity to articulate a revolutionary version of Gandhism and intensified his preexisting sympathies for communism. Amsterdam-Pleyel was born with tensions and contradictions that were never entirely resolved. Many of its political and ideological ambiguities spilled over into the French Popular Front government itself. As a symbol of unity on the left, Romain Rolland personally embodied these ambivalences.

The Amsterdam-Pleyel movement was born in the spring of 1932 as an eclectic international committee of intellectuals. The Amsterdam Congress was actually convened in Amsterdam from 27 August to 29 August 1932. Willi Münzenberg, the catalyst, was himself a colorful, renegade militant of the Communist International. Not only did Moscow distrust the pacifist ideology associated with the anticipated Amsterdam Congress, but it had not yet hammered out a Popular Front strategy nor developed a thoughtful analysis of fascism. Münzenberg's vision coincided with the desires of Romain Rolland and Henri Barbusse to generate a broad-based movement uniting disparate progressive and left-wing groups, including the communists and socialists. Historians have rightly emphasized the importance of Münzenberg, behind the scenes, preparing and administering this international gathering. An organizational genius, a brilliant tactician, and an expert in modern propaganda technique, Münzenberg orchestrated the vast assembly of "intellectual and manual workers" without the full consent of the Comintern.[37]

The call for the Amsterdam Congress and the idea of establishing an International Committee for the World Congress Against Imperialist War were triggered by the Japanese incursion into Manchuria in the fall of 1931. The Amsterdam Congress accorded antiimperialism a higher priority than antifascism. By 4–6 June 1933, when the Congress met at the Salle Pleyel in Paris, the AmsterdamPleyel movement had evolved ideologically into an explicitly antifascist mass movement. The Pleyel Congress was a direct response to Hitler's assuming the chancellorship in Germany in March 1933 and to the clamor of a distinctly fascist militancy by French rightwing movements. The Amsterdam-Pleyel movement definitely opened the French left to the idea of an alliance of French communists and socialists, which might include other progressives. In 1933 the exact nature of that coalition needed to be elaborated. Amsterdam-Pleyel subsequently became one of the eleven constituent organizations to merge with the French Popular Front. The idea of such unity was enormously popular among the worker rank and file. It also became the agency by which many partisans of the French Popular Front came to communism in the mid-1930s.

Romain Rolland participated in the Amsterdam Congress while serving as president of the International League of Fighters for Peace in 1932. Though French pacifism between the wars has not found its historian, we must remember how deeply rooted antiwar sentiment was in France, particularly in left-wing, moderate, and progressive opinion. To call the varieties of antiwar feeling a social movement is to exaggerate, but there were clearly mass support and articulate spokesmen in socialist, Radical, and anarchist circles.[38]

French communism, however, did not adequately differentiate communist anti-imperialism from pacifist anti-imperialism and unconditional opposition to war. Communists claimed to be antiwar but were not necessarily advocates of peace or nonviolence. Maurice Thorez, general secretary of the PCF, blasted the intellectual sponsors of the Amsterdam Congress as late as 28 June 1932 for their "pacifist petit-bourgeois mind," a well-worn term of Leninist reprobation.[39] From the communist standpoint, the pacifist ideology might weaken the military resolve of the Western democracies, still reeling from the war and the world economic crisis, draining their will to stand strongly against Germany or Japan if war broke out. Communists were uneasy about the penetration of pacifist ideas, fearing they might contaminate the purely proletarian and revolutionary thrust of communist doctrine and program. Furthermore, the Comintern had grave reservations in the summer of 1932 about United or Popular Front strategies (here Münzenberg was an exception), specifically about the broadness of such an alliance and the precise nature of socialist and pacifist participation. Above all, in 1932 and 1933 the communists had not yet decided to postpone the goal of a proletarian revolution in order to construct an inter-class, antifascist movement that might include the progressive part of the capitalist world. Only in 1934, after the debacle in Germany, did Moscow decide that international fascism had to be defeated first and that socialist revolution could be delayed.[40]

Romain Rolland, although publicly linked to Barbusse, campaigned in private for a pluralistic anti-imperialist, antiwar coalition. He wanted pacifists, progressives, nonconforming individuals, and class-conscious intellectuals included. The movement should not be dominated by working-class leadership and Communist Party priorities. Barbusse tried to maintain the goodwill of those noncommunists recruited to the Amsterdam-Pleyel movement, while defending the territorial integrity of the USSR, distinctly jeopardized by a militaristic Japan and by a resurgent, expansionist Germany.[41]

In publicizing for the Amsterdam Congress, Romain Rolland appealed to progressive intellectuals to end their neutrality by taking a public stand. International writers of genius graced the Committee of Initiative, including Gorky, Shaw, Russell, Wells, Einstein, Heinrich Mann, Upton Sinclair, Theodore Dreiser, and John Dos Passos. From France, Barbusse was named, along with Paul Langevin, and the pacifist intellectuals Victor Margueritte and Félicien Challaye. China was represented by Madame Sun Yat Sen, Japan by Sen Katayama. This distinguished group had the collective responsibility to oppose world war. The parliamentary leadership of the Western democracies was paralyzed. "Never was the threat heavier and more crushing. Europe is delivered to the Fascisms of the sword and of business. The stupefied democracies, betrayed by their parliamentary leaders, no longer have the force to react. A monstrous criminal outrage prepares itself." Because of the catastrophic threat of world war, to be triggered by competing imperialist systems, Romain Rolland urged intellectuals to enter into an alliance (*front unique*) with advanced workers from metallurgical, chemical, and transportation industries. An anti-imperialist coalition without the solidarity of mental and manual workers would be absurd and self-defeating.[42]

The Amsterdam-Pleyel movement aimed to group all opponents of war together in an umbrella organization. It embraced people of all parties and did not exclude members of any mass movement. All parties referred to left-wing associations in France, to "Socialists, Communists, syndicalists, anarchists, Radicals, republicans of every nuance, freethinkers and Christians, the nonparty members, all pacifist and war resisters' associations, all independent individualities."[43] Romain Rolland sought to unmask those who profited from war. The Amsterdam Congress countered the warmongers by generating a tidal wave of opinion from those revolted by war.

In promoting the Amsterdam Congress among pacifists, Romain Rolland soberly assessed the capacity of war resisters to prevent war in the West. In 1932 neither individuals nor collective antiwar groups had enough power to prevent the next war. Positioning himself on the side of "revolutionary pacifism," he called for a collective, tightly disciplined organization of war resisters who would systematically subvert the main organs of the state to prevent the unleashing of hostilities. He pushed revolutionary Gandhism to a nonviolent syndicalist conclusion, advocating a mass general strike to incapacitate production, hinder mobilization for war, and ultimately topple the state apparatus. "I believe in the invincible power of total Non-Acceptance, without violence, of a people saying No to the State that abuses them: total stoppage of every social activity, of all the wheels of State."[44]

The revolutionary nonviolent solution, however attractive as a tactical preference, was not realistic in contemporary Europe. No European satyagraha campaign could be mobilized. The European Gandhians lacked a leader, an organization, finances, and a significant number of followers. In practice, Romain Rolland suggested that there could be no war resistance unless the workers of the arsenals, building trades, and heavy industries were recruited. In the absence of a viable peace movement, he invited pacifists to collaborate with labor, each group maintaining its organizational and tactical autonomy. "Let us exclude no one!" Against the domination of big business, one had to draw on the organized workers' capacity for struggle. Moreover, pacifists had to recognize that the peace issue transcended party and doctrinal concern.[45] Urging pacifists to clarify the specificity of their "engagement," he criticized the amorphous quality of pacifist discourse. Refusal to participate in war must be linked to analysis of social injustice, the socioeconomic determinants of war, and the organizational activity, mentality, and political consciousness of the European working class. Aware that his form of revolutionary nonviolence might unleash domestic unrest, he no longer supported nonviolent techniques to the exclusion of alternative methods of action. It might be appropriate to utilize more aggressive tactics—perhaps even to risk civil war or class warfare. "We are not leaders—(we did not want to be)—but guides. We have the duty to know exactly the road [to struggle] in which we engage others."[46]

This defensive conception anticipated the alliance that became the Popular Front. Romain Rolland urged the parties and trade union movement of the left to abandon their long-term animosities, to stop competing with one another, and to mute their divergent interpretations of the present situation. The Amsterdam Congress grouped the Third and Second Internationals, voluntarily allied in opposition to European and Japanese imperialism. No international could prevail over another or outvote another. The congress ought not to break down into majority and minority factions. Emergency circumstances required strategic unity, but without collapsing tactical and ideological differences and without jeopardizing the preexisting autonomy of the constituent groups. "We want to find a terrain of agreement that worker organizations and representative individualists may employ all together against war while leaving to each its own independence, its full and free choice of means to employ."[47]

Despite the resonance of the antiwar appeal among rank-and-file workers, despite the popularity of the anticapitalist and antiimperialist sentiments expressed in the advance publicity for the Amsterdam Congress, Romain Rolland's objectives collided directly with the deep-seated hostility between communists and socialists. This historical rivalry was not overcome. Rather than join a common coalition against powerful opponents, communists continued to refer to their socialist brothers as "social fascists." Socialists, in turn, continued to denounce dictatorial tendencies in the Soviet Union and in centralized European communist parties. As late as the summer of 1932, the two worker internationals intensified, rather than diffused, their divisive relations. Vilification remained the rule, collaboration the exception. The consequences of such enmity were particularly disastrous in Germany, where a divided left failed to form a coalition against the National Socialist party.

Without official socialist participation, Romain Rolland and Barbusse could not claim that the Amsterdam Congress truly represented a unified proletarian front against war. From the first publicity about the congress in June 1932, Second International socialists balked and ultimately withheld their support for the venture. Despite exchanges of letters and even a personal meeting between Friedrich Adler, a leader of the Austrian Social Democrats and secretary of the Second International, and Barbusse in Zurich to negotiate terms, the socialists repudiated both the Amsterdam Congress and the strategy of the "United Front" against war.[48]

Adler challenged the organizational structure of the congress, protesting the composition of the executive committee. Workers should be represented to make their presence commensurate with their importance. Although intellectuals such as Romain Rolland were "sincere" and "courageous," they were essentially uncritical and easily deceived, for the congress was controlled by outright communists such as Barbusse, the international chairman, and the secretary of the World Congress, Louis Gibarti, a lackey of Willi Münzenberg. Above all, Adler feared that the Amsterdam Congress would be twisted into an antisocialist forum, not a rallying point for war resistance. The latent purpose was to create propaganda for the Soviet Union and to disrupt the socialist parties all over Europe, thus deforming the congress into a "crime against the working class."[49]

Romain Rolland and Barbusse underscored that the Amsterdam Congress was designed to be above parties, and that workers, not only intellectuals, were widely represented. To refute the charge of communist domination, they pointed out that the majority of the executive committee was noncommunist. The Third International had demonstrated its nonsectarianism by endorsing the congress even though "idealistic pacifists" were included. Adler forgot that the organizational autonomy and tactical freedom of every constituent group had been guaranteed from the beginning. Both Romain Rolland and Barbusse perceived Adler's socialist view as one of a "spirit of hostility" against the World Congress. Such a view revealed socialists' inertia and inability to innovate. Rather than promote daring ideas, they retreated once more into a posture of suspicion and denigration. Adler's obstructionism indicated the unwillingness of socialists to participate in a united front that tried to fuse the international working-class organizations with pacifist and progressive intellectuals in a mass antiwar coalition. For Romain Rolland the socialist reaction to the Amsterdam Congress replicated the loss of nerve and the inadequate social and political analysis of 1914. It reflected how international socialism had undergone a process of "embourgeoisement." Socialist leadership trusted only respectable parliamentary opposition and desired to come into power by succeeding more liberal and centrist ministries.[50]

The World Congress Against War opened in Amsterdam, 27 August 1932, in a charged atmosphere. Over 2,200 international delegates entered the immense Palace of Industry singing revolutionary songs, surrounded by red banners with the inscription: "Struggle With Us Against Imperialist War." When Barbusse appeared at 1:30 P.M., he was greeted by "frenetic ovations," and the crowd rose and spontaneously struck up the "International" in various languages. The two watchwords were "War on War" and "A Single Front." After electing a permanent international committee, the congress proceeded with the real business at hand: hammering out a strategy against imperialist war.[51]

Because of a serious respiratory illness, Romain Rolland was under doctor's orders not to attend the Amsterdam Congress. Following Barbusse's opening remarks, Romain Rolland's Declaration to the World Congress was read in his absence by the French pacifist-feminist Gabrielle Duchêne, president of the French section of the International League of Women for Peace and Freedom. Romain Rolland was explicitly identified with a pacifist position at this congress. After extending his fraternal greetings to the delegates, his Declaration commented on his evolution since World War I: "And permit the man who was marked by the title during the war, as if it were an injury, of being *Above the Battle,* to deploy the great flag of the *single front: Above all parties!*"[52] He underscored the educational value of this demonstration. Tactical divergence was tolerable if the goals of action converged. These goals constituted an anticapitalist, anti-imperialist, and uncompromising antiwar activism. Such tactical eclecticism permitted agitation and propaganda for pacifist struggle as well as for individual and mass action.

Since fascism was another form of imperialism, Romain Rolland declared that an opposition to imperialist war meant an all-out resistance to fascism:

> Among Germans, on the day after a Hitlerian coup d'état, or among those peoples dominated by fascism [*fascistisés*], it is clear that the dangers are greater, therefore it is more meritorious to risk oneself, to take a stand, against the obscure forces of nationalist suggestion, surging from the misery and despair of those who cynically exploit the Reaction.[53]

World war, wars between colonizer and colonized, class warfare, and even civil wars might break out. Against this apocalyptic backdrop, the country most in need of peace and most jeopardized by world war was the Soviet Union. He asserted that to be antifascist and anti-imperialist meant defending the Soviet Union for its own sake and for its symbolic power as "a hope and an example for all exploited peoples."[54]

The Declaration ended by addressing intellectuals in sympathy with the Amsterdam Congress, particularly doctors, teachers, and liberal professionals. They had the responsibility to act in militant struggle on the side of the class-conscious and antimilitaristic working class. Each group needed the other to form a politicized symbiotic alliance.[55]

The final program of the Amsterdam Congress was summarized in the "Manifesto of the World Congress Against War." The manifesto urged a sustained alliance of mental and manual workers to coordinate defensive action by workers, peasants, and all oppressed masses. It opposed imperialist wars, including those perpetuated by capitalist profiteers in India, Morocco, and Nicaragua and the Japanese incursion into China. It opposed war propaganda, military preparations, imperialist rivalries, the 1919 peace treaties, and the League of Nations. It posited that capitalism as an economic system had reached a crisis stage, as evidenced by the Depression and the subsequent starvation, unemployment, and unequal distribution of wealth in Western Europe and the United States. It denounced the bogey of "Red Imperialism" as a device to divide and weaken the working class. It advocated self-determination for the Soviet Union, especially in the face of contemporary capitalist threats to its existence. For mass action against war to be effective, an organized, disciplined movement was needed, with the working class playing the pivotal role. The manifesto condemned members of the Second International for their "opportunistic" collaboration with the present social order, which strengthened capitalism. This violated the principles of socialism and indicated that socialists had not evolved beyond their disastrous 1914 capitulation to war. Last, the manifesto held that pacifist resistance to war—including faith in referendums and legal channels, plebiscites, and conscientious objection—was "futile."[56]

The political orientation of the manifesto was more anti-imperialist and antiwar than antifascist. Fascism was mentioned only twice, as an indictment of the Versailles Peace Treaty, and as one instance of extreme nationalism.[57]

Though not present at the Amsterdam Congress, Romain Rolland in September 1932 wrote a summary of its achievement. He relied on the official bulletin of the World Congress Against War, reports published by pacifists, centrists, and communists, and distorted accounts in the reactionary bourgeois, socialist, Trotskyist, and Surrealist press. He received information from Madeleine Rolland, who attended the congress in his absence.[58] Statistically, the 2,200 delegates represented 30,000 worldwide associations with over "thirty million members."[59] Although the thirty million figure was surely exaggerated, it dramatized the historical significance of the event. Broad support existed for a united front against war, imperialism, and social injustice. Breaking discipline with the Socialist International, 291 socialists attended the congress. The dissident socialists understood the need for a public stand against world war and an alliance with progressive sectors of Western capitalist societies, including the communist parties and communist-dominated trade union organizations. They put aside their traditional animosity toward the Russian Revolution to sign a statement in defense of the "Soviet Revolution."[60]

Romain Rolland was heartened by the reverberations of the Amsterdam Congress in intellectual circles and among "liberal professionals." The congress was endorsed "by an elite of French intellectuals," including Georges Duhamel and André Gide. In addition,

prominent French academics, pacifists, and communist intellectuals sanctioned it enthusiastically. These "masters of pen and
thought," linked to a just cause, could ignite public opinion and
create a momentum toward future fronts. He emphasized the
democratic, nonpartisan structure of the congress: members of
many nations and political tendencies were provided with a forum
and allowed "freedom of speech." The congress did not exclusively
reflect the communist point of view.[61]

The manifesto of the Amsterdam Congress had a "composite"
and diffuse quality. Romain Rolland played no part in writing it.
The document was designed to maintain a tenuous unity among
various different political outlooks and world visions and could not
satisfy each constituent group. One could criticize the manifesto
constructively: Romain Rolland, in fact, stated that he would have
refused to sign it because of its reductionistic condemnation of
conscientious objectors. In reiterating his commitment to a militantly applied form of Gandhian satyagraha, he asserted that the
"collective Refusal" of nonacceptance could definitely paralyze the
modern state and be effective in war resistance. He completely
supported the congress in "its appeal to the union of intellectual
and manual [workers] and its appeal to organized direct action by
the proletarian masses against war." The congress succeeded in
creating "an international Committee of struggle against imperialist war."[62]

Romain Rolland's critique of the manifesto was not rhetorical.
He was prepared to resign from the committee, he told Barbusse,
unless more accurate and less "disdainful" distinctions were made
about pacifists and the role of the nonviolent resister in the Amsterdam movement. The manifesto confused the Gandhians, who
were prepared for militant forms of collective action against war,
with individual antiwar resisters, many of whom were "cowardly
and often hypocritical exploiters of a verbal and comfortable pacifism, a pacifism without risk." The Amsterdam movement attempted to coordinate both violent and nonviolent resistance to
war and capitalist imperialism. The Amsterdam Congress echoed
throughout Western Europe because it did not impose one set of
tactics or organizational priorities over another, but rather allowed
for their coexistence. If Barbusse symbolically represented the associated energies of human labor preparing for the social revolution,

Romain Rolland stood for a nonviolent nonacceptance that had its legitimate place both in the resistance to global militarism and in the construction of a durable, nonexploitive society. He would withdraw if one political means or ideological tendency were given a privileged°role. In demanding the activist rights of both Gandhian nonacceptors and individual conscientious objectors, he argued that in certain circumstances refusal to serve in the military could be a revolutionary tactic. Independent from all parties, his intention was to mediate between the scattered pacifist factions and the more organized groups of proletarians:

> I do not confuse a *tactic* of struggle with *Struggle*. I call for the foundation of a kind of General Headquarters of all parties of Revolution: violent and nonviolent, in order to elaborate a plan of action, not one plan, but a common plan, not servilely identical, but intelligently linked and coordinated.[63]

In order to retain the prestige of his name for the Amsterdam committee, the international bureau of the World Committee Against War issued a statement clarifying its position on pacifism in December 1932. This document, authorized by the Communist Parties of France, Germany and the Soviet Union, and probably written by Willi Münzenberg, stated that "conscientious objectors have their place in our ranks . . . and that unconditionally."[64] Romain Rolland, in principle, won the rectification he sought.

Following the Amsterdam Congress, in late August 1932, a public meeting took place at the Salle Bullier in Paris, along with a public demonstration by 20,000 people. Antiwar meetings were simultaneously held in Leningrad and Tashkent; 140,000 reportedly attended the Moscow gathering. By 15 October 1932, Willi Münzenberg, always held in suspicion by the Comintern hierarchy, was replaced by the more reliable Georgi Dimitrov. Dimitrov, however, was arrested in Berlin on 9 March 1933 and charged with complicity in the Reichstag fire. His arrest allowed Münzenberg to resume control.[65]

The Amsterdam movement reconvened at the Salle Pleyel in Paris, 4–6 June 1933. At this meeting, antifascism became the force cementing the alliance. The Salle Pleyel meeting, however, represented a demonstrable shift away from Romain Rolland's idea that there were no enemies on the left, toward a more coherently communist perspective. It was sponsored and financed by Moscow, and Münzenberg was more visibly in charge than at the previous meeting in Amsterdam. After June 1933 the movement was known as the Amsterdam-Pleyel movement. Romain Rolland and Barbusse remained its nominal presidents.[66]

Romain Rolland's letter to Barbusse was not his only attempt to maintain his independence while collaborating with communist front organizations. He was determined not to be an easily deceived fellow-traveling intellectual. He refused to sign a "mediocre and hollow" article called "I Accuse," written by Louis Gibarti, but carrying Romain Rolland's name. The piece was intended for the countertrial of the Reichstag fire being held in London. He never agreed to sponsor such ventures unless he could both "examine and verify the documents." Behind Gibarti, whom Romain Rolland found *sympathique* and disinterested, he suspected the expedient and contemptuous hand of Münzenberg. "*I never sign anything except that which I write myself, only after maturely studying it.*" He would not be a showpiece or simpleminded dupe of the communists, even in the name of antifascist propaganda: "I am not a man . . . to be used as a blind and passive instrument." He reminded Gibarti and Münzenberg that he had never subscribed to a political party, nor did he intend to become a communist intellectual who was "militarily regimented" or "weak in character." Communist efforts to parade Romain Rolland's name not only discredited the cause being served ("that of the proletarian revolution and the USSR") but also risked turning the French writer into an opponent—someone who might have to publicly contradict these flagrant abuses. Romain Rolland and Münzenberg exchanged letters, agreeing about the communist abuse of its fellow travelers. Communists often behaved aberrantly and shortsightedly, forgetting the importance of creating a "large movement."[67]

The Amsterdam-Pleyel movement historically ended years of isolation for the French Communist Party, opening the process of constructing a Popular Front coalition. The movement coalesced too late to be effective in the German context; its appeal was insufficient to heal the cleavages between the German Social Democratic and German Communist Parties. It formulated an antifascist alliance (first conceived of as an opposition to capitalist imperialism and to war), which would embrace progressive elements in the bourgeois world while being consistent with the goals of the international communist movement. Amsterdam-Pleyel revealed a desire to postpone the proletarian revolution in order to extinguish the threat of fascism.

The Amsterdam-Pleyel movement propelled Romain Rolland further into the political arena. As he became more engaged, he reassessed his idealism and his conviction that fascism could be resisted by words, by cultural products, or by nonviolent strategies alone. Amsterdam-Pleyel introduced him to politics 1930s-style, including some of its more distasteful sides, such as the need to make alliances with passive or opportunistic members of organized socialism, with ruthless representatives of international communism, and with paralyzed and mystified elements of the pacifist and centrist wing of the progressive bourgeoisie. Amsterdam-Pleyel further politicized him, even though he was still attempting to mediate between the left and the progressive center. His form of commitment became less linked to unrealizable goals and much more connected to the practical modalities of the European context. From the Amsterdam Congress until the signing of the Nazi-Soviet Pact, he would be committed to antifascist agitation and propaganda and to direct mass action. Amsterdam-Pleyel pushed him further away from "above the battle" metaphors, thereby marking a turn toward an all-out, unflinching resistance to fascism in general and to Nazism in particular.

Examining Romain Rolland's much-neglected *roman fleuve*, *L'Ame enchantée*, written between 1922 and 1933—the dates marking the accessions of Mussolini and Hitler, respectively—we must remember that Romain Rolland's sociopolitical commitments fused with his art. If *Jean-Christophe* was the great European novel of internationalism and cultural harmony before the Great War, *L'Ame enchantée* was the early 1930s' most potent antifascist novel. Both the story line of the novel and the trajectory of the leading characters, Annette Rivière and her son, Marc Rivière, mirror Romain Rolland's intellectual politics from 1929 to 1933—the years in which the final volumes, *L'Annonciatrice* (*The Annunciation*), were written. The Rivières pass from the world vision of liberal, nonconforming individualism to a position of critical support for the communist revolution. Antifascism was the crucial mediating factor in their evolution. Romain Rolland endowed antifascist resistance with a privileged role in the birth of a new society.

The first hypothesis of the novel was the neo-Marxist one that "the entire capitalist regime of this degenerated bourgeoisie" was indissolubly bound up with the origins, popularity, and continuance of fascism. Though he did not provide a systematic political and economic analysis of the relationship between international capitalism and the development of fascism, Romain Rolland pointed out that the "*grand bourgeois* have been wise enough to return the cudgel to their duces and their führers." The capitalist profiteers and fascist leaders cemented their parasitic relationship by the unquenchable desire to amass profits, acquire markets, and take raw materials and territory.[68]

In the novel fascism was an international movement, although Romain Rolland drew distinctions between fascist and extreme right-wing regimes in Poland, Yugoslavia, and the Balkans and between German and Italian forms. Fascist practice was characterized by its aggressive, dynamic nature and its appeal to revolt. Fascism in the novel became synonymous with conquest, imperialistic designs, and war. Fascist regimes were typified by mindless emotional ideologies and by primitive war ethics, "fighting for the sake of fighting." More significant, fascism meant "eternal imperialism," perpetual violence without a goal, contradicting any rational view of progress. Generated by desperate men without hope or vision, fascism once in power created a world of pogroms, wars, and the cynical division of the globe into conquerors and the conquered.[69]

Romain Rolland painted an unattractive portrait of Mussolini, unmasking the cult of dictatorial leadership and deflating the uncritical hero worship at the heart of the fascist social movement. The duce is portrayed as a histrionic, self-manufactured, self-aggrandizing tyrant, devoid of human sympathies, unable to love, without compassion for the weak or downtrodden. He was a willful man, capable of strong hatreds, who compensated for his "arid and burning soul" by acts of revenge and by devoting himself to the "torch of smoking action." Beyond conventional categories of good and evil, the duce was driven by his quest for glory, money, and power. Mussolini's activism, and his subsequent social programs, transformed only the surface of Italian society, not its substance. His fascist regime accommodated itself to the hierarchical and authoritarian institutions of the past, including king, church, family, and private property. He subverted more democratic alternatives—the trade unions, professional federations, and the Italian Socialist and Communist Parties. The novel concluded that "these ducis, the *condottiere*, were great butchers."[70]

As a novel of political engagement, the work moves beyond a critique and vilification of fascism to offer examples of resistance to the regime by crucial characters.[71] Preserving freedom and creativity in Europe meant not only understanding fascism but also working actively to wipe it off the globe. The young Marc Rivière allowed his bookstore in Paris to become a center of the Italian antifascist emigration in France. The refugee antifascists were articulating a "lost cause." Fascism was too firmly entrenched in Italy to be defeated by the antifascist resistance abroad. Romain Rolland accurately depicted the splits within the antifascist movement between democratic republicans and communists. These divisions weakened the antifascist forces, limiting the movement's effectiveness. Though Marc's mother, Annette, tried to conciliate between the various factions, the narrator (in obvious self-criticism) indicated that the project of leading all the "troops of the Resistance"—communists, socialists, liberals, and pacifists—in a single front against the fascist reaction was also doomed to failure. It was a "Utopian dream." Despite personal risks to himself, especially from the French secret police and from Mussolini's agents provocateurs operating in France, Marc championed the cause of the Italian antifascists by publishing antifascist books, newspapers, and brochures and by participating in antifascist agitation in Paris.[72]

Romain Rolland created poignant episodes of antifascist resistance within Italy's borders. Out of sensitivity to human suffering, the character Count Bruno Chiarenza was increasingly involved in political antifascism.[73] The gratuitous Blackshirt attack on a defenseless old colleague in Rome became his turning point. Count Chiarenza interceded for his friend in the street brawl, then testified at the court tribunal, where he transformed the victim's defense into an indictment against the fascist police, courts, and the government itself. Hounded by the secret police and Blackshirts, the count was finally forced to flee Italy. He took refuge in Paris and joined Marc

Rivière and Julien Davy, an antifascist from an older generation (antifascism also served to repair generational conflicts). Davy played the role of honorary president of the International Antifascist League.[74]

Marc Rivière's evolution within the novel from an amorphous intermediary of various ideological strains (he described himself as anti-imperialist, pro-Soviet, pacifist, and antifascist simultaneously) to one more closely connected with the Communist International and the organized French proletariat paralleled Romain Rolland's political itinerary in this period. Marc tried unsuccessfully to link the Gandhian social experiment in India with the Leninist Soviet Union, as the novelist tried to do in organizing the Amsterdam-Pleyel movement. Fascism changed the historical consciousness of the characters, modified the specific political nature of their engagement, and drastically altered their language. If fascism posed a threat to all of Europe, then the Action Française and the fascist leagues posed a potent danger in France. In a scene situated at a peaceful, legal meeting of the Secours Rouge International, held to commemorate an anniversary of the Paris Commune, he depicted a direct confrontation in which Coty's fascist troops disrupted a demonstration. Marc Rivière and Julien Davy were slated to be the principal speakers. The event ended with a riot between left and right, during which Marc, in an explosion of rage, killed one of his adversaries. Against the fascist barbarians, counterviolence was both inevitable and justifiable. The scene itself presaged a final collision between fascists and antifascists.[75]

The novel's various perspectives on fascist brutality were preludes to the climactic episode: the assassination of Marc Rivière by a gang of Blackshirt hoodlums on the streets of Florence. Italian fascism had deformed a once great city of learning and culture into a city of terror and street violence. Vacationing in Italy with his Russian-born wife, Assia, and his mother, Marc witnessed a *squadristi* assault on a harmless old man and his adolescent son. The crowd witnessing the incident remained inert, paralyzed with fear. No one but Marc dared to intervene. He leaped into the fray and was stabbed to death. Yet the meaning of his life did not perish. Annette, Marc's mother, successfully mourned her son by internalizing both the spirit and the substance of his *engagement*. She continued the antifascist resistance. After her death, the revolutionary antifascist struggle was passed on to Marc's son, Vania, thus allowing the cycle of the "Enchanted Soul" to be completed by the next generation. Marc died morally, heroically, resisting the forces that negated community, culture, social justice, and voluntary sacrifice. Fundamentally, Marc's sacrifice was neither empty nor suicidal, because it made Annette realize that "one could no longer remain outside the fight."[76]

To sharpen the struggle against fascism, Annette called for an immediate, unequivocal alliance against it. She grew intolerant of all the men, parties, and movements who took refuge in the untenable gray areas between fascism and the integral antifascist resistance. Annette's will to unify the progressive forces of the left could not be thwarted by theoretical or tactical differences of opinion. Just as she concentrated on reconciling the Communist and Socialist Internationals, so she also attempted to merge the struggle against fascism with the international opposition against colonial oppression and a sympathetic outlook on the Soviet Union and the class interests of the organized forces of labor. "The true line of demarcation between parties is between those who will and those who will not act."[77] The Rivières could no longer survive the 1930s as nonconforming individualists. Antifascism jolted them into making meaningful contact with a mass movement struggling for peace and social dignity in the world.

Before her death, Annette was stirred (as is the reader) by an extravagant gesture on the part of a character who was modeled on Lauro de Bosis, the Italian antifascist poet who flew over Rome in October 1931, dropping antifascist leaflets. De Bosis was killed on that mission. For Romain Rolland, he represented a kind of enchanted antifascism, and his flight contained a mythical as well as a political message for contemporaries. In the novel, Silvio Moroni audaciously flew his airplane over Rome, dropping leaflets to the Italian people, inciting them to revolt. Silvio Moroni was motivated by his hatred of Mussolini's dictatorship. The plane crashed; his flight ended in death, and the gesture triggered no uprising. Yet this emphatic "No" to the tyrant humiliating the Italian people symbolized antifascism as both a noble sacrifice and an act of affirmation. For Annette, Silvio's violent death, like Marc's, had tragic meaning in demonstrating that action against powerful adversaries was possible and necessary. It set a precedent for future opponents of all fascist tyrannies.[78]

Romain Rolland's perception of the international fascist menace in 1933 saturated the final volumes of *L'Ame enchantée*. He recognized the ascendancy and the offensive nature of fascism and indicated how progressive and revolutionary forces needed to regroup their ranks to prepare a defensive antifascist strategy. He grasped the historical importance of fascism's appeal as an anti-Marxist ideology, its seductiveness as a defender of order and stability. He accepted the schematic Marxist view of the class structure of fascism, namely, that the rich, influential, and economically powerful—the grand bourgeois—had handed over the instruments of state violence and control to the fascists. These shrewd capitalists did so by default, preferring the fascist hooligans who were willing to risk world war to the prospect of socialist revolution or radical reform within their own borders. France and England lacked the will to fight to protect political freedoms and human rights outside their own borders. The French and the British might balk at including the Soviets in a wider antifascist alliance. Stating that one was either for or against fascism, Romain Rolland legitimized the necessity of battle against the fascist antagonists. The former pacifist now employed military metaphors. The antifascist battle was a variant of the Hegelian dialectic of master and slave. To smash the fascists, he now held that all available instruments ought to be used, including violent ones.[79]

One passage of this novel, summarizing the discourse of antifascist engagement, represented the core of Romain Rolland's position in 1933:

> The road was blocked for the present. The Revolution in Europe allowed the Reaction the initiative to take the offensive. . . .
> The enemy made the first move. Its leaders knew how to exploit the unnecessary panic to which the chatterers of the Revolution, by their imprudent threats, had moved the troubled flocks. Throughout Europe, fascism posed itself as the defender of the moral and social order, of the woolen stocking, of the coffers of the family, of the country, of the "sick mother" and the Father God. The grand bourgeois, having with good reason lost confidence in their own energy, were wise enough to hand the bludgeon to the duces and the führers, risen from the people, whose energy was intact, and who transformed themselves from wolves to watchdogs. . . . The black or brown plague spread from one country to another; its virulence

increased with success. Even France and England, the last deposit banks of democratic freedoms, forgot how to make use of them and withdrew them from circulation.

It was no longer the time to tergiversate. Either for or against! Academic discussions for violence or nonviolence were out of season. The crucial question was of uniting all the forces of violence and nonviolence, against the block of all the forces of Reaction. All should find a place in the army: the great organized Refusal of Gandhi and the attacking troops of Lenin. Conscientious objection, strikes in factories and transport, insurrection, everything was a weapon in the battle that Annette's mind now accepted. She recognized that combat was necessary.[80]

The intellectual politics of *L'Ame enchantée* pivoted on the unity of intellectuals and workers in an international antifascist alliance. The novel recapitulated the themes of Romain Rolland's intellectual antifascism and opened vistas to a more politicized antifascism for the remainder of the 1930s, anticipating the Popular Front politics of the middle 1930s, with its emphasis on struggle and resistance.

8

Antifascist Resistance

> Antifascism is not only the vast field where liberals mingled
> with Communists as the war in Spain demonstrated. . . . It
> is a feeling, an attitude, and also a politics.
>   André Malraux, "Préface," *L'Indépendance de l'esprit*

For Romain Rolland the year 1933 was marked by a preoccupation
with the Nazis. The Weimar Republic entered its final stage when
von Hindenburg named Hitler chancellor on 30 January 1933. Romain Rolland followed events in Germany by listening to the radio
and attentively reading the German, Swiss, and French press. Living in Switzerland allowed him to think through the National Socialist phenomenon from a variety of perspectives. At first Romain
Rolland found Hitler's speeches monotonous and unintelligible.
Hitler's spoken German was bad; his orations seemed imbecilic.
The French writer did not immediately grasp how these hysterical
outbursts of "supernationalism" could appeal psychologically and
politically to large sectors of the German population. By March
1933 he no longer underestimated Hitler and his entourage: "Each
night I listen to the frenzy of these hallucinated Germans—
Goering, Goebbels, Seldte, Papen, Hitler—their husky barkings
and their raging shrieks to the crowds that applaud them." These
staged mass meetings, somewhere between religious rite and mass
theater, revealed the primitiveness at the heart of the Third Reich:
"The uninterrupted clamor of Heil! Heil!, regular and decisive like
the blows of a sabre; and the parade of musical brass instruments,
fifes, and drums; the religious national hymns; Hitler's vociferation
continues, choking on the ends of its sentences, almost like an
apoplectic fit which invokes: Thou, Master God!"[1]
    Hitler's seizure of power transformed Romain Rolland into an
integral antifascist intellectual. Having risked his literary reputation in France for his antiwar writings during the Great War, he

was ready to alienate his German public in 1933 by adopting an unrelenting anti-Nazi stand. Thus, he wrote to his German publisher: "It is inevitable that I will participate publicly against the state of violence in Germany, as much as I have against the Reaction in all countries. And at this very hour I am protesting against Hitlerian terrorism."[2]

Urged by the Association of Revolutionary Writers and Artists to respond to the National Socialist takeover, Romain Rolland penned a sharp denunciation of Hitler's regime. Typically, his first committed anti-Nazi stance began as a proclamation to humanistic intellectuals to unite against and unmask Nazi barbarism:

> At one stroke the brown plague has surpassed the black in its horror. Hitlerian fascism in several weeks has totaled more unworthy violence than ten years of its master and model, Italian fascism. The burning of the Reichstag, which it has used as a clumsy legitimation, is an act of gross police provocation, which deceives no one in Europe. Before the public opinion of the world, we denounce these outrages and lies: the entire public authority put into the hands of a party of violent reaction; full official authorization bestowed in advance on crime; all freedom of speech and thought strangled; the insolent intrusion of politics even into the Academies where the few solitary writers and artists who have preserved the courage of their opinions are expelled; the arrest of men held in the highest esteem, not only by the revolutionary parties, but among the Socialist and bourgeois liberals; the institution of a state of siege through the whole of Germany; the suspension of elementary rights and liberties on which all modern civilization is based. We appeal to all to join us in our protest, all those writers, all spokesmen for opinion, all those in Europe and America to whatever party they belong, who feel the unworthy outrage perpetrated to the essential dignity of man and citizen, and the solidarity that binds us to those who fight against the unrestrained terrorism of a reaction that is without scruples as it is without curb.[3]

Asked to endorse a large antifascist meeting organized by the Comité d'Aide aux Luttes Contre le Fascisme Hitlérien, Romain Rolland castigated the National Socialists for their unrestrained cruelty, ignorance, ethnic intolerance, and repressive policies. If he sympathized with the antifascist emigrés, he implied that real resistance to the "German executioners" would be propelled by the disciplined activity of revolutionary workers. Nazi atavism caused him to heat up his own rhetoric, comparing Hitler's excesses with acts of religious intolerance, including the atrocities of past history:

Though I am ill I do not wish that my voice should be missing at your protest meeting against the butchers of Germany. May these murderers, these torturers, be thrust aside, by the giant fist of the revolutionary masses of the world! These frenzied imbeciles, within several weeks, have flung Europe several centuries backward, beyond even the Revocation of the Edict of Nantes—to the abject time of the St. Bartholomew Massacre![4]

Romain Rolland urged his younger colleague Jean Guéhenno to open up the pages of *Europe* to such persecuted antifascist refugees as Thomas and Heinrich Mann, in order to "protest against the unheard-of criminal attacks of Hitlerian fascism, particularly in regard to free thought and the intellectuals."[5]

As early as 10 January 1933, Romain Rolland learned that the German government intended to present him with the Goethe Prize, Germany's most distinguished award for writers in the arts and sciences. The president of the Reich, von Hindenburg, personally awarded him the prize on 19 April 1933, through the German consul in Geneva.[6] Although the award was designated for the year 1932, before the National Socialists came to power, and in spite of his deep appreciation of German culture, he unequivocally declined it. He cited his opposition to Hitler's policies and the führer's perversion of German history, heroes, and ethical spirit. In rejecting the Goethe Prize, Romain Rolland inaugurated a tradition of writers refusing official literary awards because of political and cultural *engagement.* He suspected that the Germans were trying to buy off his opposition, to co-opt his sympathies for the antifascist cause.

> I keenly feel this honor, but it is painful for me to write you that in the current circumstances I cannot accept it. . . .
> But look at what is taking place in today's Germany: the crushing of freedoms, the persecution of parties opposed to the government, the brutal and infamous proscription of the Jews, all of which rouse the world's revolt and my own. You are aware that I have expressed this revolt in public protests. Such a politics will ruin Germany in the opinion of millions of men from all countries of the earth; it is a crime against humanity.
> It is impossible for me to accept an honor by a government that has made this politics its program of ideas and action.[7]

A key determinant of the Nazis' rise to power was the destructive bickering between left-wing parties in Germany, above all the

Communist and Social Democratic Parties. Accepting the Communist viewpoint, Romain Rolland indicted the Social Democrats for their inaction and divisiveness, which in turn stemmed from an inaccurate historical analysis of fascism and deep personal weakness and passivity on the part of the leadership. Antifascism was historically doomed unless antifascists risked defeat in practice:

> What affects me politically is not so much the brutal trauma of the fascist movements as the almost total abdication of the parties opposed to them. . . . *One must dare to be defeated,* but with one's weapons in hand, fighting, without asking for mercy, or consenting to agreement. . . . If they pretend, as the degenerate Socialists of today, to save their skins, to risk nothing except what is absolutely safe, then let them withdraw from the field of action. They are only good for taking notes in a library. None of the leaders of the Second International has the right to usurp direction. They have betrayed the expectations of the masses that were entrusted to them. Gandhi would condemn them no less than Lenin. For the essential point is not "violence or nonviolence," it is "to act." The worst defeat, the only irremediable defeat, is not inflicted by the enemy but by oneself.[8]

His analysis of the National Socialist seizure of power reflected his disappointment that the German left failed to unify or put aside their differences—as had been proposed in the Amsterdam Congress manifesto in the summer of 1932.[9]

Most non-Jewish antifascist intellectuals failed to situate anti-Semitism at the center of their perception of German fascist theory and practice. Here, Romain Rolland was once more the exception. He understood that the combination of racial anti-Semitism and nationalism was lethal. He insisted that all anti-Jewish policy was ignorant and barbaric, disputing the scientific and philosophical grounding for any doctrine based on ethnic supremacy. He realized that anti-Jewish opinions were specifically National Socialist in origin and that Italian fascism contained no such "stupid and disastrous racism." He predicted that the persecutions and expulsions of the Jews (he did not anticipate organized genocide) would be a heinous crime against the German state itself, not just against the innocent Jewish victims. Rolland's antifascism was internationalist, that is, fundamentally antiracist and antinationalist:

> In the unclean persecution of Jews in Germany today, one does not know whether to condemn more severely the stupidity or savagery of the rulers. . . . And the absurdity becomes grotesque (if it were

not grievously tragic) when it is the supposed nationalists who thus act as the worst enemies of their nation. . . . Hitlerism reveals itself to the eyes of the world as a usurpation of power over the great German people by savage illiterates or spiteful, malignant creatures, like Goebbels, whose weak and violent brain has been spoilt by Gobineau's ill-digested paradoxes about the "Inequality of Human Races," and by the fumes of a delirious pride intent on believing in the supremacy of his race.[10]

To denigrate the Jews was to denigrate the cosmopolitan spirit and all European thought and science. It was totally unjustifiable to charge the Jewish race with "vices and its own special infamy," given the outstanding "virtues and great gifts" Jews had historically manifested. He connected Hitler's anti-Jewish statements with police measures and illegal violence against an unarmed civilian population. Romain Rolland, the "enemy of every form of Fascism," held that the Nazis surpassed them all by the crudeness and bestiality of their anti-Jewish dogma.[11]

Romain Rolland reacted to the proscription and burning of books by attacking fascist anti-intellectualism. Intellectuals were indispensable in any peoples' struggle against fascism. If books emancipated the mind, only the disciplined action of mental and manual workers could be directed against "the despotic obscurantism of Hitler, which imprisons ideas and burns books, which tortures and kills human beings."[12]

In late May of 1933, Romain Rolland was named honorary president of the International Antifascist Committee, then planning for the large congress to be held at the Salle Pleyel in Paris. His earlier work with Barbusse on the Amsterdam Congress was sharpened by the antifascist perspective. *Front mondial* became its journal, watchword, and program. After May 1933, the Amsterdam-Pleyel movement, while turning politically toward the Popular Front, made the struggle against fascism its highest priority.[13]

It was puzzling that Romain Rolland's well-publicized anti-Nazi writings had not generated a counterattack in the Third Reich. He wondered how long the fascist press would spare his books; he expected his texts translated in German to be taken out of print and burned. On 14 May 1933, he wrote an open letter to the *Koelnische Zeitung* outlining his objections to the new "National-Fascist" Germany. He wrote as a citizen of the world who had been nourished by Goethe, Beethoven, Nietzsche, and Einstein. Hitler's ideology and action brutally distorted the Germany of the *Weltburger:*

> That Germany is being stamped out, stained with blood, and outraged by the "National" governors of today, by the Germany of the Swastika, the Germany that drives away from its bosom the free spirits, the Europeans, the pacifists, the Jews, the Socialists, the Communists, all who wish to found the International of Labor.[14]

He reminded his German audience that he had opposed the "iniquity" of the Treaty of Versailles since 1919. The führer had hatched a paranoid notion to provoke an emotional support of Germany's rearmament and expansionist aims. Although Germany had real grievances, the conspiracy theory was "a murderous error," reflecting the "delirium of despair." The emergence of National Socialism did not negate Romain Rolland's loyalty to the other Germany.[15]

His critique of the Nazi regime was well documented by witnesses who were harassed, surveyed, imprisoned, or persecuted by the Brownshirts. He had read the published accounts of victims and listened to the radio speeches of the leaders, and his complaints against German fascism were not exaggerated.[16]

Romain Rolland's open letter to the *Koelnische Zeitung* ended the brief period of benign treatment by the German press.[17] Six fascist intellectuals responded to his challenge during the months of May and June 1933. Their remarks were first published in the *Koelnische Zeitung* and then in a brochure entitled "Six Avowals of a New Germany" (1933). Rudolf Binding, the most illustrious of these writers, defended the deeper National Socialist intentions in coming to power.[18]

Romain Rolland quickly discontinued his debate with the writers clustered around the *Koelnische Zeitung*. Real dialogue with fascist intellectuals was impossible: the dissimilarity in historical, linguistic, and conceptual frames of reference was too great. The heart of the Hitlerian revolution remained "a religion of rearmament," the goal of which would be world war. National Socialism went beyond old-style nationalism, standing for a "new and more violent paroxysm" of chauvinism. He carefully read *Mein Kampf* in German and advised Western nations not to disarm in the face of Hitler's desires to conquer, so clearly spelled out in this text.[19]

Romain Rolland was sensitive to the deceptive methods used to

annex celebrated major thinkers of the past to contemporary political movements. He was deeply disturbed when Nietzsche's sister,
the disreputable ideologue Elisabeth Foerster-Nietzsche, sent Mussolini a telegram referring to the duce as "the most admirable disciple of Zarathustra." He immediately resigned from the *Nietzsche
Gesellschaft*, saying that his perceptions of the German philosopher
and poet contradicted the fascist one perpetrated by his heirs and
by the leading archivists. "I was the friend of Amendola and
Matteotti, whom Mussolini assassinated. I am the champion of
ideas that Mussolini tramples down. Thus, I have no place in an
association that glorifies the *Condottiere*."[20]

Fascism notoriously appealed to rebellious youth and to war
veterans alienated by the societies they returned to after 1918. If
antifascist resistance were to be effective, it too had to catalyze
young people. Thus Romain Rolland wrote a "Call to Youth" to
rally those with antinationalist, anticapitalist, internationalist sentiments into a "world front." Fascism in one of its "twenty masks"
remained a historical possibility in France, in view of the popularity
of the extreme nationalism espoused by the French military, the
clergy, the reactionary supporters of the church, and right-wing
jingoist, royalist, and anti-Semitic groups. Fascism threatened the
world's social development by deliberately subjugating "labor and
thought." European youth should form a common front against
the fascists, the "new Holy Alliances of Reaction."[21]

Six days before the last free election of the Weimar Republic on
27 February 1933, the Reichstag was set ablaze, beginning an unprecedented period of National Socialist violence. On 28 February
1933, the Reichstag Fire Decree was passed. Though directly aimed
at the German Communist Party, its language was loose enough to
be applied to all opponents of the government. Former Dutch communist Marinus van der Lubbe was framed as the arsonist of the
Reichstag. A public trial took place in Leipzig in which Ernst
Torgler, a leading parliamentary member of the German Communist Party, and Georgi Dimitrov, a prominent Bulgarian communist, were placed on trial for complicity in the fire. The Reichstag
fire trial catalyzed world opinion, resulting in massive rallies and
demonstrations from Rotterdam to New York City. An Antifascist
Commission of Inquiry was created in London to collect the facts of
the case and to indict the leadership of the National Socialist Party,

whom it accused of being truly responsible for the fire. Under the auspices of the World Committee for the Relief of the Victims of German Fascism, the second *Brown Book* appeared, thoroughly documenting Hitler's terror. Called *The Reichstag Fire Trial*, by the end of 1933 it had been published in German, French, English, and American editions.[22]

In arresting Dimitrov, the secretary general of the Communist International, the Nazis were putting into practice the anticommunist bias implicit in their ideology. Romain Rolland had never been deceived by National Socialist legality. The Nazis set the tone of the Third Reich immediately on taking office, by persecuting and assassinating independent intellectuals and dissidents. They legitimized their crimes by invoking anti-Marxism. Romain Rolland pointed to the murder of the Social Democrat Theodor Lessing, and to the arrest and torture of the German anarchist Erich Mühsam, to depict the degrading nature of German fascism.[23]

Whether he campaigned for the innocence and acquittal of Dimitrov, Torgler, Thaelmann, or for the arrested writers such as left-wing intellectual Karl Ossietzsky and pacifist Kurt Hiller, Romain Rolland's appeals unmasked the Nazis' terroristic methods and laid bare their abuse of the judicial process. The "true" incendiaries of the Reichstag were the upper echelons of the National Socialist leadership, including Goering and Hitler himself.[24] He depicted the accused as committed martyrs and exemplary men of decency who embodied the civilized core of Germany itself.

> And everybody knows, even in Germany, that it is not Thaelmann the man that the Hitler government is persecuting, but rather it is persecuting the principle of Communism. . . . The entire world is therefore entitled to declare that any secret sentence passed against Thaelmann would be a moral penalty against the Hitler government. The world would charge them with the murder.[25]

Romain Rolland's intervention in the Reichstag fire trial resulted in a letter of grateful acknowledgment by Georgi Dimitrov.[26] A second repercussion was the formation in France, largely under the auspices of the French Communist Party, of the Association of Revolutionary Writers and Artists (AEAR), ably directed by Paul Vaillant-Couturier. A founding member, Romain Rolland also emerged as a visible leader, along with André Gide and the young André Malraux. If he was a showpiece, he was also politically and ideologically at one with the AEAR. He shared their analysis of the current world economic crisis and their desire to reconcile workers and class-conscious intellectuals, while avoiding annexation to any political party. He agreed with their criticism of neutrality as a form of submission to the dominant class and their attempts to develop proletarian literature, to ignite people's art, and to organize a revolutionary culture in France opposed to conformist and fascist conceptions of art. He felt at home in an organization that mediated between the cultural sector and the working class. The AEAR represented over 550 engaged intellectuals. This typical 1930s communist front organization promised its members, simultaneously, independence and unity under the umbrella of antifascism. Romain Rolland offered his "Message" to the AEAR in the form of an antifascist salute. He had "chosen" sides because he found Nazi politics reprehensible. "I join in protest against the executioners of Germany, those murderers, torturers, those frenzied individuals."[27]

Romain Rolland aided antifascist refugees from Germany, Czechoslovakia, and Austria. He lent his name to the International Committee of Relief to the Prisoners and Deported of Italian Fascism, and he supported the German Library of Burned Books set up in Paris. During this time, he served as honorary president of the Amsterdam-Pleyel movement, presiding over the World Committee Against Fascism. He was particularly alarmed by events in Czechoslovakia, where crowds were hypnotized by Hitler's oratory and elaborately staged rallies. The minority of three million Germans in Czechoslovakia longed for a master and were incapable of realizing the dangers of Hitler's "hallucinated violence." This added up to a collective psychological preparation, a yielding to the "mirage of *Anschluss.*"[28]

In September 1933, Romain Rolland learned from his German editor and translator that his books had been banned in the Third Reich. The Nazi minister of the interior ordered not only that publication of his antiwar essays *The Free Spirit* (*Der freie Geist*) be blocked but also that the printer's plates be destroyed.[29] Several of Romain Rolland's friends, writing from the German concentration camps at Oranienburg, reported that *Jean-Christophe* was conspicuously displayed under a glass case with the works of Marx and Engels and the classics of Russian and German communism, in the

"museum of damned books, either burned or to be burned." He
was gladdened that the Nazi campaign to mute his opposition had
concluded. Jean-Christophe, in gesture and in spirit, was now
aligned totally with the antifascist cause: "This concentration camp
leader, this Nazi fanatic, is not wrong: against Hitlerism, against all
the tyrants who trample humanity under foot and who oppress
working people, Jean-Christophe will always display the raised
fist."[30]

Romain Rolland summed up his intellectual politics in a letter to
French pacifist intellectual Victor Margueritte. He prodded his
French comrades to distinguish between executioners and victims,
to reject any compromise or covenant with a fascist regime, and to
conceive of the ongoing antifascist combat in political terms. Hitler's presence in central Europe, coupled with the aggressive foreign policy explicitly outlined in *Mein Kampf*, made neutrality impossible. A racist, vengeful, fascist Germany was preparing for
world war; it was too late for nuanced critical analysis. World peace
could not be preserved while fascist movements stayed in power.
He now posed the antifascist struggle in Manichean form: not to
struggle against the oppressive counterrevolutionaries was to acqui-
esce. However, he remained ecumenical about the tactics best
suited to combat fascism:

> As far as I am concerned I will never make an agreement with fas-
> cism, and I am resolutely against Hitler's Germany. As for the means
> of combating it, that is another question. There are means other than
> war between nations. It is a question of supporting a non-Hitlerian
> Germany. The Leipzig trial is also a struggle. . . . Hitler must fall.
> He must, for the peace of the world depends on it. . . . Anyone who
> has read *Mein Kampf* knows the words of the secret orders, the
> excitative lessons taught to the nation; he also knows the feverish
> and continuous currents being made in Germany . . . and cannot
> doubt what awaits France and Europe momentarily, if they do not
> build a bulwark against the rise of this racism drunk with revenge
> and ready to be released by the fascist regimes, which take hold
> against all the freedoms and hopes of the world. We cannot concili-
> ate between Reaction and Revolution. We must make a choice.
> Never has the issue of choice been more clearly posed than today.[31]

French historians view the right-wing riots in Paris on 6 February 1934 as the "pivotal event of the decade, at least in internal
affairs."[32] On that day, the tenuous Republican synthesis began

visibly to unravel in the face of a challenge by indigenous reaction-ary and protofascist organizations such as the Action Française, Croix de Feu, and Solidarité Française. This day of disorder emerged from a framework of parliamentary inaction and disillu-sionment precipitated by the financial scandals of the Stavisky Af-fair. No longer could Frenchmen luxuriate smugly in their own democratic freedoms and constitutional rights, feeling that vio-lence abroad could not impinge on France. It became evident that authoritarian, nationalistic, royalist, neoromantic, and anti-Semitic enemies of the Republic existed and that they would use aggres-sive, illegal, even paramilitary tactics to gain their ends.

Romain Rolland responded to the events of 6 February 1934 by penning an impassioned appeal to "the People of Paris." He con-sciously echoed the Paris Commune and the great days of the French Revolution. He supported the general strike planned by French communists and socialists on 12 February, which temporar-ily diffused the right-wing threat and set the stage for the Popular Front coalition to be hammered out in the summer of 1934. Because of the inherent danger of the February riots, he deliberately glossed over fine distinctions between fascist movements and traditional, conservative associations. French fascism arose from an interna-tional capitalist and imperialist system in deep crisis, which ex-plained its grotesque distortions and one-dimensionality. Fascism's activist, mock-heroic, venturesome, militarist mentality coalesced into politics of desperation and cruelty. The events of 6 February proved that fascism had to be taken seriously, that it was urgent to begin orchestrated resistance, especially by those who hoped for a revolutionary solution to France's problems. He offered the idea of a people's front in which revolutionary writers joined hands with organized labor in an unrelenting battle against fascism. Romain Rol-land's call to the people of Paris recalled Michelet as much as Marx. The strategy of the Amsterdam-Pleyel movement began to take on the style and content of the Popular Front:

> Fascism is the last convulsion—which may be fatal—of the capitalist Reaction. It is the virus as an entirety of a rotten regime, the infection of which penetrates into the politics and into the State: imperialism, nationalism, racism, colonial banditry, the exploitation of the world of labor by international finance; all the monstrous forms of the

corrupt business mentality; all the ideological brutalization of its pride and servility, which the bankrupt bourgeois intelligence offers up to the service of the duces and führers, have been put into action with their strength multiplied a hundredfold.

Beware, everybody! Call out to all the forces of Labor, to the million hands of the proletarians, and to the Mind of the revolutionary writers and artists, who have remained faithful to their cause, which is our own! Between fascism and us, struggle to the death. Voltaire's words: *"Ecrasons l'infâme."*[33]

Another appeal, written for May Day 1934, rendered Romain Rolland's idea of a popular front more concrete. As a brother he asked intellectuals to abandon their priestly functions and aloofness, to take a life-affirming, activist position based on the historical presence of fascism—"the monstrous parasitism of a murderously exploiting regime." As the danger increased, his rhetoric escalated. In the face of the internal and external threat of fascism, no one could remain isolated or detached. Fascism changed everything. Antifascism became synonymous with the fusion of intellectuals and organized workers:

> The decisive battle has begun [*est engagé*]. It is no longer permissible to keep outside. . . . I make an appeal to all my fellow intellectual workers.
>
> I appeal to life against death, against that which kills, against the ravages of humanity: . . . the dictatorship of the great companies and the Fascisms drunken with blood. Proletariat, here are our hands! We are yours. Let us unite! Let us close up our ranks! Humanity is in danger.[34]

Romain Rolland was persuaded that fascism was inextricably linked with the economic interests of international capitalism. He adopted the Marxist analysis that behind each indigenous fascist movement there stood a self-interested capitalistic-imperialistic ruling class. The truth of this was frequently manifest only after the fascists came to power, betrayed their antibourgeois appeal, and became another Party of Order. Fascism, in short, was a historical mystification. It advertised itself as anticapitalist, yet it was funded and politically backed by corporate and finance capitalism—"Banks, Heavy Industry, and Big Business." Antifascists had to decipher the hidden from the surface structure of fascism—to strip the ideology of its lies, expose its propaganda machinery, and lay bare its nationalistic, hierarchical, and racist reality. Beneath every fascist regime were the class interests and iron "grip of high capitalism [*grand capitalisme*]." Profascist youth were being duped by slogans and symbolism manipulated by their fascist leaders; they were forced into military ventures at odds with their romantic and rebellious ideas. Antifascist resistance aimed to enlighten young people, especially those who could be reasoned with.[35]

Romain Rolland saw an analogy in the crushing of Austrian Social Democracy in February 1934 and the barbarous repression of the Spartacists. He vilified the role of the Catholic church in legitimizing Austrofascism; Dollfuss's clerical fascism grafted a specifically "Catholic moral and religious hypocrisy" to its feudal, reactionary, militarist, and petit-bourgeois constituency. All fascist movements employed lies, trickery, and Machiavellian devices; all were cynical, self-serving, and murderous. But clerical fascism lacked the ideological candor of Italian or German fascism. Even European liberals were offended by it, because, at its core, it jeopardized all freedom of thought and all secular progress. He praised the Viennese socialists and underscored the historical lessons of 12 February, namely, the importance of a military resistance to fascism and the imperative for the European revolutionary parties to prepare for such combat. Defeats were inspirational, if studied and not repeated. Violent conflict with fascistic movements was becoming unavoidable:

> The heroic defeat of the Viennese fighters for socialism has infused new blood into the revolutionary parties of Europe. It has produced union within their ranks. It has dispelled their illusion of a social conquest without conflict, dispelling the illusion of an evolutionary, persuasive approach to social struggle. It has taught them the virile virtues and necessary laws of action. The lesson of Vienna will not only serve Vienna. The whole world has gathered strength from it. Let us salute the heroes who paid for the lesson with their blood![36]

Romain Rolland articulated his own version of antifascist commitment to Carlo Rosselli, a leader of the Italian antifascist refugees in Paris and editor of the newspaper *Giustizia e libertà*. Integral antifascism meant absolutely no compromise with any fascist regime. Fascism in Italy could best be damaged by infiltrating the fascist syndicates. The most potent weapon against "exacerbated nationalism" was internationalism built on a global alliance of workers and intellectuals. Antifascism was part of a class struggle that had began after the Great War and its peace treaties. Antifascists had not only to embrace the distant "dream" of a classless society but also to accept authority and cohesiveness in preparing themselves for armed struggle. Fascist governments were organized militarily, highly centralized, and technologically sophisticated. Those unwilling to accept the inevitability of armed clashes with the fascists ought to resign from the ranks of the antifascist resistance: "Antifascism must be constituted in an international army having its leaders and its recruits, its iron will, and its discipline."[37]

Most antifascist intellectuals concentrated their analytical skills exclusively on the Nazis. Not so Romain Rolland. Through the efforts of the communist front organization, the Italian section of the Secours Rouge International, organizations in Paris of antifascist women refugees, committees in defense of political prisoners, and Carlo Rosselli's antifascist newspaper, he could reliably document repression in Mussolini's Italy. He also learned of the pathetic situation of Antonio Gramsci, who, despite a serious vascular disease, was serving the seventh year of a thirty-year prison sentence. He portrayed Gramsci as the exemplary communist intellectual for the 1930s. Just as the young Raymond Lefebvre represented what was best in French communism at its genesis, so the dying Gramsci symbolized the possibilities of Italian and international communism in the fascist era. It is an irony of history that the young Gramsci had a long-standing admiration for Romain Rolland, referring to him as the "Maxim Gorky of Latin Europe." Gramsci had, in fact, adopted Romain Rolland's dialectical formula for the engaged intellectual as the motto of his newspaper, *L'Ordine nuovo*. For Gramsci, this phrase condensed the revolutionary socialist process: "Pessimism of the intelligence; optimism of the will." Romain Rolland had not met Gramsci and had not known that Gramsci borrowed his aphorism.

Deeply stirred by Gramsci's history, his current agony in prison, and his intrinsic dignity, Romain Rolland penned one of the most forceful antifascist tracts ever written. Immediately translated into German, Italian, and English, it publicized Gramsci's fate as a martyr of Italian communism and helped win Gramsci's release from prison on 25 October 1934.[38]

The brochure opened with an ode to the persecuted victims of Italian fascism, with statistical evidence about those tried, sentenced, and deported by Mussolini's Special Tribunal since 1926.

For those unconvinced by statistics, Romain Rolland composed thumbnail sketches of school teachers and working-class women imprisoned for political reasons, often judged guilty by association. Instead of writing a "whole martyrology of the prisoners and deportees," he introduced his public to Gramsci—"to the greatest of the dying ones." Gramsci's ordeal symbolized the agony of the entire Italian antifascist resistance. His hopes stood for the possibilities of a liberated Italy, an Italy of human dignity, authentic culture, and social justice.[39]

Gramsci had the qualities Romain Rolland extolled in an intellectual: sensitivity, lucid intelligence, courage, the willingness to fight, and the visceral need to defend moral and political principles. Gramsci's task in the 1920s was precisely the same as Romain Rolland's in 1934: to fight for "the realization of the united front of the working class, for the theoretical revival of the Party, and for the conquest of the most advanced section of the petite bourgeoisie and intellectuals." For the broader antifascist cause, Gramsci represented the man of unbreakable spirit, impossible to humiliate, prepared to die to resist Mussolini's oppressions:

> The freedom they [the fascists] offered him, on condition that he ask for mercy—on condition that he repudiate his views—that he serenely refused to do; doing so would have been *a form of suicide*. Nor do we ask forgiveness for him. He who has faithfully fought all his life for his faith has nothing to ask forgiveness for.
>
> So, he will die. And Italian Communism will have its great martyr, whose shadow and heroic flame will guide it in future struggles.[40]

By late 1934, Romain Rolland had moved decidedly closer to a fellow-traveling position. He thought that the international communist movement shared his antifascist outlook and that the coordinated armed efforts of the European and Russian working classes were required to vanquish fascism. His "Greeting to the Spanish Revolution" signified his consciousness that the Spanish Civil War had become the crucial world arena for the fight against fascism. The former Gandhian now glorified military action against the Falange. He predicted that there would be global reverberations from the campaign in Spain. Even if defeats and bloodshed were excruciating, all revolutionary victories sprang from past failures. In offering his fraternal solidarity to the Spanish revolution, he underscored to the French the necessity of persevering in the antifascist struggle: "We make common cause with the unconquered Revolution of Spain. We owe it a debt of gratitude for its enormous sacrifices. Let us try to tend its wounds and tear their prey from the executioners!"[41]

In an article written for a Soviet journal, Romain Rolland discussed fascism's potential to germinate in France. Despite Amsterdam-Pleyel and the recently launched Vigilance, the organization of French antifascist intellectuals, the egotism, individualism, privileged status, and purely spiritual concerns of most intellectuals were alarming. The French cultural community cut itself off from constructive experiments taking place in the Soviet Union, divorced itself from meaningful forms of contact with workers, misunderstood class struggle, and isolated itself from the complex web of contemporary politics. French intellectuals smugly enjoyed their honors and narcissistically maintained their superiority. If fascism were to emerge in France, it would tap the aggressive and calculated ideology of French nationalism, especially as expressed by Action Française intellectuals. French fascism would cement the traditional antidemocratic forces: the army, the petite bourgeoisie, state functionaries, the upper clergy, and a small but powerful sector of big business and industrial combines. Moreover, French fascism would use the recent parliamentary scandals and disillusionment with the Third Republic for its own ends. Romain Rolland pinned his hopes on a coalition of youth, intellectuals, and working-class parties.[42]

Mussolini began to implement his grandiose fantasies of a new Roman Empire when his troops invaded Ethiopia in March 1935. This was a flagrant violation of Ethiopia's self-determination and a slap in the face to the League of Nations.[43] Romain Rolland reacted by abusing the duce for his unjustifiable imperialistic aggression. Fascist governments were war-making regimes: the Ethiopian war finally demystified Italian fascism. "The abominable criminal acts committed against the Ethiopian people display to the eyes of the world the monstrous face of Mussolinian Fascism." Such massacres would ultimately be devastating to the Italians themselves, for they left behind the "inexpiable rancor of the colored peoples against white civilization." Italy's penetration into Ethiopia revealed the underlying "cynicism" of fascist ideology, the "piracy" of its imperialist designs and the "greediness" of its military and economic appetite. Mussolini, the histrionic "Roman Caesar," had to be ousted. Authority had to be placed in "surer and cleaner hands," in order to prevent such "enormous and imbecilic appetites" from being transformed into policy.[44]

In a piece first entitled "Peace Is Fatal for Hitlerism," Romain Rolland modified his pacifist views in the light of new circumstances and made them consistent with integral antifascism. He subsequently revised the article's title to "Through Revolution, Peace." It became the epilogue to a major volume of essays published under the same name. Contextually, the revision reflected the threat in France of a powerful alliance of big business and nationalists who controlled the right-wing and bourgeois press. It was "the duty of every man who sees clearly to speak clearly and to assume his responsibilities." Hitler's dictatorship was a permanent danger because it amalgamated "revenge, aggression, and conquest under the Machiavellianism of his diplomatic profession of peace, which contradicts his chauvinistic publications and rabid appeals in the interior of his country." War was not the solution: to go to war with the Nazis was to fall into a trap set by the profiteers and nationalists of the capitalist West. Sincere antifascists demanded peace, for "it is not war, it is peace that is fatal for Hitlerism." Fascist regimes lacked the internal mechanisms to resolve their social and economic problems. Instead, they rearmed their populations and readied themselves for war. Without the prestige of conquest and military glory, no fascist regime could survive. Consequently, he urged the nations of Europe, including the Soviet Union, to remain united and compel Hitler to accept peace. Only desperate and destabilized countries sought war. Healthy, well-organized states recognized that war was always a "sinister adventure," that it always profited the few while sacrificing the many. Without peace, Hitler would never confront the "just demands of his people whom he has abused, deceived, oppressed, degraded and led to ruin." If world war legitimized Hitler's tyranny, then antifascists supported social revolution because they knew that any other form of peace was based on social injustice. In the contemporary framework, revolutionary class struggle and a defensive battle against fascist dictatorships took precedence over pacifist politics. Before peace could be constructed, fascism must be exterminated.[45]

On the occasion of a plenary meeting of the World Committee Against War and Fascism, held in Paris on 23–24 November 1935, Romain Rolland enthusiastically endorsed the French Popular Front, spoke of the constructive role of the Soviet Union in the world conflict against fascist imperialism, and restated the integral antifascist ideology. Mussolini's expedition into Ethiopia had unleashed an era of fascist wars. The League of Nations' reaction, although welcome, was tardy, and its sanctions had little effect. The leading members of the League, England and France, sought to preserve their own empires. "A party of treason" existed in France that wanted to undermine the Popular Front and the idea of a pact of collective security between France and the Soviet Union by negotiating a secret diplomatic treaty with the Nazis. France would sacrifice its allies in Eastern Europe and Russia in exchange for a Nazi guarantee not to invade France's borders on the Rhine. Such a plan was a gigantic miscalculation. It would only postpone a German military violation of France's borders. True peace could not conceal "imperialist and Fascist aggressions." Antifascist forces, in contrast, had to unify democratic and proletarian organizations and build a "Grand Army" that would bring together "Communists, Socialists, pacifist revolutionaries, conscientious objectors, republicans who have remained loyal to the idea of the Rights of Man of 1789, social Christians who have remained loyal to the ideal of the Gospel against the Church." Progressive intellectuals had an obligation to join in active struggle. For now, intellectuals like himself had to abandon their fantasies of the "one against all." Their talents were needed on the side of working-class revolution. The "greatest danger" was to mistake the intentions of Hitler's Third Reich. These "preachers of hate and extermination" would implement their policies unless they were decisively stopped by antifascists who personified a new order of "peace, progress, and freedom."[46]

In March 1936, Romain Rolland granted the communist poet and writer Louis Aragon an interview, published in *Cahiers du bolchevisme*, which described his situation on the eve of the electoral victory of the French Popular Front. The Great War and events in the postwar era had forced him to rethink his individualism and his affinity for contemplation divorced from practical action. "Now Romain Rolland finds himself engaged in battle, and he is forced to engage in a camp." That camp was international socialism, best exemplified by the principles of the international communist movement. He insisted that his own cultural evolution preceded his politicization. Earlier cultural projects, such as the People's Theater, were unrealizable in the period from 1897 to 1904. Because the present era was saturated with fascism, he envisioned no end to conflict in his lifetime. National Socialism had forced him to jettison any hope of a Gandhian form of resistance in the struggle against fascism. If it was chimerical to think that fascism could be opposed nonviolently then it was also absurd to think that the strategy of French integral pacifism, of "internal Resistance," would prove effective against a powerful and completely amoral enemy. Popular Front antifascism represented an active and intelligent reaction to fascist proscriptions of freedom, not a capitulation.[47]

Addressing his Bulgarian comrades, Romain Rolland admitted that antifascist struggle superseded his pacifist world view; nevertheless he called the antifascist struggle a struggle for peace:

> If . . . I am a pacifist, I am also an antifascist, and my pacifism is revolutionary. I call all free men from all countries to unite together against the fascisms which threaten all the freedoms of Europe and which are violently opposed to social progress. Every fascist movement is based on a murderous ideology of racism or dominating imperialism, which leads to wars of conquest and the enslavement of other countries and other peoples.[48]

He published two important articles in January 1936, coinciding with the formation of a coherent Popular Front coalition in France. Both were published in *Vendredi*, a weekly that staked out a non–party-affiliated but sympathetic position toward the French Popular Front. *Vendredi*, founded in November 1935, was directed by three younger colleagues of Romain Rolland: André Chamson, Jean Guéhenno, and Andrée Viollis.[49] The *Vendredi* articles and subsequent debates with French pacifist intellectuals revealed that the politics and ideology of antifascism were no longer compatible with integral pacifism. They triggered an impassioned polemic in *Vendredi* and in the pacifist, liberal, and left-wing press. These articles, later collected in a brochure entitled *Comment empêcher la guerre?* (*How to prevent war?*), marked a turning point in the history of antifascism and revealed a major divergence between antifascism and French pacifism.

"For the Indivisible Peace" completely severed Romain Rolland's connections with French integral pacifism. It singled out the periodical *Le Barrage* for censure along with two former friends, the professor and journalist Félicien Challaye and the distinguished historian Georges Michon. Present circumstances demanded that Romain Rolland repudiate the current stance of French pacifists, even old comrades whose discourse and present orientation had been inspired by his own writings and example. Now he found that pacifist position was "outside of good sense and the truth of facts." The French pacifist conception of the historical situation was deeply flawed. Pacifists did not realize that the current hour was one of deep and converging crises; their terminology was equivocal; they constantly underestimated Hitler. They set up misleading and inaccurate analogies between the present and 1914. They manifested a naive trust in the tactics of boycott and moral reprobation, which proved untenable during the Italian invasion of Ethiopia. Above all, Challaye and Michon lacked a critical analysis of fascism, particularly of Hitler's dictatorship and of his stated goals. The absence of such an analysis rendered the pacifists hopelessly anachronistic and ineffective. For Romain Rolland, National Socialism meant "delirious pride, despair, fury and misery." Hitler's foreign policy signaled expansion both into France and into the Soviet Union and Eastern Europe. Only the ignorant could deny that the National Socialists were preparing Germany for war with "tenacious and burning frenzy." That French pacifists glossed over or apologized for the führer's rearmament and plans for conquest was serious enough: that they were willing to deliver themselves and the French nation over to the Nazis without armed resistance was fatal. It betrayed the commitment to the antifascist cause.[50]

His conception of antifascism still served the cause of peace because it eliminated any prospect of a reconciliation between France and fascist Germany. Even the casual reader of *Mein Kampf* could detect Hitler's real destructiveness and the blatant hypocrisy of his assurances that he desired peace. *Mein Kampf* was "a Bible of racist hatred and of anti-French vengeance." Romain Rolland read the text in German. The führer's attempts to prevent its translation into French were a perfect example of "conscious bad faith": Hitler clearly did not wish the French to know of his anti-French and antidemocratic designs. Because Nazism was the "eternal enemy," the partisans of world peace should realize that no detente could be made with Hitler's regime. The Nazi leader's consistent refusal to sign pacts of common assistance and nonaggression with the Western democracies proved that his intentions were "criminal." It was impossible to strike political deals with an "aggressor" such as Hitler or to display weakness before him.[51]

French integral pacifists deluded themselves that a diplomatic alliance could be reached with Germany that would allow Hitler free rein to pillage Eastern Europe and "ruin our greatest ally," the Soviet Union. Pacifists were still captured by the illusion that legal methods, passive resistance, or organized Gandhian techniques could be employed effectively to stop a Nazi invasion. No organized movement of nonviolence existed in Western Europe or France, and Romain Rolland reminded Challaye and Michon that Gandhism had not yet succeeded in India, in the "country where there are more possibilities for success." By alleging that antifascist refugees were warmongers, French pacifists did themselves and these victims a great injustice. In fact, the antifascist emigrés were "living victims of the devastations caused by the savage Fascist and Nazi dictatorship": their critical perspective should be heeded, not berated. The peace he wanted was relative and situational, predicated on current realities, not on shadows and absolute ideals of faith. In the spirit of the French Popular Front, he exhorted Europeans to rally into a gigantic antifascist alliance: "Europe, let us take this in hand. Let us constitute the Ring! The Ring of Peace. And beware anyone who touches it!"[52]

European integral pacifists in the period 1933–1936 adopted an absolutist moral position best summarized in Bertrand Russell's statement: "None of the evils achieved by war is an evil as great as war itself." Romain Rolland rejected Russell's slogan in 1936 as being too unconditional. He stated that slavery was the worst of all evils, "an abyss, a nothingness."[53] The antifascist cause presumed that certain wars were worth waging, especially those linked to the liberation of oppressed peoples. Yet such pacifist intellectuals as Challaye and the Dutchman Barthélemy de Ligt persisted in calling for unilateral disarmament, preferring German occupation to the risk of world war against Hitler.

Romain Rolland's article unleashed a wide debate, including a well-publicized counterattack from French pacifists, liberals, and anarchists. Henri Bouché, an expert on Germany's military preparedness, responded that Romain Rolland suffered from "alarmism" concerning Hitler's offensive military capabilities. He predicted that Germany would reach the military level of other European powers only by 1938. Bouché affirmed that there was "still time left to organize and construct peace."[54]

Félicien Challaye opened his refutation by admitting the French writer's "preponderant" influence on his own pacifist development. Nevertheless, Challaye accused Romain Rolland of stirring up French hatred for Germany. His agitation for internal French unity returned to the concept of the Sacred Union of 1914. His advocacy of a French-English-Russian antifascist alliance, a coalition that revolved around armed resistance, meant brinksmanship with Germany. After studying Hitler's public appeals for peace, Challaye was certain that the führer wanted not revenge on France but "general disarmament." As for *Mein Kampf*, Challaye challenged Romain Rolland to read the text in its historical perspective. Hitler's anti-French utterances could be understood contextually. Hitler had written the work while serving a jail term during the French occupation of the Ruhr. The book reflected Germany's antagonism to the peace treaties of 1919 and French postwar aggression. Challaye interpreted *Mein Kampf* as merely a "maneuver for national cohesion." This already twelve-year-old book would not guide Hitler's policies as chancellor: he would be more responsible and conciliatory in office.[55]

Challaye concluded with two statements of faith. First, if war were to break out, integral pacifists would concentrate on "localizing the conflict," that is, diffusing the hostilities, preventing them from escalating into total war. Emotional slogans such as Romain Rolland's "Indivisible Peace" and "Constituting the Ring of Peace" only extended war and increased its ravages. In the eventuality of a German-Soviet military clash, Challaye proposed uncompromising nonintervention, even against the aggressor. Pacifists could legitimately use the tactics of "nonmilitary sanctions (moral, diplomatic, economic, and financial)." Second, if Hitler invaded France, "an absurd hypothesis" according to Challaye, pacifists should refuse participation in such a defensive war, even risking foreign occupation and the renunciation of basic civil liberties. Equating war with the "absolute evil," the "supreme calamity," Challaye believed that a Nazi occupation would, on balance, be less disastrous than the "deaths, ruins, and sorrows" arising from armed resistance. Challaye could more easily tolerate a fascist dictatorship than armed combat.[56]

Other integral pacifists chided Romain Rolland for his implacable stand against Hitler. Ex-Communist Georges Pioch argued that Challaye's "moral resistance" to fascism was more reasonable than Romain Rolland's proposals of "material resistance," because the latter presupposed that war was inevitable and that only armed battle could successfully meet Hitler's challenge. Just as Pioch eschewed Romain Rolland's desire for military "discipline," so he diagnosed a war "psychosis" developing in his writings, an unfortunate product of his "despair of Germany and of man." L. Cancouet lamented over Romain Rolland's departure from the pacifist position and drew analogies between the French writer's present "warmongering" rhetoric and that of such Action Française hawks as Maurice Barrès and Paul Bourget. Sylvain Brousaudier was stupefied by Romain Rolland's anti-Hitlerian stance. Expressing the strong anti-Soviet sentiments of many pacifists, he accused him of being too "worried about the defense of the USSR." For Brousaudier, the old prophet and pacifist leader had become a "partisan." He could no longer be trusted as a "guide and light." Léon Emery contested the image of the "Hitlerian monster" in Germany, suggesting that contemporary Germany lagged far behind other countries in armaments and that a negotiated peace with Hitler remained a realistic possibility. Cajoling French pacifists to be loyal to what Romain Rolland once was, Emery denounced his "caricatures" of Challaye's pacifist solutions.[57] Finally, Alain, the leading French philosopher of Radicalism, formerly an epistolary friend of Romain Rolland, penned a harsh reference to his intellectual politics in one of his *Propos:* "Romain Rolland has abandoned his role. He has spoken like a man of government; it is not his business."[58]

Romain Rolland's second *Vendredi* article, entitled "For the Defense of Peace," appeared on 6 March 1936. It reiterated his impatience with the pacifists' equivocations, their incapacity to produce a coherent definition of pacifism, and their lack of a concrete program of antiwar action. He placed the task of realizing the social revolution higher than all abstract loyalties to peace. To appreciate the present danger of German fascism was to grasp the urgency of struggles of the "exploited and oppressed" on a global level. Pacifists did not understand that Hitler wanted "to annihilate France" and that the unarmed resistance against fascism was totally futile.[59]

The metaphor "Ring of Peace" illustrated his idea of an international antifascist strategy, concretized as an alliance of France, England, and the Soviet Union for the "collective security" of all Europe. Such a coalition of the Western democracies with the USSR did not prohibit the entrance of a nonfascist Germany. Germans, however, had to prove their good faith by accepting the "obligation and guarantees" of this pact by immediately signing a nonaggression pact with these nations. Whether or not Germany participated, nothing could break the pact of collective security. There could be no world peace while fascist governments remained in power: "I will never make *my* peace with Hitlerism because of the revolt of my heart against its injustices and crimes, its proscriptions and assassinations, its debasement of humanity."[60]

The article ended with a strong statement on behalf of the Soviet Union. Admitting the USSR's "errors and weaknesses," he argued that it offered the world an example of strong opposition to fascist regimes, while its program of social reconstruction generated hopes for "social progress" and "human happiness." Antifascists had to defend the fortress of the Soviet Union for the sake of the Russians and for the real interests of progressive Western Europeans. If communist Russia fell, it would leave the West totally demoralized: the "West will have no blood to resist the iron claw of the massive reaction or its own despair—Defense of the USSR or death!"[61] The Soviet model reinforced his notion that stable world peace presupposed social revolution. French pacifists were locked into a rigid way of perceiving the world and themselves, ways outmoded now because they were based on the horrors of the World War I experience. Pacifists had a mortal fear of bloodshed and total war and they had swallowed a one-dimensional picture of the Soviet Union.

Even as he bid them farewell, Romain Rolland urged his pacifist interlocutors to face up to fascism. The time was past now for pious phrases, moral indignation, prayers, or minutes of silence. Either pacifists assumed responsibility for action against fascism, or they should retire from the political arena. What estranged him from the pacifists was his revolt against German fascism, which they did not share: that is why he repeated, untiringly, *"Fascism is the enemy that must be smashed.* I am engaged in a struggle to death against it." He departed from the pacifists with "regret, pity, but no blame." Events had surpassed their ideological comprehension and their capacity to respond creatively with politicized action. Since pacifists spoke only to themselves, he banished them from the French Popular Front: "They imagine that to defend peace they must take refuge in their boutiques, those who have never understood the true sense of the word *International,* its exigencies, its duties—the duty of struggle, duties of alliance, so that we can arrive at conquering the past for a classless society for the entire world."[62]

French pacifist intellectuals reacted violently to their "excommunication" from the Popular Front. Victor Basch, president of the League of the Rights of Man, found Romain Rolland's analysis of German fascism "pathetic." He accused the French writer of "despairing" of Germany and held that Hitler truly wanted an entente with France. Hitler could be persuaded to adhere to the principles of European collective security. Although the collapse of the Soviet Union would be a "profound disaster" for the Western democracies, Basch was unwilling to countenance any form of military antifascist alliance. He completely opposed a coalition between France and the USSR. Finally, Basch, echoing Challaye, considered any resort to injurious coercion inappropriate, even if reacting to an invasion of Hitler's armies.[63]

Michel Alexandre and Léon Emery expressed faith in the League of Nations as a viable deterrent to war. Romain Rolland, they said, criticized the tactic of boycott unfairly: it had never been rigorously applied during Mussolini's invasion of Ethiopia. Moreover, his view that the Russians would realize a "new superior humanity" was unbefitting a pacifist. Pierre Cuenat posited a synthesis of revolutionary and integral pacifism. While denouncing war and military preparations for war, he demanded "total, universal, immediate, and controlled disarmament." If war were to break out, Cuenat proposed the tactic of a united front of conscientious objectors and revolutionary pacifists working together toward the "dissipation of capitalism" as the desired goal.[64]

As late as June 1937, a writer with the pseudonym Marc Rivière, borrowed from the antifascist novel *L'Ame enchantée,* upbraided Romain Rolland for "going over to Stalin" and for promoting "international war" in his propaganda for armed resistance against Hitler. Challaye, in another article, attempted to discredit Romain Rolland by red-baiting him. Rather than address the practical issues regarding his perception of fascism and specifically of Hitler's intentions, he vituperated against Soviet communism and its gullible fellow travelers.[65]

Romain Rolland replied to the second wave of pacifist attacks on his antifascist proclamations by publishing three appeals in *Paix et liberté*, the organ of the National Committee of Struggle Against War and Fascism, formerly the Amsterdam-Pleyel committee. Hitler's strategy was to lull neighbors like France to sleep, while preparing for an invasion or for attacks against their allies, in particular the Soviet Union.[66] Pacifists erred in thinking they could "prevent war" by arguing that Hitler was conciliatory or statesmanlike or that he had legitimate grievances. Furthermore, French pacifists sterilized their doctrine by distancing themselves from mass movements committed to radical social change. The "indivisible peace of Europe" referred to one buttressed by international ties of genuine solidarity among all the peoples facing fascist aggression. His commitment to European peace excluded its imposition by a conquering Germany on a fearful or hesitant Western Europe. Peace was not enough, especially coupled with the indignities and contradictions of the capitalist social system or the deformations of fascism.

> We demand our place in the ranks of a great army of Progress, which renews the social order. Our world Peace is that of the new Revolutionary order, which can and will revise the injustices and errors of the old order. Peace and Revolution are linked. By necessity and by the irresistible élan of Revolution, Peace! And by Peace, the large, powerful, and fecund course of Revolution![67]

Antifascism and pacifism were no longer compatible. They would remain antagonistic until after the international destruction of fascism. Once the politics of fascism were broken and its ideology discredited, the social revolution could be regenerated. Only after the inauguration of a classless world would the reign of world peace be made possible. Romain Rolland was aware of the failure of the League of Nations during the Italian invasion of Ethiopia. He rhetorically asserted that "the people" themselves could serve as agents of antifascist resistance if they were united, class-conscious, internationalist, disciplined, and, above all, armed.

Antifascism emerged as a reaction to the sharp polarization and collective fears of the 1930s. For progressive intellectuals the crisis was conceived of as simultaneously moral and political. Yet historians have disregarded antifascism, thinking it too amorphous a social constituency, too indistinct a political creed, and "too vague and diffuse" an ideology to lend itself to an analytic perspective.[68]

Antifascism became the doctrine of French left-wing intellectuals in the 1930s, whether they were Marxists, communists, socialists, democrats, or heirs to the Jacobin and populist traditions. It also resonated with important sectors of the organized working class. Antifascism yielded spectacular events in the French Popular Front government of Léon Blum as well as in the massive international solidarity generated by the Spanish Civil War. Antifascism was the bridge between French communists and socialists, dominating the political discourse of the left from 1934 to 1937 and temporarily repairing the bitter rivalries and deep resentments between the left parties and trade unions. Antifascism helped fuse French enthusiasm for the successful Russian Revolution with an older, more democratic tradition in the French labor movement and with French republicanism. The cultural historian must see antifascism as a major component of the decade's climate of opinion.

To get an analytical grasp of antifascism, however, we must go to writers, not historians or sociologists. Malraux condensed its social and psychological dimension in a lapidary formula: "Antifascism is not only the vast field where liberals mingled with Communists . . . it is a feeling, an attitude, and also a politics."[69] It was a moral imperative. The politics were predominantly those of the French Communist Party's support of the French Popular Front, including intervention in Spain. The language was politicized, even militarized: the intention was to ignite the audience into action. There was pessimism that world war seemed inevitable, but also optimism that fascism could be smashed.

From 1933 until his death, Romain Rolland held that fascism in power was the world's most potent threat to the preservation and reinvention of culture. Fascism could be fought effectively if its nihilistic core could be unmasked. By 1933, he stood defiantly as an integral antifascist. Antifascism became the key reference point of his intellectual politics, the means to the liberation and self-determination of peoples. It defined all of his subsequent engaged activity. He advocated maximum resistance to fascism, by both intellectuals and the organized working class.

Romain Rolland's antifascist commitments motivated his break with pacifist theory and practice in the early months of the French Popular Front. It was responsible for his final break with Gandhi, even after Romain Rolland had extended his pacifist politics to a revolutionary, syndicalist conclusion. It made him far more receptive to the Soviet Union and to the Comintern's policies, especially after the Comintern embraced antifascism in 1935. He anticipated that the Russians would be an indispensable link in any prolonged military struggle against Hitler. By 1936, he realized that the German fascists could mobilize vast military and technological resources and that Hitler's territorial ambitions extended to Eastern Europe and Russia as well as France.

The reality of expansionist fascism finally forced him to abandon the First World War as his reference point. The need to defeat fascism meant postponing the European social revolution. Romain Rolland advocated the Marxist thesis that capitalists would opt for fascism before risking social revolution or radical reforms in their own countries. He collaborated with communist front organizations because his analyses and commitments coincided with theirs. Malraux generously assigned to Romain Rolland's antifascism "abundance, dignity, stature, and resonance."[70] In terms of Romain Rolland's intellectual politics, the rise of the French Popular Front meant that the engaged writer was explicitly antifascist. If antifascism was the high point of his politicization, it also encouraged solidarity with other intellectuals, workers, mass movements, and nations repelled by fascism, even to the point of risking world war.

9

The Politics of Critical Support

> Who fights for Communism must be able to fight and not to fight; to speak the truth and not to speak the truth; to perform services and not to perform services; to keep promises and not to keep promises; to go into danger and to keep out of danger; to be recognizable and not to be recognizable. Who fights for Communism has only one of all the virtues: that he fights for Communism.
>
> Bertolt Brecht, *The Measures Taken*

Ten days after Lenin's death, Romain Rolland eulogized the Bolshevik leader with a mixture of criticism and affection: "I did not share the ideas of Lenin and of Russian Bolshevism. But precisely because I am too individualistic and idealistic to adapt myself to the Marxist creed and to its materialist fatalism, I attach extreme value to the great individuals, and for Lenin, I have a real admiration." In the middle 1920s, he drew a parallel between Leninism and Bonapartism, suggesting a will to power in both ideologies and a hardening of the revolutionary impulse into tyranny. Both Lenin and Napoleon were disciplined, activist, innovative, and highly authoritarian. Both practiced political expediency, combining a moral vision and a dictatorial style that radically transformed their epochs. Lenin's self-abnegation and "will of steel" had fused with communist doctrine to produce a powerful religious faith. "Never before had human action produced a master of men, a more absolutely disinterested dominator."[1]

Responding to P. Kogan's address "Western Revolutionary Art," Romain Rolland argued that Leninism drastically simplified cultural and political activity. His own alternative was more vitalistic and opposed to state policy restricting scientific research or artistic production. The "class-against-class mentality" was a mechanistic and dangerous form of dogma. All attempts to legitimize dictatorships were sophistic rationalizations of oppression. Romain Rolland's vision pointed to universalism, self-reflection, and voluntary political association rather than to the Leninist emphasis on proletarian domination. Nor did he accept the inevitable triumph of the victimized slave through violent social confrontations and political collisions. He feared the Leninist hegemony both in its political practice and in its ideological line. A revolutionary intellectual existed outside of a party or social movement.

> As I understand it, the truly revolutionary mind never permits the congealing of forms of life. . . . The truly revolutionary mind tolerates no social falsehood. It is incessantly at war with every prejudice. . . . It is as armed against the new prejudices of the Proletarian Revolution as it is against the old prejudices of bourgeois democracy, . . . for in its eyes every social and political form marks only an hour on the dial. The art issued from it must function to uphold freedom against all. [To uphold] the whole truth. . . . On the road to truth we often find ourselves the companions of the revolutionary proletarians. But free companions. Not enrolled. . . . And working not for the domination of one class but working for all men. We shall not tolerate it that one class of men be either oppressive or oppressed.[2]

After the Rollandist periodical *Europe* refused to publish a novella by Maxim Gorky that was critical of Bolshevik functionaries, Romain Rolland upbraided the editor, Léon Bazalgette, for allowing politics to bias aesthetic judgment. If *Europe* were to provide a corrective to the "detestable influence" of the *Nouvelle Revue française,* the worth of literature had to be determined according to its artistic and human value. "In art there are no parties of Left or Right." *Europe* could express the editors' personal views and "prejudices" but should also offer essays with contrasting points of view. The Parisian literati were blind to the internal realities of the Soviet Union, ignorant of its language, and misinformed about its social and cultural conditions. They stressed only the "grandeur" of the revolution. Romain Rolland never denigrated its stunning accomplishments, but *communisant* French intellectuals seemed oblivious to the Russian Revolution's "ignominies," that is, "the suffering, ruins, cruelties and imbecilities that weigh on millions of innocents."[3]

During Romain Rolland's Gandhian period, in the 1920s, he maintained that there were essential similarities between fascist and communist methods: the use of violence, one-dimensional political philosophies, the party spirit, and the systematic curtailment of both traditional civil liberties and intellectual freedom. He chose to remain autonomous.[4]

In May 1927, Romain Rolland replied to charges by the Parisian anarchocommunist weekly *Le Libertaire* concerning the Soviet secret police and government persecutions of Russian anarchists and Social Revolutionaries. Although the sources could not be verified, it appeared that the Soviets had arrested their political opponents. Twentieth-century politics made him realize that "the worst is always certain" and that expediency was the motor force of all systems of government. Yet the Russians had no monopoly on repression or hypocritical rhetoric: "Every government, whether it is imperialist, bourgeois, fascist, or communist unfailingly does everything that it condemns in its adversary, and everything that condemns it and its ideas to failure and to ruin." Soviet abuse of power was reprehensible because it was directed against former participants in the October Revolution, the "old comrades of its ordeals and sacrifices." The French writer called for a general amnesty of Russian anarchists and Social Revolutionaries, an end to the mutual resentments between the Bolsheviks and their fraternal opponents. He urged a unified front against common enemies as an antidote to Bolshevik extolling of force. The European left would perceive this as an act of good faith. By amnesty he meant emptying the prisons in "good sense and magnanimity." The slogan "Russia is in danger" suggested that the Soviets' existence was threatened externally by European imperialists and hostile neighbors, while it remained unprepared for war or invasion. The Soviets undermined the ongoing social experiment by circumscribing individual freedom within their borders. If the Soviet revolution were crushed, not only the Russian peoples but also the entire world "will be thrown back several stages," deprived of a practical opportunity to implement progressive social ideals. His judgment on Bolshevik repression was mixed: "Whatever have been the injustices, stupidities, and often even the crimes of the Russian Revolution, the Russian Revolution represents the greatest, the most powerful, and most fecund social effort of the modern world."[5]

The French communists pounced on his interpretation of Soviet repression with a sectarian article by Jean Brecot in *La Vie ouvrière*. Brecot regretted Romain Rolland's association with the "counterrevolutionary" anarchist weekly *Le Libertaire*, whose anti-Soviet campaign was "wedded to the general bourgeois attack against the USSR." Brecot challenged the evidence of repression in Russia, suggesting that the documents were suspect, "provided by emigrés and by members of the old czarist aristocracy." Romain Rolland's anticommunist formulas derived from his "passive and pacifist attitude," which was fundamentally metaphysical and "above the battle." The French writer misunderstood class struggle and lacked the political acumen to distinguish between various forms of government. He lumped them together indiscriminately and "condemned them equally." If he worked "at a Citroën factory," he would grasp the "great economic laws" of class conflict and the practical modalities of the political arena. Brecot disagreed that the Soviet government should collaborate with its political renegades. Amnesty for the anarchists and Socialist Revolutionaries was strategically unwise. It might unleash civil war in Russia, thus fulfilling the wish "of all the anti-Bolshevik forces in the world."[6]

Reverberations of his *Libertaire* polemic reached the Soviet Union. On 2 September 1927, Anatole Lunacharsky, the broad-minded people's commissar of education, requested Romain Rolland's collaboration with the new review *Revolution and Culture,* which was to be a literary supplement to *Pravda.* Lunacharsky assured him that his writings would be published uncensored in accurate translations, though the editorial board reserved the right to comment on any article submitted. Despite their divergences from him, Soviet writers accorded him "great respect." Lunacharsky predicted that the association "will be imminently useful to our public."

> Your reply to the newspaper *Le Libertaire* has shown us, at the first attempt, that your objective wisdom is superior to the hesitations of many intellectuals who sometimes call themselves our friends. That does not mean that I agree with all that you have written in this letter; but the magisterial political tone is just and morally elevated.[7]

Romain Rolland accepted Lunacharsky's invitation cautiously. He agreed to contribute an occasional article, writing as a "free Frenchman." If he opposed the European bourgeois press campaign to debunk the Russian Revolution, he knew also of major injustices emanating from the Bolsheviks themselves. To counter the anticommunism of the "hypocritical reaction" and to unmask the plots of the "international Profiteers," he emphasized the "grandeur," "historical necessity," and progressive aspects of the Soviet Revolution. He would not endorse the unnecessary excesses of Soviet communism: "My aversion for certain of its political methods, too connected to the worst errors of the reactionary politics that it combats, for its narrowness of doctrine and for its dictatorial spirit. I have condemned without regard its duplicity and its violence." He realized the monumental innovativeness of this great social revolution: internal democracy and self-criticism were the best assurances that it would remain "the powerful vanguard of human society." To persuade Western intellectuals to sympathize with the Soviet cause, Communist Party leadership had not only to upgrade its simplistic slogans but also to jettison the mindless posturing so prevalent in Soviet Marxism. Intellectuals would resist such alliances until the Soviets demonstrated a consistent antifascist perspective that incorporated a thoroughgoing commitment to human dignity, enlightened self-reflection, and basic individual freedoms: "You will rally the phalanx of vigorous minds, which refuses its obedience to dogma whatever it may be, and which leads a struggle against all Fascisms, whether of the right or left."[8]

Asked by the Society of Cultural Relations between the USSR and Foreigners (VOKS) to commemorate the tenth anniversary of the Soviet Revolution, Romain Rolland hyperbolically celebrated the event as "the greatest anniversary of social history." Professing his revolutionary fraternity as a non-Marxist French intellectual, he glossed over the ethnic, geographical, historical, and cultural differences between his Russian comrades and himself. He stressed instead a powerful unifying bond—labor. Labor created abundance, vitality, gave meaning to life; labor was more than just the "spirit of life," it was the "sole king of the world." The Russian Revolution's supreme accomplishment was to establish the dignity of labor as its operative social principle. The USSR was the world's strongest barrier to "all the imperialisms, fascisms, and obscurantisms" currently on the rise in Europe. In modern Russia existed the possibility of a collaboration between mental and manual labor. As a "Republic of Labor," the Soviet Union had already surpassed the most advanced socioeconomic achievements of the French Revolution while avoiding some of its "errors and crimes." After one decade, the Soviets appeared to have avoided the bloodthirstiness of the Terror, the chaos of internal disunity and civil wars, and the destabilization of the rapid succession of government. The enemies of these revolutions were similar: the coalition of the European reaction, dictated by the interests of big capital and the military, with Great Britain the most flagrant of all. To date, the communist revolutionaries surpassed the French Jacobins in political wisdom. Rather than export their ideas by war or by conquest, they were dedicated to building "their own house in a reliable manner." Rather than replace the old regime with a new structure of privilege, they fostered a relatively egalitarian form of construction within their own borders. The Russian Revolution on its tenth anniversary symbolized a hope for the world's future.[9]

The anarchocommunists of *Le Libertaire* strongly contested Romain Rolland's salute to the Soviet Union. Russian emigré N. Lazarevitch alleged that the Frenchman failed to distinguish between the Soviet people and the Soviet rulers. Anarchists still faced torture in prisons, and worker sovereignty did not exist in the USSR. In fact, the dictatorship of the proletariat exploited the majority of Russian workers, many of whom were "crushed in mines and factories."[10]

Romain Rolland cited the impartial study by the liberal Italian Catholic Guido Miglioli, *The Soviet Village* (1927), to document the élan of the Soviet peoples and to underscore the "immense" achievements of only ten years. Lazarevitch's analysis was one-sided, omitting that in the USSR "the development of good and evil are mingled in gigantic proportions." To object to Soviet crimes without praising its creative initiatives was polemical and contrary to disinterested inquiry; such analyses were misguided. Compared to the social stalemate and political regression in postwar Europe, the Russian model stood as a significant "island" of progress. Romain Rolland consistently refused to adopt the perspectives of ultra-leftist or anarchist groups during the interwar period. Instead he called for a common front, an interclass leftist alliance against the political and social injustices of the reaction: "I do not defend a party. . . . When I think of the Tenth Anniversary of the October Revolution, I do not think of Stalin, Bukharin, Trotsky, or Zinoviev—or of Lenin. I think of the broken chains of the fallen Bastille. Now the work must be finished, for other Bastilles remain."[11]

To Lazarevitch, Romain Rolland's articles exemplified how the Soviets cynically exploited his reputation and naivety. He was "involuntarily" situated on the side of the intellectual idealist, which accounted for his biases "against the proletariat."[12]

Romain Rolland replied that he was unable to separate the realities of the Soviet government and the Russian people. If Romain Rolland's allegiances were with the intelligentsia, how could Lazarevitch explain his "lively sympathies" for the Russian Revolution, despite his explicit disclaimers: "I am . . . at least the only non-Bolshevik, noncommunist, nonpolitical intellectual who has spoken for the Russian Revolution at the present time." Lazarevitch did not understand that much of his life had been spent deflating the intellectual class of its superiority. He rejected *Le Libertaire*'s *ouvrièrist* view as a presumptuous and reductionistic form of dogma: "I do not believe in [the class dogma] of the workers unless you enlarge the name to all those who live of and *for* their Labor, as I live also."[13]

Romain Rolland's tenth anniversary greetings to the Soviet Union triggered an emotional polemic by two Russian emigré writers, Constantin Balmont, a poet, and Ivan Bounine, a distinguished writer who in 1933 became the first Russian winner of the Nobel Prize for Literature. In two open letters published in the anticommunist daily *L'Avenir*, the exiled Russians accused the Frenchman of "shaking hands with assassins." According to Balmont, the Soviet regime was synonymous with massive destruction. The majority of the Russian population opposed the Bolshevik regime. Bolshevik abuses included censoring all printed material, denying religious liberties, plundering the peasantry, throwing millions out of work, and executing or destroying the sanity of leading Russian intellectuals.

Bounine exhorted Romain Rolland to return to the role of "world conscience" and "humanitarian." The French Nobel laureate ought to repudiate the "brigands and band of ill-doers who have devastated and exhausted Russia over the last ten years." Bounine supplied him with ghastly information from noncommunist sources and appealed to him as a well-informed, liberal-minded Russian writer, not an "obtuse reactionary." He summed up his disillusionment in one sentence:

> If certain of us hate the Russian Revolution it is solely because it has atrociously offended the hopes that we have put into it; we hate in it what we have *always* hated and will always hate: the tyranny, the arbitrariness, the violence, the hatred of man for man, of one class for another, the baseness, the imbecile cruelty, the trampling of all

divine prescriptions and of all the noble sentiments; in short, the triumph of the muzzle, of the villainous.[14]

Romain Rolland acknowledged that the world of these two "representatives of human nobility" was irrevocably shattered. The emigré writers were destined to live out their existence in psychological and cultural exile in a world that received them with "indifferent egoism or intolerable pity." He distrusted the current allies of Balmont and Bounine. They had become "instruments" of the European reaction, the "monied imperialist moral order" that wanted to crush the Soviet Revolution, not to restore the Russia for which these artists yearned. The imperialists wanted a dependent Russia they could manipulate to their own advantage. Knowing that the anti-Soviet Russian writers had developed a mental framework that prevented them from being reconciled to the revolutionary regime, Romain Rolland wrote for self-clarification. It was practically impossible to have dialogue with a "martyred writer."[15]

Balmont and Bounine failed to appreciate the historical context of the Russian Revolution and how that context decisively affected its first decade of existence. The Bolsheviks contended with the heritage of czarism as well as with severe, converging crises—the cataclysmic effects of the First World War, foreign invasion, and a civil war followed by a period of famine, epidemics, and massive population dislocations. After the final squelching of the European revolution in the early 1920s, the Soviet Union stood completely isolated internationally and menaced by internal opponents, its borders surrounded by enemies.[16]

Although he was publicly "disgusted and horrified by their ferocious errors and crimes," Romain Rolland was convinced that the Soviets were creating a new world. An impartial observer had to be "struck by the original reconstruction and vigorous renewal" taking place there. Profoundly uprooted emigrés clung to rigid ideas fueled by frenetic rage against the Soviet state. They conspicuously omitted all mention of Soviet achievements. As a corrective, he highlighted educational, technical, scientific, and social advances taking place in the USSR. Bolshevik collectivization and the establishment of worker and peasant councils promised glorious results, reversing centuries of stagnation and mystification. Having radically broken with the past, the Russian communists were building a new world that would benefit their children and grandchildren. Underscoring the "joy," the "health," and the "vital sprightliness" of Russian youth, he explained Soviet exuberance in terms of a collective sense of purpose.[17]

Balmont and Bounine's allegations that his information on the USSR derived from Communist Party sources were misleading. Romain Rolland distrusted the orthodox line of every political party and had always refused to compromise his intellectual independence by joining one. His pro-Soviet sentiments stemmed not from politics but from his historical imagination. He was kept informed of Soviet affairs by travelers, scholars, and writers, many of whom visited him in Switzerland after their journeys to the USSR. These witnesses represented the spectrum of classes, countries, opinions, professions, and ideologies. Over two-thirds had begun their investigations unsympathetic to communist ideas. The sincerity and aptitude for observation of such men as Georges Duhamel, Luc Durtain, Max Eastman, Scott Nearing, Guido Miglioli, and Maya della Torre were irrefutable.[18]

The fellow traveler's task was to support the revolution in a balanced and analytical manner, which was impossible for the exiled Russians. He criticized the policies of curtailing human freedoms within Russia just as he advocated that the Soviets openly discuss substantive issues. Romain Rolland was particularly appalled by the institution of domestic espionage, predicting that "the monstrous organ of the secret police" might denature Russian life.

> Another disgrace, worse still, so degrading that we shall not dream of dissimulating, that inspires in us, as in you, a limitless disgust, is informing. We contemptuously denounce this ignoble poison that withered the soul of a nation, and to which too many souls in Russia have become accustomed.[19]

While acknowledging abuses of power, the Russian Revolution had to be preserved in an open-ended manner to enable it to fulfill its destiny. "It is the hope, the miserable hope, of the human future." It was Balmont's and Bounine's "hope," in spite of themselves. The Soviet Revolution inspired Romain Rolland with a tragic pessimism about historical advance: "human progress, which the proscribed Condorcet affirmed with intrepid serenity before he committed suicide, is brought about at the price of millions of sacrifices."[20]

Romain Rolland's play *Les Léonides* (1928) addressed itself to the perception of a social revolution by its historically conscious emigrés and victims. It rendered the dialogue with Balmont and Bounine an art form. Romain Rolland created an implausible situation in which the two leading characters, both exiled to Switzerland in the late 1790s, resolved their seemingly insurmountable political and attitudinal differences. The final agreement between emigré aristocrat Prince de Courtenay and the outlawed Jacobin Mathieu Regnault was a synthesis of old and new France, implying that a purposeful mutuality could be generated after ten years of revolution. Using the Leonid meteor showers as a symbol of movement and reconciliation, the play demonstrated that the old was inevitably destroyed and that the new emanated from it.[21] The problematic was whether there could be cooperation instead of bloody collision between the extremes of the ideological spectrum. This question crystallized Romain Rolland's dilemma as an engaged writer in the late 1920s, when he found himself writing as an idealistic Gandhian attempting to blunt violent extremes and at the same time maintain a critical but supportive perspective on the USSR.

Romain Rolland's relations with the Romanian writer Panaït Istrati (1884–1935) disclosed his ambiguous sympathy for the Soviet Union in the late 1920s and early 1930s. In addition, it revealed the ways in which he reflected on criticism of Russian communism deriving from an extreme left or ex-communist perspective.

Istrati was a creatively disturbed, self-taught man of letters, much closer to the tradition of picaresque than to proletarian literature. This traveler with a taste for danger and excitement was also a rebel and a passionate individualist. He developed original narrative forms and spun enchanting, ingenious autobiographical tales. After a suicide attempt in 1921, Istrati composed a desperate letter to Romain Rolland in Switzerland.[22] This letter began a complicated but deeply felt relationship between the two writers. Romain Rolland was captivated by Istrati's storytelling genius and his remarkable mastery of the French language after only seven years' practice. Istrati's prose was marked by its tragic cheerfulness, its sparkle and lucidity. In a 1923 preface to Istrati's *Kyra Kyralina*, Romain Rolland celebrated him as a "new Gorky from the Balkans" (*un Gorki balkanique*).[23]

Romain Rolland helped launch Istrati's literary career. Royalties, publishing contracts, and fame were not long in coming. Twenty years older than Istrati, he empathized with the Romanian's longings for "friendship" but also played the role of disciplinarian. He exhorted Istrati to create: "I do not expect hysterical letters from you. I expect books. Produce them: they are more important and more lasting than you, who are merely the vessel containing their seeds."[24]

His direct experience of poverty among the marginal and abandoned peoples of Eastern Europe and Asia Minor led Istrati to join the Communist Party in the mid-1920s. Communism represented to him the possibilities of fellowship extended to an entire community. To honor the tenth anniversary of the October Revolution, Istrati toured the Soviet Union for sixteen months in 1927–1928, criss-crossing from the Siberian north to the western Caucasus. He knew Russian and various national dialects. Because of his ties to Romain Rolland, Gorky granted him an interview. What Istrati saw was disillusioning: his faith in Soviet communism suddenly crumbled. In 1929, he published a three-volume work describing and interpreting his voyage, called *Vers l'autre flamme.*

Istrati exposed the bureaucratic and doctrinaire aspects of the Soviet communist organization, the privileges party functionaries enjoyed in everyday life, and aspects of injustice and of gross insensitivity toward the masses. He unmasked the pervasive role of spying and denunciation throughout Russian society. His outrage sprang from the harassment and imprisonment of comrades by the Soviet police system. *Vers l'autre flamme* articulated the revolutionary anarchist perspective of dissident Russian intellectuals, which in the late 1920s closely paralleled that of the Trotskyist opposition. Istrati was one of the earliest disillusioned communists to lay bare glaring abuses in the Soviet Union. His works also contained much exaggerated, even sophistic, criticism. His prose could be self-discrediting and his hyperemotionality often interfered with the logical argument and the coherent grounding of his perceptions. Yet passages describing human degradation and the stifling of intellectual life in the USSR were prescient.[25]

Romain Rolland responded to Istrati's exposé as if it were a betrayal. The French press, already anti-Soviet, widely publicized Istrati's reports. Romain Rolland was heartbroken by the volumes but not in the least persuaded by them. Istrati's assessment, he alleged, had been influenced by Victor Serge and other dogmatic "anti-Moscow revolutionary anarchists"; Istrati's account was not balanced by countervailing research findings or by an acknowledgment that the dissidents' framework might itself be distorted. Istrati's picture was marred by the "frenetic excess of his customary passion, as he stabs Russia as a whole." Lacking objectivity and restraint, Istrati twisted the virtue of fellowship into a vice. He magnified the jailing and harsh treatment of his close friends in order to take revenge on the Soviet government, but he totally discounted the self-sacrifice being channeled into building Soviet society. Istrati had told him privately that two of the volumes published under his name had been written by friends. Romain Rolland felt that many of Istrati's comrades were neither personally decent nor politically trustworthy. To deceive the public about authorship was to act in bad faith and did not inspire Romain Rolland with trust in the accuracy of the account.[26]

He did not hide his differences from Istrati. It was unconvincing to "stigmatize an entire regime" on the evidence of concrete injuries to particular individuals. He did not contradict the fact of Soviet excesses, but he questioned Istrati's emphasis and challenged his interpretative zeal.

> For your friends, the innocents, heroes, voluntary martyrs, everything is confusedly concealed in a stream of abuse. Your justice is the supreme injustice. It is iniquitous to generalize about one hundred million beings from the dirtiness [*malpropretés*] of a dozen, or of a hundred. The only one to profit from this infuriated revenge is the Reaction. . . . You could have gotten to the essentials of this business without denying what is healthy in Russia, and what deserves to be saved, defended, exalted.[27]

He did not dispute the substance of Istrati's report on specific cases of political repression in the USSR. He never regarded Istrati as a counterrevolutionary agent, nor did he employ other derogatory epithets to dismiss his charges. He questioned the logical and historical strategy of drawing universal conclusions from isolated factual examples. Nor did Romain Rolland endorse the revolutionary anarchist or the Trotskyist critique of the origins and inherent evils of Stalinism. While they were unmistakably gifted, these ultra-leftists had their own axes to grind. Their analyses were often self-serving and rhetorical, tactically divisive and extremist in relation to European left-wing politics. He had felt estranged from the anti-Stalinist ultra left since its genesis, not seeing a huge difference between its denunciations of the Soviet Union and those of the European right. He never embraced a contemporary report on the Soviet situation that eliminated references to the accomplishments and progressive nature of the experiment.

If he disavowed the extreme left's use of Istrati, he found the communist reply equally reprehensible. He refused to toss books by ex-communists such as Istrati into the intellectual ashcan of history. *L'Humanité's* labeling Istrati a counterrevolutionary agent or capitalist spy left Romain Rolland with "disgust and contempt" for communist journalism. The "blindness and stubbornness" of the French communist press reflected nothing but venom; PCF analogies were appalling if not ridiculous. They lambasted Istrati for not toeing the party line, while praising Barbusse for being a "people's writer" or "proletarian" artist simply because his public pronouncements were consistent with the Comintern.[28] The Istrati episode revealed that the age of ideological posturing had begun. The engaged writer was challenged to preserve his free moral perspective, not to be swept away by the polarization of politics and culture into the neat left/right categories so characteristic of the discourse of the 1930s. It took courage to resist the splitting and fragmentation of the left: many disillusioned writers, following Istrati's precedent, might drift into despair or cynicism. That, too, was a dead end.

By 1929, Romain Rolland viewed political repression in fascist regimes as typical of both the ideology and politics of fascism. Violence and nihilism were its essence. Yet as a fellow traveler, he separated Soviet abuses from Soviet construction, acknowledging acts of cruelty but seeing them as oversights, not representative policy. They did not negate the vast industrialization, the economic planning, the cultural effervescence, and the regeneration of an entire continent. In the Soviet Union, the whole was considerably greater than the parts, the socialist humanist core compensating for the internal errors, violences, and deformations.[29]

In a debate with the Romanian pacifist intellectual Eugène Relgis, author of *The Pacifist International* (1929), Romain Rolland took issue with pan-European ideas. They disguised nationalism and revived an archaic form of Eurocentrism. As he evolved from a revolutionary Gandhian position, he grew closer to a politicized version of fellow traveling. Romain Rolland used his debate with Relgis to reply directly to Julien Benda's *Treason of the Intellectuals* (1927). Benda's concept of the mind was abstract, Platonic, and even frozen; his superordinate ideas transcended history. In upholding the privileges of a "clericature of the mind," Benda deprecated political activity. He was blind to the contemporary mesh of politics and culture, and his metaphysics clouded the intellectual's responsibility to social justice: "Never shall I tire of denouncing the injustices of action, and of working for the amelioration of social conditions." Though not formally affiliated with a party or association, Romain Rolland no longer considered himself an apolitical writer. Intellectuals ought not to denigrate the field of politics, which touched all aspects of life, including "sustenance, labor, [and the] freedoms."[30]

Intellectuals were obliged to understand the roots of poverty to eliminate, or at least reduce, its staggering impact. "[The intellectual] has no right, in the name of the mind, to disdain material realities that are the basis and the first condition of the mind. . . . Before everything else, we must think of reducing their misery." The counterpolitical attitude was untenable in a crisis-ridden era. Romain Rolland's mission as a writer impelled him to make his literary skill available to class-conscious workers struggling politically to free themselves from material poverty:

> I am the servant of the hungry, the exploited, the oppressed. Before giving them, if I can, the treasures of the mind, I owe them bread, justice, and freedom. My very participation in the privileged realm of intelligence provides me the means, imposes on me the duty, of effectively aiding the community—by illuminating, if I can, the right road and the dangers that beset it. No, I will not turn my back on politics.[31]

By 1930, Romain Rolland's fellow traveling pivoted around the defense of the Soviet Union. Today the USSR is a political, industrial, and military superpower. But from his vantage point, the country's existence was threatened by the "International of Business," a term designating American and European corporate capitalists, imperialists, reactionaries, clerical hypocrites, and fascists with multiple masks. The titanic effort of Soviet social reconstruction required peace in order to reach completion. He called for an end to the doctrinal and tactical divisions among progressive European friends of the USSR. He urged a collective alliance against "the most filthy reaction: that of money, of the sabre, of the cudgel, of the tiara." Convinced that there was a conspiracy against the Soviets, he urged European public opinion to lobby against the militaristic sectors, to prevent an unholy "crusade against the rebellious reds." The left could unite against the common enemy without accepting "Moscow's political direction." He was particularly distressed by the role of the bourgeois nationalist press and the church in stirring up antagonisms to the Russian communists. They invoked the canons of religious morality, justice, and civilization to justify "the foulest kind of Reaction." Western anti-Soviet propaganda was motivated by the fear that the Five-Year Plan might succeed and become an exportable model. He predicted that within three years the Soviets would be industrially and militarily capable of "defying your assaults."[32]

His perception of the Soviet Union figured in a debate with Gaston Riou over the issue of pan-Europeanism in early 1931. Romain Rolland declared himself "anti-European." His public ought to liberate themselves from outdated notions of the nation-state and democratic ideologies camouflaging empire; beneath the sublime principles of the United States of Europe lay the interests of big business. He defended the Soviet Union because an organized, international campaign threatened to encircle and subdue the communist state.[33]

The anti-Soviet conspiracy was masterminded by multinational corporations, particularly the iron and steel industries and the huge oil and gasoline companies such as Standard Oil. These cartels colluded with White Russian emigrés, mercenary armies in the Balkans, and the reactionary political parties of Europe and America. The Western democracies had perverted their historical, legal, and philosophical origins by functioning as empires. The public required information unavailable through media controlled by nationalist or capitalist interests. Europe was an antiquated idea unless Russia were included. He also called for an immediate revision of the 1919 peace treaties and urged Europeans to ready themselves for an extended period of decolonization in Asia, Africa, and the Islamic world. He pointed to the Moscow trials of November–December 1930, which consisted of charges against L. K. Ramzin and Russian technicians accused of "wrecking," to illustrate that the USSR was truly in danger. He never questioned the validity of the charges against Ramzin, presuming that he was "guilty of sabotage and treason."[34] Just as he would not protest publicly against other revolutionary tribunals and purge trials in communist Russia in the mid- and late 1930s, Romain Rolland's silence reflected his belief in an internal conspiracy against the Soviet experiment.

Provoked by Serge Radine's articles in a Swiss newspaper expressing "uneasiness over the 'materialism' of Communist thought," he addressed himself to the elusive question of "idealism versus materialism." These labels concealed more than they revealed. Romain Rolland was historically conscious of fifty years of "filth" shielded by the banner of "idealism." Neither ideological nor semantic differences mattered: what mattered were the concrete accomplishments and the degree of sacrifice involved by those participating in Soviet planning. "The entire question is to know if the movement of construction in the USSR is going toward a more just human organization—the only just and fruitful one. And I believe it is." The Russian communists should be evaluated in terms of quantifiable achievements, not compared to a "hypothetical paradise." Critics of the Russian Revolution should focus on the principle of the social division of labor: "The problem is to divide and distribute labor equally. And by the sole fact of this equitable division, to restore to millions of human beings the right to leisure and the possibility of individual development." Calling for a realistic assessment of Soviet deeds, he was unable to resist mythical allusions: the Soviet experiment was a "Herculean labor." Soviet internal violence was a distortion, resulting from the desire to "clean up their Augean stables." The Gandhian Romain Rolland was becoming less easily disgusted by the role of expediency and less moralistic about the role of compromise and coercion in the work of social reconstruction: "One has no right to be squeamish because the builders have had to soil their hands." The young Soviet leadership inspired confidence in that they were pragmatic visionaries who knew how to implement policy. Soviet sympathizers should not be put off by communist "dogmas and errors" and should remember Russia's backwardness and the disadvantageous framework in which the Bolshevik Revolution was made. Europeans "had much to learn" from the Soviet leadership. For the moment, only a provisional evaluation could be made. Ultimately history would be the judge of Russian accomplishments and misdeeds.[35]

Romain Rolland answered a query by two Soviet literati, the autodidact and gifted proletarian writer Fedor Gladkov and the constructivist Ilya Selvinsky, who upbraided him in the leading Soviet literary review, *Literaturnaya gazeta*, for being an "individualist" and a "humanist." His "comrades" should know that he was one of the Soviet Union's most "loyal friends and defenders" in Europe. He contested the self-righteous tone of contemporary Russian writing and the dismissal of all other forms of struggle as absurd, outdated, or idealist. Just as there were hypocrites who mouthed humanitarian rhetoric in the West, so there were impostors, scoundrels, and self-aggrandizing individuals within communist circles. Communists who demonstrated a capacity for faith and self-sacrifice were "individualists without knowing it—and (without knowing it?) the true champions of humanity." He voluntarily entered the Soviet camp carrying with him a European heritage of critical and creative freedom, a method and tradition not always present among Soviet militants and intellectuals. Soviet writers ought to have the largeness of mind not to reject him, to set aside their parochialism and attempt to integrate what was valid in his aspirations and cast aside what was not.

> I bring to you, I bring into your camp, the camp of the workers who are masters of their destiny, the sacred banners of freedom of thought and humanity. Do not reject them! Be proud of them! Rejoice that they come to fight on your side. . . . The gods of the old world, *freedom, humanity*, are deserting the camp of your enemies. They are coming over to you. Welcome them! And grasp the hand of he who leads them to you. They shake your hand—Fraternally.[36]

Romain Rolland now exalted the Soviet Union as a workers' haven for those who opposed fascism, imperialism, and integral nationalism and for those who were authentically committed to a republic of emancipated laborers. Still mediating between the Gandhian and fellow-traveling ideologies, he began to veer more toward the Soviet Union than toward India. Yet his idea of the USSR remained mythical: a society founded on socialist humanist principles, which promoted self-scrutiny and which tolerated no forms of racial, ethnic, hierarchical or social privilege. This mythical notion implicitly criticized the reality of dictatorship in the Soviet Union and debunked the monolith of party privilege and narrow Marxist sectarianism.[37]

Gorky's writings and political itinerary became the themes to which Romain Rolland appended his views on the USSR. He began to revise and blur the distinctions between the fellow-traveling and the communist writer. Gorky's rallying to the Bolshevik government and ideology became a foil for criticism of Western intellectuals and questions about the cherished values of "liberalism and individualism." Gorky's social origins, his roots in the Russian peasantry and artisanat, his experiential knowledge of the common people, and his voluntary decision to embrace the Russian Revolution suggested an end to the long-standing isolation of the intellectual from the masses. Events in Russia now made a mutually beneficial union between workers and thinkers possible, allowing them to focus their energies toward common projects.

> The independent mind is . . . condemned to die if we do not succeed in transforming it in full humanity, in this "black earth," which is the Laboring people. Gorky has come from there. Now he is one with the very conscience of the proletariat. He is its intellectual crown. They are inseparable from one another.[38]

Western intellectuals substituted an "aristocracy of the mind" for an aristocracy of birth, which they had helped to destroy before and after the great French Revolution. Art and literature supplanted religion as the "opium" of the French intellectuals. Taking refuge in aestheticism, formalism, or involuted philosophical discourse, French thinkers offered plausible rationalizations for complacency about pressing social realities. Apathy and cynicism were the rule, engagement the exception. Notwithstanding the extraordinary moment of the Dreyfus Affair, intellectuals entered the social arena reluctantly and cautiously; most sustained their revolt "for only a brief moment." From his perspective of critical support for the Soviet Union, Romain Rolland judged intellectuals irresponsible: "They have deadened the public conscience, supplied men with alibis to escape from social responsibility, chapels in which to shut themselves up and take refuge from reality, pretexts to turn

their backs on action and to say: 'I wash my hands of injustices.' "[39]
Even the most clear-sighted, from Flaubert and the birth of modernism, exempted analytic understanding from action. The times no
longer permitted writers to be "above the battle" or to retreat to the
island of an "independent mind." The writer's isolation and ethical
conscience were ambiguous legacies.[40]

Writing a preface to Gorky's *Eux et nous* (1931), Romain Rolland
openly identified with Gorky the communist intellectual. At the
same time, the dichotomy made him uncomfortable: it was paranoid and Manichean, even for an era of crisis when engagement
was mandatory. He clung to the oceanic idea of an alliance among
left-wing workers and progressive intellectuals. His concept of
choice was not nearly as sharp or exclusive as that of Gorky, whom
he preferred to think of as guide and preserver of culture.

> This Gorky . . . a privileged person of art and intelligence, a master
> writer, passing over with all of his genius and glory to the camp of
> the Revolution, and addressing the intellectuals of Western Europe
> from the other side of the barricade. I, too, cross over to that side of
> the barricade, and grasp Gorky's fraternal hand.[41]

The Soviet Revolution provided and restored culture to the Russian people. Gorky, the "shock" writer, took exaggerated positions
because of the great deeds being accomplished in Soviet Russia,
particularly the narrowing of the cultural gap between the elites
and the masses.[42]

Just as Gorky found Western individualism "limited," Romain
Rolland upbraided liberalism in the light of its "deformities." The
Soviet Union fortified the intellectual capacities and nourished the
emotional needs of its citizens, allowing the individual to achieve
"the free development of all his strengths and aptitudes." In decadent Europe, one found a stupefied and languid intellectual sector,
the embodiment of subjective "sterility" and "pessimism." Gorky
was correct that "class, race, nationalism, and religion" thwarted
creative freedom. European intellectuals who advocated an extreme individualism only imprisoned themselves in a "prideful illusion." "The will of the mass, in its greatest moments of creative
action, *assigns itself a goal inaccessible to a single individual, however
much a genius he might be.*"[43]

Gorky's passage into the communist camp, his dedication to the task of Soviet construction, and his revolutionary fervor all added up to a significant tribute to the Revolution itself, suggesting that the best of secular culture might be preserved and updated in the USSR. Gorky understood both the "grandeur" of their epoch and the need for disciplined sacrifice to actualize the historic task. Romain Rolland emphasized the international and universal dimension of the Soviet experiment, its potential fusion of freedom and necessity. The Bolshevik Revolution testified not to the inspired leadership of the Communist Party but to the masses seeking self-expression and self-determination: "A people of 160 million works not only for itself, but for all of humanity, by showing humanity the miracles created by the intelligently organized will of the masses."[44]

He did not cite Gorky's congratulatory passages about the Communist Party and the dictatorship of the proletariat. Nor did he endorse the Leninist line on imperialism. From these omissions we can infer that he did not wholly approve of Soviet organization and policy. He never embraced the crucial features of Marxism-Leninism as a model of the transition from capitalism to socialism. He made no mention of Stalin and so lent no credibility to the emerging personality cult.

Romain Rolland's autobiographical essay "Good-bye to the Past," composed on Easter Sunday 1931, constituted a major reevaluation of his antiwar writings from a fellow-traveling vantage point. His farewell to the Gandhian position reflected his perception of international fascism and reappraisal of the Russian Revolution after fourteen years. His antiwar utterances from 1914 to 1919 had mourned for the butchered millions and at the same time indicted those responsible for their murder: "orators, thinkers, Churches and Governments."[45]

But that historical juncture was past. The unresolved tension of his pacifist writing had been between absolute freedom of the mind and active commitment to socialist revolution, partly inspired by the Russian example. In 1917, Romain Rolland had refused Lenin's offer to join him in his return to Russia, believing that such an affiliation with Bolshevism would compromise his integrity and autonomy. He was never prepared to be a professional revolutionary on Leninist terms or to adopt Bolshevik tactics, since he was "repelled by the sanguinary violence of their methods."[46] In 1931, however, he repudiated abstractions and cosmic ideals to uphold "truth in action," that is, ideas that were modifiable by being put into practice. He gradually gave up his illusions about a Western intellectual elite, having learned, painfully, that his ideas were only possible for an exceptional self-disciplined and ascetic minority. He extended his critique of the wishful "democratic ideology," begun in *Liluli*, to the "bourgeois ideology" as a whole. The twenties had revealed that modern nationalism was inextricably linked to expansionist corporate capitalism. One could no longer oppose the idols of the fatherland without taking strong positions against imperialism and militarism. The Soviet Union alone was a restraint to world war and global domination by the strong over the weak. He now trafficked in the Hegelian-Marxist dialectic of master and slave and cited Marx with approval. Formerly, mature class-conscious workers were few and isolated. The contemporary working-class struggle was remarkable in its doctrinal coherence, its organizational structures, its demonstrated leadership, and its rank-and-file solidarity. Despite the "weariness and torment" occasioned by Soviet politics, Romain Rolland's new frame of reference was not the Great War but the dangers of international fascism, the global conflict between capitalism and socialism, and the creative possibilities of socialist revolution:

> Then, how the very march of events, Ananke, which Marx reduced to the iron law of economic materialism, and which, severing the world into two camps, daily witnessed the gulf between the colossus of International Capitalism and that of the other giant, the Union of Proletarian Workers, had ineluctably led me to cross the abyss and range myself on the side of the USSR.[47]

Romain Rolland played a peripheral role in the Aragon Affair of 1932. Here he differentiated his moralistic fellow-traveling commitment from the Surrealist and the Communist Party postures.

Louis Aragon's poem "Front rouge," first published in Russia in 1931, appeared in French in *Littérature de la révolution mondiale* early in 1932. At the time, Aragon was both a Surrealist and a Communist. "Front rouge" can hardly be regarded as a masterpiece, but its incantatory celebration of the Soviet Union, its call for mutiny in the army, and its violent harangues against rightwing leaders such as Frossard and Déat scandalized the public. The poem blasted Socialist parliamentary reformists Léon Blum and Joseph Paul-Boncour, unequivocally urging its readers to murder these politicians:

> Fire on Léon Blum
> Fire on Boncour Frossard Déat
> Fire on the trained bears of social democracy

French authorities indicted Aragon and charged him with incitement to assassination. If convicted, he faced a five-year prison sentence. To defend the creative license of his Surrealist-Communist colleague, André Breton published a pamphlet ironically entitled *Misère de la poésie* (1932).[48] At the same time, Breton tried unsuccessfully to rally leading French writers to Aragon's cause, arguing that "Front rouge" must be understood as an example of "poetic freedom," not as politics or journalism. Both André Gide and Romain Rolland declined to endorse Breton's defense of Aragon. Breton published Romain Rolland's refusal in the same pamphlet, commenting on his inability to comprehend poetry.

Romain Rolland's letter firmly disavowed the Surrealist support of Aragon. There was no radical distinction between writing and action, especially when both text and context were saturated by politics. It was an evasion of moral responsibility to hide behind formal aesthetic principles or abstract notions about psychic life. Surrealist modernism contradicted his concept of the engaged writer's accountability for his words and images. Those who failed to remember the past, or who remembered selectively, participated in a crime ("the forgetting of a crime is a crime"). To attack the sham of the bourgeois judiciary, the Surrealists should remain conscious of the link between ideas and action. Maurras's murderous writings against Jaurès before the Great War were a case in point. After Jaurès's assassination, neither Maurras nor the Action Française assassin was punished for the murder this form of writing encouraged. Instead of defending Aragon's right to publish exaggerated poetry along dubious modernist lines—a poem divisive for the French left in that it exhorted Surrealists and communists to do violence to socialists—Romain Rolland insisted that adolescent invocations of aggression had disastrous historical repercussions. If there were to be no enemies on the left, socialists and communists would have to recognize their common enemies (the extreme right), while intellectuals clarified the ideological nature of the struggle.

Vituperation against Blum deflected energy and did not raise political consciousness. His intellectual politics contrasted fundamentally with the Surrealists, whom he saw as infantile and irresponsible:

> I do not sanction the terms of the protest that you have communicated to me. I do not approve of them for the honor of Aragon himself or the Surrealists.
>
> I ask you to do honor to yourselves by distinguishing yourself from the remainder of writers, attributing to you the will that nothing that you write be "literature," that everything that you write be an act. It ill becomes you to take refuge behind the screen of symbolism or of poetic "interiorism."
>
> We are combatants. Our writings are our weapons. We are responsible for our weapons as are our worker and soldier comrades. Instead of denying them, we should accept our responsibilities for them. Let each of us be judged individually for the arms he employs![49]

Though begun in November 1929, *L'Annonciatrice*, the final volumes of Romain Rolland's epic novel *L'Ame enchantée*, were not completed until April 1933.[50] Considering that its writing extended from the time of the Wall Street crash to Hitler's seizure of power, one would not expect the images of "soul" or "enchantment" to figure so centrally. Romain Rolland fused the mystical and the political, transposing his fellow-traveling views into the thought and actions of his leading characters. His intellectual politics at this moment were characterized by a pre–Popular Front type of engagement, broadly antifascist and pluralistic, but with pacifists now excluded from the progressive coalition. The social awareness of the Rivière family mirrored the problematic of commitment in the early 1930s. In Chapter 7, I analyzed *L'Ame enchantée*'s negations in terms of its integral antifascist ideology. The novel's positive vision turns on the coming to communism of the enchanted soul, that is, the Western humanist intellectual. In tracing the ambiguities of this voyage, Romain Rolland depicted the psychological dimensions of fellow traveling for an entire generation. His engagement announced the birth of a different kind of intellectual, one who participated in the creation of an innovative social and cultural community.

The Rivière family endured an extended, often painful, process of self-reflection. Deciphering deceptive forms of commitment became as crucial as participating in valid ones. Romain Rolland unmasked official 1930s pacifism as a hypocritical attempt to derail rebellious action or co-opt revolutionary engagement. Beneath the platitudes of pacifism were the harsh realities of preparation for war, profits from the armaments industry, and the cynical attempt to destroy the workers in body and spirit. Those currently mouthing the rhetoric of peace were almost all the unrepentant chauvinists of the Great War. Their high-minded language hid the forces that blocked radical change and encouraged passive acceptance of the status quo.[51]

Marc Rivière functioned as an intellectual with communist sympathies. He liberated himself from the paralyzing constrictions of European thought: the legacy of Cartesian rationalism and French skepticism, the undervaluation of emotions, and the self-referential tendencies of modern French art. But instead of celebrating the intrinsic healthiness of free thinking, the bewildered Marc wondered if consciousness itself might not be an illness.[52]

Depicting Marc's evolution from detachment to an *engagé* stance, Romain Rolland harshly condemned theories that could not be modified in the light of new circumstances and revised in application. He scorned those who played promiscuously with thinking as if there were no priorities in the realm of ideas. As he employed the metaphor of engagement more often, he contrasted it with the tactics of political evasion: "Thus, the intellectuals escaped any painful contact with the real, with rough hands, dirty hands and blood. They made use of their ideas, their prostitutes, to escape the responsibilities and risks of social action."[53]

Romain Rolland showed that a majority of French intellectuals refused to align themselves with the organized working class out of their own sense of class superiority. Although most French intellectuals arose from either the working class or the petite bourgeoisie, most had gained middle-class status through education or acquiring a veneer of culture, the result of social mobility. Once they "arrived," these individuals appointed themselves "watchdogs" over the national patrimony of art and knowledge. The intellectuals' disdain for the popular masses masked a deep current of self-hatred. Their denial of their origins had reactionary implications for all concerned.[54]

Marc assumed the impossible task of repairing the extreme splits that characterized interwar European cultural life, especially between the thinkers who refused to act and the militants who acted without reflection. He became a man of thought who risked taking action, thereby achieving a partial synthesis of thinking and will. *Engagement* mediated between culture and politics. It allowed Marc to advocate a principled defense of human dignity while participating in specific struggles against humiliation, beginning with total opposition to all forms of fascism. The verb *engager* signaled a new style of intellectual life, which neither devalued the self nor diluted politicized forms of struggle; to not engage in battles was to be defeated in advance.[55]

Marc discovered that there were degrees of engagement. Several intellectuals in the novel took committed stands that stopped short of direct political action. In the early 1930s Marc realized that intellectuals acting alone were powerless. Their protests were ritualized verbal performances, lacking originality, influence, or the ability to operate on a number of levels at once. The protest of the left-wing writer was another bogus strategy in the intellectual's arsenal of self-deception. He expressed Romain Rolland's own ironic critique of the interminable statements of position by committed Parisian intellectuals, including himself.

> A very small number of writers—always the same ones—were sufficiently lacking in appetite to protest. But their protests, as thin as themselves and just as monotonous, to which Marc added his, evoked no echoes; they were repeated every week, with the crimes they described. In the end, they passed unnoticed. Or the good public grew bored, saying: "What again!" . . .
> Marc himself became infected with the boredom, felt disengaged from the rain of protests without action. They ended by becoming an evasion for one's conscience, a side door one slipped through, to fly from the dangers of action, or a painful confession of impotence. When he had signed a dozen, his heart failed him and his angry hand broke the pen on the *M* of his signature. And instead of his name, he wrote the word of five letters [*merde*].[56]

For the protagonists of *L'Ame enchantée*, engagement was elaborated into a 1930s world vision of socialist humanism, balancing the negativities of antifascism, and promising an oceanic fellowship with the class-conscious masses. Both were indispensable to a durable socialist alternative to fascism and liberal democracy in collapse. Engagement supplied these fictional characters with the courage to die while resisting oppression. "Where there is no impulse to resist, there is nothing to lose."[57]

In the novel, the historical reality of the USSR served as a corrective to Romain Rolland's pronounced idealism about historical change. At first, the Soviet Union was only a disorienting "enigma" to the main characters: "The USSR gave him vertigo."[58] Soon it was recognized as a "necessary counterweight" to reactionary Western nations. Beneath fellow traveling was a conception of the anti-Soviet conspiracy that typified 1930s political discourse on the left. Several characters uttered pro-Soviet sentiments not because they admired the Soviet Union or agreed with communist methods of analysis or practice, but because they opposed the enemies of Russian communism.

> Thus he found himself daily more deeply engaged in the battle against the whole clan of the anti-Soviet coalition. Not that he did not detest Communism; but he hated and despised their adversaries. Now he no longer had a choice. A fight to death was being engaged [*s'engageait*]. He felt himself being surrounded by their spies and police agents, and he employed them against his own, who were sometimes the same.[59]

The anticommunists combined ideological hatred for communism as an economic system with demonizing Bolshevik leaders. Members of the anti-Soviet camp were Machiavellian: they did not hesitate to employ spies, police, mercenary armies, diplomatic alliances, political leverage, and economic blockades to encircle and strangle the Russians.

The fellow-traveling characters in this novel viewed the Soviet Union as a young, isolated, undeveloped nation equally vulnerable to its hostile European neighbors on the West and to an aggressive Japan on its East. They never perceived the USSR as a superpower with expansionist ambitions, never believed that it possessed the industrial or military capacity to defend itself against fascist militarism.

French Marxism in the 1930s responded to Marc's need to be contemporaneous and linked to the forces of historical change. Yet Marxism remained closed to Marc, its Hegelian roots foreign to his allegiance to the Kantian categorical imperative. He was unable to integrate Marxism with his idealist, individualist sense of self, nor was he drawn to Marxist historiography, theorizing, or political economy. He read selected passages of Marx's works, not entire treatises, so he rarely glimpsed the power of Marxist epistemology. He attended the tedious meetings of communist militants more out of guilt than enthusiasm. Though he resisted Marxism on a visceral level and acquired an insufficient Marxist culture, he found something compelling about revolutionary socialism. It was lucid and it was designed to meet political and economic necessity:

> [The self] would only touch the Marxist field with the tip of a disdainful nose. This humiliating preeminence of the "economic" over the "psychic" revolted him. Yet he and his mother had painfully "paid" to learn what it costs to come up against the "economic" and that it has to be taken into account. But he and his mother were romantics—shall we call them outdated? or eternal?—whose real purpose in life is to vindicate their independent souls against all the fatalities that oppress them.[60]

In voicing his solidarity for politicized groups of French workers and students, Marc attacked the capitalist colossus at its sources. He was quickly designated a "public danger" in France. Nationalists, protofascists, and centrist coalitions assaulted him in print. The Soviet Union's program of planning was a positive alternative to crisis-ridden Europe after the collapse of the world economy and the ascendancy of fascism. For Marc, the Soviet Union had to be preserved so that its anticapitalist, anti-imperialist, and antifascist model could come to fruition. Fifteen years of revolutionary practice meant that the idea of social revolution was no longer a utopian abstraction.

Though distanced from his uncommitted intellectual peers, Marc, like his creator, remained uneasy about affiliating with the rebellious masses.[61] He agonized over and ultimately refused to endorse the inequities and ideological rigidities that were inevitable in communist associations. The fellow-traveling writer was destined to remain outside the Communist Party, suspect to members and equally suspect to the bourgeois cultural establishment. Romain Rolland provided his cast of fellow-traveling characters with a variety of opinions about the Soviet Union, thus outlining options for European progressives in the 1930s. The older generation of nineteenth-century intellectuals, described as gentle Nietzscheans, offered an empathic but world-weary judgment of Russian communism, shrewdly seeing the Soviet experiment as a mixture of atrocious follies and remarkably vital projects:

> They were curious as to the Labors of the Russian Revolution, and they followed them with a sympathy which did not exclude criti-

cism; but it was that of aged friends, who regretted that they could not take their part in the suffering and even in the youthful errors engendered by a Truth, a new Life.[62]

Marc wanted to mediate among Russian Bolshevism, the French intellectual left, and the working class. By publishing inexpensive translations of Marxist and revolutionary classics, he not only educated the French (and prepared the foundations for more rigorous research into Marx's thought for future generations) but also alerted his public to the urgency of thoughtful action. Marxism implied a rational understanding of social and political struggle. It showed the intellectual and educated worker the necessity of disciplined action. The quite different attitude of Marc's mother, Annette, toward these texts, which she helped translate, reflected her deeper understanding of historical process.[63]

The impulsive Assia, Marc's wife, articulated a wholehearted, unsubtle defense of the USSR. Assia represented the emotional commitment of the true believer, the ardent procommunist who, disillusioned by the brutalities of Russian communism, would become an equally ardent anticommunist. To her, the Soviet Union stood for something universal, hopeful, and pure. It was antifascist to its core. A cult of personality or severe social distortions occurring in Russia were unimaginable to Assia.[64]

Marc expressed Romain Rolland's deep ambivalence about fellow traveling. He distrusted Communist Party discipline, secrecy, doctrine, determinism, homogenization of culture, and bureaucratic organization. He hated the overemphasis on violence and proletarian class conflict. He was appalled by the despotic imposition of "correct" modes of inquiry and cultural forms onto others. He irreverently protested against all the "imposed Gods." Marc found the authoritarian tendencies among the French Communist Party leadership equally foreign to his own need for democratic tolerance, reflective insight, and empathic understanding. He never legitimized the "iron hand of ideological, social, economic, and police dictatorship."[65] Soviet brutality and the network of terror were no less destructive than the harsh repression of the czarist regime they had supplanted.

Unconvinced by the dialectical acrobatics of Marxist intellectuals in the 1930s and distressed by their sophistic blurring of facts, Marc refused to accept the priority of ends over means. Such a refusal was essentially moral. The communist intellectual viewed the Soviet Union as a model of social revolution and industrial development. The fellow traveler recognized that French workers would be inspired by the Soviet Revolution but urged them not to follow it like a blueprint. Social revolution had to be commensurate with each country's history and level of civilization:

> The French workers had no experience as yet of the social combat in which they were about to engage. No doubt they would acquire it at the price of more than one disaster, as had revolutionary Russia before 1905. With this essential difference: that the USSR now existed as an example and support. They must learn from the strategic school of Moscow, but with the knowledge of the resources proper to France, to the country's mental needs, and the tenacious attempts of the old Parties of Revolution—free from the wounds of past campaigns and from its young unions. Marc, henceforth, applied himself to the task. He was still only a pupil.[66]

Several factors explain the pro-Soviet sentiments of the fellow-traveling characters. Soviet planning contrasted vividly with chaotic Europe and the "imbecility of the old world" in the world depression. Soviet educational campaigns compared favorably to Western anti-intellectualism and consumerism. The novel stressed the measurable achievements of the Russian people, the faith of the youth, and the pride of the workers—a combination of self-abnegation and construction that led Marc to believe that "no sacrifice is disproportionate to such a goal." If a god was being born in the Soviet Union, that god was purposeful, intelligent action. Modern capitalism in crisis was the degraded religion, representing the trinity of "War, Commerce, and Piracy . . . three in one, consubstantial."[67] In the hands of "Marxist, materialist, atheist youth," communist projects would realize "social welfare and happiness." The energy of Russian communism was irresistible. Its monumentality appealed to Romain Rolland's sense of heroism and its ideology appealed to his need for something to believe in. He celebrated the "supremacy of Labor, free, equal, and sovereign."

The cosmopolitan and internationalist Marc knew that the class struggles of French workers were related to those of the colonized in Indochina, China, Africa, and Central and South America. Mirroring Romain Rolland's work with the Amsterdam-Pleyel movement, Marc tried to construct a broad, pluralistic Popular Front.

> So Marc continued to sell and publish books and pamphlets of antifascist, anti-imperialist, pro-Soviet, pro-Gandhian, etc., propaganda . . . without deciding to take up a clearly defined position among these various lines of battle. He was trying to make himself the link between the armies and to lead them (utopian dream) to make a common front against the massive forces of the Reaction. Of course he did not succeed.[68]

His mythical version of the Soviet Union did not blur Marc's awareness of tensions and blunders. The novel's committed characters wagered on the Soviet experiment. It was Italian fascism that sobered them and finally showed them capitalism's adaptive tendencies and its ability to absorb its radical opposition.

Paradoxically, Marc's assassination at the hands of Blackshirts consolidated Annette's subsequent *engagement*. The character of Annette—the enchanted soul—symbolized the transition between two epochs and two conceptions of revolution, the bourgeois French Revolution and failed French revolutions of the nineteenth century and the victorious materialist October Revolution. She bridged the ideas of Michelet and Marx, Péguy and Lenin, the supporters of the Amsterdam-Pleyel movement and Gramsci. Mourning her son did not push her to disavow communist front activities. These fictional fellow travelers tragically realized that only through "the voluntary sacrifice of a generation" could a revitalized and just world be born. That meant risking transient injustices to realize the desired end: "Certainly he [Marc] could not overthrow the enslaving order without binding himself to a new, but consented to, temporary, contract of servitude, which was for an end that made sacrifices legitimate."[69]

The specter of fascism alerted Annette to the pressing necessity for politicization and self-renunciation. Antifascism meant transcending her lifelong individualistic revolt, her own brand of nonconformist, freewheeling feminism. She allied with those ready to fight to crush the fascists, to defend a fragile and encircled USSR. Above all, Annette made the transition because of her desire to prepare Europe's terrain for a social revolution. Annette joined the "grand army of the Revolution" by stamping *engagement* with a 1930s neo-Marxist legitimacy. The novel climaxed with a passage advocating the primacy of labor, a vision of the harmonious relationship between two prototypical groups—factory workers and writers. The final victory of labor signaled an end to stale middle-class morality and the necessity for "illuminating a new morality." That task was relegated to the future, beyond the achievement of a classless society.

Annette struggled without seeing her efforts come to fruition. Her grandson, Vania, would implement the work begun by his father and grandmother. He, like his teachers, would engage in battle cheerfully, maintaining an inner state of calm and impartiality, without taking the slogans or abstractions of his engagement terribly seriously.[70]

Romain Rolland's novel elevated fellow traveling to a potent strategy against international fascism. At the same time, fellow travelers, in alliance with the working class and often with communist organizations, initiated the extended process of constructing a humane, peaceful, classless society without a disastrous gap between mental and manual workers. Fellow-traveling engagement provided the characters of *L'Ame enchantée* with the courage to resist and linked them to those who acted consciously to transform their society. It married contemporary radical politics to self-reflective forms of introspection:

> In short, both were following the track that led to their true goal, to the first action that is the maturity of every full life. It was their proper line of development. It was adapted to that of the epoch, marching toward the necessary Revolution. In the great upheavals of the earth, little streams follow the same slope as the rivers, and all mingle their waters.[71]

L'Ame enchantée is engaged literature in that it advances a critical and nuanced fellow-traveling perspective. Its attitude toward communism set the stage for and resonated with left-wing intellectuals during the Popular Front era.

10

The Cultural Politics
of the Popular Front

I think that Communism will make dignity possible for
those with whom I am fighting.
                    André Malraux, *La Condition humaine*

The Popular Front era, 1934 to 1937, unfolded against a backdrop of
sharp political polarization and collective fear. Writers gave expression to profound social cleavages, making manifest what had been
hidden in earlier epochs. The impact of the Great Depression, the
ascendancy of international fascism, particularly after Hitler's seizure of power in 1933, and strategic shifts on the part of Stalin and
the Communist International in favor of Popular Front alliances
converged to produce a reevaluation of the intellectual's role in the
struggle for political and social justice.

Antifascist intellectuals provided the French coalition with moral
authority, prestige, ideological legitimacy, a rhetoric of hope, and a
cultural effervescence in the theaters, cinema, universities, and artistic associations. Left-wing artists such as Romain Rolland participated in or supported experiments in popular education: worker
universities, agitprop theater, social cinema, and the proliferation of
Houses of Culture. Generation gaps closed: Malraux and the almost
seventy-year-old Romain Rolland shared the presidency of the
World Committee Against War and Fascism. The Popular Front's
cultural politics were marked by a moderate, fraternal spirit and a
willingness to work within the legal and institutional framework of
the Third Republic. If the elected leaders could not be persuaded to
take action, then direct appeals to the population were launched.

Antifascism was the cement of the Popular Front coalition. Its
temporary unity depended on the collaboration of individuals and
groups in a broad interclass alliance. It could not have existed
without the consent of nonproletarian social classes. The heteroge-

neous people's front updated the democratic and Jacobin heritage of the French Revolution, attempting to reconcile diverse sectors of the French population with the organized working class. Malraux characterized it as "Michelet's revenge on Marx." There was a universal, patriotic quality to its appeal, a populist and vaguely socialist underpinning rather than a sectarian emphasis on class against class.

Romain Rolland's Popular Front sympathies changed his reception within communist circles. His election to the Russian Academy of Sciences in 1932, the Amsterdam-Pleyel movement's shift into a more aggressive antifascist, pro-Soviet line in the summer of 1933, and his evolution from a revolutionary Gandhian position toward a more politicized fellow traveling enhanced his standing.[1] French and Soviet communist writers effusively welcomed his voluntary offer of fellowship. They blunted the critical edge of his writings on the Soviet Union, playing down his deliberate distance from the Communist Party apparatus and his ambivalence toward Leninist action and doctrine. They conspicuously praised the political content of his journalism, criticism, and fiction, particularly the concluding volumes of *L'Ame enchantée*.

At sixty-seven, the man of letters and former pacifist spokesman became a showpiece of the international communist movement, a prototype of the new intellectual. Communist writers hyperbolically asserted that his political and philosophical evolution was complete. His entry into the revolutionary camp meant more than the arrival of an exceptional talent with an impeccable reputation; it bridged Europe's lasting cultural achievements and the Soviet attempt to preserve and revolutionize culture. Romain Rolland brought with his "energetic and intransigent" communist sympathies a cultural legacy that included Shakespeare, Goethe, Beethoven, and Tolstoy. "The works of Romain Rolland and, above all, *L'Ame enchantée* are the prototypes of a new literature, of the only literature that in our day has a reason for existing."[2]

To commemorate the tenth anniversary of Lenin's death, Romain Rolland reflected on the great Bolshevik's life and work. The Bonapartist Lenin of the 1920s, the man of dictatorial will and political expediency, gave way to a Popular Front Lenin acceptable to the fellow traveler. Lenin fused art and action. He was so profoundly stirred by Beethoven's sonatas that he protected himself against their beauty by not listening to the music; he would not let art deflect him from his revolutionary *métier*. The Lenin of 1934 was not simply a master of the Kremlin, but a devotee of Turgenev and Tolstoy. Romain Rolland read about Lenin's humanism in French translations of Russian studies by Guirinis, Krupskaya, Gorky, and Stalin. Romain Rolland endorsed a Marxist understanding of people and culture; he no longer trusted "universalism." He vilified "apolitical" or "neutral" bourgeois writers. Lenin's insight into Tolstoy's works demonstrated that towering masterpieces of literature were bound by historical necessity. The artist was never "disengaged from the atmosphere of his time." The contradictions within Tolstoy's works reflected the social and intellectual tensions of Russia before the 1905 Revolution.[3]

He portrayed Lenin as an artist of revolution, not a ruthless professional revolutionary, one who transformed political struggle. His philosophical world view merged with the often pitiless task of social upheaval. Lenin "realized in himself, as no other, the historical hour of human action that is the proletarian Revolution." He achieved a "perpetual communion with the elementary forces manifested in the masses."

Because he understood that revolution was not chaos but part of the normal order of things, Lenin shifted the practice and theory of revolution into a "metaphysic." He complemented his incisive sense of the real with a powerful but disciplined ability to dream. Identification with the masses gave him an energy and self-confidence. He mastered the laws of social life and bent them in a revolutionary direction. He gave expression to dreams in the framework of what was historically possible: "Thus, his dream was action." He exhorted his party comrades to dream, but to combine dreams with "serious" attention to the external world in order to "realize our fantasy scrupulously."[4]

The Soviets echoed his spirited defense of the USSR at the First Soviet Writer's Congress, held in August 1934, but not attended by Romain Rolland. In his didactic address, "Contemporary World Literature and the Tasks of Proletarian Art," Karl Radek, an important communist journalist who often served as a spokesman for Stalin, lavished praise on Romain Rolland and glorified his solidarity with the international proletariat. As an example of "great revolutionary literature," *L'Ame enchantée* documented the history of a

bourgeois intellectual who moved into the revolutionary camp after reconciling his old humanist "vacillations." His fellow traveling
refuted the tendentious charge that no literary talent could support
the working class and still produce a major work of art.[5]

Romain Rolland's critical essay "Panorama" was completed on 1
November 1934; it formed the introduction to an anthology of his
engaged writings, *Quinze Ans de combat* (1935), surveying the continuities and discontinuities of his intellectual politics from 1919. By
the word "combat" he underscored the impassioned controversies
he had waged with competing intellectual coteries, political movements, and ideologies. He tried to neutralize his reputation of being above all battles, to demonstrate that there had been no rest or
retreat. The central theme of "Panorama" was the relationship of
political commitment to humanism, how the European intellectual's perception of the Soviet Union altered the tasks and responsibility of the writer.[6]

In no other sustained piece of prose did he explore his relationship to Marxist thought and reflect on the problematic of socialist
humanism. Like most of his French contemporaries in the late
1930s, Romain Rolland had read Marx unsystematically and mostly
in translation. He did not grasp the technical, philosophical, or
economic component of Marx's thought; rather, he extrapolated
the kernel of humanism, especially from the earlier, anthropologi-
cal Marx, just becoming available to most Europeans. He was captivated by Marx's writings on alienation and his critique of idealism.
In the corpus of his writings only here did Romain Rolland quote
from Marx's early texts, including *The Holy Family* (1845), *On the
Jewish Question* (1843), and *Preparatory Notes to the Holy Family*. He
then applied Marx's analytical tools to his own development as an
intellectual idealist. Socialist humanism suggested a way out of
idealist mystification.[7]

In his analysis of Feuerbach and the left Hegelians, the young
Marx demonstrated that notions of abstract liberties always masked
estrangement from oneself, one's community, and the products of
one's labor. Marx understood that the freedoms codified in the Declaration of the Rights of Man and Citizen were inherently bourgeois
in that they crystallized the mentality of the "small property owner."
They stood as barriers to higher, more social aspects of freedom. Romain Rolland redefined humanism as a synthesis of the rational and

the oceanic, as "the sense of the truly human, complete, conscious, the communion of the one with all." Meaningful intellectual activity reduced the discrepancies between "real and *abstract being*" and pointed the way toward "the natural and logical coexistence of Communism with *humanism.*"[8]

Assisted by Marx's "lucidity," Romain Rolland unmasked the ideals in which he had trafficked. Upholding the integrity of the individual and freedom of conscience might have been tenable in previous historical periods (as before and during the Great War). A contemporary articulation of these "word fetishes" seemed "naive," an indirect apology for abuses of power that had been justified by these former "noble and pure human ideals."[9]

To posit unrealizable ideals as the motor force of history was self-defeating. When intellectuals transformed freedom and equality into nonreferential and nonhistorical essences, they were contributing to another alienating form of knowledge. His immersion in Marx's texts made Romain Rolland aware that he could not be sincerely committed "to building a new order" unless he was vitally connected to a mass political movement capable of both understanding and implementing this goal.[10]

The Russian Revolution's commitment to socialist humanism obliged him to clarify his relationship to the "powerful Communist movement." The Soviets were making positive strides toward the construction of a new social order. Yet as a fellow traveler and not a Communist Party member, he maintained his critical posture toward Soviet distortions, the unnecessary violence and stupidities perpetrated by the revolutionary regime. He still detested the "dictatorial spirit" of the Communist International, the doctrinal inflexibilities, and the "abuses" of communist propaganda. He indirectly criticized Stalinism by discussing the inadequacy of Soviet leadership after Lenin's death.

There was a great gap between Marx's cogent theory and contemporary communist practice. In Romain Rolland's perspective, however, the Soviet Union was an open-ended experiment capable of rectifying itself. The Soviet Revolution derived from "historical necessity." European writers were obliged to educate the public about this new experiment, indirectly enabling it to survive. Promoting world peace remained "the base of all my social thought," but he was increasingly aware that international capitalism gave rise to fascism of every variety. The USSR promised a deterrent to the inherent evils of capitalist economies in crisis. A viable strategy against fascism and world war was a crucial goal of his international Popular Front activities. Like other fellow travelers from the peace movement, he equated communism with antimilitarism and anti-fascism. Although world war would disrupt the USSR's "fecund social development," peace could be only a respite; he predicted that a clash between fascism and communism was inevitable.[11]

In contrast to fascist anti-intellectualism and disdain for culture, Romain Rolland appreciated the multidimensional quality of cultural work underway in the Soviet Union in 1934. The Marxist view of "the totality" was not far removed from the Rollandist notion of the oceanic feeling: both suggested that a harmonious relationship was possible between free beings voluntarily participating in a rationally organized and productive community. He was seduced by the discernible advances of the Russians in the areas of science, technology, literature, and cinema; he was persuaded that the Soviets wanted to proliferate and honor important forms of culture, not simply to launch engineering projects.[12]

He remained cautiously optimistic that the concept of labor might be sufficiently broad to implement a "just, free, better-ordered humanity." He quoted Stalin's clever metaphor for writers, "engineers of human souls," and he accepted the equalitarian proposition that no form of labor was superior to another. But he realized that the achievement of a mutually liberating relationship between intellectuals and the proletarian masses would require years of struggle. He urged the communists to remain conscious of their own prejudices. One served the USSR best by retaining a healthy concept of "independence in the Revolution," namely, a toleration of democracy, criticism, cosmopolitanism, internationalism, and irreverence within party ranks. Socialist humanism was a sham unless the Soviet people were granted freedom of speech as well as freedom to work.[13] He fought for a form of socialism that preserved basic individual liberties.

"Panorama" did not pay homage to Stalin's simplifications and vulgarizations of Marxism. It did not endorse Stalin's program of socialism in one country, his Russian nationalism, or the emerging cult of personality around the Soviet leader. Romain Rolland mentioned the "dictatorship of the proletariat" merely as a "fatal and severe stage" of the revolution. The "transitory violence" of the revolutionary upheaval was unfortunate, not to be magnified into a major theoretical construct.[14] It was less significant than the everyday work of building a society along socialist humanist lines. Not accidentally, his most transparently pro-Soviet essay concluded not in celebration of Stalin or the party dictatorship, but with a quotation from the brilliant fellow-traveling French writer André Malraux. Malraux, addressing the First Congress of Soviet Writers in November 1932, stressed the humanistic potential still to be realized in the USSR, which would protect individualism and creativity.[15]

Asked by his comrades at *Commune* about his relationship to his audience, Romain Rolland could not separate "why" he wrote and "for whom." Writing was a necessity: it was his form of "thinking and acting." Rejecting the static notions of optimism and pessimism, he wrote to catalyze others into action: "I have always written for *those who march.*" Currently, he felt most connected to the organized masses of proletarian workers whose vision coincided with their "Union of Soviet Socialist Republics," and who waged a prolonged battle for the "establishment of a human community without frontiers and class." His version of communism included the idea of conquest. Communists were not contaminated by self-interest or excessive compromise. The engaged intellectual wrote for "the avant-garde of the army on the march," and the masses, in return, replenished the writer's energies. He was not discouraged by the intellectuals who were terrified by massive social change: "We writers launch the rallying cry to the sluggish." Apparently delighted by these remarks, Aragon referred to the old French master as "one of the first *Soviet* writers in France."[16]

He differentiated his fellow traveling from the agitprop methods adopted by Henri Barbusse, France's leading communist intellectual of the era. After his celebrated controversy with Romain Rolland in the early 1920s, Barbusse joined the French Communist Party and became a leading spokesman for Russian communism in Western Europe. His collaboration with international communism was accompanied by a narrow conception of intellectual commitment predicated on total loyalty to the party. From 1923 to 1934, Barbusse functioned as one of French communism's most visible organizers and journalists, a bridge to army veterans and progressive intellectuals. As Barbusse's energy became focused on communist causes, his creative work deteriorated. Contemporaries such as Romain Rolland were aware of the inferior quality of his art, the absence of complexity in his scholarship, the conspicuous lack of imagination in his biographies. Barbusse's decline as an intellectual left a huge gap between the stirring pages of *Le Feu* and the obsequious prose and maudlin hero worship of *Staline* (1935). The creative writer in Barbusse was eclipsed by the organizer of conferences and the orator at huge demonstrations.[17]

Romain Rolland remained fond of Barbusse; they agreed on certain causes and on substantive social issues but disagreed on fundamental ways of mobilizing political support and achieving cultural goals. Romain Rolland had glimpsed the dangers of outright Communist Party membership during their open debate; Barbusse's ten years of militancy confirmed that he had betrayed the writer's *métier*.

In the last personal letter written before Barbusse's death, Romain Rolland sketched his critique of the Communist Party intellectual, differentiating his own independence and allegiance to progressive struggles. Barbusse forgot that the writer's chief obligation was to be "truthful and logical and especially courageous." Honesty and coherence did not mean avoiding political engagement, but they required that "the writer must be loyal to himself." Nowhere was Barbusse's abandonment of good faith more manifest than in his public appeals to other intellectuals. Romain Rolland was irritated by the "certainty" of Barbusse's rhetoric and his use of "military commands." Barbusse had mastered a crude form of communist thinking: his discourse specialized in forms of intolerance, and he persuaded through "imperatives," employed the "language of theoreticians of economy" in inappropriate contexts, and intimidated by mouthing pseudoscientific, "correct" modes of analysis. He alienated humanist French intellectuals by the "haranguing tone of meetings."[18]

By the middle of the 1930s, fellow travelers tended to distinguish Soviet communism and German fascism sharply by their respective attitudes toward cultural freedom. The first appeared to promote cultural activity, whereas the second seemed totally hostile to it, subordinating it to ideological priorities or the exigencies of a mass movement. In his public writings Romain Rolland appeared to accept this contrast. But as the Victor Serge affair would illustrate, he had many private reservations concerning it.

Victor Serge was a writer of exceptional ability and productivity who held editorial and administrative positions in the Communist International in the 1920s. He was half-Russian and half-Belgian. His political leanings before the Bolshevik Revolution were anarchosyndicalist. While living in Russia in the twenties, Serge emerged as an articulate critic of Soviet programs and foreign policy. He was one of the earliest opponents of Stalinism and may have coined the term "totalitarian" to describe bureaucratization and organized repression in the Soviet state. The Soviets regarded Serge as a thorn in their side. They designated him a member of the Trotskyist counterrevolutionary deviation. Serge was arrested by the Soviet police in 1933 and exiled to the Ural Mountains. It was alleged that he was an accomplice in Kirov's murder. Serge's detention and persecution became a cause in left-wing circles in France, Switzerland, and Belgium. Socialist Magdeleine Paz campaigned for Serge as a victimized political prisoner, defending his right to publish on humanitarian grounds. By the summer of 1935, agitation was mounting in France for some action on the case. The Surrealists joined in the clamor, embracing Serge's rights according to the principles of free speech.[19]

The Victor Serge affair climaxed at the moment of the International Writers' Congress for the Defense of Culture, convened in Paris at the Mutualité in June 1935. Several speakers agitated for Serge's release. Censorship and detainment of a dissident writer resembled the methods of fascism. André Gide interceded for Serge, even though he made pro-Soviet pronouncements at the congress. Romain Rolland was traveling in the Soviet Union at the time and carried on personal diplomacy for Serge with leading Soviet authorities and with Stalin himself. Stalin promised a thorough inquiry. Yagoda, head of the Soviet Police, was unable either to turn up incriminating evidence or to get a confession of wrongdoing. As a result of Romain Rolland's intervention, Serge was finally released from captivity and granted permission to leave the Soviet Union with his family.[20]

Serge and Romain Rolland were on friendly terms although they disagreed on matters of political ideology. Serge had attacked him during the debate with Barbusse, offering sarcastic remarks about his advocacy of intellectual independence. During Romain Rolland's Gandhian phase, Serge had vilified him for his petit-bourgeois mystifications. He opposed the strategy of the Amsterdam-Pleyel movement as unrealistic and contrary to the needs of the European working class. Despite their formidable differences, however, the two corresponded, knew one another's work, and were mutually concerned about repression in the Soviet Union. Romain Rolland volunteered to be Serge's intermediary during his years of imprisonment, forwarding his manuscripts from Switzerland to his Paris publisher. Serge and he suspected that these manuscripts were being intercepted. He "often intervened . . . with Soviet authorities in [Serge's] favor." In his eyes Serge was "a writer of great talent." Moreover, he felt attached to Serge's most active supporters in Europe, especially Jacques Mesnil.[21]

What troubled him was Serge's "political personality." His allies used his arrest to "insult the Soviet government." Though he lacked corroborative evidence, he guessed that Serge had joined a small sect of disgruntled ultra-revolutionaries. Serge had an extremist past; he had reprimanded Lenin for not applying "revolutionary violence" in the first year of the October Revolution. The Serge affair placed Romain Rolland in an awkward situation. He intervened as a diplomat to Soviet authorities to secure Serge's freedom without endorsing Serge's political analysis or promoting Serge's anti-Soviet sentiments to his European admirers. The specific injustice against Serge could not be generalized into a full critique of Stalin's tyranny. His goal was to mediate between Serge and Soviet authorities without fueling anti-Soviet propaganda in Europe and America. A lapidary sentence summed up the dilemmas of critical support for the fellow-traveling intellectual: "Let us help Serge, but let us not permit serving him to be used against the Union of S[ocialist] R[epublics]!"[22]

Romain Rolland made a four-week summer visit to the USSR in 1935. Publicly he extolled the virtues of the Soviet system, toning down his earlier reservations. Privately, he remained critical of internal Russian policies. Much of his political journalism now appeared in communist organs or in the fellow-traveling press. For an article in the PCF's *Regards*, he replied both to the "hateful excitations" of French pacifism, specifically the pacifists clustered around *Le Semeur*, and to the use of the Kirov assassination to create anti-

Soviet propaganda. Those who approached the USSR without a historical perspective would never achieve a "just appreciation" of its accomplishments. By using their own political tradition and value system to evaluate the Soviet experiment, American centrists missed the crucial point that "the proletarian Revolution had never bragged of liberalism and was never made by liberal promises." The Russian Revolution provided a dynamic alternative to the "pseudoliberalism" of the West, in particular its "laissez-faire" system, which was simply an "instrument in the hands of the most powerful, richest, and most crafty."[23]

Romain Rolland offered a metapolitical argument to support the dictatorship of the proletariat. To achieve the peace and social freedoms implicit in a well-organized classless society, it was necessary for the Russians to establish a *"provisional,* but absolute" class dictatorship. He did not examine the contradictions of a "provisional absolute," as he had done as a freewheeling critic and Gandhian in the 1920s. The Soviet government was determined to vanquish the old order. They reacted with "rigor and energy" against external or internal enemies. It was quite probable that conspirators orchestrated Kirov's assassination of 1 December 1934. If in fact a "conspiracy by young, violent, and irreflective men" existed, it was proper for Soviet authorities to take strong measures against it. World opinion would readily exploit Soviet "abuses." He still opposed "exceptional tribunals and summary arrests." Sorting out the reality of plots from the brutality of the Soviet apparatus of repression was not easy. After studying the available documents and reading the "acts of accusation and avowals" in the communist press, he was convinced that the one hundred men charged with the crimes were not "innocent." Nevertheless, he hoped that they would receive a fair hearing, conducted with normal judicial procedure, so that their verdicts would be "judged in broad daylight."[24]

His detractors obscured the fact that he was no longer the same man who had written *Above the Battle;* he identified himself as the author of *L'Ame enchantée,* an antifascist fellow traveler. He noted that the USSR employed comparatively less state terror in the service of socialist causes than had the Jacobins and Robespierre in the service of republican causes, even though the Russians faced "greater danger." Romain Rolland was unable to predict whether the Soviet leadership would retain their moderation, preventing dangerous "exceptional procedures" from being unleashed. Anti-Soviet critics declaimed against Stalin while remaining impervious to the repressions of reactionary governments in Spain and elsewhere: they were indifferent to the "state of almost permanent crime that reigns in fascist states in Europe." "We must judge social action not from the empyrean of abstract and comfortable ideas but from the heart of action."[25]

Romain Rolland's trip to the Soviet Union lasted from 23 June to 21 July 1935 and was spent mostly in Moscow and its immediate vicinity. It was his only visit. In the summer of 1935, Moscow was experiencing great enthusiasm for the Soviet Constitution, which was nearing completion. The period was characterized by a general loosening of controls. He could not know that the Soviet Constitution, so egalitarian and democratic on paper, would never be implemented, or that the climate of liberalization would be followed by one of terror in which an entire generation of revolutionaries and innocent victims would be exterminated. The Soviet society he glimpsed was not truly representative of Russia as a whole. As he did not read or speak Russian, he relied on his half-Russian wife, Marie Koudachef, to translate. This severely hampered his capacity to establish rapport with Russians he encountered. In recognition of his sympathies for the Russian Revolution and his reputation as a world conscience and major literary figure, he was accorded a fraternal welcome. While part of this warmth may have been a genuine expression of Russian exuberance, Soviet authorities clearly orchestrated his travels and commanded the open demonstrations of affection for him. A four-week stay conducted under these circumstances could only furnish impressions, not definitive conclusions.[26]

His Soviet visit was highlighted by his stay at Gorky's residence and by a series of meetings with top government and cultural officials, including members of the Central Committee of the Russian Communist Party. He was granted two interviews with Stalin, a rare honor for a European man of letters. Romain Rolland's impressions were printed in a posthumous account in 1960, four years after Khrushchev's Twentieth Party Speech, during a period of partial de-Stalinization within communist circles in France. This extract, taken from his Journal of June–July 1935, and called "A

Sojourn at Gorky's," contained some critical remarks on Soviet policies, ideology, and leaders that remained unpublished in the 1930s. He clearly suppressed them at the time.[27]

Although he enjoyed Gorky's candor and earthiness, Romain Rolland was shocked by his "brutality," evidenced in his Manichean division of the world into allies and enemies of Soviet communism. Adversaries, in Gorky's view, had to be "crushed as enemies and bastards." Observing Stalin during a ceremonial meal, Romain Rolland commented on the Soviet leader's "maliciousness." (Lenin had spoken of Stalin's "rudeness.") Stalin's sense of humor was sadistic. He teased others for being "too serious," and he "intimidated by making pleasantries." Stalin punctuated his "tough form of joking, bantering, and making fun" with "good-hearted laughter." The vignettes of Stalin were decidedly negative: "He has the humor of a buffoon or practical joker, [and he] is a little rough and peasant in his witticisms."[28]

After viewing two Soviet films, Eisenstein's *Potemkine's Revolt* and *The Mother*, Romain Rolland was struck by their "bloody and sinister vision." Soviet cinema exuded a kind of primitive hatred that was abundant in this new society. He deplored the Russians' tendency to copy American techniques and tastes rather than develop their own. He expected divergence between Soviet and Western forms of culture and was disappointed by the inability of the Russian leadership to converse in any language other than their own. This "regrettable" fact made him wonder about the depth of Soviet internationalism. He was disturbed by flagrant intolerance within the Soviet educational and political systems.

Romain Rolland's public statements did not reflect his uneasiness. Before leaving the Soviet Union, he proclaimed in an open letter to Stalin that he was "fraternally linked to the Soviet People." He universalized the appeal: more than "the ardent center of the international proletariat," Russia was a symbol of "world progress" and of "humanity as a totality." He campaigned to protect the communists from their enemies, not out of allegiance to Marxism or the principles of class conflict, but to serve the Russian population and the world by creating a positive alternative to declining capitalism and expansionist fascism. In a rare expression of public praise for Soviet Communist Party officials, the French writer applauded their "tireless struggle" and "heroic élan," persevering against "a thousand obstacles."[29]

In October 1935, he published a summary of his impressions of the Soviet Union in *Commune*, a leading fellow-traveling journal. He underscored the "vitality" of Soviet society. He had personally witnessed the "unanimous sentiments of the people" in live demonstrations and in letters received from every Russian region. The Soviet masses were expressing deeply felt emotions, not acting "from dictated orders." Yet he crystallized his image of Soviet élan in the pejorative phrase "collective psychosis." The Russian masses externalized their enthusiasm while participating in a "psychosis of faith, joy, and assurance in the truth and victory of a cause which these millions of men incarnate in the world."[30] He did not explain or explore its dangerous, volatile, unrealistic and disordered aspect.

The leadership of the Central Committee impressed him with their practical intelligence and their confidence in the efficacy of planned communitarian activity and in the scientific rigor of Marxist conceptualizations. Soviet leaders blended willfulness and subtle intelligence in a philosophical doctrine "embracing the totality of human problems." The dialectical nature of Marxism was tempered to meet the needs of social action and adapt to new situations. The Soviet leadership's tactical flexibility easily accommodated the "relative and changing necessities of action." His portrait was not of ruthless technicians of power: he detected a "faith at the moral base of all the important leaders." There was a "passionate disinterestedness" among the political vanguards and an absence of "poisoned egotism." Individual personalities grasped that "with them or without them" their project would succeed.[31]

For those who drew a fallacious comparison between communism and fascism, he now differentiated the two systems. Having accepted the totalitarian analogy in the 1920s, he attempted to dismantle it in the mid-1930s. Unlike Stalin, Mussolini was preoccupied only with personal power and glory. Issuing from a "violent pessimism" and a pseudophilosophical "base of nothingness," the fascist governments centered on the "monstrous pride" of the leader, the "sinister grandeur" of territorial conquests, the neglect of qualitative social changes, and the failure to resolve the problem of political succession. Stalin and his "great Bolshevik companions" were, in contrast, fearless optimists, without illusions. Orienting themselves to the future, they anchored their social construction to the "Marxist Gospel," which provided them with both a "materialist dynamic" and a historical schema of "ineluctable laws of human development." If they were "realists," Soviet leaders were also motivated by a "social idea of justice and panhumanism that is more idealist than human dreams."[32]

After seventeen years of planned construction, the Soviet people's confidence in the revolution was "enlarged, enlightened, and ennobled." He glimpsed a latent communitarian heroism on the part of the Russian masses; there was a willingness among them to "sacrifice voluntarily" for the future. The observable achievements of Soviet labor were historically unprecedented, setting an example to the world. The second generation of Soviet leaders would probably surpass the current one in "amplitude" and in efficient, less disruptive techniques of industrialization. His brief trip to the USSR reinforced his notion that Soviet success was bound up with the "best hopes of the world."[33]

In an open letter to a Swiss pastor in answer to the "slanderers" of the USSR, he refuted the charges that Soviet Russia was an authoritarian dictatorship with an expansionist foreign policy opposed to peace, whose internal policies were anti-Semitic and antireligious. Romain Rolland was aware of communist "errors and injustices," distortions derived from the historical genesis of the Revolution. Far more significant was the "heroic" daily construction of an industrial society out of the debris of backwardness, war, civil war, and famine. To counter the insinuation that the Soviet communists coerced the masses into happiness, he invoked the millions of illiterate and exploited people who had suffered under the czarist regime. The prerevolutionary ruling class, with the complicity of the church, had saturated the masses with "religious and lay ignorance," enabling the "exploiters" to perpetuate their control over the Russian economy and society. The communists were beginning to reverse this prerevolutionary pattern. One of their toughest battles was to "disintoxicate" the Russian population from "their moral prejudices as well as their dogmatic practices."[34]

The Soviets desired world peace in order to complete their domestic projects. They built a "powerful army" to deploy against their enemies—the most dangerous being German fascism—in event of an invasion. The Russians sought diplomatic and military alliances with the European democracies and joined the League of Nations in September 1934. Such tactics did not demonstrate "bad faith or political Machiavellianism." The Antifascist Front was a "conditional alliance," calling for a settling of accounts with Hitler before returning to "the state of permanent combat that still exists against the capitalist States." The Soviet leadership demonstrated "good sense" in maintaining an international stand against fascism. Nor had the communists capitulated in their reaction to the Italian invasion of Ethiopia. Although diplomats such as Maxim Litvinov, Soviet foreign minister during the Popular Front era, were truly anti-imperialist and antifascist, they were "realistic" enough to understand the limits of the current historical situation. They were not deceived by "idealistic rhetoric" or tempted by unilateral forms of brinkmanship. If the Soviet Union alone went to war against Mussolini, they would have weakened their logistical position in Europe once general warfare was declared.[35]

Although the Soviets were opposed to the development of Zionism on their own "terrain," this did not prove they were anti-Semitic. The regime considered racism fundamentally "repugnant" to its basic legal and ideological principles. Ethnic minorities and various nationalities were treated with "perfect equality." Jews were conspicuously visible in important occupations "up to the highest positions in government." As a direct antidote to the Nazis' aggressive anti-Jewish policies, the Russians established the experimental community of Birobidjan as a refuge for the "Jews persecuted in the Balkans and in Germany." Romain Rolland refused to accept unnuanced denunciations of the Soviet Union's policies on religious persecutions. To discuss this issue, each allegation had to be examined specifically. As far as he knew, "religions are protected in the USSR up to the present."[36]

The Soviet government faced violent conspirators attempting to sabotage or topple the regime. Fascist Germany now financed and stimulated the anti-Soviet "conspiracies and assassinations." Romain Rolland pointed to the Kirov murder to illustrate the depth of the "frenetic opposition" to the most able of Soviet administrators. Stalin behaved less "radically" than had his counterparts in the

French Revolution's period of Terror. So far no "evil had been inflicted" on Zinoviev and Kamenev, suggesting perhaps that Stalin "resisted the wave of anger after Kirov's death."

He used the forum of a debate with Julien Benda to advance the fellow-traveling position. Benda's notion of nonapplied intelligence was sophistic. He interpreted Benda's preoccupation with the "frozen world of abstract ideas" as encouragement for the "*combinazioni* of the present masters." Benda's style of intellectual life kept thinkers self-deceived and removed from the dangers to be encountered in the "domain of the real." Intellectuals had to test their formulations with scrupulous regard to political and social realities. Not acting on one's perceptions of the world was the greatest example of human treason. Intellectuals refined the "special weapon" of intelligence, but there was no inherent "superiority" in this weapon: "It would be nothing without the arms of our proletarian companions." By forging a community of mental and manual labor, the Soviets showed their understanding of the seminal role of the politically active writer, those "*engineers of souls*," who helped to "inaugurate a more just, freer, better ordered humanity."[37]

Benda erred by opposing "realism of action" to "idealism of thought" and by resurrecting the discredited Platonic separation of mind and body. The USSR's social experiment was designed to resolve these dualisms. The "*new man*" emerging under these novel conditions was a potentiality, someone who might achieve liberation in a society without the alienating distortions of class, racism, nationalism, or religious prejudice. Individuals could attain a "universal harmony" of thought and action because they concentrated on the unfolding of emotional and intellectual capacities in a society uncontaminated by "nationalism and militarism." One did not have to be a Russian or a communist to grasp the USSR's significance: it was "*our* Soviet country."[38]

The publication of two volumes of Romain Rolland's selected essays, *Quinze Ans de combat* (1935) and *Par la révolution, la paix* (1935), extensively documented his itinerary as an engaged writer. *Quinze Ans de combat*, published by Editions Rieder in their "Collection Europe," reflected his status as a Popular Front fellow traveler. *Par la révolution, la paix* appeared in the Communist Party–financed Editions Sociales Internationales in the "Collection Commune" series sponsored by the AEAR.

These two volumes, coupled with the trip to Moscow, were warmly received by French and Soviet communists. Vladimir Pozner underscored Romain Rolland's evolution from antifascist to fellow traveler. The Frenchman, with his self-imposed exile, had always sought a "human country." His fellow traveling refuted the rationalizations of intellectuals who refused to participate actively in politics: "Let his example be meditated upon and followed." Pozner applauded his ability to strike a balance between a pro-Soviet stance and integrity as an independent voice.[39]

Nicolai Bukharin's "Greetings to Romain Rolland" celebrated the writer's high moral character. Bukharin's style illustrated the way the top Soviet party apparatus lavished praise on its illustrious fellow travelers. The leading Soviet communist theoretician portrayed Romain Rolland as "artist, musician, thinker, personification of human nobility, a man with a courageous and intrepid soul." The Soviet Union was touched by his understanding of the "struggle and victory of the proletariat." The Soviet people regarded him as a "glorious friend," welcoming him to the USSR with a "warm embrace."[40]

The extreme left in France reprimanded Romain Rolland in his current incarnation as antifascist and Popular Front fellow traveler. They articulated a critique of his intellectual politics still current among the non-Stalinist left in France. Marcel Martinet lashed out at him for becoming "Stalinized." Instead of supporting the Bolshevik Revolution in its young and exuberant period, he postponed his devotion until 1935, when it had ossified into "reason of State." Incessantly searching for heroes and examples of courage, he obscured the truth that "in the business of the working class and revolution, high personalities like Romain Rolland do not count, no personalities count." Soviet influence over the French proletariat was lamentable, dragging "our working class from stupidity to swinishness." The conversion of intellectuals into easily manipulated instruments of the Soviet regime, or Russian foreign policy, was pathetic. Those writers designated "engineers of souls" were in fact puppets; Stalin's concept of "socialism in one country" meant in practice the substitution of nationalism for internationalism. Martinet denounced the all-pervasive repression in the USSR. The Soviets exiled Trotsky, deported Riazanov, starved Serge, committed summary executions, and submitted workers to constant

police surveillance. Soviet "violence" not only perverted the principles of socialism but also rendered both the communist and fellow-
traveling protests against fascism palpably "ridiculous."[41]

Romain Rolland's visibility as a fellow traveler triggered an
angry denunciation by Leon Trotsky, who now saw him as an
apologist for the Stalinist bureaucracy. The former humanitarian
emerged as "the advocate of Thermidorean terror." He demonstrated analytical strength in the realm of "psychological perception" but never displayed "political clarity or revolutionary flair."
Trotsky was alarmed by the French writer's factual ignorance
about the Kirov assassination and felt that his public statements
lacked "prudence." Drawing from his own previous association
with Zinoviev and Kamenev and his knowledge of the internal
mechanisms of the Kremlin, Trotsky stated that it made no "political sense" for either to have participated in a conspiracy antitheti-
cal to the "conceptions, goals, and political past of both men." Romain Rolland legitimized Stalin's campaign of reprisal against
former revolutionaries without using "Marxist analysis" and without being a revolutionary himself. Dismissing Romain Rolland's
political writings as "categorical and unreliable," the exiled Russian revolutionary compared the "psychological system" of the
French academics with the functionaries of the Stalinist bureaucracy. Many French academics, he added, were "professional
friends of Mussolini." Romain Rolland, too, had become an authoritarian personality cut off from the masses.[42] Trotsky's polemic was written with a personal and ideological ax to grind and
disregarded Romain Rolland's record as an antifascist intellectual.
Trotsky did not acknowledge Romain Rolland's protest, despite
long-standing political disagreement, when governmental authorities had expelled Trotsky from France in 1934.[43]

In October 1935, Romain Rolland penned an introduction to a
volume of collected essays entitled, significantly, *Compagnons de
route* (the French term for fellow travelers), in which he paid homage
to his lifelong literary companions. The volume included writings
on Empedocles, Shakespeare, Goethe, Renan, Hugo, and Tolstoy,
with a concluding piece on Lenin. He now glimpsed the possibility
of synthesizing Europe's cultural legacy with the revolutionary tradition of Russia: "The assimilation of Goethe's spirit with the forces
and laws of eternal Becoming is a permanent Revolution, which will

complete itself . . . in the present People's Revolution." The young Marx's writing optimistically pointed toward "the synthesis of thought and action." Europe's current impasse could not be resolved without "practical activity" and "social action." His fellow-traveling position fused dream and action. "Two maxims, paradoxically, which complete each other: 'We must dream,' says the man of action [Lenin]. And the man of the dream [Goethe]: 'We must act!' "[44]

Louis Aragon's "Interview with Romain Rolland, Engineer of Souls," brought together two artists of different generations, sensibilities, and cultural backgrounds. Romain Rolland embodied the potential in Stalin's term "engineer of souls" by facing the social responsibilities of the writer, always remaining "open to the future." Aragon described him as an important ideological "precursor" of the Popular Front. Romain Rolland now believed that the socialism being constructed in the USSR was "the only full and integral completion of individuality." In his own words: "Since the war my social sense has asserted itself and with it the necessity of an army, a campaign plan, and a party." Aragon underlined Romain Rolland's hostility to fascism in tracing his evolution to a procommunist perspective. Resistance to fascism would be ineffective if organized on Gandhian or pacifist lines. National paralysis of will could be prevented if the International of Labor "imposed peace on the world." The fellow-traveling intellectual worked for peace by expanding the struggles of the Popular Front on an "international scale." Aragon summed up his presence as "guide, master, and neighbor close to the heart of our country's proletariat."[45]

During the Popular Front era, French Communists placed Romain Rolland in a distinguished line of writers whose lives and works were unalterably opposed to cultural elitism, social hypocrisy, and political oppression.[46] For Malraux, Romain Rolland and André Gide were antidotes to Action Française writers and right-wing university professors. Their style of intellectual life opposed class inequalities, racial exclusivism, and imperialist policies: "France is not Racine, it is Molière; not de Maistre, it is Stendahl; it is not the Fascist poets under Napoleon III, but Hugo; not the academic signatories [endorsing Mussolini's invasion of Ethiopia] but Gide and Romain Rolland."[47]

For an inquiry on the "decline of ideas of freedom and progress" in Europe, Romain Rolland contrasted Western paralysis with the Soviet Union's efforts to construct a just society. Current Soviet planning made European decadence appear even more regressive than the militarism unleashed during the Great War. Intellectuals were part of the European malaise. Culture had become an "opium of the people," a retreat from the real world. If freedom and progress were to be meaningful values, they had to be struggled for on a daily, practical level. He sanctioned an assault on those oppressive institutional structures of the "bourgeois democracies" that denied workers an opportunity to realize their intellectual and productive potential.[48]

If formerly he was a "citizen of the world," he now regarded himself as a "worker of the world." The project of restoring to labor its dignity and productive power made him abandon his visions of world unity through music, Franco-German reconciliation, East-West dialogue, or the strategies of revolutionary Gandhian ideology. From 1927 to 1935 there had been a "slow, continuous, and reflective evolution of the mind" toward communism. His social philosophy sprang from two central assumptions: "the communion of all the living and the unity of the human species; and the indivisibility of thought and action." In the era of the Popular Front, there was no discrepancy between supporting the Soviet Union and adhering to these values. The USSR's existence proved that ideas and practice could be linked. Thought divorced from action was an "abortion or a treason."[49]

Romain Rolland's seventieth birthday was celebrated in late January 1936 in an atmosphere pervaded by the optimism of the French Popular Front. For a brief moment, the reclusive, mystical writer, in Swiss exile, became a living presence, signifying cultural and political unity for the French left. The idea of "no enemies on the Left" resonated with the readiness of French Communists, Socialists, and Radicals to put aside their differences to form a progressive interclass coalition. French pacifists were no longer a part of the unity. Romain Rolland was composing the *Comment empêcher la guerre?* essays which excommunicated French integral pacifists from the Popular Front alliance. It was a unique (and short-lived) moment in French cultural history: the man whose antiwar writings had been "treasonous" and "anti-French" twenty years earlier was now being showered with effusive praise, as an exemplar of the French man of letters, extending the tradition of the Enlightenment philosopher and the socially conscious writer of the nineteenth century. A party was held to honor his seventieth birthday in the main hall of the Palais de la Mutualité in Paris, where dignitaries of the French left, including Léon Blum, Gide, Malraux, and many French communists, feted him. André Gide presided over this *soirée d'hommage*. Romain Rolland was praised for his internationalism, his perspicacious reading of contemporary political trends, and his willingness to revise his position in view of changing circumstances. Tributes to him were printed in the communist and fellow-traveling press, most particularly in *L'Humanité, Regards, Commune, Europe,* and *Vendredi*.[50]

Romain Rolland became the symbolic grandfather of the Popular Front: a reassuring presence, standing for fellowship on the left, the authentic defense of culture, uncompromising resistance to fascism, and strengthening the Soviet Union geopolitically by lobbying for an alliance of collective security. He was spokesman for a progressive coalition of nations, classes, world views, sexes, and generations. Even his long-standing enemies temporarily stopped denigrating him as a writer and deriding him as a sentimental conscience. Gide retracted harsh comments about Romain Rolland being "above the battle" during the Great War. The two fellow travelers shook hands and endorsed the same Popular Front causes. Praising him for incarnating "the honor and glory of France and of all humanity," Gide embraced the very spirit of the Popular Front.[51] (This appearance of fraternal unity was deceptive, however, and would be quickly shattered. Conflicting perceptions of the Soviet Union would transform Gide and Romain Rolland into irreconcilable opponents within the year.) In three successive articles, Marcel Cachin defined the French Communist Party's position, reporting hyperbolically that the "entire Popular Front had celebrated Romain Rolland at the Mutualité." He was elevated into "the most glorious intellectual of our epoch."[52]

In the spring of 1936, on the eve of the French Popular Front's electoral victory, Romain Rolland called for a new "people's theater." What he had campaigned for during the Dreyfus Affair had been premature historically. During the Popular Front era, its intellectual allies not only took energy from the working classes but also produced lasting literary masterpieces. Revolutionary theater outstripped other art forms in its potential for heightening political

awareness and mobilizing the masses: "Theater is a place of immediate communion; plays serve as the daughters and mothers of
action." The conservative and centralized French state feared the
"irruption of mass emotion and revolutionary energies" from a
politicized people's theater and would never sponsor such a project. The bourgeois state would deflect the concept of decentralized
Houses of Culture or blunt the radical edge of the experiment. If
peace presupposed a social revolution, then a people's theater
would thrive only "through Revolution." To prepare the "people of
Paris" for the future cultural revolution, Romain Rolland advised
using the huge theater of Trocadero, which was designed to house
a massive audience and permit crowds on stage. Class-conscious
antifascist intellectuals had to prepare for a "renewal of the present
world." He urged progressive writers to enter into alliances with
organized labor without losing sight of conflict: "It is necessary for
the minds to prepare the victory. We are the arm, voice, and faith
of history's human combat."[53]

After the Popular Front government came to power in May 1936
under the direction of Léon Blum, the first Socialist and Jewish
premier of France, Romain Rolland attempted to conciliate between
disparate elements on the left and center-left. In *Clarté*, the monthly
review of the World Committee Against War and Fascism and the
Amsterdam-Pleyel movement, he urged the masses of France to
push their democratic sovereignty to its limits. He was inspired by
the spontaneous wave of sit-ins initiated by French workers in May–
June 1936. French proletarians proved their maturity by inaugurating a "movement of unprecedented strikes, and they demonstrated
magnificent discipline and showed to an amazed world a People-
King, master of its destinies." Opposition to the "audacious infamy"
of fascist dictatorships cemented the Popular Front alliance. The
common denominator was political resistance. The integral pacifists
ought to be excluded from the Popular Front: they were blind to "the
amassed dangers of fascism"; they advocated a naive and short-
sighted policy of French isolationism, giving the fascists "carte-
blanche to extend and destroy our friends and allies"; they were
unwitting "auxiliaries of fascism." Romain Rolland called himself an
integral antifascist, which presupposed a readiness "to come immediately to the aid of those in every country struggling desperately
against fascism" and to orchestrate a sustained policy of "vigilance

and universal defense" allowing the "Laboring Peoples" to take direction of governments and institutions.[54]

His initial impression of Blum's Popular Front was ambivalent. Romain Rolland now cautiously approached Blum after avoiding him for over three decades. Brushing aside a long-standing personal animosity and differences with Second International socialism over the Great War and the Amsterdam-Pleyel movement, he wrote a letter of reconciliation in early February 1936. He thanked the socialist leader for his "generous words" spoken at the Mutualité soirée honoring Romain Rolland's seventieth birthday. Their current comradeship was based on common struggles and common dangers: "The more threatened you are, the more I have wished for a long time to shake your hand."[55]

Only one week later, Blum was assaulted by a gang of Action Française thugs in Paris and nearly killed. Romain Rolland conveyed his sympathies through socialist journalist Amédée Dunois, wishing Blum a speedy recovery. He urged Blum to use the occasion to "extinguish" the danger of future Action Française provocations. Yet his pleasure over the Popular Front victory was qualified. Blum's electoral success was only a "conditional" first stage, marked by internal "compromises" and "risks." The new coalition should institute social and economic reforms, developing policies that might serve as models for other democratic governments. The Blum government was tenuous. There could be no blossoming of the French Popular Front, Romain Rolland wrote to Lucien Roth, unless the threat of French fascism was checked: "Although I don't like Blum (whom I have nevertheless learned to appreciate), I am happy that he is now, for the moment, the leader of an antifascist Popular Front."[56]

After the Spanish Popular Front government was established in February 1936, and especially after Spanish Republicans tried to mobilize Blum's government to their aid, Romain Rolland's attention shifted to foreign policy. The issue became urgent when the Spanish Popular Front urged Blum to intervene in Spain after 20 July 1936. Romain Rolland endorsed *Vendredi's* solidarity with the Republicans, hoping that Blum's government would intervene immediately: "Whatever be the dangers of the present hour, the worst danger is abstention through the prudence of the French government."[57]

In his declarations in favor of the Spanish Popular Front, he depicted the cause of the Spanish people as identical to that of the freedom-loving French. The Spanish Civil War unmasked the hegemonic designs of Hitler and Mussolini. The crushing of the Spanish Republicans would lead first to a fascist Spain, then to a general world war, ultimately pitting fascists against antifascists. Fascist military strategy made the "encirclement" of France a top priority. French nonintervention was not a benign form of neutrality; it was a blind and ill-advised sacrifice of the Spanish people and their legally elected government. Nonintervention was "iniquitous and monstrous"; it allowed Franco, with Hitler's and Mussolini's financial and military assistance, to destroy the Spanish revolution. He legitimized the use of all necessary means to assist Republican Spain: "To defend the peoples of Spain is to defend peace, the peace of France, of the West, of the world. . . . They are our brothers and our avant-garde."[58]

His propaganda for the Spanish Republicans clearly aimed to catalyze the progressive Jacobin sentiments of the French Popular Front. He was convinced that only a genuine people's movement could be counted on in the antifascist struggle in Spain. He campaigned to explode French neutrality and isolationism, endorsed by Blum's government. The Spanish cause was consistent with the interests of Popular Front France. There was no way to avoid a direct confrontation with the fascist enemy. The Western democracies should not yield to fascist challenges or bluffs. His appeals mirrored the justification offered by members of the International Brigades, who risked their lives and reputations to fight in Spain. The Spanish Civil War was the decade's great showdown. The cause of the Spanish Republicans was identical to the struggle to defend culture, to secure social justice, to smash barbarism, and ultimately to establish a durable and reasonable peace. The International Brigades struggled "against the murderous power of the past."

> Humanity! Humanity! I call upon you, the people of Europe and America! Help Spain! Help ourselves! Help yourselves! It's you, it's all of us, who are threatened![59]

Romain Rolland sided with the Spanish Republicans with the full knowledge that Hitler and Mussolini contributed armaments and economic aid to Franco's forces. If Franco came to power, the fascists would acquire military leverage in Europe and possibly in North Africa. After the bombing of Madrid and Barcelona, the fascists would shell London and Paris. He deplored the violence unleashed against innocent Spanish women and children, the gratuitous destruction of hospitals, nurseries, and civilian quarters. In Spain, the disarmed and the disabled were perishing along with the world's greatest art treasures. Authentic antifascism was fraternal; his contemporaries had no option but "to speak out, cry out, and act." Aiding Spain would demonstrate the solidarity of people of goodwill everywhere: "Come to the aid of Spain! Come to our aid, to your aid! Remain silent and tomorrow it will be your sons who perish!"[60]

Deeply moved by the tragedy of the Spanish Republicans and the courage of the International Brigades, incensed by flagrant fascist violations of the Non-Intervention Pact, he composed a strong letter to Premier Blum. He empathized with Blum's desire to help Spain without triggering a civil war in France, plunging into a general European war, or splitting his own divided Socialist Party. The political resolution of this dilemma should not violate the principles of the antifascist Popular Front, both in Spain and in France. The French Popular Front should divorce itself from England's desire to crush the Spanish Republicans. Holding that "the defeat of Spain is the defeat of France," he advised Blum to take decisive action. If the French Popular Front government failed to resist this "ambush of the fascisms against Spain's legal government and people," then Blum would be responsible for betraying the principles of democratic socialism, jeopardizing France's honor and security, and increasing the "insolence and greediness of fascism." Spain was France's neighbor. The two Popular Front coalitions were brothers. Because France possessed sufficient military might and could legitimize its entry into the Spanish Civil War, Romain Rolland predicted that French intervention would not precipitate general war. The Republic of Spain should not be allowed to "suffocate."[61]

Blum's refusal to intervene actively in the Spanish Civil War was a bitter disappointment to Romain Rolland. Such a display of "weakness of will" would have terrible repercussions for that part of France that was antifascist and for the Spanish people. World peace was damaged by cowardly capitulation to fascist violence. He grew increasingly intolerant of all policies of "concession and compromise" to fascist movements.[62] Simultaneously, he moved even closer to the communist camp. He perceived that Soviet aid to the Spanish Republicans was constructive, and he was convinced that the politics of collective security would have safeguarded Republican Spain. In a flurry of open declarations and appeals, he tried desperately to ignite public opinion to pressure Blum for French aid to Spain. As the fighting continued, he employed more emphatic slogans, associating the Spanish people's struggle against fascism with "the fight for culture, freedom, and the independence of all men and peoples." Spain was now the chief arena of the antifascist struggle. If the "Ring of Peace" were to be broken there, then fascist expansionism would escalate.[63]

Franco's ideologues took a perverse pleasure in proliferating sadistic anti-intellectual slogans. The two most infamous ones, "Down with the intelligentsia!" and "Long Live Death!" reinforced Romain Rolland's perception that antifascist resistance was commensurate with the defense of cultural life. To the International Congress of Antifascist Writers, meeting in Valencia, Spain, in July 1937—during the Civil War—he penned the following greeting:

> In these moments the civilization of the entire world is united in these capitals; a world menaced by the airplanes and bombs of the fascist barbarians, as it was in antiquity by the barbarian invasions. . . .
>   Glory to this nation of heroes, to these knights of the spirit, to this alliance of two faces—the power of the popular masses and their elected leaders! May this alliance serve as an example to the great democracies of Europe and America! May this alliance, strengthened in combat, safeguard the progress and liberty of the world![64]

On the anniversary of the defense of Madrid, he indicted the French and English policies of nonintervention in Spain. The fighting in Spain had an "epic grandeur" because the stakes were so high and because the choices were so clear. The Spanish Republicans represented not only the right of the Spanish people to self-determination but the very struggle for human dignity. He wrote about Spain from the moral and political perspective of the International Brigades, those who "gloriously lent witness to the present fraternity of peoples."

They feel with sorrow and revolt the unworthy treason of their governments who refuse to support the Spanish Republic, who sacrifice the defenders of Western freedom, and who have made the cowardly and perfidious Comedy of Non-Intervention a machine of suffocation.[65]

During this period, on 18 June 1936, Maxim Gorky died. In a moving tribute, Romain Rolland marked the event as "humanity's greatest bereavement since the death of Lenin." No other important writer had played so prominent a role in the cultural history of a postrevolutionary society. Gorky functioned as overseer of Soviet culture and adviser to Communist Party leaders. He died, tragically, before the implementation of the Soviet Constitution.[66] Romain Rolland's leave-taking mingled veneration and sorrow. If Barbusse's death had distanced Romain Rolland from the leadership of the French Communist Party, Gorky's death diminished his ability to influence the Soviet Communist leadership and signaled the beginning of the end of the engaged intellectual's impact in the 1930s.

At the height of enthusiasm for the Popular Front government, Romain Rolland's play *Le 14 juillet* (1902) was performed in Paris at the Alhambra Theater on 14 July 1936. These theatrical performances climaxed the cultural life of the French Popular Front. They reflected the euphoria and aspirations of the coalition and the visibility of its intellectual followers.[67] The play glorified the people of Paris for forcibly taking a stand against tyranny and conquering the Bastille. The production brought together some of the most gifted artists on the French left. Old and young, communist and noncommunist, they voluntarily joined their expertise in different genres and mediums. The music was composed by Milhaud and Honegger. Pablo Picasso designed a stage curtain, which evocatively combined mythological and political symbolism. In the context of the victorious Popular Front, Romain Rolland's dream of a people's theater appeared to move toward fruition. The center and left press responded to *Le 14 juillet* with great acclaim.[68] The playwright suspended his exile from Paris and made a rare public appearance at the play's opening night. He was greeted with thunderous applause by the politicized audience. To the image of intellectuals marching hand in hand with leaders of the French communist and socialist parties should be added the sight of the septuagenarian Romain Rolland, celebrated by the Popular Front spectators at the Alhambra

Theater, still standing for an indivisible left-wing alliance against fascism. For that brief moment, he was recognized as the cultural symbol of Popular Front unity against the fascist threat.

To commemorate the revival of his play and to draw the historical parallels between the Popular Front and the French Revolution, Romain Rolland penned his "Fourteenth of July: 1789 and 1936," integrating the Soviet Revolution into the populist and Jacobin spirit of the Popular Front. The crucial lesson of 1789 was that the people must "seize action by the mane." The slogan of that day— "*A la Bastille!*"—helped to "unite and direct the forces of revolutionary action." Other "factual and symbolic" Bastilles remained to be taken. The respective constituencies of the 1789 Revolution and the 1936 *Rassemblement populaire* were similar: each was composed of "middle- and lower-class elements, lawyers, artisans, and proletarians." Both were interclass alliances cemented by shared sentiments and values, common enemies, and a common political orientation. He reminded his contemporaries that the original Bastille had been taken by force, not simply by an act of faith. New armies might be necessary to assault other Bastilles—a clear if indirect reference to the Spanish Republican cause.[69]

The "bad conscience" of the Old Regime still existed a hundred and fifty years later, however updated and disguised in the "new feudalism of finance and industry with their vassals of the intelligentsia and the press." His "comrades" of 1936 ought not to flinch in the face of new oppression. Jaurès's cautionary words, written about reprisals after the Bastille was taken, were still pertinent: "Proletarians, remember that cruelty is a reminder of servitude, for it certifies that the barbarism of the oppressor regime is still present in us!" The Popular Front was designed to resist fascism, not to imitate fascist methods of intimidation or repression. In the spirit of moderation, and contrary to the model of Soviet communism, Romain Rolland counseled the Popular Front to minimize the violence in social struggles: "This violence was the ransom of the Old Regime's totality of cruelty."[70]

Romain Rolland's intellectual politics during the French Popular Front provide a crucial point of entry into the era. He was integrally connected to the origins, contradictions, victories, and defeats of the Popular Front. He contributed to the opening created by this brief political and cultural experiment, which took place under adverse circumstances. Dialogue between the classes inspired hope for social change and heightened militancy among the working class. This was reflected in the famous sit-in strikes of May–June 1936, which produced the Matignon Agreements. In a decade saturated with slogans, the call for unity between mental and manual workers did not seem to be empty posturing. It resonated with its partisans as a harbinger of the future communal society.

Most accounts of the cultural politics of the Popular Front are highly biased for and against.[71] Much art and culture of this period has been dismissed as agitprop, "low" or "dishonest." Critics of committed literature have labeled it didactic, self-righteous, unable to withstand close scrutiny—in short, a betrayal of art, or worse still, a new religion.[72] Clearly not all socialist and antifascist sentiments were easily expressed in revolutionary form.

The cultural politics of the Popular Front era marked the turning point between Romain Rolland's critical and uncritical fellow traveling.

Once again, his perception of fascism accounted for the shift. Beginning in 1933 and culminating in 1936, the European democracies appeared to be in an emergency situation. Searching for an antifascism of integrity and action, he joined the call for a grand unity between the progressive wing of the bourgeoisie and the working class. He opposed the rhetorical, conciliatory antifascism of Blum's government and pointed to the example of the Soviet Union's concrete aid and sponsorship of the International Brigades fighting in Spain.

The Popular Front transformed Romain Rolland's intellectual engagement. His fellow traveling became less nuanced, more prone to gross dichotomies in its basic opposition of fascism and antifascism. He still considered himself a spokesman for the oppressed but now focused on the victims of fascism. Fascism must be smashed before the struggles of the working class, the unemployed, the colonized, and the culturally deprived could be resumed. He welcomed the thrust toward a democratization of culture and politics in France, which meant increased participation by social classes who had historically been excluded. He vastly preferred Popular Front–style governments to the centralization, secrecy, and authoritarianism of Stalin's regime. At the same time, he realized he could no longer influence internal policies in the USSR or the Communist International.

His own ideology syncretized, somewhat amorphously, anti-fascism, anti-imperialism, and socialist humanism. In his mind, this ideology was most coherently exemplified in the Comintern's support of the Spanish Republicans. He glossed over, or dismissed as divisive propaganda, charges that the Soviet Union took its revenge on noncommunist components of the Spanish left.[73] The Popular Front permitted him to raise the question of cultural as well as social revolution—who ought to play a vanguard or rear-guard role, what ought to perish or be retained in the new society. The cultural politics of the Popular Front temporarily made him feel less isolated and promised the intellectual a more active role in the making of a revolutionary society. Even the generous idea of no enemies on the left had a built-in disclaimer, namely, that the left required an inflexible opposition to all forms of fascism.

The inspirational collective consciousness on the left appeared to integrate an awareness of history, community, and international solidarity. The authenticity of this solidarity was tested in extreme situations, as in Spain, or in the struggle against right-wing leagues in France. Romain Rolland's advocacy of a collective consciousness on the left was neither utopian nor aesthetic. Circumstances denied him the luxury of playing the role of conscience of the left. He compromised the absolute nature of his moralism, primarily because it was necessary to choose in a crisis. The central unifying elements of his vision remained fraternity and the oceanic bonds generated by resistance to the fascist enemy and the fascist threat to human dignity.

For the rest of the 1930s, he was silent about the distortions of Soviet communism. To have publicly condemned the internal or foreign policies of the USSR would inevitably have weakened the antifascist cause.

He now entered a period of uncritical fellow traveling.

11

The Politics of Uncritical Support

Perhaps later, much later, the new movement would arise—
with new flags, a new spirit knowing of both: of economic
fatality *and* the "oceanic sense." Perhaps the members of the
new party will wear monks' cowls and preach that only purity of means can justify the ends. Perhaps they will teach
that the tenet is wrong which says that a man is the quotient
of one million divided by one million, and will introduce a
new kind of arithmetic based on multiplication: on the joining of a million individuals to form a new entity which, no
longer an amorphous mass, will develop a consciousness
and an individuality of its own, with an "oceanic feeling"
increased a millionfold, in unlimited yet self-contained space.
                              Arthur Koestler, *Darkness at Noon*

Several factors converged to solidify Romain Rolland's sympathies
for Soviet communism and the PCF in the declining years of the
French Popular Front. During the Popular Front era, the French
Communist Party evolved from a minority revolutionary party into
a mass political movement with a permanent base among organized
workers. From 1932 to 1936 the PCF changed its political orientation,
temporarily patched up its historic quarrel with French socialists,
and left its seclusion. The national presence of the PCF was evident
not only in the huge increases in membership and electoral strength,
but also in its attraction for intellectuals, students, and members of
the liberal professions. Reversing its chronic suspicion of intellectuals and lifting its rigid controls of artistic life, the party openly
courted writers and sponsored avant-garde cultural projects. Many
of the most significant artistic experiments of the era took place
under the aegis of the PCF or the PCF-dominated trade union organization.[1]

As the French communists repudiated their parochial politics of
the 1920s, their simplistic class rhetoric, and their dismissal of
intellectuals and interclass alliances, they began to take more re-

sponsible stances on internal French policies and on foreign affairs.[2] In view of Romain Rolland's prior political itinerary, he was very receptive to PCF positions in 1936. He agreed with the PCF's desire to press Blum's government for armed intervention in Spain, and he endorsed the party's current stance on fascism. He understood the historical reasons for its close ties to the Soviet Union. He developed esteem for the leadership of the PCF. General secretary Maurice Thorez, the self-styled *fils du peuple,* echoed several of Romain Rolland's phrases in his own Popular Front journalism, most notably the defense of collective security formulated in the phrase "the Ring of Peace." Romain Rolland reciprocated in July 1936 by indicating to "Comrade Thorez" that he "entirely approved of the Party's firm and wise politics." He identified himself with precisely the same struggles that the PCF was committed to, "the great cause of the international Proletariat and for the defense of world Peace."[3]

Romain Rolland was simultaneously arguing in *Comment empêcher la guerre?* that the Western democracies had to contain and challenge fascist expansionism by forming a solid military alliance with the USSR. The clarity and strength of the PCF stance on Spain illustrated the bankruptcy and defensiveness of Blum's neutrality. The Popular Front government took the course of least resistance. Blum remained paralyzed by fear of internal tensions within the Socialist-Communist-Radical alliance, thereby violating the people's trust in it. Blum's rhetorical commitment to "Peace and Freedom" was undermined by his cautious isolationist policy and his vague, nonfighting antifascism. Meanwhile, the Soviet Union and Western communist parties were providing arms, men, and money, not to mention propagandistic support, to the Spanish Republicans. Blum's failure to intervene in Spain and to sign a political-military alliance with the Soviet Union was unrealistic, in the light of the global thrust toward a military showdown between fascists and antifascists.[4]

On a more subjective level, as they had been during and immediately after World War I, Romain Rolland's writings were either omitted or vitriolically dismissed in the various cultural organs of the French extreme right, the pacifist right and center, the Radical center, the Socialist center and right, and the extreme left. He had stood for Popular Front cultural unity and had become a symbol of the Popular Front intellectual; he had been celebrated and glorified;

but by the fall of 1936 Romain Rolland was appreciated only by the communist and fellow-traveling press.[5]

André Gide's trip to the Soviet Union and the publication of his book *Return from the U.S.S.R.* in November 1936 triggered a scathing denunciation by Romain Rolland on the front page of *L'Humanité*. The violent reaction provoked by Gide's book effectively destroyed the tenuous cultural unity of the French Popular Front and of the Association of Revolutionary Writers and Artists. Intellectuals took sides for or against Gide's perceptions of Soviet communism and Stalinism. In a large, inexpensive Gallimard edition Gide's *Retour* sold 100,000 copies in two months. The Popular Front weekly *Vendredi* published an extract that reached a quarter of a million influential readers. The text was discussed and reviewed throughout France.[6]

Romain Rolland's response showed a complete lack of sympathy, except in the salutation and closing regards to his communist "comrades." "The U.S.S.R. Has Seen Others Like Him" does not bear scrutiny as a review at all. It never addressed the substance of Gide's critique of Soviet communism.[7] The tone was sarcastic and vindictive. Coming after the writings of Istrati, Victor Serge, and a host of disillusioned communists, Gide's book struck Romain Rolland a crushing blow. He portrayed Gide as someone who acted in bad faith by consciously violating the engaged intellectual's task. This review was the culmination of his long-standing personal animosity toward Gide. The *Nouvelle Revue française* had ignored or denigrated his work for twenty-eight years. In this rejoinder, his spitefulness spilled over into slander, reasoned analysis gave way to ad hominem argument. He resented Gide's stature as France's leading man of letters, and he envied the huge popular success of this essay. Gide's pro-Soviet speeches delivered in the Soviet Union contradicted the vicious anti-Soviet remarks published in France. He accused Gide of allowing "his celebrity to be exploited by the enemies of the USSR." He was incensed by the timing of the book: not only would it be misused by the anti-Soviet press, but it also coincided with a climactic moment in the Spanish Civil War when the Republicans were fighting against overwhelming odds for Madrid. Its appearance weakened the antifascist French Popular Front and those who wished for an alliance of the Western democracies with the Soviet Union. Gide failed to overcome his personal narcissism and failed to perceive that the great social causes of the moment, specifically antifascism and support for the "universal workers' fatherland, founded by the October Revolution," transcended the writer's preoccupation with himself. Romain Rolland was temporarily beside himself with rage. "This bad book is, besides, a mediocre book, astonishingly poor, superficial, childish, and contradictory."[8]

Events in the Soviet Union far surpassed individual judgment, in Romain Rolland's view. The USSR stood for a revolutionary form of social advancement and economic development. One needed a historical consciousness to comprehend its significance. The work of the revolution required of the intellectual personal responsibility and a tenacious loyalty to the revolutionary process, both of which Gide totally lacked. Unlike Gide, who had never met Stalin, Romain Rolland had interviewed him twice and found the leader to be accessible and unpretentious, addressing him as "you" or as "comrade." It was wrongheaded to label him "the master of peoples." He quoted Stalin's phrase "Modesty is the ornament of the true Bolshevik" to refute Gide's argument of an emerging cult of personality in the USSR. He cajoled his audience to remain "unshakable in our battles."[9] In his declamation against Gide and in his identification with the Soviet experiment, as well as in his increasingly desperate portrayal of the antifascist struggle, Romain Rolland crossed the line from critical to uncritical fellow traveling. His subsequent reputation as an engaged writer would suffer from that decision and from this ill-tempered review.

Gide replied directly in his *Afterthoughts on My Return to the U.S.S.R.*, published in June 1937. He returned to his earlier view of Romain Rolland's inadequacy as a writer. More injurious, he raised serious questions about Romain Rolland's integrity, implying that the elderly writer's engagement with communism severely compromised him as a man of principle.

> Romain Rolland's response gave me pain. I never cared very much for his writings, but at any rate I hold his moral character in high esteem. The cause of my grief was the thought that so few men reach the end of their life before showing the extreme limits of their greatness. I think that the author of *Au-dessus de la mêlée* would pass a severe judgment on the Romain Rolland of his old age.

Gide disliked the asymmetries in Romain Rolland's view of justice. As a fellow traveler, Romain Rolland vilified fascism but not the deep-seated and well-known Soviet abominations: "Those who have the ideals of justice and liberty at heart, those who combat for Thaelmann—the Barbusses, the Romain Rollands and their like—have kept silent, still keep silent."[10]

In two articles published in *L'Humanité* in January 1937, Romain Rolland focused on the Spanish Civil War. The first was coauthored with Largo Caballero and La Pasionaria: here a Spanish socialist, a Spanish communist, and a French engaged writer joined hands in solidarity. The Soviet Union was aiding the Spanish Republicans and the International Brigades. The PCF consistently urged the Blum government to intervene in Spain. Romain Rolland lavished praise on the Soviet Union as "the great country of Socialism" and the French Communist Party "as the true representative of the people of France and its international mission."[11] He admired the PCF's historical evolution to its current Popular Front stance, especially against the "mortal threat of German and Italian fascist imperialisms." He contrasted Blum's weakness and uncertainty to the PCF's leadership, to which he hyperbolically attributed "wisdom, patience, and a firm political sense." The French communists understood that nonintervention in Spain jeopardized French "political security" along with the "necessary success" of the democratic cause. He expressed fraternity only with those willing to fight to the death for antifascist ideals: "Even if my voice is weak, it is for peace and freedom, it is for our brothers of Spain who defend them against the reactionary *condottieri's* aggression."[12]

In letters written in 1936, Romain Rolland's old colleague from *Demain*, Henri Guilbeaux, tried unsuccessfully to press him to speak out against the Moscow purge trials.[13] Guilbeaux had evolved from impassioned Bolshevik to violent anti-Stalinist. In *The End of the Soviets* (1937), Guilbeaux disavowed his communist loyalties. He borrowed information from Gide, Victor Serge, and Kléber Legay to attack the fellow travelers. He accused them of becoming "puppets in the hands of Stalinist functionaries" and acquiescing in the face of Soviet bureaucratization, Stalin's cult of personality, the widespread execution of Octobrists, and the perversion of the revolution's ideals. As Gide's "principal maligner," Romain Rolland ignored the internal reality of Soviet conditions and refused to address the serious social distortions deriving from "Stalin's omnipotence." Gide acted with "real courage," whereas Romain Rolland attacked

Gide through cowardly character assassination: "He is denounced as a homosexual for propagandistic purposes." In Guilbeaux's text, the geopolitical polarities of the 1930s were compressed into the politics of personal slander. Guilbeaux catalogued his grievances against the French fellow traveler in a chapter called "Romain Rolland's Marriage of State, Prisoner of the Kremlin." Romain Rolland's fellow traveling stemmed from his 1934 marriage to the half-French, half-Russian Marie Koudachef, a communist sympathizer. "Higher-ups" in Stalin's bureaucracy had sent her on a "special mission" to woo the French writer away from the influence of his pacifist and liberal sister, Madeleine Rolland. Romain Rolland, in short, was married to a Stalinist agent, which explained his uncritical support for the USSR despite his knowledge of the USSR's misrepresentation of history, Stalin's execution of "Lenin's comrades," and the restrictions on workers and "persecutions of peasants in Russia." After she became his secretary in 1929, and especially after the consummation of this Soviet "marriage of State," it was impossible to see the French writer without Madame Marie Romain Rolland being present. She allegedly filtered all critical perspectives that he might have had on international communism. It was regrettable, Guilbeaux concluded, that he was being so "shamefully exploited" by the communist leadership. He now served as a substitute for Barbusse, a literary showpiece who allowed himself to be manipulated by the "craftiness of the Kremlin masters."[14]

Romain Rolland read Guilbeaux's book and was furious about its insinuations. He privately broke relations with him, accusing his old comrade of libel and replying that such charges were defamations. To attack Romain Rolland's ideological leanings was one thing; to smear his marriage was betrayal. He also broke with a friend who favorably reviewed Guilbeaux's book, explaining that the "violation of my personal life was something not to be countenanced."[15]

As the French Popular Front coalition unraveled, Romain Rolland's fellow traveling became increasingly controversial outside communist circles. He, in turn, published almost exclusively in the PCF or *communisant* press. In the spirit of the French Popular Front, he endorsed the concept of decentralized Houses of Culture that would be democratic, firmly antifascist, and linked to a tradition of French skepticism, including Molière, Voltaire, and Anatole France.

That tradition established the writer as a "combatant of the mind," using critical reason and satire against superstition and tyranny. He subsequently wrote appeals for political prisoners in Nazi Germany, denouncing the fascist regime for suspending civil liberties and using violent coercion: "Hitler's regime is a regime of terror, a dictatorship, that maintains itself by force." Speaking for the silent, arrested victims of German fascism, he brought Nazi concentration camps to Western attention and attempted to cajole the European democracies out of their inertia: "Hitler counts on silence and on the forgetting of the Western democracies who are betrayed by the cowardly weaknesses of their governments. But he is deceived. We do not forget the forfeiture of the oppressors nor the heroism of the oppressed."[16]

In a brief salute to the French Communist Party at its Ninth Party Congress, held from 25 December to 29 December 1937, he praised the party for its rapid growth over the preceding few years, its humanistic "enlargement" of thought, and its ability to incarnate the "most profound forces of France." At the same time, the PCF championed the international causes of the masses, rallying its rank and file to the ideal of the "Universal Union of Workers." The PCF was the "indestructible pivot of the Popular Front." "I view the great Party that derives from Marx and Lenin as the most logical and most firm representative of social justice. I feel mentally and emotionally linked to it."[17]

Earlier in the month of December 1937, communist critic Georges Sadoul compared Romain Rolland's place in twentieth-century literature to that of Voltaire in the eighteenth century and Hugo in the nineteenth. Sadoul studded his review of the *maître*'s latest book, *Compagnons de route* (1936), with superlatives: "Romain Rolland joins the genius of Stalin to the genius that inspired the works of Leonardo da Vinci. Romain Rolland is the most complete and clearsighted mind of our time."[18]

Turning to Romain Rolland's positions on Stalin's purge trials, we must remember that he never condemned or criticized these procedures in a public statement.[19] Nor did he endorse, justify, or applaud them. The French writer whose career as an engaged intellectual was built on speaking out against injustice reacted, paradoxically, with silence.

The difficulty in explaining his silence is compounded by his expressed desire to remain an untainted conscience, oriented toward an oceanic contact with the masses. The politics of the late 1930s no longer allowed such purity. He held that events in Spain, the French Popular Front, and the all-out campaign against fascism took precedence over criticism of internal Soviet affairs. He could not rely on accurate facts or unprejudiced information about Soviet politics in the crisis-ridden 1930s: reports were colored by the biases of writers or editorial boards. It became virtually impossible to read a balanced or unemotional view of the Soviet Union after 1936. For years Romain Rolland asserted that the bourgeois and nationalist press discredited itself in reporting on Russian communism, as did the socialist, pacifist, and centrist media. The extreme left in France, whether Trotskyist, revolutionary syndicalist, or anarchist, relied too extensively on Victor Serge and Magdeleine Paz or on Leon Trotsky's "vindictive diatribes." He dismissed their accounts as "exaggerated" or completely paranoid. He distrusted critics of the Soviet Union who maintained deep-seated personal grudges against the government. Moreover, he suspected that there might be collusion between the Trotskyist extreme left, Hitler's Gestapo, and other European fascist movements, including Mussolini's government. He considered their "independence of opposition" untenable in the current context and hypocritical given their former roles in polemicizing against and purging revolutionary opponents.[20]

Influenced by the PCF press and by his own interpretation of contemporary circumstances, he accepted the theory that a real conspiracy existed against the Soviet system. Both Kamenev and Zinoviev had dubious pasts. They were accused of being "renegades and traitors" and were expelled from the Communist Party in 1927 and 1932. Both proclaimed their guilt in this crime. There was no reason to assume that their confessions were forced or invented. The real issue of the Moscow trials was "corruption." After studying French translations of the court proceedings in the 604-page *Procès du centre antisoviétique trotskiste* (1936), he was convinced that the accused had committed villainous acts. It was logical and inevitable that plotters might desire to topple the regime. The French writer suspected that Trotsky may have masterminded these intrigues, as Radek charged. He rejected Georges Duhamel's coverage of the trial as being uncritical, unhistorical, and overly indebted to Victor Serge. Duhamel portrayed the accused as "empty and flattened-out puppets," not spirited revolutionaries fighting for their lives. Duhamel injected his own "academic consciousness" into his journalism, distorting it even further.[21]

To clarify the issues, Romain Rolland drew parallels between the Moscow purge trials and the period of the French Revolutionary Terror. He never doubted the "historical justification" of Danton's "condemnation." He cited Albert Mathiez's *Etudes robespierristes* for historical precedents of revolutionary treason countered by severe punishment: "Danton had also betrayed the Revolution." If counterrevolutionaries emerged in revolutionary situations, revolutionary regimes ought to be expected to punish these traitors harshly.[22]

Yet there was another side to Romain Rolland's perception of the Moscow trials, a private and moral one. Although he offered a historical justification, he agonized over the purges: "I feel pain and affliction at the Revolution torn between the furious duels of ideology, exacerbated by personal rancor and hate." The second wave of trials confirmed his "apprehensions and repulsions" over the first. He knew that innocent men and women were being victimized by Stalin's purges, though he was unable to grasp the scope of the systematic terror. "I no longer rejoice over what happens in the USSR. The malady of arrests and executions has gone on too long."[23] He was disturbed about the way Stalin's regime not only devoured its loyal opposition but also justified its repression in the name of high-sounding ideological principles.

Despite his public silence regarding the purges, Romain Rolland still operated within communist circles as a spokesman for human rights. When he learned of the persecution, arrest, and disappearance of Soviet citizens for political reasons, he interceded for their release. In the summer of 1937, he wrote a personal letter to Stalin, urging the Soviet leader to commute the sentences of Alexander Aroseff, the Moscow-based president of VOKS, and Aroseff's wife. Romain Rolland no longer exaggerated his influence or the willingness of the Soviet authorities to respond to such requests with compassion: "I am writing Stalin (without very much hope!)."[24] These intercessions were on behalf of innocent, highly reputable individuals caught in the momentum of Soviet repression. Because Barbusse and Gorky were dead, Romain Rolland used his notoriety and his connections with French Communist Party officials such as Maurice Thorez, international communists such as Georgi Dimitrov, and Soviet leaders, including Stalin himself, to guarantee that his appeals for human rights went through proper channels and were taken seriously. He never threatened to attack communism in public or to repudiate his fellow-traveling views if his appeals went unheeded. He alerted communist officials to particular errors and miscalculations on their part without breaking his faith in the overall cause of international communism.

Hearing of the arrest and detention of Oscar Hartoch, an eminent professor of medicine at the University of Leningrad, Romain Rolland realized that the purge was out of control. All his letters of inquiry went unacknowledged. He had received "no official answer since Gorky's death."[25] Through Thorez, he pressured Dimitrov to investigate the facts in the Hartoch case. He reminded the Bulgarian Communist Party leader that after Dimitrov's own arrest in Nazi Germany, he had been instrumental in securing his release. In the spirit of mutuality, Dimitrov ought to reciprocate. Romain Rolland was flabbergasted that a man with Hartoch's "inoffensive politics" could be charged with a "serious inculpation of any action directed against the regime." Hartoch was probably being persecuted by the police or the network of Soviet informants, "compromised by suspect relations or by thoughtlessness and ignorance." Romain Rolland argued on humanitarian grounds, asking for detailed information about Dr. Hartoch, underscoring that Hartoch's sister was a personal friend. Moreover, the request was urgent because of the doctor's failing health. Without challenging the fairness or health of the Soviet judicial system, he advised the Soviet leadership to behave more empathically toward the close relatives of its victims, to "conciliate its rigor with a little pity for innocents (friends and parents) who suffer from the detention of the accused."[26] He never concluded that the political repression under Stalin represented a form of fascism on the left.

He was saddened by the Soviet policy of secrecy. Regardless of Moscow's treatment of individuals, Romain Rolland remained convinced that the general cause transcended specific injustices: "Moscow knows well that whatever is done with regard to my request, I will hold to my unbreakable affection for the USSR." Six weeks later, he wrote another letter to Thorez, expressing his irritation at Dimitrov's failure to answer. He interpreted communist silence as a personal slight, not an indirect admission of generalized guilt.

The absence of dialogue reflected "a lack of regard and a lack of humanity which hurts me cruelly." Soviet indifference to his human rights appeals did not alter his "deep loyalty to the great cause that we serve. It is infinitely above all individualities."[27]

In early March 1938, the German writer Hermann Hesse asked him to intercede for two "absolutely innocent" persons being persecuted in the Soviet Union. Hesse urged him to write directly to Stalin on behalf of the writer Karl Schumuckle and the economist Valy Adler, daughter of Alfred Adler.[28] Romain Rolland, in turn, lamented to Hesse that he was unable to secure the release of his own personal friends in Russia. Alluding to Oscar Hartoch, he mentioned having written to Stalin twice and to other prominent Soviet leaders. The result: not "one single word in answer." Since the beginning of the purges two years earlier, Romain Rolland's petitions for "a number of other arrested or disappeared men" were greeted with "silence." Consequently, his influence was probably negligible, especially on behalf of people he did not know. With uncharacteristic resignation, he admitted that his effectiveness had diminished to zero since Gorky's death: "The 'philosophes' (as they said in the time of Jean-Jacques) no longer matter to the masters of power."[29] The Communist International no longer cared whether it alienated its progressive noncommunist intellectuals. As far as communist relations with intellectuals went, the Popular Front period was over.

The announcement of the third show trial in Moscow with Bukharin, Rykov, and Yagoda as central figures caused Romain Rolland further anguish. Yet he did not break his public silence. In a letter to the French communist intellectual Jean-Richard Bloch he wrote that the "trial in Moscow is a torment." He predicted that the "effects in America and France would be damaging to the internal unity of the New Deal and to salvaging unity out of a deeply split Popular Front." Writing to the Marxist sociologist Georges Friedmann, he indicated his full awareness of Stalin's dictatorial policies. The purge trials extended Stalin's authoritarian style. Before speculating on the "reasons for Stalin's leadership cult," he acknowledged that the cult "has often angered me as it has angered you." Stalin's policies were an exaggerated, perhaps paranoid, reaction to the existence of a real conspiracy against his government. He was creating a "new icon" of himself, deliberately forcing it onto the minds of the Russian masses to protect himself "against the will of criminal attacks."[30]

These letters document that Romain Rolland knew much more about deformations of the Russian Revolution under Stalin than he stated in public. His appeals for compassion and pity from high-ranking Russian Communist leadership toward their innocent victims indicate his recognition of significant abuses within the Soviet system. He knew that Stalin, having consolidated power, was implementing a policy of terror. Yet as a European antifascist, he was not prepared to return to a position of critical support for the Soviet Union. The general emergency made it impossible to criticize Stalin's terror while remaining positive about other aspects of Soviet construction and agreeing with the Communist International's public record of antifascist activity and propaganda.

Sensing that his literary reputation and intellectual influence were eclipsed in France, especially as the French Popular Front moved toward collapse, Romain Rolland was exceptionally proud of the reception his works received in the Soviet Union. By November 1937, the Russians had published 1,300,000 copies of his literary works in translation, making him one of the most accessible French authors in the Soviet Union; he bragged that the "French language is read less in France than in foreign countries."[31]

Late in December 1937 he ended his twenty-four years of self-imposed exile in Villeneuve, Switzerland. He returned to the French provinces, not to Paris, reestablishing his roots in his own native soil, the countryside of his early childhood and boyhood. He purchased a "small but comfortable" house in Vézelay, a picturesque town perched in the sweet hilly countryside of Burgundy and known for its splendid Romanesque cathedral. He justified his move politically and symbolically, saying that he could no longer abide Swiss opportunism—the country seemed to be veering toward fascism—and that he wanted to demonstrate his solidarity with the declining French Popular Front. Suffering from intestinal and pulmonary illnesses, he left Switzerland because he could no longer "breathe free air" there, for the "contagion of the 'brown plague' or the 'black' has spread." France would be his final resting place. It represented the fragile legacy of freedom and the democratic possibilities of the Popular Front:

"My place is in the France of the Popular Front—and much more so now that it is threatened."[32]

In an open declaration on the front page of *L'Humanité*, entitled "The Mission of France in the World," he desperately called for a union of French writers, artists, and scientists against the fascist menace. The time for "prolonged dissension and internal combats" was over. Because France's "common welfare" was jeopardized, he urged progressive Frenchmen to "be silent on differences," that is, on conflicting interpretations of Soviet repression within the USSR, the French Popular Front, and the Spanish Civil War. He exhorted Popular Front France to remain the "last continental bastion of freedom." The Spanish Civil War proved that weakness in the face of fascism only made "the adversary arrogant and powerful." Antifascist intellectuals ought to emphasize consensus in this moment of dire crisis: "Let's call a truce to our disagreements."[33]

By the spring of 1938, Romain Rolland was disguising mixed feelings about French communism. He felt an affinity for the PCF's policies on foreign affairs and esteemed certain communist intellectuals and artists enormously. High on his list were Aragon, Paul Nizan, Jean-Richard Bloch, Paul Vaillant-Couturier, Georges Friedmann, Roger Garaudy, and Léon Moussinac. A true socialist society required the voluntary consent of intellectuals with the organized working class; it needed the "cooperation and harmony of its free individual forces." Significant tasks for the Marxist intellectuals remained for the future: "It is our true task as writers, following Marx, to disengage virilely the real man from the abstract man, and to lead him to the threshold of a reign of *true freedom*, by showing as Marx did, the coexistence, or the coincidence, of Communism with humanism."[34]

After the fall of the Spanish Republic, he was certain that Czechoslovakia would be the next target of fascist aggression. Western politicians appeared willing to sacrifice the territorial integrity of the Czechoslovakian nation in return for some diplomatic or political deal with the unscrupulous Nazis. In early September 1938, the French writer sent a telegram to British prime minister Neville Chamberlain and to French president Edouard Daladier, strenuously warning them against allowing the German fascists to occupy Czechoslovakia:

We are convinced . . . that the French and English governments must obtain immediately an accord among democratic powers, in order to prevent by rigorous concord and by energetic measures those criminal violations perpetrated by Hitler against Czechoslovakian independence and integrity, and consequently against European peace.[35]

French intellectual pacifists, led by the lyrical novelist Jean Giono, blasted Romain Rolland for his telegram. They countered with a telegram of their own to the democratic heads of state, laying bare his "lies." Giono, Alain, and Victor Margueritte exhorted Chamberlain and Daladier to negotiate with, not threaten, Hitler. The words "prevent . . . by energetic measures" signified war.[36] This open exchange was the epilogue to the *Comment empêcher la guerre?* debate of early 1936. Once again, French integral pacifists opposed integral antifascism and counseled appeasement with Germany. This debate would reverberate in Vichy France, when intellectuals and militants agonized over the choice between collaboration or resistance. Many of the integral pacifists would collaborate, at least passively. Many antifascists became both active and passive resisters.

On 29 September 1938, Daladier and Chamberlain signed the Munich Accords with Hitler. To deflate Chamberlain's declaration that the agreement meant "peace in our time" and to reverse Munich's numbing effect on internal French politics, Romain Rolland composed a rejoinder. Published on the front page of *L'Humanité*, its title summarized its contents: "The Munich 'Peace' Is a Degrading Capitulation." Appeasing Hitler only accelerated the momentum of fascist pride, greed and expansionism. Having gained leverage in central Europe, the Nazis would soon make France a target. The real losers in this false peace, besides the Czechs, were those committed to the idea of an antifascist France: "But if we all love and want peace, we must consider that the one of Munich is a degrading capitulation that furnishes new arms against France."[37]

After the Munich Accords and Hitler's provocative overtures toward Czechoslovakia, Romain Rolland reminded himself that the German fascists used anticommunism as a pretext to legitimize their plans for world conquest. Hitler blended anti-Semitism and anticommunism to justify his assault on the remnants of Popular Front coalitions and Western democracies. The Munich Accords demonstrated that the führer used manipulation and "heinous lies" to serve his own interests: "Hitler represents the democracies as 'Judeo-Communist'; he wants to kill them." As a student of German history and culture, Romain Rolland was seldom astonished by political developments there. Yet Hitler's excesses horrified him. He could not fathom the "facility with which German souls are taken by [Hitler's] combination of mysticism and violence. Hitler and the peoples following him are a formidable monster." This frenzy was particularly evident at the National Socialist mass rallies, where millions were hypnotized by the führer's "hallucinated personality," cruel oratory, and Wagnerian theatrics.[38]

After reviewing the various political disasters of the year, he dubbed 1938 a "year of mourning." Western democracies, particularly France, had to assume the burden of "shame and remorse" for both the "delivery" of Czechoslovakia to the German fascists and the "abandonment" of Spain to Franco. He considered worthy of praise the intervention in Spain by a "few, heroic volunteers," the fighters in the International Brigades, who risked life and limb for the Spanish Republic. The Popular Front was dead; he now promoted antifascism by emphasizing its nationalistic dimensions. "We know that on the earth of Spain, it is France they defended."[39]

Romain Rolland privately expressed his displeasure with the PCF's domestic policy in letters to general secretary Maurice Thorez. Thorez should prevent a "collision" between organized workers and the armed forces in a demonstration called for on 30 November 1938. Such a clash would weaken the unity of France and thereby benefit Hitler. Urging Thorez to end the Communist campaign of "furious exaggerations" and "verbal violence" against Daladier's government, he pointed out that this rhetoric only served the reaction. It smacked of self-defeat. The Communists would be labeled "antinational" in the French context. Although Daladier capitulated to German fascism in signing the Munich Accords, he was neither "a traitor nor a swindler," as the Communist press portrayed him. History would sufficiently admonish him for his miscalculation. The Communists, even if they were able to maintain an alliance with the Socialists, not a probability after Blum's second government collapsed, possessed neither the resources nor the power to sustain national unity. To safeguard the country's military and psychological readiness for war and to preserve the PCF as an autonomous party, he pressed Thorez to give the "example of discipline and sacrifices." Preserving democratic France was now identical with the "cause of international social-ism." Any other activity would result in "anarchy and confusion in which the enemy would profit." He closed his letter by sending his "respect and faith in the future to La Pasionaria."[40] Clearly, Romain Rolland's commitment to antifascism and to the Republican struggles in Spain and France far outstripped his endorsement of Thorez's parochial maneuverings.

Just as *L'Ame enchantée* explored the dimensions of critical support for communism in the early 1930s, the epic drama *Robespierre* addressed the ambiguities of uncritical support in the framework of the Moscow purge trials. This was Romain Rolland's last play and artistic summary, composed for his Theater of the Revolution cycle. He designed the play to be read, pondered, and interpreted rather than performed. It expressed his revised perceptions about a revolutionary upheaval that failed to live up to his mythical and humanistic hopes for it. *Robespierre* was a self-reflexive play without being apologetic or self-congratulatory. It did not offer an easy way out of the dilemmas of fellow traveling. In the preface, he admitted that he postponed writing it until he turned seventy-two. He was unable "to take possession of the subject" until the year 1938, when the parallels between France during the last months of the Terror and Russia during Stalin's purges were quite unmistakable.[41]

The play addressed three converging problems: the fatality of revolutionary action at a moment of crisis, the dilemmas of a complex revolutionary personality confronted with difficult options, and the assessment of a social revolution from a divided perspective of sympathy for the revolution's goals and revulsion at its systematic terror. In recreating the "moral truth" of the "hallucinated drama of the last months of the French Revolution," Romain Rolland was coming to terms with events in Stalin's Russia, which were equally "hallucinated" in the eyes of a moralist.[42] Although his uncritical fellow traveling took the form of public silence in the face of Stalin's aberrations, he explored his conscience about these events in this play. In a climate of suspicion and irrational frenzy, everything seemed possible, including the perversion of the specific ideals and accomplishments of a social revolution; a subtext of the play was the destruction of the idea of social revolution itself.

Romain Rolland's historical description of the summer of 1794 easily fit that of Russia 145 years later, in the period of the trials and the global ascendancy of fascism: "And the thousand and one daily suspended dangers of death—foreign wars, internal wars, invasions, conspiracies, assassination, mutual distrust—the illness of suspicion and the delirium of persecution."[43]

Napoleon once said that "politics is the modern fatality." Romain Rolland tragically interpreted that remark to embrace the dynamics of twentieth-century mass politics. Revolutionary leaders were compelled to make choices that honored or undermined a revolution. In *Robespierre,* the critical issue was how to save the Republic in a situation of unprecedented crisis. The play explored the problem of constructing the edifice of military dictatorship, dominated by a powerful but flawed leader, in order to preserve the revolution. Romain Rolland's characters refused this choice. Stalin accepted it. Instead of instituting a dictatorship, Robespierre persuaded his followers and adversaries with words. He was put to death. The revolution ended, its results remaining open to erosion and to interpretation. Revolutions created Manichean choices. Robespierre eliminated the centrist Danton and the extreme leftist Hébert in order to protect the Republic against its enemies, just as Stalin had purged Bukharin and Trotsky. Robespierre anchored his social and political philosophy in Enlightenment thought; Stalin in Marxism-Leninism. As a Jacobin, Robespierre was opposed to the domination of privilege. In order to realize his rational and progressive ideals, Robespierre adopted violent measures leading to unpredictable results. Lies, betrayals, accusations, and the guillotine were substituted for the decent aspirations of the Enlightenment.[44]

Romain Rolland had no intention of glorifying Robespierre. He presented a balanced portrait of Robespierre as the man who dominated the French Revolution. Thinking that he incarnated virtue, Robespierre pushed self-righteousness to extremes. He was tragically "isolated from the world." Robespierre refused to risk dictatorship to save the Republic, a decision pivoting on the notion of popular sovereignty. Robespierre's dedication to popular rights paralleled the contemporary struggle against fascism. Dictatorship equaled fascist forms of government (*les faisceaux de la dictature*).[45]

Stalin's purges illustrated the "delirium of persecution" as perti-
nently as the worst bloodbaths of the Terror. Stalin's European
contemporaries wondered how to justify Soviet crimes historically
in the name of the lofty goals and noble principles of socialist
humanism. Here Romain Rolland faltered: the purges were neither
socialist nor humanist. If historians were to judge these events,
they would have to be impartial and imaginative, not simply the
"servants of success."[46]

In spite of his good intentions, Robespierre performed real evil.
Romain Rolland, too, in sympathizing with the monumental Russian Revolution, refused to protest major acts of evil. The Terror,
counterposed against the reality of Stalin's purges, illustrated the
impossibility of maintaining the élan of social revolutions, of preventing the revolution from degenerating into crime or totalitarian
dictatorship. The politics of uncritical support for socialist revolutions by the artistic or intellectual community would be tarnished,
perhaps discredited, for another generation. The reality of a republic
that protected popular sovereignty and preserved human freedoms
was lost: "The Republic, the country [*patrie*], all is lost. All our hopes
in reason, in justice, in virtue. Humanity is condemned." The European fellow traveler observing the events in Soviet Russia expressed
deep anguish about the historical significance of events thus: "The
forces of circumstances have led us, perhaps, to results we had not
foreseen."[47]

Romain Rolland confessed to having been swept away by wishful
impulses. As a fellow traveler, he was overwhelmed by the logic of
revolutionary upheaval, transformed into an unwilling accomplice
to the crimes: "I have not sought to idealize them. I have spared
neither the ones their errors nor the others their faults. I, myself,
have been taken by the great wave that carried them. I have seen the
sincerity of all the men who exterminate themselves, and the terrible
fatality of Revolutions. It is not of *a* time. It is of all times."[48] The most
damaging fatality of revolution was the inevitable slide from idealism to extermination. The engaged intellectual was not immune
from this process of debasement. In *Robespierre* he questioned
whether his own humanistic form of engagement might be nullified
by the heinous results of Stalin's excesses. In Stalin's purge trials,
the European fellow traveler observed the destruction of an oceanic
feeling of community between intellectuals and manual workers;

this contact was twisted into the cynical expediency of dictatorial power politics, where individuals became numbers and where sensibility, consciousness, and morality were extinguished.

The literature on fellow traveling has been monographic or thematic. The case histories examine the particularities of a writer's fascination with communism; they draw no general or comparative conclusion.[49] The thematic scholars propose overarching theses: that fellow-traveling writers came to communism as a new form of religion; that their sympathies with communism demonstrated the potency of the liberal, enlightenment tradition; that communism legitimized their deep alienation from their own society and social class; or that communist commitment reflected profound self-deception (the last concludes that they were "guilty of fecklessness, dilettantism, arrogance").[50] Although there is some merit in each of these points of view, they tend to be decontextualized. They rob the intellectual in question of complexity and self-doubt. They reduce the problematic of fellow traveling by mixing critical analysis with condescension, self-righteousness, and downright hostility.

This account has elucidated Romain Rolland's fellow traveling by tracing its emergence from his itinerary of engaged stands. Fellow traveling cannot be comprehended outside of the specificities of the Popular Front era: it was historically relative, a reaction to cataclysmic events in the 1930s, above all the proliferation of fascist movements and the perceived inevitability of world war. In an era saturated with expansionist fascism, fellow traveling derived from a sober, defensive reassessment of European realities. It also recognized the improbabilities of a pacifist opposition to fascism, and the weakness of a conciliatory diplomatic approach to fascism by the European democracies and social democrats. Fascism could not be resisted without the firm resolve of the organized working class in Europe and without the military might of the Soviet Union. The collapse of the Republican cause in Spain powerfully illustrated what occurred if the antifascist élan could not be maintained in practice as well as in principle.

The most inexplicable aspects of Romain Rolland's fellow traveling were not his public statements in support of Soviet policies, the existing Soviet leadership, and ongoing projects of social planning. What was constructive in the USSR made the contrast with European paralysis more vivid. His statements on the emergence of a "new man," the practical wisdom of communist leadership, and the depths of the communist desire to defend culture seem hopelessly naive and wishful from a historical retrospect of fifty years. Yet this study has also documented his private doubts and disclaimers regarding Soviet Marxism and communist representatives in France, even in the most uncritical phase of his fellow traveling.

After making a career of conscientious protests, Romain Rolland neither endorsed nor criticized the most glaring communist excess of the era, the Moscow purge trials. It is not easy to reconcile committed writing and silence. Was this silence a betrayal of his own version of engagement? The fellow traveler refused to equate communism and fascism. He differentiated sharply between their governments, ideologies, leaders, and goals. To keep alive the hope of a Europe free from fascism, the fellow-traveling writer had to know when to keep silent, when public pronouncements no longer clarified issues, when protest might demoralize or divide the pockets of active resistance to fascism. Circumstance no longer permitted a critical, freewheeling dialogue within socialist and communist circles—no longer permitted the left-wing intellectual to remain tolerant, compassionate, irreverent, and free to infuse utopian ideas and artistic imagination into existing left movements. Romain Rolland's silence revealed his sense of desperation and mirrored the Manichean choices in an era of collapsing options. To purists, this silence may seem reactionary, even reprehensible—a collusion with atrocity, especially in someone who knew the concrete abuses and injustices perpetrated by the communists. Yet in the late 1930s, coinciding with the decline of the Popular Front, silence was a compromise consistent with an unyielding antifascism. The politics of uncritical fellow traveling corresponded to a historical juncture where debate and analysis could no longer illuminate individual and collective choice. Silence became a last resort, an attempt to maintain balance and lucidity, even if it implied an acquiescence toward communist dogma and tyranny.

Romain Rolland celebrated the one hundred fiftieth anniversary of the French Revolution in 1939 with an article called "The Necessity of Revolution." This was his last essay published in *Europe* during his lifetime. He contrasted the French revolutionary experience with the contemporary state of the European democracies, obliquely commenting on the current deformations of the Russian Revolution.

He set up the philosophical writings of Turgot and Condorcet and the Declaration of the Rights of Man and Citizen to argue the essential identity between revolutionary activity and the maturation of reason. Revolutionary militancy since 1789 proved a universal point: that people could make history rationally regardless of the obstacles in their way. Revolutionary upheavals marked humanity's consciousness of its own power to change the environment, underscoring the possibilities of coherent action in which "man takes possession of himself and the world." Revolutions, then, were points of departure that could "and *must* be surpassed." The health of the revolutionary process depended on a sovereign people who were allowed to "judge and revise freely" the principles of any government. Twentieth-century social revolution created a disparity between free reason and revolutionary construction directed from above. Elliptically referring to the Soviet Union, he alleged that a "fearful distrust" of reason produced a kind of "bodyguard" that enclosed the revolution within narrow parameters. The revolution, rather than being the "protector," became a prisoner within its own confines, masochistically turning on itself, fearing dialogue, crushing dissent.[51] By inference, the Stalinist phase of the purge had pushed the Russian Revolution in an irrational direction.

To prevent "criminal usurpation" by a revolutionary regime, the people needed full freedom of inquiry and complete access to information. An educated populace served as a corrective to revolutionary centralization. The government must be accountable, "the principles and rules of government submitted to the free examination of every citizen."[52] Civil liberties and political rights were absent in Stalin's Russia. Romain Rolland preferred Popular Front–style governments to Stalin's dictatorship of the proletariat and his domestic network of terror; but the Popular Front had failed, leaving a major political and cultural void.

Aware that Europe was caught in the "snares of lying dictatorships that support ignorance and delirium," he proclaimed the necessity for a revolution that would bring to fruition the initiatives started in 1789. He no longer had the Soviet model in mind. All revolutionary achievements were regressions unless the three goals of Condorcet's *Credo* were fulfilled: "Destruction of inequality between nations; progress of equality in a people itself; and finally, the perfectability of man."[53] Romain Rolland's enlightened, populist

internationalism hardly tallied with Stalin's "socialism in one country" in 1939.

On 23 August 1939, the Soviet Union and fascist Germany
signed a pact of nonaggression. The unexpected news of the Nazi-
Soviet Pact struck like a lightning bolt in the community of French
communist intellectuals and fellow travelers. Though not all the
terms were clarified until the Russian invasion of Finland in the
winter of 1939–1940, the pact wreaked havoc among the members
of the French intellectual left. For Romain Rolland, the alliance of
Hitler and Stalin created more difficulties than the purges: it called
into question his twelve years of friendship with the Soviet Union.
His own analysis of fascism, coupled with politicized antifascist
activities, had cemented his ties with the French communists and
the Comintern. The Nazi-Soviet Pact forced him to rethink his
decision to choose between uncritical fellow traveling and antifascism. Now that the two irreconcilable enemies and divergent ideological systems made a diplomatic alliance, he could either denounce the pact publicly, voicing his considerable reservations
about domestic Soviet policies and foreign affairs, or he could remain silent. Silence seemed to be the lesser of evils, even though
he felt that the Soviets had broken faith with antifascism and betrayed the interests of international communism. The communists
abandoned the Western democracies at the critical moment when a
military confrontation with fascism was inevitable.

The Nazi-Soviet Pact snuffed out Romain Rolland's last hopes
for a French interclass unity and for an equalitarian internationalism. The "Ring of Peace" had been smashed by the Russian communists themselves. He wrote Jean Cassou, editor of *Europe,* to indicate his awareness of the "sorrowful disarray" among the editorial
board of the review. Fellow-traveling writers such as René Lalou
and Luc Durtain reacted to the pact by publishing violent protests
and resigning from *Europe.* Communist writers such as Bloch and
Aragon published "absurdly obstinate" pieces that cynically defended the realism of the German-Russian alliance. In view of this
confusion, Romain Rolland agreed with Cassou that *Europe* should
temporarily suspend publication.[54] The major Rollandist journal of
the interwar years ceased to exist until after the Second World War.

He praised Cassou for his "just moderation" and contrasted it
with the "violent panic" of Lalou and Durtain and the "desperate

acceptance" of Bloch and Aragon. Rather than precipitate further schisms in the editorial board, Romain Rolland urged a "momentary retreat." Massive disillusionment with the USSR or toeing the party line were now beside the point. Every statement and accusation would be emotionally "exploited by different points of view." Silence was justified when polemics no longer clarified the issues: "We must wait and be silent until events slacken a little in the crisis."[55]

However, after "reading and meditating on the text of the Pact," and especially after learning that the Soviet Union forced the rupture of the British-French-Soviet diplomatic conference, he "addressed his resignation to the Association of the Friends of the Soviet Union." This symbolic act was done privately because he did not want his resignation to be "brutally exploited by the adversaries of the Soviet Union." The association ought to be dissolved because it had "no cause to exist now under its present form."[56] This quiet gesture ended Romain Rolland's engagement as a fellow-traveling intellectual.

The Russians, he conjectured, accepted the pact for "political reasons" or because of a Nazi "imperative" or "ultimatum." The Soviet Union had "gravely failed in its duties in this conflict." The Soviet diplomatic alliance with the fascists simultaneously betrayed the Western democracies and dishonored the Communist International. The former were left isolated and weakened against the fascist threat. The Soviet Communist Party "sacrificed" the loyal parties of France, Great Britain, and other countries. European communists would be tainted with "suspicion" and subjected to the "vengeance of the reaction." The Nazi-Soviet Pact might ultimately be assessed as a "horrible political blunder," or an "error," despite its Machiavellian designs. Whatever the pragmatic explanation for this alliance, he judged that it would "remain unpardonable."[57]

His disillusionment with the Nazi-Soviet Pact was not a temporary sentiment or a brief explosion of rage. He shared Georges Friedmann's "reaction" to it as a "double blow": it "had broken the confidence and faith" of nonfascist European countries and shocked non-Soviet communists and fellow travelers around the world. Counseling Friedmann against "unnecessary passion and weakness" with regard to the pact, he justified his own silence about

Soviet complicity with German fascism. If they were among the "first and most tenacious" opponents of fascism, they knew that one overwhelming responsibility remained: "Union in combat against Hitlerism." Although the pact shifted the international balance of power, he asserted bitterly, "it is not we who have changed." Despite the communists' reversal of their policies, antifascist French intellectuals ought to unite their shrunken ranks in order to prepare the all-out fight against fascism. In waging this battle, he exclaimed, "combatants of the mind have one other duty: lucidity."[58]

Romain Rolland wrote a public letter to President Daladier affirming his absolute antifascism, even after the withdrawal of the Soviet Union from an alliance with European countries. His unalterable opposition to fascism transcended his fellow-traveling activities, remaining at the root of his intellectual politics in the 1930s. His desire to liquidate fascism was linked to his commitment to democracy and civil liberties:

> In these decisive days when the French Republic rises to bar the road to Hitler's tyranny, which is flooding Europe, permit an old fighter for peace—who always denounced barbarism, perfidiousness, and the unbridled ambition of the Third Reich—to express to you my complete devotion to the cause of the democracies, of France and the world, in such danger today.[59]

He responded to Hitler's invasion of Poland on 1 September 1939 and to the subsequent declaration of war with characteristic equanimity. Europe was being "delivered over to monsters." He reappraised his thirteen-year antifascist campaign as a failure. In these circumstances, despair and defeatism were inappropriate reactions. It was crucial "to maintain a firm and clear mind."[60] With absolute power invested in Hitler and now unleashed in war, he expected the most terrible devastation: "Hitler is a half-mad somnambulist who thinks himself inspired and whose imagination has been deformed by poorly digested false (racist) science and by Wagner's extravagances." National Socialism meant "war, destruction, and . . . degradation": only military combat could wipe out German fascism.[61]

Overcoming the Nazis remained the focus of his intellectual politics from 1939 until his death on 30 December 1944. Until the German fascists were defeated, their ideology discredited, and political methods dismantled, no work toward democratic socialist reconstruction could be completed:

> I believe that all efforts of every Frenchman should converge from this moment on toward this chief if not exclusive goal: the total elimination of German fascism. *Delenda est.* After, one can discuss [other things]. But first, crush the monster. This is a question of life and death. I have never varied on that.[62]

It was in this pessimistic mood, but with the spirit of lucid antifascism, that Romain Rolland prepared himself for the ordeal of total war in the winter of 1939.

Conclusion:
Pessimism of the Intelligence,
Optimism of the Will

> What I especially love . . . is this intimate alliance—which
> for me makes the true man—of pessimism of the intelli-
> gence, which penetrates every illusion, and optimism of the
> will. It is this natural bravery that is the flower of a good
> people, which "does not need to hope to undertake and to
> succeed to persevere," but which lives in struggle over and
> above suffering, doubt, and the blasts of nothingness be-
> cause his fiery life is the negation of death. And because his
> doubt itself, the French "What do I know?" becomes the
> weapon of hope, barring the road to discouragement and
> saying to his dreams of action and revolution: "Why not?"
>
> Romain Rolland, review of
> R. Lefebvre's *The Sacrifice of Abraham*

When Britain and France declared war on Germany on 3 September 1939, Romain Rolland was seventy-three years old. He lived in
Vézelay and occasionally traveled to his Left Bank apartment on 89,
boulevard du Montparnasse to conduct literary business or to consult with a physician about his failing health. The "phony war" in
France lasted six weeks, from 10 May until 25 June 1940. France's
defeat and the fall of the Third Republic were followed by Nazi
occupation and the "phony regime" of Vichy France, in which
Pétain and his entourage collaborated with the German fascists and
took their revenge on the French Popular Front. Consistent with
his mature intellectual politics of the 1930s, Romain Rolland remained unalterably antifascist. He regarded the era as reflecting
"the tidal wave threat of the barbarous tyranny of Hitler's Third
Reich."[1]

His final years were marked by chronic illnesses of the heart,
lungs, intestines, and eyes. Problems of everyday life were exacerbated by difficulties in walking and breathing, lack of food, anxi-
eties about the sales of his books, intellectual isolation, and separation from friends and acquaintances. Many of his closest colleagues

did not survive the Second World War. In 1942, he learned of the suicide of his Viennese translator and biographer, Stefan Zweig, who was unable to tolerate the horrors of exile, total war, and the shattering of the Europe of his youth. Romain Rolland and his wife were deeply concerned about the safety of his Russian stepson, Serge Koudachef, who was fighting in the Russian Army, and who was later killed in action.[2] Living in solitude in Occupied France severely taxed the elderly writer's inner resources. It appeared that his idealism had been useless, that the ensemble of his campaigns for humanitarian, political, and cultural causes had failed miserably. Yet he remained cautiously optimistic about his ideals and about the future.

Well-meaning friends urged him to leave France and seek shelter in the United States. He felt too old and disabled, and too culturally distant from America, to uproot himself. As his economic situation worsened, he anticipated royalties from American translations of his *Memoirs* and his multivolume *Beethoven*. Undoubtedly, his life was extended by the tireless aid and tenderness of his wife, Marie Romain Rolland, who nursed him, kept visitors and informers away, and provided invaluable administrative and secretarial services to him. Blurring the line between personal and political and social history, he characterized the era of Vichy France as the "weary, dark, somber years of moral oppression and illness."[3]

Unable to participate in meaningful resistance, he restricted his activities to literary creation. As in other tormented periods of his life, writing became a source of consolation and revitalization. Rather than be overwhelmed by the bigotry, conservatism, and mindless clerical nationalism of Vichy France, he worked, retaining a "serene soul and clear mind."[4] Because the present was so dreadful, he looked back to the past, including the period of his own intellectual apprenticeship, taking courage from the moral stature of his earliest cultural heroes. During this period, he completed the final volumes of his massive *Beethoven*. In 1943, he finished both *The Ninth Symphony* and *The Last Quartets*.[5] No better contrast could be made between the two Germanys: Hitler's cruel vision of Aryan purity and global conquest against Beethoven's vision of fraternity and creative joy. Reflecting on Beethoven's last years and hearing his glorious music were an escape from the bleak conditions of Occupied France. The biography was an extended meditation on musical genius and on the historical and psychological components of the composer's imagination. It explored the strength of will that enabled Beethoven to overcome personal obstacles to produce sublime, life-affirming works of art. Romain Rolland managed to conclude his oeuvre with a literary masterpiece, a two-volume biography of Charles Péguy, in whose independent journal he had published his earliest engaged writing at the beginning of the century. *Péguy* contained much autobiographical data, but it was, above all, a "moral portrait" underscoring the subject's "independent faith and passion for freedom."[6]

Romain Rolland's age and infirmities kept him from active opposition to the Nazis and the Vichy government, but he was in solidarity with the French Resistance movement. Given his public political commitments in the 1930s, Vichy France authorities considered him dangerous. They labeled him, pejoratively, an "antifascist." The Vichy police monitored his house, opened his correspondence, spread rumors, and assembled data in a classified dossier. The harmless old man of French letters was a ready target for police intrusion, even for persecution. The gendarmerie was located across the street from his residence, and surveillance was relatively easy. Marie Romain Rolland feared that his arrest or assassination was a distinct possibility. Not until influential Parisian friends interceded did the zealous Vichyite subprefect back off from petty but potentially injurious harassment. *Jean-Christophe* was placed on the index of books banned by Vichy's state secretary of public instruction in February 1941.[7] It was alleged to corrupt French adolescents. An abridged version was removed from the educational syllabus in the French national school system. Attentive to the cultural politics of repressive states, Romain Rolland held Vichy authorities accountable for this act of censorship and intellectual terrorism: "It is its fashion of practicing the politics of collaboration."[8]

He wrote letters to a young member of the French Resistance, Elie Walach, a Jew born in Poland in 1921, who had emigrated to France in 1929 and been recruited into the communist Resistance. Walach's early membership was exceptional. The majority of French communists became active in the Resistance only after June 1941, following the Nazi invasion of the Soviet Union. For the French writer, Walach represented the "ardor and spontaneity" of the antifascist Resistance movement. Walach joined the Resistance on 1 March 1940 and was captured by Vichy authorities on 27 February 1941. He was imprisoned, interrogated, and tortured for months without disclosing information; he was finally murdered on 27 July 1941.[9]

Romain Rolland's first letter to Walach articulated their shared, uncompromising antifascist sentiments. He did not, however, exaggerate the impact of intellectual opposition in these extreme circumstances. Such claims would have been grandiose and disrespectful of the concrete dangers of those actively resisting, whose lives were on the line. He recognized the need for a collective, military assault on fascism:

> Those of us [alive] today when the word cannot be of significance . . . can only be brave and patient and lead in common the combat against Hitlerism, until it is vanquished. For if it is not, all that we love and respect will perish: our France, our freedoms, and our great hopes. Hitler must be vanquished.[10]

Romain Rolland predicted that world war and Vichy France's Catholic and nationalistic bigotry, including its horrific policies toward Jews, workers, and intellectuals, would be transient phenomena. Police states run by narrow-minded, reactionary oligarchies were destined for short historical duration. He persisted in believing that hatred among people and nations could be overcome and that the eventual reconciliation of humanity might still occur. Fascism had to be obliterated for that hope to germinate. He would neither live to see these ideals realized nor witness a regenerated France forge the "victory of the human spirit" out of the ruins of the Occupation.[11]

He was inspired by the young, activist intellectuals of the French Resistance, particularly those steeled in the underground. Their words and deeds eloquently testified to a minority's will to fight degradation. This new breed of French intellectual might continue the tradition of intellectual engagement he had participated in, legitimized, indeed partly invented. He clearly felt that his style of commitment, fusing morality and politics, was being passed on to the generation of the Resistance, which gradually took on the form and content of politicized engagement and was a powerful impetus toward social and cultural renewal: "And in the clandestine literature and in the liberated press, one has already heard great voices— young and moving, for the most part. I have trust."[12]

In August 1944, Paris was liberated and the end of European hostilities seemed near. Charles de Gaulle received a kind of popular coronation in Paris on 26 August 1944. As an epilogue to a career of intellectual politics, Romain Rolland's last article warmly endorsed the engaged writers emerging historically from the Resistance. His commemoration of intellectuals killed by the German Occupation or by French collaboration was read in his absence at the Sorbonne on 9 December 1944. He established a continuity between the left-wing and antifascist politics of the 1930s and the Resistance politics of the early 1940s. The moral and political awakening among the intellectual youth of France in the period between the two wars reached its climax during the Occupation. Resistance intellectuals came from diverse classes, regions, and political, religious, and ideological backgrounds. Their common denominators were purity, generosity, a capacity for sacrifice, and above all an antifascist passion. This new generation of insurgents and their heirs represented France's profound mission in the world, namely, to overcome passivity in fighting to defend human freedom: "Each of the young deaths has affirmed the life and victory of France and Freedom."[13]

Romain Rolland last appeared in public at the Russian Embassy in Paris on 7 November 1944. He expressed skepticism about having accomplished his role as an engaged writer. These self-doubts were perhaps connected to the Russian setting, where he was obligated to maintain his tact, or to his bad conscience for not having spoken out about deformations in Soviet communism during the late 1930s. His theme on that occasion in 1944 was the writer, self-disclosure, and the connection to the reader: a characteristic Rollandist preoccupation and one of the central problems in the conception of engaged literature. Respecting his audience's need for hope, he admitted that he had remained silent at various "moments," despite reflection on and knowledge of the issues: "Even in his Diary, even in his Memoirs, there are things he must be silent on. . . . A writer cannot expose himself completely. . . . And yet I am one of those who will have confided the most."[14]

Romain Rolland died in Vézelay on 30 December 1944. He was seventy-nine years old. One last episode of impassioned debate surrounded him. He was the first celebrated man of French letters to die after France's liberation. The choice of a final resting place became a battle among leading Parisian writers; intellectual politics extended to burial. Several distinguished writers launched a journalistic campaign to have his ashes transferred to the Panthéon. Aragon, among others, vociferously rallied communist and left-wing opinion. The cry was *"Romain Rolland au Panthéon!"* He deserved this honor, Aragon asserted, because he was "the symbol of the *Sacred Union against Fascism and for France.*" As the left lobbied for this official recognition by the French state, they were answered by the center and the post-1945 new right. Jérôme Tharaud, writing in *Le Figaro*, demanded that Péguy's ashes be transferred to the Panthéon alongside Romain Rolland's. (No mention was made of the fact that Péguy died in 1914.) Tharaud's desire, read between the lines, was to balance Romain Rolland's internationalism, pacifism, cosmopolitanism, antifascism, and fellow traveling with Péguy's Catholicism, his reassuring mysticism, and his amorous feelings for France. To complicate matters further, and perhaps to ensure a stalemate, the Catholic philosopher Gabriel Marcel and the Gaullist Maurice Schumann insisted that Henri Bergson, who had died in 1941, also belonged in the Panthéon. They maintained that the ashes of two such fin de siècle vitalists as Romain Rolland and Péguy should not be placed there without those of the author of *Creative Evolution.*[15]

The public struggle over Romain Rolland's corpse was a signal of the beginning of the post–World War II realignment in France and the emergence of Cold War politics. The episode marked the end of a temporary period of Resistance unity, which stemmed from opposition to the common enemy. Once that enemy disappeared, the death of an eminent but controversial writer unleashed new ideological battles in the context of French intellectual politics.

Appropriately, Romain Rolland's posthumous testament effectively ended the debate: his wish was to be buried quietly, nonreligiously, and privately in Burgundy, next to the graves of his parents in Clamecy.[16]

Romain Rolland can be viewed as the key transitional figure in the history of engaged French intellectuals. His mature life as a writer practically spanned the time between Zola's Dreyfusard "J'accuse"

(1898) and Sartre's existential formulations about engagement in *What Is Literature?* (1947). He lived through and reflected on every major crisis of the Third Republic. He witnessed France's decline from a global to a peripheral power. In that fifty-year period, he not only named his form of activism *"engagement"* but also entered into periodic dialogue with other intellectuals about it. He personally laid the foundation for intellectual engagement, its possibilities, and its contradictions. Both his adventures with commitment and his self-criticism legitimized the committed style. His life and work demonstrated that twentieth-century writers need not retreat from political reality or ideological involvements.

Methodologically, I have situated Romain Rolland's intellectual politics by placing his writings into their proper historical framework. He belonged to an era quite unlike our own, although his cultural and political interrogations are pertinent. All of his work questioned what it meant to be an intellectual. He trafficked in ideas, spoke out on controversial issues, and allowed himself to be transformed by contemporary history. Romain Rolland belonged to the nineteenth century in that he aspired to be an exemplary intellectual, maintaining an elevated notion of intellectual responsibility. He lived in the present but was profoundly rooted in the culture and politics of the past. He developed a taste for puncturing hypocrisy, unmasking lies, and decoding mystifications. False idealism always represented to him the most dangerous cultural force. He demonstrated an equal taste for cultural preservation and affirmation. He regarded himself as a fixed point for others to follow, but always with humility and with the notion that he was continually in process, evolving and rethinking his earlier positions. This book has mapped out an itinerary of distinctly twentieth-century engaged stands, not dramatic conversions without mediations. In this sense, engagement modified engagement: one commitment in context became a frame of reference and a springboard for advance or regression. There were definite periods of partial to total disengagement and introspection. Disengagement was also part of the dialectic.

Romain Rolland assumed a prophetic voice because he intuited patterns in human behavior and understood the tragedy of historical repetition. If history repeated itself without human knowledge, people would never gain mastery over their own lives. He realized most of his contemporaries were emotionally and intellectually unprepared to hear his message. He was a moralist who concerned himself with universal issues, who linked a particular abuse to all-encompassing principles; one example of cruelty reverberated for all of humanity. He advanced a totalizing but tragic view of the individual in society based on the novelist's technique of critical realism. His oceanic sensibility allowed him to feel an intimate contact with other human beings who struggled. At moments, he felt indissolubly merged with them into a larger whole. The oceanic feeling existed alongside his analytical faculties. It enabled him to transcend the boundaries of language, ethnicity, history, and culture. The oceanic sense was never anti-intellectual, but it distrusted critical intelligence stripped of visceral emotions, devoid of compassionate understanding for human suffering.

Romain Rolland aspired to express his moral views with courage, regardless of the receptivity of his audience. Rarely shrill, often polemical, but always courteous, he occasionally became sentimental and self-righteous about his own ethical stance. Yet he fully realized the limitations of conscience in a field dominated by political, economic, social, or military power. If appeals to conscience were futile, if articulating the grievances of history's victims meant defending lost causes, he persisted nevertheless with the conviction that potential openings could be discovered among those in power or those who were destined to come to power. Protest and subsequent politicized resistance might make the masters of power ill at ease.

There was a dialectic of intellectual engagement in his career, summed up elegantly in the phrase "Pessimism of the intelligence, optimism of the will." In positing a necessary tension between pessimism and optimism, intelligence and will, thinking and revolution, he sharply distinguished the committed writer from his disengaged contemporaries. The loss of tension unbalanced the writer's tenuous situation at the interface of politics and culture, where power relations and cultural production intersected and critical analysis was always difficult. Pessimism of the intelligence meant being able to see glaring, as well as subterranean, sources of misery and to uncover those relationships in the present that worked against human dignity and fulfillment.

Optimism of the will was a leap into action that enabled the engaged writer to struggle for hopeless causes and to resist co-optation and the status with which modern societies rewarded illustrious writers. It affirmed renewal even in the face of chaos and devastation. In Romain Rolland's case, it may have involved a willful rechanneling of aggressive energies into culturally sanctioned modes of behavior.

The dialectic "Pessimism of the intelligence, optimism of the will" implicitly acknowledged every person's right to choose to be an intellectual. An intellectual life was open to the possibilities of reflection and self-reflection. It granted the individual an active and critical connection to the community. To be an engaged intellectual, as Sartre brilliantly formulated it, was to be aware that one was already engaged, that one's life was contemporaneous by necessity. Engagement encouraged intellectuals to use their knowledge, historical consciousness, imagination, and emotion to make responsible choices in the present, as well as to pass on a cultural legacy.

Romain Rolland was both an exponent and practitioner of *littérature engagée*. He applied it experimentally in novels, plays, biographies, essays, journalistic pieces, protests, appeals, manifestos, and also in his private correspondence and diaries. Writing was a means of igniting his audience to create a society that would guarantee human rights without the alienating aspects of class, caste, nationalism, militarism, or privilege. No society was truly free unless *esprit*, that untranslatable French noun meaning mind, spirit, soul, wit, and sensibility, was expressed by every individual in a spontaneous and self-determining manner. The engaged writer viewed reflection as a form of action. Those who reflected were enjoined to revise their analyses in the light of changing circumstances. Engaged writers took full responsibility for their writings and their actions: no alibis, no excuses, no self-deception. The reciprocity of the writer and reader was the paradigm for radical social change and authentic dialogue. The engaged intellectual understood the implicit power of words to inspire and transform readers. Words informed, relaxed, and consoled, while tapping into the deepest strivings of the human soul. Engaged writings were mediations, transferring energy between texts and audience.

Once the engaged writer became more involved in political activity, writing took on new parameters and encountered new limitations. Romain Rolland was at times confronted with impossible choices. His commitment was simultaneously to social revolution and to democratic freedoms, including intellectual independence. In revolutionary crises, as the Soviet Union illustrated in the late 1930s, it was often impossible to salvage both the socialist revolution and the guarantee of individual human rights. Nothing he could say or do would shift the momentum of the revolution's slide toward tyranny. This dilemma forced him to maintain his sympathies for socialist revolution while remaining outside the French Communist Party, the Communist International, and all other left-wing political parties and social movements.

In his reflections on the world wars, social revolutions, counter-revolutions, and the massive social and economic dislocations of his era, Romain Rolland developed a new intellectual style, formulating a language of engagement that combined the negative and the positive. The negative emphasized lucidity, the writer's need to be analytical and in sharp antagonism to anti-intellectual, antiprogressive, and antidemocratic forces. He negated political and cultural values that denied the oppressed an opportunity to develop their mental and emotional lives. Engagement was a powerful way of rebelling against the embourgeoisement, bureaucratization, and professionalization of French intellectual life. He also criticized those aspects of socialist and Marxist orthodoxy that stifled the imagination, worked against dialogue, and trampled on human rights. The engaged writer reflected on himself while contesting specific grievances within the larger framework. One single abuse, one known injustice, resonated for all people. The key unit of discourse was always humanity. The positive was expressed as a sensation of fusion, of the potent mutuality and freedom implicit in human contact. Romain Rolland described this deep sense of oneness with the environment and with other individuals as "oceanic." Oceanic optimism gave him a sense of purpose and meaning, even in defeat, and reminded him, particularly in adverse circumstances, that people could make and comprehend their own history.

The writer's existence in the twentieth century was anomalous. Writers consumed while not producing. No price could be placed on them, no value assigned to their activities. But the engaged writer was not simply an articulate impostor on the stage of history. Romain Rolland's tragic vision transcended static nineteenth-century values such as honor, genius, virtue, and courage. He could synthesize in a single passage the idealism of William of Orange, the doubts of Montaigne, and the activist fervor of the French Revolution. As an engaged writer, he kept toleration, self-reflexive knowledge, and the will to change the world in dialectical relation to one another. "Pessimism of the intelligence, optimism of the will" was his legacy to this century. That dialectical blend of negative and positive, realism and idealism, self-knowledge and self-affirmation, linked to a mature historical sense of the possibilities of a rationally organized social community, allows the writer to act, to mediate, to contest, and to dream all at the same time.

Notes

The following abbreviations have been used in the notes:

ARR   Archives Romain Rolland, Paris.

BV   *Un Beau Visage à tous sens. Choix de lettres de Romain Rolland (1886–1944)* (Paris, 1967).

G-RR   *Gandhi et Romain Rolland. Correspondance, extraits du Journal et textes divers* (Paris, 1969). Translated into English as *Romain Rolland and Gandhi Correspondence* (New Delhi, 1976), trans. R. A. Francis.

HH-RR   *D'une rive à l'autre. Hermann Hesse et Romain Rolland. Correspondance et fragments du Journal* (Paris, 1972).

JAG   Romain Rolland, *Journal des années de guerre* (Paris, 1952).

JG-RR   *L'Indépendance de l'esprit. Correspondance entre Jean Guéhenno et Romain Rolland* (Paris, 1975).

JRB-RR   *Deux Hommes se rencontrent. Correspondance entre Jean-Richard Bloch et Romain Rolland (1910–1918)* (Paris, 1964).

LG-RR   *Correspondance entre Louis Gillet et Romain Rolland* (Paris, 1949).

PRP   Romain Rolland, *Par la révolution, la paix* (Paris, 1935).

QAC   Romain Rolland, *Quinze Ans de combat* (Paris, 1935). Translated into English as *I Will Not Rest* (New York [1935]), trans. K. S. Shelvankar.

RR-MvM   *Choix de lettres à Malwida von Meysenbug* (Paris, 1948).

RR-SBGG (1959)   *Chère Sofia. Choix de lettres de Romain Rolland à Sofia Bertolini Guerrieri-Gonzaga (1901–1908)* (Paris, 1959).

RR-SBGG (1960)   *Chère Sofia. Choix de lettres de Romain Rolland à Sofia Bertolini Guerrieri-Gonzaga (1909–1932)* (Paris, 1960).

RT-RR   *Rabindranath Tagore et Romain Rolland. Lettres et autres écrits* (Paris, 1961).

CHAPTER 1

1. For more theoretical studies, see Philip Rieff, ed., *On Intellectuals* (New York, 1969); Lewis A. Coser, *Men of Ideas: A Sociologist's View* (New

York, 1970); Alvin W. Gouldner, *The Future of Intellectuals and the Rise of the New Class* (New York, 1979).

2. Theodore Zeldin, *The French* (New York, 1982), 394–413, also see Theodore Zeldin, *France, 1848–1945*, 2 vols. (Oxford, 1977), 2:243–345. Régis Debray, *Teachers, Writers, Celebrities: The Intellectuals of Modern France*, trans. David Macey (London, 1981), 39–94. Raymond Aron, *The Opium of the Intellectuals*, trans. Terence Kilmartin (New York, 1962), 203–324; J. E. Flower, *Writers and Politics in Modern France, 1909–1961* (New York, 1977). Michel Foucault, "Truth and Power," in *Power/Knowledge: Selected Interviews and Other Writings, 1972–1977*, ed. Colin Gordon (New York, 1980), 127–133.

3. See George L. Mosse, "Fascism and the Intellectuals," in *The Nature of Fascism*, ed. S. J. Woolf (New York, 1969), 205–225; Robert Soucy, *Fascism in France: The Case of Maurice Barrès* (Berkeley, Calif. 1972); and Zeev Sternhell, *Maurice Barrès et le nationalisme français* (Paris, 1972).

4. Michel Winock, *Histoire politique de la revue "Esprit," 1930–1950* (Paris, 1975); J.-L. Loubet del Bayle, *Les Non-conformistes des années 30* (Paris, 1969).

5. Daniel Guérin, *Ni Dieu ni maître: Histoire et anthologie de l'anarchisme*, 2 vols. (Lausanne, 1969); Jean Maitron, *Histoire du mouvement anarchiste en France* (Paris, 1955).

6. David L. Schalk, *The Spectrum of Political Engagement* (Princeton, N.J., 1979), 3–25.

7. Jean-Paul Sartre, *Sartre by Himself*, trans. Richard Seaver (New York, 1978), 63.

8. Micheline Tison-Braun, *La Crise de l'humanisme*, 2 vols. (Paris, 1958, 1967), 1:463–502; 2:54–58, 168–171, 257–271.

9. H. Stuart Hughes, *Consciousness and Society* (New York, 1958); George L. Mosse, *The Culture of Western Europe* (New York, 1961); Wilson H. Coates and Hayden V. White, *The Ordeal of Liberal Humanism* (New York, 1970), vol. 2.

10. Julien Benda, *The Treason of the Intellectuals*, trans. Richard Aldington (New York, 1969); David L. Schalk, *Spectrum of Political Engagement*, 26–48.

11. Jean-Paul Sartre, *What Is Literature?* trans. Bernard Frechtman (New York, 1965).

CHAPTER 2

1. Sigmund Freud, *Civilization and Its Discontents*, in *The Complete Psychological Works of Sigmund Freud*, standard ed., trans. James Strachey, 24 vols. (London, 1953–1974) (hereinafter cited as *Standard Edition*), 21:64.

2. Ibid.; Sigmund Freud, "A Disturbance of Memory on the Acropolis: An Open Letter to Romain Rolland on the Occasion of His Seventieth Birthday" (1936), *Standard Edition* 22:238, 248.

3. Letters from Sigmund Freud to Rolland, 4 March 1923, 29 January 1926, 13 May 1926; Freud to Victor Wittkowski, 6 January 1936, in *Letters of Sigmund Freud, 1873–1939*, trans. Tania Stern and James Stern (London, 1970), 346, 365, 371, 423.

4. David James Fisher, "Reading Freud's *Civilization and Its Discon-*

tents," in *Modern European Intellectual History: Reappraisals and New Perspectives,* ed. Dominick LaCapra and Steven L. Kaplan (Ithaca, N.Y., 1982), 251–279; David James Fisher, "Sigmund Freud and Romain Rolland: The Terrestrial Animal and His Great Oceanic Friend," *American Imago* 33 (Spring 1976): 1–59; David S. Werman, "Sigmund Freud and Romain Rolland," *International Review of Psycho-Analysis* 4 (1977): 225–242; Jeffrey Moussaieff Masson, *The Oceanic Feeling: The Origins of Religious Sentiment in Ancient India* (Dordrecht, 1980), 33–50.

5. Letter from Rolland to Freud, 5 December 1927, *BV,* 264–266.

6. Letter from Freud to Rolland, 14 July 1929, *Letters of Sigmund Freud,* 388.

7. Freud, *Civilization and Its Discontents, Standard Edition* 22:68.

8. Letter from Freud to Rolland, 19 January 1930, *Letters of Sigmund Freud,* 392–393.

9. Romain Rolland, *The Life of Ramakrishna,* trans. E. F. Malcolm-Smith (Calcutta, 1970), 6–7; this first appeared as *Essai sur la mystique et l'action de l'Inde vivante. La Vie de Ramakrishna* (Paris, 1929).

10. Romain Rolland, *Le Voyage intérieur (Songe d'une vie)* (Paris, 1959), 19–26, 40; William T. Starr, *Romain Rolland: One Against All* (The Hague, 1971), 11–21; Stefan Zweig, *Romain Rolland: The Man and His Work* (1921; New York, 1972), 3–7; Ronald A. Wilson, *The Pre-War Biographies of Romain Rolland* (1939; New York, 1972), 1–5.

11. Rolland, *Voyage intérieur,* 139–173; Starr, *Romain Rolland,* 33–44; Wilson, *Pre-War Biographies,* 21–26; Zweig, *Romain Rolland,* 23–31; René Cheval, *Romain Rolland, l'Allemagne et la guerre* (Paris, 1963), 94–116.

12. Letter from Rainer Maria Rilke to Princess Marie von Thurn und Taxis-Hohenlohe, 17 April 1913, in *Letters of Rainer Maria Rilke,* trans. Jane B. Greene and M. D. H. Norton (New York, 1972), 92.

13. Zweig, *Romain Rolland,* 45–47.

14. Ibid., 8–11; Wilson, *Pre-War Biographies,* 6–12.

15. Starr, *Romain Rolland,* 176, 200; Cheval, *Romain Rolland, l'Allemagne et la guerre,* 29n.6.

16. Romain Rolland, *Mémoires* (Paris, 1956), 21–35.

17. Rolland, *Voyage intérieur,* 27–41.

18. Romain Rolland, *Le Cloître de la rue d'Ulm. Journal de Romain Rolland à l'Ecole normale (1886–1889)* (Paris, 1952); Rolland, *Mémoires,* 36–71.

19. Rolland, *Cloître de la rue d'Ulm,* 313; on the Sorbonne of this period, see Steven Lukes, *Emile Durkheim: His Life and Work* (New York, 1972), 373–375. Also see Robert J. Smith, *The Ecole Normale Supérieure and the Third Republic* (Albany, N.Y., 1982).

20. Romain Rolland, *Les Origines du théâtre lyrique moderne. Histoire de l'opéra en Europe avant Lully et Scarlatti* (Paris, 1895).

21. Romain Rolland, *De la décadence de la peinture italienne au XVIᵉ siècle* (1895) (1931; Paris, 1957); Rolland, *Mémoires,* 195–196.

22. Rolland, *Mémoires,* 222.

23. Zweig, *Romain Rolland,* 32–36; Jacques Robichez, *Romain Rolland* (Paris, 1961), 31–32, 47–48, 55–56.

24. Romain Rolland, *Péguy,* 2 vols. (Paris, 1944), 1:40–41, 137–143.

25. Ibid., 15–41.

26. Rolland, *Cloître de la rue d'Ulm,* 17, 80–81, 85–86, 89, 145, 148.

27. Ibid., 73–74.

28. Claude Digeon, *La Crise allemande de la pensée française (1870–1914)* (Paris, 1959), 519–533; Allan Mitchell, *The German Influence in France After 1870* (Chapel Hill, N.C., 1981).

29. Romain Rolland completed eight plays in a projected cycle of twelve for his *Théâtre de la Révolution.* The following list is in thematic order and indicates year of publication:

Pâques fleuries. Prologue (Paris, 1926)

Le 14 juillet (Paris, 1902)

Les Loups (Paris, 1898)

Le Triomphe de la raison (Paris, 1899)

Le Jeu de l'amour et de la mort (Paris, 1925)

Danton (Paris, 1900)

Robespierre (Paris, 1939)

Les Léonides. Epilogue (Paris, 1928)

See Romain Rolland, *Les Tragédies de la foi: Saint-Louis, Aërt, Le Triomphe de la raison* (Paris, 1913); and Rolland, *Le Théâtre de la Révolution: Le 14 juillet, Danton, Les Loups* (Paris, 1909).

Various dimensions of the French popular theater have been studied in David James Fisher, "Romain Rolland and the Ideology and Aesthetics of the French People's Theatre," *Theatre Quarterly* 9, no. 33 (1979): 83–103; David James Fisher, "The Origins of the French Popular Theatre," *Journal of Contemporary History* 12 (1977): 461–497; David James Fisher, "Romain Rolland and the French People's Theatre," *Drama Review,* March 1977, 75–90; "People's Theatre in France Since 1870," *Theatre Quarterly* 6, no. 23 (1976); Michael Ragon, *Histoire de la littérature prolétarienne en France* (Paris, 1974), 134; Denis Gontard, *La Décentralisation théâtrale* (Paris, 1973), 21–41; Emile Copfermann, *Le Théâtre populaire, pourquoi?* (Paris, 1969), 22; Léon Moussinac, *Le Théâtre des origines à nos jours* (Paris, 1966); Jack Lang, *L'Etat et le théâtre* (Paris, 1968), 109–110; Helen W. Machan, "The Popular Theatre Movement in France," Ph.D. diss., University of Illinois, 1950; Maurice Edgar Coindreau, *La Farce est jouée: Vingt Ans de théâtre français* (New York, 1942), 153–177; Jacques Copeau, "Le Théâtre populaire," *Théâtre populaire,* no. 36 (1959): 91–94; Marcel Doisy, *Le Théâtre français contemporain* (Brussels, 1947), 232–233; Jean-Richard Bloch, "Le Théâtre du peuple. Critique d'une utopie," in *Carnaval est mort* (Paris, 1920), 27–40.

30. Romain Rolland, "Préface à mon théâtre" (1892), *Textes politiques, sociaux et philosophiques choisis,* ed. Jean Albertini (Paris, 1970), 118–119.

31. Ibid., 119–123; for an analysis of Romain Rolland's "critical realism," see Georg Lukács, *Realism in Our Time,* trans. John Mander and Necke Mander (New York, 1964), 93–94, 96, 97–103, 105, 108; Lukács wrote a short essay on Romain Rolland's *Colas Breugnon* in *The Historical Novel,* trans. Hannah Mitchell and Stanley Mitchell (New York, 1963), 322–332.

32. Romain Rolland, "Réponse à l'enquête sur la critique dramatique," *Revue d'art dramatique,* 5 February 1899, 160–161.

33. Romain Rolland, "La Poison idéaliste," *Revue d'art dramatique,* July 1900, 661–665; reprinted in Romain Rolland, *Compagnons de route. Essais littéraires* (Paris, 1936), 17–22.

34. Romain Rolland, "Enquête sur la Comédie-Française," *Revue naturiste*, 1 October 1901, 62–65.

35. On Pottecher's People's Theater of Bussang, see Fisher, "Origins of the French Popular Theatre," 463–465; Gontard, *Décentralisation théâtrale*, 21–41.

36. Letter from Rolland to Maurice Pottecher, 27 November 1897, ARR.

37. Rolland, *Mémoires*, 281–295.

38. Ibid., 247, 262–264, 275.

39. Ibid., 284–288; letters from Rolland to Lucien Herr, 1 February 1898, 15 December 1898, cited in Robert J. Smith, "A Note on Romain Rolland in the Dreyfus Affair," *French Historical Studies* 7 no. 2 (Fall 1971): 284–287; Michael R. Marrus, *The Politics of Assimilation: The French Jewish Community at the Time of the Dreyfus Affair* (Oxford, 1971).

40. Rolland, *Mémoires*, 289–290.

41. Ibid., 283; Christophe Charle, "Champ litteraire et champ du pouvoir: Les Ecrivains et l'Affaire Dreyfus," *Annales, ESC* 32, no. 2 (March–April 1977): 240–264; Jean-Denis Bredin, *The Affair: The Case of Alfred Dreyfus*, trans. Jeffrey Mehlman (New York, 1986), 275–285, 520.

42. Rolland, *Mémoires*, 291, 316; Antoinette Blum, "Romain Rolland face à l'Affaire Dreyfus," *Relations internationales*, no. 14 (Summer 1978).

43. Ibid., 286; Rolland, *Voyage intérieur*, 164–165.

44. Letter from Rolland to Malwida von Meysenbug, 22 May 1898, RR-MvM, 233.

45. Rolland, *Mémoires*, 290–291.

46. Romain Rolland, "Préface" (January 1909), *Le 14 juillet. Théâtre de la Révolution* (Paris, 1926), vi.

47. Rolland, "Préface" (June 1901), *Le 14 juillet*, 3.

48. Romain Rolland, *Le Théâtre du peuple. Essai d'esthétique d'un théâtre nouveau* (Paris, 1926), 74–85, 171–191. This work was originally published in *Cahiers de la Quinzaine*, 24 November 1903; first published in book form in 1904; a tenth edition was published in 1913. I cite the thirteenth edition of 1926. It appeared in English as *The People's Theater*, trans. Barrett H. Clark (New York, 1918); Clark's translation, now out of print, omitted a critical chapter on people's festivals. One segment of Romain Rolland's text has been reprinted in *The Theory of the Modern Stage*, ed. Eric Bentley (Baltimore, 1968), 455–470; another segment, entitled "Theatre for the Real People," appeared in *Theatre Quarterly* 6, no. 23 (1976): 17–23.

49. Cheval, *Romain Rolland, l'Allemagne et la guerre;* Marcelle Kempf, *Romain Rolland et l'Allemagne* (Paris, 1962); Michael Kelly, *Modern French Marxism* (Baltimore, 1982), 5–23; Daniel Lindenberg, *Le Marxisme introuvable* (Paris, 1975); George Lichtheim, *Marxism in Modern France* (New York, 1965); Claude Willard, *Les Guesdistes* (Paris, 1965).

50. Rolland, *Mémoires*, 240, 241, 244.

51. Ibid., 292, 293, 294, 296–298, 314; letter from Rolland to Louis Gillet, 18 January 1901, LG-RR, 117–118.

52. Letter from Rolland to Gillet, 22 January 1901, LG-RR, 121.

53. Rolland, *Mémoires*, 251, 295, 312.

54. Rolland, *Le 14 juillet*, 7; first published in *Cahiers de la Quinzaine*, 20 March 1902; published in English as *The Fourteenth of July*, trans. Barrett H. Clark (New York, 1928).

55. Rolland, *Le 14 juillet*, 125–138.

56. Rolland, "Préface" (June 1901), *Le 14 juillet*, 3.

57. Letter from Rolland to Firmin Gémier, 11 January 1902, ARR; also see Romain Rolland, "Variante. Pour une représentation de fête populaire avec orchestre et choeurs," *Le 14 juillet*, 138–149; Rolland, "Note sur la dernière scène," ibid., 150–151; David Sices, *Music and the Musician in Jean-Christophe* (New Haven, Conn., 1968), 105–110; and Romain Rolland, "Le 14 juillet," *L'Art du théâtre*, 18 June 1902, 107–111.

58. Letters from Rolland to Julien Tiersot, 12 February 1902, 8 May 1902, ARR; Romain Rolland, "La Musique pendant la Révolution," *Pages libres*, no. 80 (12 July 1902): 35–36.

59. Letter from Rolland to Malwida von Meysenbug, 31 December 1899, *RR-MvM*, 273.

60. Romain Rolland, "Le Théâtre du peuple," *Cahiers de la Quinzaine*, 24 November 1903.

61. Rolland, *Théâtre du peuple*, 65, 106–107.

62. Ibid., 108–112.

63. Ibid., 64–65.

64. Ibid., 106–107.

65. Letter from Rolland to Sofia Guerrieri-Gonzaga, 22 May 1903, *RR-SBGG (1959)*, 116.

66. Rolland, *Théâtre du peuple*, 153–168.

67. Ibid., 169.

68. Letter from Rolland to Henrik Ibsen, 5 July 1894, *BV*, 43–46; Ibsen replied in a letter dated 23 July 1894, "Your letter inspired me with a very lively sympathy." ARR.

69. Romain Rolland, "Préface" (January 1908), *Vie de Beethoven* (Paris, 1969), 13–18.

70. Romain Rolland, *Vie de Michel-Ange* (Paris, 1964), 209.

71. Rolland, *Mémoires*, 310. *Lives of Illustrious Men* included *Vie de Beethoven* (Paris, 1903), *Vie de Michel-Ange* (Paris, 1906), and *Vie de Tolstoï* (Paris, 1911).

72. Romain Rolland, "Préface" (March 1927), *Vie de Beethoven* (Paris, 1969), 7–10.

73. Romain Rolland, "Richard Strauss," in *Richard Strauss and Romain Rolland: Correspondence, Diary, and Essays*, ed. Rollo Myers (Berkeley, Calif., 1968), 175–195; originally published in *Revue de Paris*, 15 June 1899.

74. Rolland, *Vie de Beethoven* (Paris, 1969), esp. 98–102.

75. Rolland, *Vie de Tolstoï* (Paris, 1959), 1–4.

76. Ibid., 156–174.

77. Letter from Rolland to Tolstoy, 16 April 1887, *BV*, 17–19.

78. Letter from Tolstoy to Rolland, 4 October 1887, *Compagnons de route*, 237–246; first published in *Cahiers de la Quinzaine*, 25 February 1902.

79. Romain Rolland, "Introduction à une lettre de Tolstoï," *Compagnons de route*, 219–223; Rolland, "In Memoriam Léon Tolstoy," ibid., 224.

80. Rolland, *Vie de Tolstoï* (Paris, 1959); translated by Bernard Miall as *Tolstoy* (Port Washington, N.Y., 1972).

81. Rolland, *Vie de Tolstoï* (Paris, 1959), 111–125.

82. Ibid., 170–171, 174.

83. Ibid., 159–168.

84. Ibid., 4, 18; for the influence of Hugo and Michelet on him, see Romain Rolland, "Le Vieux Orphée: Victor Hugo" (1935), *Compagnons de route*, 198–217; Rolland, *Mémoires*, 265–266; and Rolland, *Théâtre du peuple*, 85–86.

85. Letter from Rolland to Malwida von Meysenbug, 10 April 1900, *RR-MvM*, 281.

86. See Romain Rolland, *Pour l'honneur de l'esprit. Correspondance entre Charles Péguy et Romain Rolland* (Paris, 1973).

87. Letter from Rolland to Malwida von Meysenbug, 30 December 1901, *RR-MvM*, 305–306.

88. See the bibliography in Bernard Duchatelet, "Des débuts de Jean-Christophe (1886–1906)," 2 vols., doctoral thesis, University of Lille, 1975, 1:781–793.

89. Romain Rolland, *Jean-Christophe* (Paris, 1966), 1562; English trans. Gilbert Cannan (New York, 1913), 473.

90. Ibid., 1559, 1562 (English, 470, 474).

91. Ibid., 983, 1024, 1062, 1077 (English, 361, 405, 448, 463).

92. Ibid., 801, 1115, 1024, 1055, 1072, 1077, 1138, 1435 (English, 168, 395–396, 405, 439, 458, 463, 52, 353).

93. Ibid., 942, 943–944, 1008–1009, 1282 (English, 317, 318–319, 387, 194); also see Victor Brombert, *The Intellectual Hero: Studies in the French Novel, 1880–1955* (Chicago, 1960), 21–22, 25, 33, 38, 138, 157, 160–161; William M. Johnston, "The Origin of the Term 'Intellectuals' in French Novels and Essays of the 1890's," *Journal of European Studies* 4 (1974): 43–56.

94. Rolland, *Jean-Christophe*, 987, 993, 995–996, 1062, 1068, 1257, 1325 (English, 365, 370, 373, 448, 453, 167, 242).

95. Ibid., 1176 (English, 91); and Romain Rolland, "Dialogue de l'auteur avec son ombre" (March 1908), *Jean-Christophe*, 635–639. *Jean-Christophe* was dedicated "to the free souls of every nation who suffer, who struggle, and who will vanquish." See Paul Claudel, "La Pensée religieuse de Romain Rolland," in *Accompagnements* (Paris, 1949), 62–88; Pierre Sipriot, *Romain Rolland* (Bruges, 1968).

96. Starr, *Romain Rolland*, 124–145; Zweig, *Romain Rolland*, 157–237; letter from Rolland to Charles Péguy, 14 June 1913, *Pour l'honneur de l'esprit*, 340.

CHAPTER 3

1. Letter from Rolland to H. G. Wells, 1 July 1911, *BV*, 95–96.

2. Letter from Rolland to Alphonse Séché, 14 January 1914, *BV*, 118–120; also see letters from Rolland to Jean-Richard Bloch, 14 January 1912 and 16 January 1913, *JRB-RR*, 99–100, 177–179.

3. Letter from Rolland to Louis Gillet, 6 July 1914, *LG-RR*, 280; see also letter from Rolland to Jean-Richard Bloch, 14 January 1912, *JRB-RR*, 99. In this period Romain Rolland completed his second novel. See Romain Rolland, *Colas Breugnon. Bonhomme vit encore* (Paris, 1919); Romain Rolland, *De Jean-Christophe à Colas Breugnon. Pages de journal* (Paris, 1946); Stefan

310 *Notes to Pages 39–43*

Zweig, *Romain Rolland: The Man and His Work* (1921; New York, 1972), 241–253; William T. Starr, *Romain Rolland: One Against All* (The Hague, 1971), 172–174.

4. Henri Giordan, ed., *Romain Rolland et le mouvement florentin de "la Voce"* (Paris, 1966).

5. Letter from Rolland to Sofia Bertolini Guerrieri-Gonzaga, 23 September 1913, *RR-SBGG (1960)*, 184; Rolland, *De Jean-Christophe à Colas Breugnon*, 106.

6. For a day-by-day account of Romain Rolland's activities during the Great War, see the magnificent *Journal des années de guerre* (Paris, 1952) (*JAG*), surely one of the most stirring intellectual documents produced during this period.

7. Romain Rolland, *Au-dessus de la mêlée* (September 1915), reprinted in *L'Esprit libre* (Geneva, 1971), 53–55; letters from Rolland to Bloch, 21 September 1914, 24 September 1914, *JRB-RR*, 270–278.

8. Roland N. Stromberg, *Redemption by War: The Intellectuals and 1914* (Lawrence, Kans., 1982), 39–60, 153–156; Robert Wohl, *The Generation of 1914* (Cambridge, Mass., 1979), 1–41; Sandi Cooper, "Liberal Internationalism Before World War I," *Peace and Change* 1 (1973): 11–19; Sandi Cooper, "The Guns of August and the Doves of Italy: Intervention and Internationalism," *Peace and Change* 7, no. 1–2 (Winter 1981): 29–43.

9. See Romain Rolland, "Lettre ouverte à Gerhard Hauptmann" (24 August 1914), *L'Esprit libre*, 57–59; Romain Rolland, "Pro Aris" (September 1914), ibid., 61–69; and Romain Rolland, "Au-dessus de la mêlée" (15 September 1914), ibid., 70–83 (reprinted in English translation of *Au-dessus de la mêlée*, titled *Above the Battle*, trans. C. K. Ogden [Chicago, 1916], 19–55).

10. Romain Rolland, "Jaurès" (1 August 1915), *L'Esprit libre*, 165–172 (*Above the Battle*, 181–192). Also see Romain Rolland, "Lettre à ceux qui m'accusent" (17 November 1914), *L'Esprit libre*, 104–110; and Romain Rolland, "Les Idoles" (4 December 1914), ibid., 111–120.

11. Romain Rolland, "Inter Arma Caritas" (30 October 1914), *L'Esprit libre*, 90–100 (*Above the Battle*, 76–92); and Romain Rolland, "Le Meurtre des élites" (14 June 1915), *L'Esprit libre*, 154–164 (*Above the Battle*, 168–180).

12. Rolland, "Au-dessus de la mêlée," 77 (*Above the Battle*, 47).

13. Rolland, "Au-dessus de la mêlée," 82 (*Above the Battle*, 55).

14. Rolland, "Au-dessus de la mêlée," 74 (*Above the Battle*, 43); and Rolland, "Les Idoles," 116–118 (*Above the Battle*, 115–119).

15. Rolland, "Inter Arma Caritas," 100 (*Above the Battle*, 91).

16. Romain Rolland, "Littérature de guerre," *L'Esprit libre*, 143 (*Above the Battle*, 153); also see Romain Rolland, *Clérambault. Histoire d'une conscience libre pendant la guerre* (1920; Geneva, 1971), 148.

17. Rolland, "Inter Arma Caritas," 100 (*Above the Battle*, 91).

18. Rolland, "Lettre à ceux qui m'accusent," 107 (*Above the Battle*, 101–102).

19. Rolland, "Pour l'Europe," *L'Esprit libre*, 121 (*Above the Battle*, 122); Romain Rolland, "Pour l'Europe: Un Appel de la Hollande," *L'Esprit libre*, 125–127 (*Above the Battle*, 127–130).

20. Rolland, "Les Idoles," 117–118 (*Above the Battle*, 116–117).

21. René Cheval, *Romain Rolland, l'Allemagne et la guerre* (Paris, 1963), 476–583; William T. Starr, *Romain Rolland and a World at War* (Evanston, Ill.

1956), 97–114; David James Fisher, "Pacifism and the Intellectual: The Case of Romain Rolland," *Peace and Change* 7, no. 1–2 (Winter 1981): 85–96.

22. Cheval, *Romain Rolland,* 564–565; Starr, *Romain Rolland and a World at War,* 130–136.

23. Letter from Rolland to his mother, 18 December 1914, in *Je commence à devenir dangereux. Choix de lettres de Romain Rolland à sa mère (1914–1916)* (Paris, 1971), 45; Cheval, *Romain Rolland,* 584–697; Starr, *Romain Rolland and a World at War,* 137–198.

24. Romain Rolland, "Introduction" (6 April 1931), *L'Esprit libre,* 29–31; see also Rolland, *Above the Battle,* 14.

25. *JAG,* 558, 1129–1131; Cheval, *Romain Rolland,* 594–599; telegram from V. I. Lenin to Henri Guilbeaux, 8 April 1917, *The Letters of Lenin,* ed. Elizabeth Hill and Doris Mudie (New York, 1937), 423; also see Alfred E. Senn, *The Russian Revolution in Switzerland, 1914–1917* (Madison, Wis., 1971), 162, 213.

26. Shaul Ginsburg, *Raymond Lefebvre et les origines du communisme français* (Paris, 1975), 25–27, 29, 37–38, 80; Christian Gras, *Alfred Rosmer (1877–1964) et le mouvement révolutionnaire international* (Paris, 1971); Robert Wohl, *French Communism in the Making* (Stanford, Calif., 1966), 58.

27. Letter from Rosa Luxemburg to Luise Kautsky, 17 December 1917, in Rosa Luxemburg, *Letters to Karl and Luise Kautsky, 1896 to 1918,* trans. Louis P. Lochner (New York, 1925), 211–212.

28. Letter from Lenin to V. A. Karpinski, 13 September 1915, in Vladimir Ilyich Lenin, *Oeuvres* (Paris, 1959), 36:351.

29. Romain Rolland, *"Le Feu* par Henri Barbusse" (February 1917), *L'Esprit libre,* 245; *JAG,* 496.

30. Romain Rolland, "Ara Pacis," *L'Esprit libre,* 179–181; Rolland, "Aux peuples assassinés," ibid., 189–197; Rolland, "Un Grand Européen: G. F. Nicolai," ibid., 262–298.

31. Romain Rolland, "Tolstoy: L'Esprit libre," *L'Esprit libre,* 207–210; Rolland, "A Maxime Gorki," ibid., 211–212; Rolland, "Voix libres d'Amérique," ibid., 218–221; Rolland, "Pour E. D. Morel," ibid., 235–236.

32. Romain Rolland, "Introduction" (June 1919) to *Les Précurseurs,* in *L'Esprit libre,* 178; letter from Rolland to René Arcos, 19 December 1920, indicating that he had received twenty death threats during the war, ARR.

33. Rolland, "Pour E. D. Morel," 236; Romain Rolland, "Pour l'Internationale de l'esprit" (15 March 1918), *L'Esprit libre,* 322–331.

CHAPTER 4

1. Sigmund Freud, "Thoughts for the Times on War and Death" (1915), *The Complete Psychological Works of Sigmund Freud,* standard ed., trans. James Strachey, 24 vols. (London, 1953–1974)14:274–302.

2. Benedict de Spinoza, *A Political Treatise,* in *The Chief Works of Benedict de Spinoza,* trans. R. H. M. Elwes (London, 1883), 314.

3. Romain Rolland, "Pour l'Internationale de l'esprit" (1918) in *L'Esprit libre* (Geneva, 1971), 322–331; for other perspectives on Romain Rolland's pacifist intellectual stance, see David James Fisher, "Pacifism and the Intellectual: The Case of Romain Rolland," *Peace and Change* 7, no. 1–2 (Winter 1981): 85–96; René Cheval, *Romain Rolland, l'Allemagne et la guerre*

(Paris, 1963), 681–699; William T. Starr, *Romain Rolland and a World at War* (Evanston, Ill., 1956), 162–169, 173–174, 207–208.

4. Letters, Rolland to Maxim Gorky, 18 March 1917, 27 January 1919, ARR; *JAG*, 1052; Jean Perus, *Romain Rolland et Maxim Gorki* (Paris, 1968), 45–52.

5. Letter from Rolland to Rabindranath Tagore, 26 August 1919, *RT-RR*, 27–28; *JAG*, 1272–1273; letter from Rolland to Paul Vaillant-Couturier, 30 March 1919, *JAG*, 1777.

6. Romain Rolland, "Romain Rolland et l'Espéranto," *La Vie ouvrière*, 6 August 1919; Rolland, "L'Opinion de Romain Rolland sur l'Espéranto," *La Vie ouvrière*, 23 April 1920.

7. Letter from Rolland to Upton Sinclair, 22 August 1919, Upton Sinclair MSS, Lilly Library, Indiana University, Bloomington, Indiana.

8. Romain Rolland, "Pour bâtir la cité libre de l'esprit" (1 November 1918), *JAG*, 1637.

9. *JAG*, 242, 699, 1113.

10. Ibid., 1129–1131, 558, 644–645; for Henri Guilbeaux's attitude toward Romain Rolland, see his "L'Age nouveau et les intellectuels," *Demain*, August–September 1918, 198; on Guilbeaux, see Alfred Senn, *The Russian Revolution in Switzerland* (Madison, Wis., 1971), 37, 141, 162, 174, 180, 213, 227–228.

11. Romain Rolland, "Journal inédit (1919–1920)," *Europe*, November–December 1965, 201–204, 207; and *Journal intime*, carnet 32, May 1920–July 1920, 28, 56–57, 74, 183, ARR.

12. Romain Rolland, "A la Russie libre et libératrice" (1 May 1917) in *L'Esprit libre*, 205–206; first published in *Demain*, 1 May 1917; republished in *Le Populaire*, 22 July 1919.

13. *JAG*, 1227–1228, 1366, 1426, 1537, 1547–1548, 1577; letter, Rolland to Jean-Richard Bloch, 24 October 1918, *JRB-RR*, 375–380; letter from Rolland to Monsieur B., 26 January 1919, *JAG*, 1700.

14. Romain Rolland, "Pour nos frères de Russie. Contre le blocus affameur" (23 October 1919), *QAC*, 31–32; first published in *L'Humanité*, 26 October 1919.

15. Romain Rolland, untitled article, *La Vie ouvrière*, 22 October 1919.

16. *JAG*, 915, 1010, 1131, 1139, 1167–1168, 1183, 1365, 1784.

17. For Lenin's views on imperialism, see Vladimir Ilyich Lenin, *Imperialism, The Highest Stage of Capitalism* (1917; Moscow, 1964), 185–304; for his views on pacifism, see Lenin, "Bourgeois Pacifism and Socialist Pacifism" (1917), *Collected Works* (Moscow, 1964), 23:177–194.

18. *JAG*, 1342, 1366, 1367, 1426–1427, 1537, 1547–1548, 1577.

19. Ibid., 1700, 1782, 1784; letter from Rolland to Bloch, 24 October 1918, *JRB-RR*, 375–380.

20. *JAG*, 152, 766, 802, 1205, 1343, 1524, 1661–1662; letter from Rolland to Jean Longuet, 22 August 1918, *BV*, 158–159; letter from Rolland to Bloch, 24 November 1918, *JRB-RR*, 380; also see Peter Nettl, *Rosa Luxemburg* (Oxford, 1969), 486–489.

21. Romain Rolland, "Janvier sanglant à Berlin," *QAC*, 11–30; first published in *L'Humanité*, 16–18 February 1919; also see Romain Rolland, "Sur un martyr," *L'Avenir international*, no. 13 (January 1919): 36–39; *JAG*, 1704.

22. *JAG*, 1704.

23. Rolland, "Janvier sanglant à Berlin," *QAC*, 27–29.

24. Ibid., 11, 12, 15.

25. Ibid., 27.

26. Ibid., 30.

27. Romain Rolland, "Journal inédit (1919–1920)," *Europe*, November–December 1965, 181–182.

28. *JAG*, 66, 969, 1002, 1053–1054, 1368, 1431, 1537, 1654; for Romain Rolland's public positions on Wilson, see Romain Rolland, "Lettre ouverte au présidente Wilson" (November 1918), *L'Esprit libre*, 332–333; and Rolland, "Une Lettre de Romain Rolland à Jean Longuet," ibid., 334; the letters were published in *Le Populaire*, 18 November 1918 and 4 December 1918, respectively.

29. *JAG*, 1661, 1665; also see 1696–1697, 1738, 1776, 1799, 1822, 1828–1829, 1832.

30. Romain Rolland, "Une Lettre de Romain Rolland à Jean Longuet" (4 December 1918), *L'Esprit libre*, 334 n. 1 (dated June 1919); also see Romain Rolland, *QAC*, 186; *Journal intime*, carnet 30, July 1919–October 1919, ARR. Romain Rolland refused to contribute an article to *L'Art libre* on Wilson in 1924, accusing the ex-president of profound insincerity and "failure of internal truth"; see letter from Rolland to Paul Colin, 6 February 1924, ARR.

31. Nicole Racine, "The *Clarté* Movement in France, 1919–1921," *Journal of Contemporary History* 2, no. 2 (April 1967): 195–208; Annie Kriegel, "Naissance du mouvement Clarté," *Mouvement social*, no. 42 (January–March 1963): 117–135.

32. *JAG*, 1824.

33. Ibid., 1272, 1273, 1777.

34. Letter from Rolland to Henri Barbusse, 23 June 1919, *JAG*, 1831–1832.

35. Letter from Rolland to Barbusse, 14 June 1919, *JAG*, 1828.

36. *JAG*, 1826; also see the letters of collective resignation from seven Rollandists to the *Clarté* group, 18 June 1919, signed by Charles Vildrac, Georges Chennevière, F. Crucy, Léon Werth, Albert Doyen, L. Bazalgette, Paul Signac; ibid., 1830.

37. *JAG*, 1824–1825; letters from Rolland to Marcel Martinet, 10 July 1919; to Edouard Dujardin, 10 July 1919; to Edouard Dujardin, 4 September 1919, ARR.

38. Letters from Rolland to Barbusse, 17 June 1919; 23 June 1919, *JAG*, 1829, 1831–1832.

39. Romain Rolland, "Journal inédit (1919–1920)," entry of 14 December 1919, *Europe*, November–December 1965, 185.

40. Ibid., 184–185, 187–188; Romain Rolland, Henri Barbusse, Georges Duhamel, "Appel pour le premier Congrès de l'Internationale intellectuelle," *L'Humanité*, 23 January 1920; *Clarté*, 24 January 1920. See also letters from Rolland to Raymond Lefebvre, 31 December 1919, 4 January 1920, 15 January 1920, 19 February 1920, ARR; Shaul Ginsburg, *Raymond Lefebvre et les origines du communisme français* (Paris, 1975), 114–116, 119–122; Racine, "The *Clarté* Movement in France, 1919–1921," 203.

41. *JAG*, 1726–1727, 1744–1748; on Morel, see Sheldon Spear, "E. D. Morel's U.D.C. International," *Peace and Change* 7, no. 1–2 (Winter 1981): 97–108.

42. Letter from Rolland to E. D. Morel, 30 March 1919, *JAG*, 1778.

43. Letters from Rolland to Amédée Dunois, 6 January 1919, 24 June 1919, ARR; Pierre-Jean Jouve, *Romain Rolland vivant* (Paris, 1920), 217–219n.1.

The Declaration first appeared as "Fière déclaration d'intellectuels," *L'Humanité*, 26 June 1919, 1; it was also published in *L'Art libre*, June 1919; *La Feuille*, June 1919; *Rassegna internazionale*, July 1919; *Forum*, August 1919; *Demokratie*, 18 July 1919; *Foreign Affairs*, August 1919; *New York Times Current History Magazine*, October 1919; and *The Liberator*, December 1919. It was reprinted in Romain Rolland's *Les Précurseurs* (1919), in *L'Esprit libre*, 337–342; and his *QAC*, 1–6. For contemporary echoes, see Paul Souday, "Une Déclaration d'intellectuels," *Le Temps*, 27 June 1919; Marcel Martinet, "Les Intellectuels et la guerre," *La Vie ouvrière*, 2 July 1919; F. Vandérem, *Le Miroir de lettres* (Paris, 1919), 112–116. The following is a national breakdown of those who signed the Declaration:

France: Alain, Raoul Alexandre, René Arcos, Henri Barbusse, Charles Baudouin, Léon Bazalgette, Edouard Bernaert, Lucien Besnard, Jean-Richard Bloch, Louise Bodin, Samuel Buchet, Dr. E. Burnet, Alphonse de Chateaubriant, Georges Chennevière, François Crucy, Paul Desanges, Fernard Després, Albert Doyen, Georges Duhamel, Edouard Dujardin, Amédée Dunois, Gustave Dupin, Dr. Joseph Fiévez, Waldemar George, G. Georges-Bazile, Jean Guéhenno, Augustin Hamon, Pierre-Jean Jouve, C. A. Laisant, A. M. Labouré, Raymond Lefebvre, Marcel Martinet, Emile Masson, Alexandre Mercereau, Luc Mériga, Mathias Morhardt, Georges Matisse, Madeleine Matisse, A. Pierre, August Prenant, Gabriel Reuilland, Romain Rolland, Jules Romains, Nelly Roussel, Han Ryner, Dr. Schirardin, Edouard Schoen, P. Schultz, Edouard Schneider, Séverine, Paul Signac, Dr. Robert Sorel, Gaston Thiesson, Jules Uhry, Paul Vaillant-Couturier, Charles Vildrac, Dr. Wacker, Léon Werth.

Germany: G. van Arco, Albert Einstein, W. Foerster, Leonard Frank, H. von Gerlach, Ivan Goll, Wilhelm Herzog, Hermann Hesse, David Hilbert, Käthe Kollwitz, Max Lehmann, Heinrich Mann, A. Moissi, Paul Natorp, Georg F. Nicolai, Nithack-Stahn, H. Paasche, Hélène Stoecker, Fritz von Unruh, H. Wehberg, Franz Werfel.

Italy: Enrico Bignami, Roberto Bracco, Benedetto Croce, Amaldo Lucci, Attilio Cimbro, Marie Cimbro-Bonnet, Confucio Cotti, Dino Muratore, Dr. Enrico Lenzi, Dr. Elsa Castagneri.

Belgium: Paul Colin, Georges Eekhound, J. F. Eslander, Frans Hellens, Georges Khnopff, Frans Masereel, Mélot du Dy, Jacques Mesnil, Edmond Picard, Henry van de Velde.

Switzerland: Ernst Bloch, Dr. Robert Eder, August Forel, Charles Hofer, Professor Ragaz, H. Roorda van Eysinga.

England: Edward Carpenter, Lowes Dickinson, Roger Fry, Bertrand Russell, Israel Zangwill.

Sweden: Verner von Heidenstam, Ellen Kay, Selma Lagerlöf, Carl Lindhagen.

Catalonia: M. Lopez-Pico, Alfons Maseras, Eugenio d'Ors, Paul M. Turull, Emilio H. del Villar.

Holland: Dr. L.-G. Brouwer, Dr. Frederick van Eeden, J. C. Kapteyn.

Austria: Dr. A. H. Fried, Stefan Zweig.

Russia: Paul Birukof, Maxim Gorky, Nicolas Rubakin, L. de Wiskovatov.

Hungary: Monseigneur Alexandre Giesswein, Andreas Latzko.

Poland: Dr. M. de Rusiecka.

Greece: Georges Donvalis, Yannios.

United States: Jane Addams, Sherwood Anderson, Van Wyck Brooks, Waldo Frank, Frederick P. Hier, B. W. Huebsch, John Haynes Holmes, Horace B. Liveright, Edgar Lee Masters, Scott Nearing, Upton Sinclair, Alfred Stieglitz, Louis Untermeyer, Oswald Garrison-Villard.

India: Ananda Coomaraswamy, Rabindranath Tagore.

Argentina: Dr. Manuel Galvez.

Brazil: Benedicta Costa.

The appeal was also signed by over 100 Spanish writers and scholars, the signatures collected by Emilio H. del Villar; 28 professors from the University of Turin; 56 professors and students from Piedmont; and 617 individuals from central Europe, whose signatures were collected by Georg F. Nicolai and published in his brochure, *Romain Rollands Manifest und die deutschen Antworten* (Charlottenburg, 1919).

44. Romain Rolland, "Déclaration de l'Indépendance de l'Esprit," *L'Esprit libre,* 337–338.

45. *JAG,* 16 March 1919, 1769–1771.

46. Ibid., 1770.

47. Romain Rolland, "The Intellectuals: Their Failure—Their Opportunity," *Foreign Affairs* 1, no. 2 (August 1919): 5–6; this was reprinted in *QAC* as "Pour l'union des travailleurs des mains et de l'esprit (commentaire à la Déclaration de l'Indépendance de l'Esprit)," 7–10.

48. Rolland, "The Intellectuals," 5.

49. Ibid., 6.

50. Ibid., 5.

51. Ibid., 6.

52. Ibid.

53. Romain Rolland, "Déclaration de l'Indépendance de l'Esprit," *L'Esprit libre,* 342.

54. Perus, *Romain Rolland et Maxime Gorki,* 53, 57–64, 73.

55. Romain Rolland, Dedication to *Les Précurseurs (1919),* in *L'Esprit libre,* 175.

56. Letter from Rolland to George Bernard Shaw, 25 April 1919, *JAG*, 1796.

57. *JAG*, 1771; Jouve, *Romain Rolland vivant*, 218 n. 1.

58. *JAG*, 126, 1007.

59. Letter from Rolland to Shaw, 25 April 1919, *JAG*, 1796.

60. Letter from Shaw to Rolland, 7 May 1919, *JAG*, 1815.

61. Ibid.

62. Letter from Rolland to Shaw, 28 May 1919, *JAG*, 1817.

63. Letter from Shaw to Rolland, 27 June 1919, cited in *PRP*, 13–14.

64. Letter from Rolland to Shaw, 29 June 1919, *PRP*, 14.

65. Letter from Shaw to Rolland, 10 July 1919, *PRP*, 14 n. 1.

66. *QAC*, lxiv; *PRP*, 14–15.

67. Max Eastman, "A Letter to Romain Rolland," *The Liberator*, December 1919, 24–25; for Romain Rolland's relations with Eastman during the war, see Romain Rolland, "Voix libres d'Amérique" (August 1917), *L'Esprit libre*, 222–234.

68. Eastman, "Letter to Romain Rolland," 24.

69. Ibid., 25.

70. Letter from Rolland to Max Eastman, 5 December 1919, *BV*, 161–162; Rolland, "Journal inédit (1919–1920)," 183–184.

71. Rolland, "Journal inédit (1919–1920)," 183.

72. Letter from Rolland to Waldo Frank, 21 March 1920, ARR.

73. *JAG*, 510–515, 1284–1286, 1762, 1771.

74. Ibid., 1820.

75. Letters from Albert Einstein to a colleague in Breslau, 17 August 1919, and to a liberal professor in Potsdam, 18 August 1919, cited in *Einstein on Peace*, ed. Otto Nathan and Heinz Norden (New York, 1965), 31–32.

76. *JAG*, 1817.

77. Romain Rolland, "Un Grand Européen: G. F. Nicolai" (15 October 1917), *L'Esprit libre*, 262–297; *JAG*, 802, 1600–1602, 1607–1609, 1756–1769, 1771.

78. Nicolai, *Romain Rollands Manifest*, 27. Some of the signers included Alfred Adler, Johannes R. Becher, Edouard Bernstein, Max Brod, Martin Buber, Richard Dehmel, Kasimir Edschmid, Albert Einstein, August Forel, Wilhelm Foerster, Leonard Frank, Ivan Goll, Walter Gropius, Wilhelm Herzog, Hermann Hesse, Kurt Hiller, Hermann Kantorowicz, Karl Kautsky, Annette Kolb, Käthe Kollwitz, Andreas Latzko, Carl Lindhagen, Emil Ludwig, Heinrich Mann, Walter Rathenau, Arthur Rosenberg, René Schickele, Artur Schnabel, Arthur Schnitzler, Wilhelm Steckel, Hélène Stocker, Ernst Toller, Kurt Tucholsky, Fritz von Unruh, Franz Werfel, Kurt Wolff, Stefan Zweig.

79. Karl Kraus, in Nicolai, *Romain Rollands Manifest*, 54–56.

80. *JAG*, 574, 606; also see Roland N. Stromberg, *Redemption by War: The Intellectuals and 1914* (Lawrence, Kans. 1982), 74–75, 150.

81. Letter from Benedetto Croce to Rolland, 9 April 1919, *JAG*, 1792, 1864.

82. Letter from Rolland to Croce, 18 April 1919, *BV*, 160.

83. Letter from Charles Gide to Rolland, May 1919, *JAG*, 1817–1818.

84. Letter from Charles Richet to Rolland, May 1919, *JAG*, 1818.

85. *QAC*, lxiv, n. 1; also see *JAG*, 1814.

86. For a sample of the positive responses, see letter from Israel Zangwill to Rolland, May 1919, *JAG*, 1818–1819; E. D. Morel, "Contributions from Abroad," *Foreign Affairs*, 1 (August 1919): 5; letters from Louis Untermeyer to Rolland, 28 September 1919, ARR; from Stefan Zweig to Rolland, 20 March 1919, 23 March 1919, 7 April 1919, 14 April 1919, ARR; Hermann Hesse to Rolland, 2 May 1919, *HH-RR*, 61; Alain to Rolland, 29 June 1919, *Salut et fraternité. Alain et Romain Rolland* (Paris, 1969), 79–80; Jean Guéhenno to Rolland, 4 July 1919, *JG-RR*, 15; August Prenant to Rolland, June 1919, *JAG*, 1820; Rabindranath Tagore to Rolland, 24 June 1919, 4 October 1919, *RT-RR*, 25–26, 29–30.

87. Letter from Bertrand Russell to Rolland, 7 April 1919, *JAG*, 1790.

88. Ibid., 1791.

89. *JAG*, 1792.

90. Ibid., 1814.

91. Letter from Rolland to Russell, 4 June 1919, *JAG*, 1819; Russell had proposed on 4 May 1919 to revise paragraph 3 of the Declaration, ibid., 1818.

92. Letter from Rolland to Russell, 4 June 1919, *JAG*, 1819.

93. Ibid.

94. Ibid., 1820.

95. Letter from Rolland to Russell, 23 June 1919, ARR.

96. Letter from Rolland to Russell, 16 March 1920, *BV*, 162–163.

97. Letter from Rolland to Pierre-Jean Jouve, 9 June 1919, cited in Jouve, *Romain Rolland vivant*, 263.

98. Ibid., 262–263.

CHAPTER 5

1. David James Fisher, "The Rolland-Barbusse Debate," *Survey*, no. 2/3 (91/92) (Spring–Summer 1974): 121–159; Jean Albertini, "Barbusse et Rolland," *Europe*, September 1974, 119–129; Jean Albertini, "Controverse entre Henri Barbusse et Romain Rolland au sujet de l'Indépendance de l'Esprit," in *Textes politiques, sociaux et philosophiques choisis*, ed. Jean Albertini (Paris, 1970), 182–190; David Caute, *Communism and the French Intellectuals, 1914–1960* (London, 1964), 80–83.

2. Charles S. Maier, *Recasting Bourgeois Europe: Stabilization in France, Germany, and Italy in the Decade After World War I* (Princeton, N.J., 1975); Felix Gilbert, *The End of the European Era, 1890 to the Present* (New York, 1979), 204–254; Philippe Bernard, *La Fin d'un monde, 1914–1929* (Paris, 1974), 121–167.

3. Ronald Tiersky, *French Communism, 1920–1972* (New York, 1974), 23–53; Nicole Racine and Louis Bodin, *Le Parti communiste français pendant l'entre-deux-guerres* (Paris, 1972), 89–102; Jederman, *La 'Bolchevisation' du P.C.F. (1923–1928)* (Paris, 1971); Robert Wohl, *French Communism in the Making, 1914–1924* (Stanford, Calif., 1966), 396–432; Jacques Fauvet, *Histoire du parti communiste français*, 2 vols. (Paris, 1964), 1:67–82.

4. Annie Kriegel, *Aux origines du communisme français, 1914–1920. Contribution à l'histoire du mouvement ouvrier français*, 2 vols. (Paris, 1964); Annie Kriegel, *Le Congrès de Tours. Naissance du parti communiste français* (Paris, 1964).

5. Daniel Lindenberg, *Le Marxisme introuvable* (Paris, 1975), 221–230;

George Lichtheim, *Marxism in Modern France* (New York, 1966), 1–68; Wohl, *French Communism in the Making*, 441–454.

6. Lindenberg, *Marxisme introuvable*, 230; Lichtheim, *Marxism in Modern France*, 67–68; Annie Kriegel, *The French Communists: Profiles of a People*, trans. Elaine P. Halperin (Chicago, 1972).

7. Letter from Rolland to Jean Longuet, 19 March 1921, ARR.

8. *QAC*, xvii.

9. Letters from Rolland to Jean-Richard Bloch, 30 January 1920, 28 March 1920, 17 September 1920, 20 September 1920, ARR. In this final letter, Romain Rolland hyperbolically asserted that "a book is worth an army."

10. Romain Rolland, *Liluli* (Geneva, 1919; English trans. New York, 1920).

11. Letter from Rolland to Istar de Thionville, 13 May 1920, *BV*, 164.

12. Rolland, *Liluli*, 116–118, 188, 189, 190, 199–200.

13. Letter from Rolland to Bloch, 20 December 1921, ARR; also see letters from Rolland to Louise Cruppi, 9 February 1919, 25 February 1919, ARR. For a discerning discussion of *Liluli* as a work of art, see Pierre-Jean Jouve, *Romain Rolland vivant (1914–1919)* (Paris, 1920), 280–293.

14. Romain Rolland, *Pierre et Luce* (Geneva, 1971), 41–42; first published in Geneva in 1920, English trans., *Pierre and Luce* (New York, 1922).

15. Letters from Rolland to Paul Colin, 23 February 1920, 27 February 1920, ARR.

16. Romain Rolland, *Clérambault. Histoire d'une conscience libre pendant la guerre* (Geneva, 1971); first published in Paris in 1920; translated by Katherine Miller as *Clérambault: The Story of an Independent Spirit During the War* (New York, 1921).

17. Romain Rolland, "Introduction à l'un contre tous" (March 1917), *Clérambault*, 82.

18. Rolland, *Clérambault*, 367.

19. Ibid., 148.

20. Ibid., 281.

21. Ibid., 269.

22. Ibid., 293.

23. Ibid., 368.

24. Eugen Weber, *Peasants into Frenchmen: The Modernization of Rural France, 1870–1914* (Stanford, Calif., 1976), 99, 295, 297, 544 n. 11.

25. David James Fisher, "Pacifism and the Intellectual: The Case of Romain Rolland," *Peace and Change* 7, no. 1–2 (Winter 1981): 88–90.

26. Jean Maxe, "L'Idole 'l'européen' Romain Rolland," *Cahiers de l'anti-France* 1 (Paris 1922): 10, 13, 67, 91; for earlier attacks on Romain Rolland by the French extreme right, see Henri Massis, *Romain Rolland contre la France* (Paris, 1915); J. M. Renaitour, Stéphane Servant, and Paul-Hyacinthe Loyson, *Au-dessus ou au coeur de la mêlée?* (Paris, 1916); Isabelle Debran, *M. Romain Rolland, initiateur du défaitisme* (Geneva, 1918).

27. Letter from Rolland to Cruppi, 7 December 1922; also see Rolland, *Journal intime*, December 1920, 43, ARR.

28. André Gide, "Réflexions sur l'Allemagne," *Nouvelle Revue française*, 1 June 1919, 46n; André Gide, "Journal sans dates," *Nouvelle Revue fran-*

çaise, 1 July 1919, 278: "His book (*Jean-Christophe*) never seems better than when translated."

29. Albert Thibaudet, "La Conscience libre et la guerre," *Nouvelle Revue française,* no. 88 (1 January 1921): 67–80; Frederick John Harris, *André Gide and Romain Rolland: Two Men Divided* (New Brunswick, N.J., 1973), 71–85; on the intellectual importance of the *Nouvelle Revue française,* see Herbert R. Lottman, *The Left Bank: Writers, Artists, and Politics from the Popular Front to the Cold War* (Boston, 1982), 32–34; Régis Debray, *Teachers, Writers, Celebrities: The Intellectuals of Modern France,* trans. Francis Mulhern (London, 1981), 60–75.

30. Letters from Rolland to Bloch, 12 October 1920; to Pierre Abraham, 26 July 1932, ARR.

31. Paul Colin, *La Vertu d'héroïsme et Romain Rolland* (Brussels, 1919); Stefan Zweig, *Romain Rolland, der Mann und das Werk* (Frankfurt, 1920), English trans. 1921, Russian 1923, French 1930; Pierre-Jean Jouve, *Romain Rolland vivant (1914–1919)* (Paris, 1920); Jean Bonnerot, *Romain Rolland. Sa vie, son oeuvre* (Paris, 1921); Marcel Martinet, *Pages choisies de Romain Rolland,* 2 vols. (Paris, 1921).

32. Stefan Zweig, *Romain Rolland: The Man and His Work* (New York, 1972), v; Stefan Zweig, *The World of Yesterday* (Lincoln, Neb., 1964), 265–267.

33. Jean Albertini, Introduction to *Avez-vous lu Jean-Richard Bloch?* (Paris, 1981), 9–140.

34. Letter from Bloch to Rolland, 27 January 1920, in Romain Rolland, "Journal inédit (1919–1920)," *Europe,* November–December 1965, 196; Bloch had favorably reviewed Romain Rolland's works. See "Colas Breugnon. Un Livre gai," *L'Humanité,* 7, 8, 9 June 1919; Jean-Richard Bloch, "Le Théâtre du peuple. Critique d'une utopie," *Carnaval est mort* (Paris, 1920), 27–40.

35. Letter from Rolland to Bloch, 30 January 1920, in Rolland, "Journal inédit (1919–1920)," 196–198.

36. Romain Rolland, "Un Livre de Raymond Lefebvre. *Le Sacrifice d'Abraham,*" *L'Humanité,* 19 March 1920, 1.

37. Raymond Lefebvre, Review of *Les Précurseurs,* in *Le Populaire,* 11 January 1920.

38. On Barbusse, see Annette Vidal, *Henri Barbusse. Soldat de la paix* (Paris, 1953); Vladimir Brett, *Henri Barbusse, sa marche vers la clarté, son mouvement Clarté* (Prague, 1963); "Henri Barbusse," *Europe,* January 1969, 3–77; "Henri Barbusse," *Europe,* September 1974, 3–241.

39. Romain Rolland, "*Le Feu* par Henri Barbusse" (February 1917), in *L'Esprit libre* (Geneva, 1971), 237–245.

40. Letters from Rolland to Raymond Lefebvre, 31 December 1919, 4 January 1920, 12 January 1920, 15 January 1920, 19 February 1920, and esp. 10 March 1920, ARR.

41. Romain Rolland, *Journal intime,* cahier 29, 32, ARR.

42. Rolland, *Journal intime,* cahier 30, 28; letters from Rolland to Bloch, 20 September 1920; to Stefan Zweig, 26 July 1919, ARR. Also see *QAC,* xvi, lxv.

43. Letter from Rolland to Bloch, 10 April 1920; Rolland, *Journal intime,* cahier 29, 32, ARR.

44. Rolland, "Journal inédit (1919–1920)," 187; the conversation with Duhamel was dated 17 December 1919.

45. Henri Barbusse, *Le Couteau entre les dents. Aux intellectuels* (Paris, 1921).

46. Ibid., 14, 36.

47. Ibid., 47, 60–62, 74, 77, 80.

48. Henri Barbusse, "L'Autre Moitié du devoir. A propos du 'Rollandisme,' " *Clarté*, no. 2, 3 (December 1921): 25–28; the text was also published in *Journal du peuple*, no. 31–32 (31 January–1 February 1922). The entire Rolland-Barbusse debate in chronological order was published in *Textes politiques*, 190–233.

49. Barbusse, "L'Autre Moitié du devoir," in *Textes politiques*, 12–194.

50. Ibid., 194, 198–199.

51. Ibid., 193, 194, 199, 200.

52. Ibid., 194, 195, 197, 199.

53. Ibid., 196, 197, 198.

54. Romain Rolland, "Lettre ouverte de Romain Rolland à Henri Barbusse," *L'Art libre*, January 1922, 1–2; republished in *Clarté*, no. 6 (1 February 1922): 126–127; *Rassegna internazionale* 4:14–17; *Journal du peuple*, no. 33 (2 February 1922); *The Nation*, 8 February 1922; *Les Humbles*, March 1922. All of Romain Rolland's open letters to Barbusse were included in *QAC*, 43–59, translated into English as *I Will Not Rest*, trans. K. S. Shelvankar (New York [1935]), 127–145.

55. Romain Rolland, "Lettre ouverte de Romain Rolland à Henri Barbusse," *Textes politiques*, 202, 204.

56. Ibid., 202, 203, 204–205.

57. Ibid., 202, 204.

58. Ibid., 203, 204.

59. Ibid., 203.

60. Ibid.

61. Ibid., 204, 205, 206.

62. Ibid., 205.

63. Henri Barbusse, "Lettre à Romain Rolland à propos du Rollandisme," *Clarté*, no. 6 (1 February 1922): 127–128; also published in *Journal du peuple*, no. 36 (5 February 1922) and *L'Art libre*, February 1922, 19; *Textes politiques*, 206–209.

64. Romain Rolland, "Deuxième Lettre à Henri Barbusse," *L'Art libre*, February 1922, 17–19; also published in *Journal du peuple*, no. 47 (16 February 1922); *Textes politiques*, 209–218.

65. Rolland, *Textes politiques*, 209–210.

66. Ibid., 210, 211, 213.

67. Ibid., 211, 213.

68. Ibid., 213.

69. Ibid.

70. Ibid., 214.

71. Ibid., 216–217.

72. Ibid., 217–218.

73. Henri Barbusse, "Réponse de Henri Barbusse," *Clarté*, no. 10 (1 April 1922): 221–225; also in *Journal du peuple*, no. 92 (2 April 1922); no. 94 (4 April 1922); *Textes politiques*, 218–227.

74. Barbusse, "Réponse de Henri Barbusse," 219, 223, 226.
75. Ibid., 224, 225, 226.
76. Ibid., 220.
77. Ibid., 220, 221, 222.
78. Ibid., 226–227.
79. On the trial of the Social Revolutionaries, see Roy A. Medvedev, *Let History Judge: The Origins and Consequences of Stalinism*, trans. Colleen Taylor (New York, 1972), 381–384.
80. Romain Rolland, "La Révolution et les intellectuels. Lettre aux amis communistes," *L'Art libre*, April 1922, 49–50; also in *Journal du peuple*, no. 117 (29 April 1922); *Textes politiques*, 227–233.
81. *Textes politiques*, 230; for Romain Rolland's information about the Social Revolutionaries, see *QAC*, lxvi–lxvii.
82. Rolland, "La Révolution et les intellectuels," *Textes politiques*, 228, 229, 230.
83. Ibid., 232–233.
84. Ibid., 230, 231.
85. Ibid., 231.
86. Ibid., 232–233.
87. Letters from Rolland to Barbusse, 18 January 1922; to Colin, 27 December 1921, 1 January 1922; Rolland, *Journal intime*, 1 January 1922, 81–82, ARR.
88. Letters from Rolland to Edouard Dujardin, 20 January 1922; to Colin, 9 January 1922, ARR.
89. Amédée Dunois, "A propos du 'Manifeste communiste,' " *L'Humanité*, 10 March 1922, 1.
90. Romain Rolland's letter was published in *L'Humanité*, 12 March 1922.
91. Amédée Dunois, "Neutralité est impossible," *L'Humanité*, 12 March 1922, 1.
92. Marcel Martinet, "Les Intellectuels et la révolution," *L'Humanité*, 25 March 1922, 1; Martinet wrote an earlier piece on the same themes, "La Révolution et la liberté," *L'Internationale*, 8 March 1922.
93. Albert Mathiez, "L'Elite européenne et la Terreur," *Clarté*, no. 14 (June 1922): 323.
94. Romain Rolland, "L'Elite européenne et la Terreur. Réponse à Albert Mathiez," *Clarté*, no. 16 (1 July 1922): 372–373; republished in *Journal du peuple*, 13 July 1922; see also Albert Mathiez, "Réplique à Romain Rolland," *Clarté*, no. 16 (1 July 1922): 373–374.
95. Letters from Rolland to Colin, 3 February 1922, 10 February 1922, 27 February 1922, 3 March 1922, 6 March 1922, ARR.
96. Romain Rolland, "Deuxième lettre de Rolland à Barbusse," *Textes politiques*, 215–216.
97. "L'Indépendance de l'Esprit. Réponses à l'appel de Romain Rolland," *L'Art libre*, no. 3 (March 1922). The following intellectuals participated in the debate: René Arcos, Georg Brandes, Léon Bazalgette, Georges Chennevière, Paul Colin, Jean Debrit, Georges Duhamel, Edouard Dujardin, Luc Durtain, Gustave Dupin, Kasimir Edschmid, Fernand Gouttenoire de Toury, Pierre-Jean Jouve, Annette Kolb, Andreas Latzko, Frans Masereel, Heinrich Mann, Marcel Martinet, Jacques Mesnil, Jules Romains,

René Schickelé, Fritz von Unruh, Charles Vildrac, Henry van de Velde, Léon Werth, and Stefan Zweig.

98. Edouard Dujardin, "L'Indépendance de l'Esprit," 36–37; Marcel Martinet, ibid., 39–40. Martinet and Pierre Monatte had visited Romain Rolland on 18 March 1922. See Rolland, *Journal intime,* cahier 32, 123, ARR; Kasimir Edschmid, *L'Art libre,* no. 4 (April 1922): 50–51.

99. Fernand Gouttenoire de Toury, "L'Indépendance de l'Esprit," 38; Léon Werth, ibid., 42.

100. See P.-J. Jouve and Charles Vildrac, "L'Indépendance de l'Esprit," 39, 42, respectively.

101. Joseph Rivière, "Enquête Romain Rolland–Henri Barbusse," *Cahiers idéalistes,* June 1922, 126–127; Marcel Millet, ibid., 123–124.

102. Fabrice, "Romain Rolland et Henri Barbusse," *Le Libertaire,* no. 158 (3 February 1922); Maurice Wullens, "Romain Rolland et Barbusse," ibid. no. 160 (17 February 1922); Fabrice, "Littérateur," ibid., no. 160 (17 February 1922); André Colomer, "La Révolution et le prolétariat," ibid., no. 165 (24 March 1922); André Colomer, "Philosophie ou révolution," ibid., no. 168 (14 April 1922); Génold, "Le Bon Grain et l'ivraie," *Revue anarchiste,* no. 5 (May 1922); Han Ryner, "Rollandists," *Journal du peuple,* no. 99 (9 April 1922); Marceline Hecquet, "De la non-coopération," *Journal du peuple,* no. 179 (29 June 1922).

103. *QAC,* xxiii–xxix; letters from Rolland to Colin, 21 April 1922; to Maxim Gorky, 20 December 1921, 21 January 1922; letters from Gorky to Rolland, 3 January, 25 January 1922, ARR.

104. Letters from Rolland to Colin, 23 April 1922; to Einstein, 21 April 1922; to Ernst Robert Curtius, 19 January 1923, ARR; also see Joseph Kvapil, *Romain Rolland et les amis d'Europe* (Prague, 1971), 86–109; Pierre Abraham, "La Naissance d'une revue," *Europe,* September–October 1973, 6–13.

105. *QAC,* lxx.

106. Romain Rolland, *L'Ame enchantée,* vol. 1, *Annette et Sylvie* (Paris, 1922).

107. Letter from Rolland to Paul Seippel, 28 May 1922, ARR. During the heat of the debate, Romain Rolland interceded on behalf of Barbusse's candidacy in the Cercle Littéraire Internationale. See letters from Rolland to Léon Bazalgette, 9 March 1922; to Bloch, 3 March 1922, ARR.

108. Romain Rolland, "Le Banditisme du capital aux Etats-Unis. Une Lettre de Romain Rolland," *L'Humanité,* 15 June 1922, 1.

109. "Lettre de Romain Rolland," *Journal du peuple,* no. 87 (8 July 1922); "Le Procès des S.R. russes," *Journal du peuple,* no. 196 (16 July 1922); Rolland, *Journal intime,* 12 July 1922, ARR.

110. Letter from Rolland to Marcel Martinet, 18 July 1922; Rolland, *Journal intime,* 18 July 1922, ARR.

111. Letter from Rolland to Martinet, 13 July 1922, ARR.

112. Leon Trotsky, "Le Drame du prolétariat français," *Clarté,* no. 22 (1 October 1922): 507–511; Leon Trotsky, "Une Pièce qui est une date," *L'Humanité,* 7 October 1922, 1; the *Clarté* piece first appeared in Russian in *Izvestia,* 16 May 1922; in English in *Labour Monthly,* 22 August 1922; reprinted in *Trotsky on Literature and Art,* ed. Paul N. Siegel (New York, 1970), 148–161.

113. Letter from Rolland to Frans Masereel, 11 October 1922, ARR.

114. Rolland, *Journal intime*, October 1922, 49–51, 56, ARR. A year later, Romain Rolland argued for an education that stressed free inquiry and opposed every church mentality: "And churches—all clericalism (bourgeois or proletarian)—that is the enemy!" *L'Ecole émancipée*, no. 45 (1 September 1923): 2–3; Victor Serge defended Soviet forms of collective education in his rebuttal and accused Romain Rolland of taking flight into an abstract form of neutrality; see Victor Serge, "Au-dessus de la mêlée sociale," *L'Ecole émancipée*, no. 4 (14 October 1923): 49–51.

115. Letter from Rolland to Edouard Dujardin, 2 March 1922, ARR.

CHAPTER 6

1. Romain Rolland, "Europe and the Coloured Peoples," *Foreign Affairs* 1, no. 11 (1 May 1920): 1; Romain Rolland, "A Letter from Romain Rolland," *Foreign Affairs* 2, no. 12 (June 1921): 185.

2. Romain Rolland, "The Iron Net," *Survey* 56, no. 9 (1 August 1926): 495–496; for the full version of this article, see letter from Rolland to Paul Kellog, 18 November 1925, *BV*, 227–230.

3. Rolland, "Iron Net," 496.

4. Romain Rolland, "L'Appel aux intellectuels. Une Lettre de Romain Rolland," published in *La Liberté* (Cairo), no. 981; letter is dated 18 December 1924, ARR.

5. Romain Rolland, "Réponse de Romain Rolland, 'Que pensez-vous de la guerre du Maroc?' " *Clarté*, no. 76 (15 July 1925): 271; Rolland, "Appel aux travailleurs intellectuels. Oui ou non, condamnez-vous la guerre?" ibid., 285; this appeal was also signed by Barbusse and the *Clarté* group, the *Philosophies* circle of Norbert Guterman, Henri Lefebvre, Pierre Morhange, and Georges Politzer, as well as by Marcel Martinet, Georges Pioch, Charles Vildrac, and Léon Werth.

6. Rolland, "Réponse de Romain Rolland, 'Que pensez-vous de la guerre du Maroc?' " 271.

7. Rolland, "Iron Net," 495, 496.

8. Ibid.

9. Ibid. Also see Romain Rolland, "Protestation contre l'invasion du Nicaragua par les troupes des Etats-Unis," *Front uni des travailleurs et intellectuels de l'Amérique latine* (1927), ARR.

10. Romain Rolland, "Adresse aux étudiants et travailleurs indo-chinois en France" (17 May 1926), *QAC*, 69–71; this first appeared in the monthly Indochinese newspaper, *Viêt-Nam-Hön*, published in Paris; also see letter from Rolland to Cheng Tcheng, 13 January 1927, ARR. For Romain Rolland's influence on Chinese intellectuals, see T. B. Kin-Yn-Yn, "La Renaissance Chinoise et l'influence de Romain Rolland," *Europe*, 15 September 1927, 101–108.

11. Letters from Rolland to Count Richard Coudenhove-Kalergi, 14 September 1925, *QAC*, xxx; and to Louis Rougier, 14 November 1924, ibid., xxxii–xxxiii; also see Romain Rolland, "Sur Pan-Europe," ibid., 97–98; this was first published in *L'Effort* (Lyons), 28 January 1930; for a full critique of pan-European ideas, see Romain Rolland's debate with Gaston Riou, summarized in his "Europe, élargis-toi, ou meurs." *QAC*, 112–126.

12. Romain Rolland, "Le Pact Kellog," *Monde*, no. 12 (25 August 1928): 1; "Le Pact Kellog et la comédie de la paix," *L'Effort*, 30 October 1928; "Contre le traité de paix," *Cri des peuples*, 10 February 1929; "Contre la guerre. Un Appel de Romain Rolland," *Monde*, no. 67 (14 September 1929): 3; "La Piraterie de la paix," PRP, 19–26; this first appeared in *Europe*, 15 November 1929, 431–436; Russian trans. *Izvestia*; "Il faut réviser les traités" (30 October 1931), PRP, 107–109; "Il faut réviser les traités," PRP, 110–111, first published in *L'Effort*, January 1932; and "Il faut réviser tout l'ordre social" (23 April 1932), PRP, 112–118.

13. See Peter Brock, *Twentieth Century Pacifism* (New York, 1970). Though Brock's essay is excellent on British, Indian, and American varieties of pacifism, it is scanty on Continental peace movements.

14. Romain Rolland, "Message à la Volonté de paix," PRP, 100–104, first published in *Volonté de paix*, no. 5 (October–December 1928); Romain Rolland, "Réponse à l'exposé d'Eugen Relgis," in Eugen Relgis, *L'Internationale pacifiste* (Paris, 1929), 27–29; see Jean Train, "Sur Romain Rolland," *Mère éducatrice*, no. 7–9 (July–September 1929): 5.

15. These debates are discussed in David James Fisher, "Romain Rolland and the Question of the Intellectual," Ph.D. diss., University of Wisconsin, 1973, 320–372.

16. Romain Rolland, "Contre la loi militaire," PRP, 144 n. 1; this first appeared in *Europe*, no. 53 (15 May 1927): 62. Also see Romain Rolland, "Postface," in Marianne Rauze, *L'AntiGuerre. Essai d'une doctrine et d'une philosophie de l'antimilitarisme en 1923* (Niort, 1923), 187–192; this was reprinted as "Contre du pacifisme négatif," in PRP, 93–97. One of the leading advocates of peacetime civil service was the Swiss Pierre Cérésole; see Pierre Hirsch, ed., *Bon Voisinage. Edmond Privat et Romain Rolland* (Neuchâtel, 1977).

17. Romain Rolland, "Le Devoir des intellectuels contre la guerre," PRP, 143–148; first published in *L'Avenir social* (Brussels), 1 May 1927.

18. Jean Biès, *Littérature française et pensée hindoue. Des origines à 1950* (Paris, 1974), 9–351; Edward W. Said, *Orientalism* (New York, 1979), 166–197, 226–254.

19. David James Fisher, "Pacifism and the Intellectual: The Case of Romain Rolland," *Peace and Change* 7, no. 1–2 (Winter 1981): 91–94; R. A. Francis, "Romain Rolland and Gandhi: A Study in Communication," *Journal of European Studies* 5 (1975): 291–307; David James Fisher, "Romain Rolland and the Popularization of Gandhi, 1923–1925," *Gandhi Marg*, 18, no. 3 (July 1974): 145–180; Biès, *Littérature française et pensée hindoue*, 357–428; Margaret W. Fisher, "Introduction" to Romain Rolland, *Mahatma Gandhi* (New York, 1973), 5–36; V. V. Ramana Murti, "Romain Rolland and Gandhi," *Gandhi Marg*, no. 37 (January 1966): 40; Pierre Meile, "Gandhi, ou la sagesse déchaînée," in M. K. Gandhi, *Autobiographie ou mes expériences de vérité* (Paris, 1964), 6; Camille Drevet, "Gandhi in France," *Gandhi Marg*, no. 4 (October 1959): 302.

20. Paul Clay Sorum, *Intellectuals and Decolonization in France* (Chapel Hill, N.C., 1977).

21. Joseph J. Doke's *M. K. Gandhi, An Indian Patriot in South Africa* (London, 1909) was the first book on Gandhi.

22. René Grousset, *Histoire de la philosophie orientale* (Paris, 1923); *Histoire de l'Asie* (Paris, 1924), vol. 2; and *Le Réveil de l'Asie* (Paris, 1924). See also René Guénon, *Introduction aux doctrines hindoues* (Paris, 1921), and *L'Orient et l'Occident* (Paris, 1924).

23. "Les Appels de l'Orient," *Cahiers du mois*, no. 9–10 (February–March 1925). Participants included Gabriel Audisio, Henri Barbusse, André Breton, Paul Claudel, André Desson, Florent Fels, Claude Ferrière, André Gide, René Guénon, André Harlaire, Franz Hellens, Dinet and Sliman ben Ibraham, Sylvain Lévi, René Lalou, Henri Massis, Paul Masson-Oursel, André Maurois, Romain Rolland, Sédir, Fritz von Unruh, and Paul Valéry.

24. Henri Barbusse, "Les Appels de l'Orient," *Cahiers du mois*, no. 9–10 (February–March 1925): 244; André Breton, ibid., 250–251.

25. Paul Valéry, "Puissance de choix de l'Europe," *Cahiers du mois*, no. 9–10 (February–March 1925): 16–17.

26. Henri Massis, "Mises au point," *Cahiers du mois*, no. 9–10 (February–March 1925): 30–38; also see "Henri Massis nous parle de la Grande Asie de Romain Rolland et Rabindranath Tagore," *Journal littéraire*, no. 42 (7 February 1925): 4; Henri Massis, *Défense de l'Occident* (Paris, 1927). For an introduction to Massis, see Robert Wohl, *The Generation of 1914* (Cambridge, Mass., 1979), 5–18.

27. This was well articulated by Sylvain Lévi's "Distinction," *Cahiers du mois*, no. 9–10 (February–March 1925): 11–13; and André Gide, "Les Appels de l'Orient," ibid., 18; also see Sylvain Lévi's *L'Inde et le monde* (Paris, 1926).

28. Romain Rolland, "Les Appels de l'Orient," *Cahiers du mois*, no. 9–10 (February–March 1925): 322.

29. For Romain Rolland's personal reaction to the works of Massis and Lévi, see letters to Kalidas Nag, 18 July 1924, ARR; and 2 May 1925, *RT-RR*, 132; also see Romain Rolland, *L'Inde. Journal, 1915–1943* (Paris, 1951), 46, 289, 411, 488; he preferred the scholarly works of Paul Masson-Oursel to those of Lévi and Massis. For Romain Rolland's thoughts on Europe's degeneration, see his conversation with Tagore, 24 June 1926, *RT-RR*, 183.

30. Rolland, *L'Inde*, 39–40. In addition, see letter from Rolland to Hermann Hesse, 5 April 1923, *HH-RR*, 100–101; Hesse replied on 6 April 1923, ibid., 101–103. Hesse's ability to absorb Eastern religious ideas was related to his marginal position in European intellectual currents.

31. Romain Rolland, "Au P.E.N. Club de Londres (Pour la première réunion internationale du Club Internationale des Ecrivains)," 1 May 1923, *QAC*, 59–61; first published in *Europe*, 15 June 1923, 102–105. Romain Rolland, "'Sur l'occupation de la Ruhr," *QAC*, 61–62; first published in *Rassegna internazionale*, July 1923, and in *Libres Propos*, 6 October 1923, 218. Romain Rolland, "Appel aux français pour venir en aide aux malheureux d'Allemagne," *QAC*, 62–64; this first appeared in *Europe*, 15 February 1924, 233–234; *L'Universel*, February 1924, 1; and *Revue européene*, no. 13 (1 March 1924): 72–73; letter from Rolland to Ernst Toller, 20 November 1924, ARR; also consult *QAC*, 71.

32. Rolland, *L'Inde*, 9–11.

33. Ibid., 12–13; also see Romain Rolland, *Les Précurseurs* (1919; Ge-

neva, 1971), 191; Rabindranath Tagore, "Le Message de l'Inde au Japon," trans. Andrée Jouve, in Romain Rolland, *A la civilisation* (Paris, 1917), 25–30.

34. Letters from Rolland to Tagore, 26 August 1919, 10 April 1919, 25 April 1921, *RT-RR*, 26–28, 21–22, 34–35; also see Rolland, *L'Inde*, 19–27.

35. Rolland, "Avant-Propos pour *La Danse de Civa* d'Ananda Coomaraswamy," *L'Inde*, 598–604; this first appeared in Ananda Coomaraswamy, *La Danse de Civa*, trans. Madeleine Rolland (Paris, 1922). Letter from Rolland to Dilip Kumar Roy, 24 February 1924, in D. K. Roy, *Among the Great* (Bombay, 1945), 86–89; also published in *G-RR*, 208–210; English translation, *Romain Rolland and Gandhi Correspondence*, trans. R. A. Francis (New Delhi, 1976), 23–25; also see letters from Rolland to Maxim Gorky, 4 April 1922, 16 September 1922, 8 February 1923, 4 October 1923, 1 August 1924, 16 October 1924, ARR; from Rolland to Roy, 1 October 1924, *Among the Great*, 60–62.

36. Romain Rolland, *Mahatma Gandhi* (Paris, 1924), 14.

37. Letters from Rolland to Nag, 21 October 1924, *RT-RR*, 118–119; from Rolland to Marcel Martinet, 1 November 1924, ARR. From 1923 to 1924, *Revue européene* was more receptive than *Europe* to the Indian cultural influence; it published "Deux Poèmes de Tagore," trans. P.-J. Jouve, no. 8 (1923): 21–23; and C. F. Andrews, "Une Journée avec Mahatma Gandhi," no. 21 (1 November 1924): 47–54; with an introduction by Romain Rolland.

38. Rolland, *L'Inde*, 18.

39. Ibid., 34–35.

40. Ibid., 39. Rolland acknowledged his intellectual debt to Nag in *Mahatma Gandhi* (Paris, 1966), 9; see letters from Rolland to Nag, 14 August 1922, *G-RR*, 172, and 12 November 1922, ARR.

41. Romain Rolland, "La Réponse de l'Asie à Tolstoï" (May 1927), *Vie de Tolstoï* (Paris, 1959), 214–231; first published in *Europe*, 15 July 1928, 338–357; "Lettre écrite par Tolstoï deux mois avant sa mort, à Gandhi," in Rolland, *Vie de Tolstoï*, 331–335. For Romain Rolland's relations with Tolstoy and Tolstoy as a bridge between Gandhi and Romain Rolland, see Romain Rolland, *Monsieur le Comte. Romain Rolland et Léon Tolstoy textes* (Paris, 1981), 135, 139, 149, 166–167.

42. Letter from Rolland to Nag, 21 December 1922, *G-RR*, 173.

43. Letter from Rolland to Nag, 12 November 1922, ARR; also see letters from Rolland to Louise Cruppi, 25 January 1923; to Paul Colin, 25 January 1923; to Maurice Delamin, 7 February 1923, *G-RR*, 175, 175–176, 177–178; to Colin, 25 January 1923; to Paul Amann, 9 February 1923, *G-RR*, 175, 180. The biography was published in three parts in *Europe*, 15 March 1923, 129–163; 15 April 1923, 267–310; 15 May 1923, 427–454; the concluding remarks of the final chapter were published under the title "L'Evangile de la nonviolence," in *Libres Propos*, 16 June 1923, 72–74. It was released in book form by the French publisher Les Editions Stock in 1924, and translated into English by Catherine P. Groth as *Mahatma Gandhi: The Man Who Became One with the Universal Being* (New York, 1924; reprint, New York, 1973). I will cite the definitive French edition of 1966.

44. Rolland, *Mahatma Gandhi*, 27, 28–29.

45. Ibid., 64.

46. Ibid., 15, 35, 47–48.
47. Ibid., 48, 73.
48. Ibid., 49–50.
49. Ibid., 109–112.
50. Ibid., 59; also see 21, 69, 95–96.
51. For representative historical evaluations of the events at Chauri Chaura, see D. G. Tendulkar, *Mahatma: The Life of Mohandas Karamchand Gandhi* (Bombay, 1951), 2:101–123; B. R. Nanda, *Mahatma Gandhi: A Biography* (London, 1958), 235–237; Francis Watson, *The Trial of Mr. Gandhi* (London, 1969), 184–185; Rolland, *Mahatma Gandhi,* 89, 96.
52. Rolland, *Mahatma Gandhi,* 96.
53. Ibid., 84–85.
54. Ibid., 44, 48.
55. Erik H. Erikson, *Gandhi's Truth: On the Origins of Militant Nonviolence* (New York, 1969), 229–254; Rolland, *Mahatma Gandhi,* 86.
56. Ibid., 85; V. V. Ramana Murti, "Romain Rolland and Gandhi," *Gandhi Marg,* no. 37 (January 1966): 40, observes that Romain Rolland draws his portrait from "a Tagorean viewpoint."
57. Rolland, *Mahatma Gandhi,* 85.
58. Ibid., 113.
59. Romain Rolland, "L'Inde depuis la libération de Gandhi," *Europe,* 15 April 1924, 507–514. This essay served as the "postface" in later editions (see Rolland, *Mahatma Gandhi,* 117–126) but is not included in the English translation. Gandhi was released from prison on 2 February 1924.
60. Romain Rolland, "Introduction à *La Jeune Inde,*" *G-RR,* 349–361; first published in *Revue européene,* no. 20 (1 October 1924): 1–15. This served as Romain Rolland's introduction to the French abridgment of Gandhi's *Jeune Inde* (Paris, 1924), trans. Hélène Hart; English translation in *Rolland–Gandhi Correspondence,* 509–519.
61. Rolland, "Introduction à *La Jeune Inde,*" 514.
62. Ibid., 513.
63. Rolland, *Mahatma Gandhi,* 21, 43 n. 25, 111; Romain Rolland cited M. N. Roy, *India in Transition* (Geneva, 1922), and M. N. Roy and Evelyn Roy, *One Year of Non-Cooperation* (Calcutta, 1923), adding that these brochures "set forth the communist thesis, in opposition to Gandhi," ibid., 130.
64. Despite the popularity of Romain Rolland's volume on Gandhi, it was ignored by reviewers. Three rare but not substantive reviews are Charles Henry Hirsch, *Mercure de France* 165 (1 July 1923): 191–192, and 175 (1 November 1924): 793; Jean Caves, "Le Nihilisme européen et les Appels de l'Orient," *Philosophies,* no. 2 (15 May 1924): 190–195; and Paul Souday, "*Mahatma Gandhi* de R. Rolland," *Le Temps,* 13 March 1924. Letters from Rolland to Luc Durtain, 1 June 1923; to Waldo Frank, 17 June 1923; to Stefan Zweig, 22 March 1924; *G-RR,* 192, 196, 212.
65. Ram-Prasad Dube, "Les Aspects sociaux au mouvement Gandhi dans l'Inde," *Clarté,* no. 8 (1 March 1922): 188–191.
66. M. N. Roy, "Le Congrès national de Gaya. Vers la disparition du quiétisme de Gandhi," *L'Humanité,* 3 March 1923, 3.
67. Executive Committee of the Communist International, "Les Crimes de l'impérialisme brittanique," *L'Humanité,* 19 March 1923, 3.

68. Henri Barbusse, "Révolutionnaires d'Orient et d'Occident. A propos de Gandhi," *Clarté*, no. 39 (13 July 1923): 314.

69. Ibid., 315.

70. Ibid., 316.

71. Ibid., 317.

72. Ibid., 317–318.

73. Ibid., 318.

74. Ibid.

75. Ibid., 319.

76. Ibid., 320; Evelyn Roy's "Mahatma Gandhi. Révolutionnaire ou contre-révolutionnaire?" *Clarté*, no. 46 (November 1926): 437–439, was critical of both Barbusse and Romain Rolland; *Clarté* had evolved to an extreme left position by 1926.

77. Letters from Rolland to Jacques Mesnil, 12 March 1923; and to J. Taupin, 12 March 1923, *G-RR*, 188, 188–189.

78. Letter from Rolland to Roy, 24 February 1924, *G-RR*, 209.

79. Letter from Rolland to C. F. Andrews, 24 September 1924, *G-RR*, 218. Romain Rolland noted in March 1924 that his portrait of Gandhi was proscribed in the Soviet Union (ibid., 432).

80. Letter from Rolland to Andrews, 24 September 1924, *G-RR*, 217–218.

81. For the text of Gandhi's statement, see M. K. Gandhi, *Non-Violence in Peace and War* (Ahmedabad, 1962), 1:29–30, which first appeared in *Young India*, 12 December 1924.

82. Rolland, journal extract, January 1924, *G-RR*, 437–438. For *Le Matin's* exploitation of Gandhi's statement, see "Gandhi refuse de l'argent offert par Moscou pour fomenter la révolution aux Indes," *Le Matin*, 20 January 1925, 1.

83. Letter from Rolland to Roger Avermaete, 28 July 1924, *G-RR*, 215.

84. Letter from Rolland to Gandhi, 24 February 1924, *G-RR*, 13–14.

85. Letters from Rolland to Gandhi, 1 October 1925, *G-RR*, 15; from Madeleine Slade to Rolland, 12 November 1925, ibid., 15–16; from Gandhi to Rolland, 13 November 1925, ibid., 16; journal extract, 14 September 1925, ibid., 439–440. Also consult Madeleine Slade, *The Spirit's Pilgrimage* (New York, 1960).

86. Letter from Gandhi to Rolland, 22 March 1924, *G-RR*, 14.

87. Rolland, journal extract, December 1924, *G-RR*, 437.

88. Letter from Gandhi to Emil Roniger, October 1926, *G-RR*, 26 (English translation in *Rolland-Gandhi Correspondence*, 77); also published in *Liber Amicorum Romain Rolland*, ed. Georges Duhamel, Maxim Gorky, and Stefan Zweig (Zurich, 1926), 155.

89. Letter from Rolland to Slade, 26 September 1926, *G-RR*, 22–23 (*Rolland-Gandhi Correspondence*, 72).

90. *G-RR*, 23 (*Rolland-Gandhi Correspondence*, 73).

91. Romain Rolland, "Hic et Nunc" (22 November 1926), in *Le Voyage intérieur* (Paris, 1959), 374–379.

92. Letters from Rolland to George Lenard, 8 March 1928; to Reginald Reynolds, 19 September 1930, *G-RR*, 240, 253 (*Rolland-Gandhi Correspondence*, 410, 423). Romain Rolland also used the line from Spinoza as the epigraph to *Mère et fils* (1927), in *L'Ame enchantée*, 431.

93. Rolland, "Hic et Nunc," 375, 376, 379.

94. Letter from Rolland to Slade, 10 December 1927, *G-RR*, 30–32 (*Rolland-Gandhi Correspondence*, 88–90); letters from Slade to Rolland, 6 January 1928, 12 February 1928, *G-RR*, 32–33, 34–35 (*Rolland-Gandhi Correspondence*, 90–91, 93–94); letter from Gandhi to Rolland, 17 February 1928, *G-RR*, 36–37 (*Rolland-Gandhi Correspondence*, 95–96); letter from Rolland to Slade, 21 January 1928, *G-RR*, 33 (*Rolland-Gandhi Correspondence*, 91–92).

95. Letter from Rolland to Gandhi, 8 March 1928, *G-RR*, 39–41 (*Rolland-Gandhi Correspondence*, 99–102); M. K. Gandhi, "My Part in the War," and "A Spiritual Dilemma," in *An Autobiography: The Story of My Experiments with Truth* (New York, 1971), 346–348, 348–350.

96. Letter from Rolland to Gandhi, 7 March 1928, *G-RR*, 41 (*Rolland-Gandhi Correspondence*, 101).

97. Letters from Rolland to Gandhi, 16 April 1928, 17 February 1928, *G-RR*, 46–48, 51–53 (*Rolland-Gandhi Correspondence*, 111–114, 128–130).

98. Message from Rolland to Reginald Reynolds for Gandhi's birthday, 1 October 1930, *G-RR*, 254–255 (*Rolland-Gandhi Correspondence*, 141).

99. Letter from Rolland to Gandhi, 10 September 1931, *G-RR*, 61–62 (*Rolland-Gandhi Correspondence*, 147–148); letter from Rolland to Slade, 9 November 1931, *G-RR*, 65–68 (*Rolland-Gandhi Correspondence*, 156–159).

100. Rolland, journal extract, December 1931, *G-RR*, 70 (*Rolland-Gandhi Correspondence*, 163–164); the full text of Gandhi's visit is recorded in *G-RR*, 69–127.

101. Geoffrey Ashe, *Gandhi* (New York, 1969), 311–312; Louis Fischer, *The Life of Mahatma Gandhi* (New York, 1962), 298–301.

102. Rolland, journal extract, *G-RR*, 73–76 (*Rolland-Gandhi Correspondence*, 168–171).

103. Rolland, journal extract, *G-RR*, 75–76 (*Rolland-Gandhi Correspondence*, 169–170).

104. Rolland, journal extract, *G-RR*, 83–85, 86, 115–116 (*Rolland-Gandhi Correspondence*, 179–181, 183, 217–218).

105. *G-RR*, 97–98, 114–117, 118–119 (*Rolland-Gandhi Correspondence*, 195–197, 216–217, 218–219). Only the revolutionary syndicalists covered Gandhi's visit to Europe; see D. Guérin, "Gandhi à Paris," *Révolution prolétarienne*, no. 122 (December 1931): 306–309. Gandhi replied to Monatte's question (posed by Romain Rolland) in *Révolution prolétarienne*, no. 123 (January 1932): 5–6.

106. Rolland, *L'Inde*, 315–321, 338.

107. Ibid., 353, 362–364, 376–380.

108. Ibid., 320, 364.

109. Ibid.

110. Letter from Gandhi to Rolland, 20 December 1931, *G-RR*, 129.

111. Rolland, *L'Inde*, 423; dated 1933.

112. Letter from Rolland to Gandhi, 2 January 1932, *G-RR*, 134–135, (*Rolland-Gandhi Correspondence*, 245–248). This letter was neither completed nor mailed because of Gandhi's arrest in India.

113. *G-RR*, 135.

114. Romain Rolland, *Le Voyage intérieur. (Songe d'une vie)* (Paris, 1959); Rolland, *Beethoven. Les Grandes Epoques créatrices de l'Héroïque à l'Appassionata* (Paris, 1928); Rolland, *Goethe et Beethoven* (Paris, 1930); Rolland,

Essai sur la mystique et l'action de l'Inde vivante. *La Vie de Ramakrishna* (Paris, 1929) and *La Vie de Vivekananda et l'évangile universel*, 2 vols. (Paris, 1930).

115. Rolland, *L'Inde*, 262; also see letters from Rolland to Albert Crémieux, 8 February 1928; to Swami Ashkananda, 4 October 1927; to Swami Shivananda, 12 September 1927, ARR. Letter from Rolland to Roy, 22 August 1928, in Roy, *Among the Great*, 51–54.

116. Rolland coined the term "oceanic sensation" in a letter written to Sigmund Freud on 5 December 1927 (*BV*, 264–266); see David James Fisher, "Sigmund Freud and Romain Rolland: The Terrestrial Animal and His Great Oceanic Friend," *American Imago* 33, no. 1 (Spring 1976): 1–59; and David James Fisher, "Reading Freud's *Civilization and Its Discontents*," in *Modern European Intellectual History*, ed. Dominick LaCapra and Steven Kaplan (Ithaca, N.Y., 1982), 251–279.

117. Letter from Rolland to Freud, 17 July 1929, ARR. Also see Romain Rolland, *The Life of Ramakrishna*, trans. E. F. Malcolm-Smith (Calcutta, 1970), 4–5, 6–7; Rolland, *The Life of Vivekananda and the Universal Gospel*, trans. E. F. Malcolm-Smith (Calcutta, 1970), 254. For a study of Romain Rolland's religiosity, see Paul Claudel, "La Pensée religieuse de Romain Rolland," in *Accompagnements* (Paris, 1949), 62–88.

118. The following is a list of Romain Rolland's "Courrier de l'Inde" articles: "Courrier de l'Inde. La Déclaration de guerre de l'Angleterre à l'Inde," *G-RR*, 383–393 (first published in *Europe*, 15 February 1932, 250–260); "Courrier de l'Inde II. Echec au Roi!" *G-RR*, 394–406 (first published in *Europe*, 15 March 1932, 416–427); "Courrier de l'Inde III. Révolution, le chef invisible," *G-RR*, 406–417 (first published in *Europe*, 15 May 1932, 108–119); "Le Christ des Indes," *G-RR*, 417–419 (first published in *Journée internationale pour l'Inde*, 6 October 1932); "Tagore et Gandhi pendant le jeune," *L'Inde*, 559–562 (first published in *Europe*, 15 November 1932, 448–551); "Vers l'unité de l'Inde par l'entente Hindoue-Musulmane," *L'Inde*, 559–562 (first published in *Europe*, 15 January 1933, 107–110); "Documents sur l'Inde," *L'Inde*, 568–572 (first published in *Europe*, 15 February 1933, 254–257); "Pour les condamnés de Meerut," *L'Inde*, 573–577 (first published in *Europe*, 15 April 1933, 593–597); "Les Resolutions du Congrès National de Toute L'Inde, à Calcutta" (May 1933), *L'Inde*, 578–581 (first published in *Europe*, 15 June 1933, 273–276).

119. Letters from Rolland to Lucien Price, 25 December 1931; to Stefan Zweig, 30 December 1931; to Marcel Lob, 1 January 1932; to Ré Meynard, 17 January 1932; *G-RR*, 284–287, 287–291, 295, 300–301.

120. Letter from Rolland to Waldo Frank, 26 January 1932, *G-RR*, 301–302. Also see letters from Rolland to Reginald Reynolds, 12 July 1933; to Eugene Lagot, 4 November 1933; to Saumyendranath Tagore, 14 November 1933; *G-RR*, 316–318, 320, 321–322. For Romain Rolland's attempts to bridge the communist and Gandhian movements, see "Entretien entre Romain Rolland et S. Tagore," *G-RR*, 330–332.

121. Letter from Rolland to Gandhi, 14 April 1932, *G-RR*, 154–157 (*Rolland-Gandhi Correspondence*, 302–305).

122. Gandhi had attacked socialist theory and practice in his "Adresse au Congrès de Bombay," *Europe*, 15 March 1935, delivered in September 1934. Also see letter from Gandhi to Madeleine Rolland, 28 March 1935, *G-RR*, 162–163. For Romain Rolland's reactions, see *PRP*, 74 n. 1; and

Rolland, journal extract, *G-RR*, 340–343 (*Rolland-Gandhi Correspondence*, 324–327).

123. Romain Rolland, "Acte de reconnaissance d'un homme d'Occident à Gandhi" (February 1939), *G-RR*, 420–422 (*Rolland-Gandhi Correspondence*, 345–348).

124. See Joan V. Bondurant, *The Conquest of Violence: The Gandhian Philosophy of Conflict* (Berkeley, Calif., 1971), for the connection between Gandhism and the liberal democratic ideologies; Erikson, *Gandhi's Truth*, for the correspondences between Gandhism and psychoanalysis; and George Woodcock, *Mohandas Gandhi* (New York, 1971), for the link to anarchist ideas.

CHAPTER 7

1. Letter from Rolland to Louise Cruppi, 15 February 1922, ARR; also *QAC*, xl.

2. Letter from Rolland to Cruppi, 1 November 1922, ARR.

3. Letter from Rolland to Sofia Guerrieri-Gonzaga, 27 July 1922, *RR-SBGG (1960)*, 287; letter from Rolland to Cruppi, 8 February 1923, ARR.

4. Letter from Rolland to Guerrieri-Gonzaga, 31 December 1922, *RR-SBGG (1960)*, 290–291; letter from Rolland to Cruppi, 13 September 1923, ARR.

5. Rolland, *Journal intime*, December 1924–December 1925, ARR; letter from Rolland to Umberto Zanotti-Bianco, 31 August 1925, ARR.

6. Letters from Rolland to René Arcos, 31 August 1925; to Léon Bazalgette, 7 September 1925; to Jean-Richard Bloch, 5 September 1925 and 15 October 1925, ARR.

7. Romain Rolland, "Contre la guerre et ses agents provocateurs," *QAC*, 66–67; first delivered as an address to the French League of the Rights of Man, Drôme and Ardèche sections, 19 April 1926.

8. Romain Rolland, "*Vita sine libertate, nihil,*" *QAC*, 67; this was first a letter written to Henry Torrès, 23 April 1926.

9. Romain Rolland, "Lettre à Filippo Turati" (1 May 1927), *QAC*, 67–68; Romain Rolland, "La Veuve de Matteotti séquestrée," *Le Populaire*, 3 October 1927, 3. For a description of the weekly *La Libertà* and for information on the activities of Turati and Claudio Treves, see Charles Delzell, *Mussolini's Enemies: The Italian Antifascist Resistance* (Princeton, N.J., 1961), 58.

10. Henri Giordan, ed., *Romain Rolland et le mouvement florentin de "la Voce"* (Paris, 1966). Giovanni Amendola's tribute to Romain Rolland appeared in *Liber Amicorum Romain Rolland* (Zurich, 1926), 393–394.

11. Letter from Rolland to Giorgio Amendola, 22 May 1926, in Giordan, *Romain Rolland et la mouvement florentin de "la Voce,"* 355–356; also see *QAC*, xl; published in Italian in Giorgio Amendola, *Communismo antifascismo resistenza* (Rome, 1967), 411–412.

12. Romain Rolland, *L'Inde. Journal, 1915–1943* (Paris, 1951), 109–119, 126–127, 134.

13. Letter from Rolland to Gaetano Salvemini, 5 July 1926, *RT-RR*, 147.

14. Letter from Rolland to Rabindranath Tagore, 11 November 1926, *RT-RR*, 78; also see the conversation between Rolland and Tagore, 25 June 1926, ibid., 187–191.

15. Letter from Rolland to Kalidas Nag, 6–7 July 1926, *RT-RR,* 149–151.
16. Letter from Rolland to Salvemini, 5 July 1926, *RT-RR,* 147; also see Rolland, *L'Inde,* 138–146, 157, 159–166, 179, 182–192. For Tagore's final statement on Italian fascism, see "Tagore en Italie," *Europe,* 15 August 1926, and *L'Humanité,* 16 August 1926. See Romain Rolland, "Lettre à *The Indian Daily Mail,*" *L'Inde,* 184–185, for a protest against the spread of pro–Italian-fascist propaganda in India.
17. Letter from Rolland to Madame Thérèse Dispan de Floran, 31 January 1927, ARR.
18. Letter from Rolland to Salvemini, 28 May 1927, *BV,* 248–251; also see *QAC,* lxxiv.
19. Romain Rolland and Henri Barbusse, "Aux esprits libres, contre le fascisme," *Bulletin du Comité de défense des victimes du fascisme et de la terreur blanche* (February 1927), *QAC,* xlii; in a letter to Barbusse dated 28 January 1928, Romain Rolland condemned this bulletin for its communist invective and propaganda, ARR.
20. Letter from Rolland to Heinz Haeberlin, 3 March 1927, in Pierre Abraham, *Romain Rolland* (Neuchâtel, 1969), 135.
21. Letters from Rolland to Henri Barbusse, 30 November 1926, 10 February 1927, ARR.
22. Letter from Rolland to Barbusse, 28 January 1928, ARR.
23. Letter from Rolland to Barbusse, 28 October 1928, ARR.
24. Romain Rolland, "M. Romain Rolland prend position," *Clarté,* no. 5 (15 January 1927): 158; Marcel Fournier had challenged Romain Rolland in *Clarté,* no. 4 (15 December 1926): 124.
25. Letter from Rolland to André Berthet, 30 October 1928, ARR.
26. Romain Rolland, "Avertissement à l'Amérique" (10 September 1926), *QAC,* 72–73. Romain Rolland also protested the abuse of justice in the Sacco and Vanzetti case; see "Lettre à un ami Américain sur le meutre judiciaire de Sacco et Vanzetti," ibid., 74–78; first published in *Europe,* 15 October 1927, and *The Nation,* 28 September 1927.
27. Romain Rolland, "Au *Flambeau* d'Egypte," 14 October 1929, *BV,* 284–286; letter from Rolland to Charles Lecôeur, 28 June 1930, ibid., 305–307.
28. Romain Rolland, "Sur pan-Europa" (28 January 1930), *QAC,* 97–98; this first appeared in *L'Effort* (Lyons) as an address to secular educators for a conference organized by the League of the Rights of Man.
29. Romain Rolland, "Le Gouvernement reste muet sur les massacres du 1ᵉʳ mai. Une Protestation de Romain Rolland contre le repatriement forcé de Tao à Saigon," *L'Humanité,* 12 May 1931, 1.
30. Rolland, journal extract, 16 March 1931, ARR.
31. Romain Rolland, "Un Meeting grandiose et vibrant pour la libération de Tao en faveur de l'indépendance de l'Indochine," *L'Humanité,* 20 May 1931, 1; this reappeared as "Politique coloniale," in *L'Oeuvre sociale* (Besançon), no. 463 (18 July 1931): 1.
32. Romain Rolland, "Romain Rolland appelle à la lutte révolutionnaire," *L'Humanité,* 4 November 1931, 3; also see his review of Pin Yin's *Une Jeune Chinoise à l'armée révolutionnaire,* in *L'Intransigeant,* 18 July 1931. For a discussion of Romain Rolland's impact on contemporary Chinese intellectuals, see T. B. Kin-Yn-Yn, "La Renaissance Chinoise et l'influence de Romain Rolland," *Europe,* 15 September 1927, 101–108.

33. Romain Rolland, "The Action of the League Against Imperialism," *Anti-Imperialist Review*, 1, no. 3 (January–February 1932): 209; also signed by Barbusse and Gorky.

34. Romain Rolland, "Pour les condamnés de Meerut," *QAC*, 189–197; first published in *L'Humanité*, 18 March 1933; *Europe*, 15 April 1933; *The World Tomorrow*, 14 September 1933; reprinted in *L'Inde*, 573–577.

35. Rolland, "Pour les condamnés de Meerut," 192.

36. Romain Rolland, "Pour les condamnés de Saigon en Indochine," *QAC*, 197–198; this first appeared in *Monde*, no. 273 (26 August 1933): 13. Romain Rolland became one of the honorary presidents (along with Barbusse, Paul Langevin, and Victor Margueritte) of the Committee for Amnesty and Defense of Indochinese and Colonized Peoples; see Rolland, "Message de Romain Rolland," in Félicien Challaye, *Souvenirs sur la colonisation* (Paris, 1935), xiii, 138.

37. Key literature on the Amsterdam-Pleyel movement includes E. H. Carr, *The Twilight of the Comintern, 1930–1935* (New York, 1982), 385–399; Babette Gross, *Willi Münzenberg* (New York, 1974), 223–246; Helmut Gruber, "Willi Münzenberg: Propagandist For and Against the Comintern," *International Review of Social History* 11 (1965): 188–210; Helmut Gruber, "Willi Münzenberg's German Communist Propaganda Empire, 1921–1933," *Journal of Modern History* 38, no. 3 (September 1966): 278–297; Daniel H. Brower, *The New Jacobins: The French Communist Party and the Popular Front* (Ithaca, N.Y., 1968), 17–18, 39–41, 54–55, 102, 105, 142–143; Georges Lefranc, *Histoire du front populaire* (Paris, 1965), 36–47; Jacques Fauvet, *Histoire du Parti communiste français* (Paris, 1964) 1:116–118; Maurice Thorez, *Fils du peuple* (Paris, 1960), 79–80; Nicole Racine, "L'Association des Ecrivains et Artistes Révolutionnaires (A.E.A.R.)," *Mouvement social*, no. 54 (January–March 1966): 29–47; André Legendre, "Bibliographie," *Cahiers de l'Institut Maurice Thorez*, no. 1 (April 1966): 165–181; Claude Willard, "Les Intellectuels français et le front populaire," *Cahiers de l'Institut Maurice Thorez*, no. 3–4 (October 1966–March 1967): 115–124.

38. Nathanael Greene, *Crisis and Decline: The French Socialist Party in the Popular Front Era* (Ithaca, N.Y., 1969); Peter J. Larmour, *The French Radical Party in the 1930s* (Stanford, Calif., 1964); Stanley Hoffmann, "Paradoxes of the French Political Community," in *In Search of France*, ed. Stanley Hoffmann et al. (New York, 1965), 23–24, 33. See the entries by Sandi E. Cooper, David James Fisher, James Friguglietti, and David Schalk in *Biographical Dictionary of Modern Peace Leaders*, ed. Harold Josephson (Westport, Conn., 1985).

39. Maurice Thorez, "Pourquoi les communistes iront à Genève," *L'Humanité*, 28 June 1932, 1; earlier Marcel Cachin had exhorted the congress to be "practical and realistic." See "*L'Humanité* sera au congrès mondial contre la guerre," *L'Humanité*, 17 June 1932, 1.

40. Carr, *Twilight of the Comintern*, 396–427; Ronald Tiersky, *French Communism, 1920–1972* (New York, 1974), 54–95; George Lichtheim, *Marxism in Modern France* (New York, 1966), 34–68.

41. Letter from Rolland to Barbusse, 10 September 1932, ARR. Guessler Normand, "Henri Barbusse and his *Monde* (1928–1935)," *Journal of Contemporary History*, Spring 1976, 173–197. Also see the joint appeal signed by Rolland and Barbusse, "Appel de Romain Rolland et Henri Barbusse,"

leaflet issued by Comité contre la guerre impérialiste, Bibliothèque Nationale, Paris, Imprimés no. 2638.

42. Romain Rolland, "La Patrie est en danger!" *PRP*, 27, 28; first published in *L'Humanité*, 1 May 1932, and in *Pravda*.

43. Romain Rolland, "Contre la guerre. Rassemblement!" (1 June 1932), *PRP*, 29.

44. Romain Rolland, "Appel à la Ligue des Combattants de la Paix" (10 June 1932), *PRP*, 34.

45. Ibid., 36.

46. Romain Rolland, "Lettre à Victor Méric," 12 July 1932, *PRP*, 40.

47. Romain Rolland, "Lettre à Albert de Jong" (31 July 1932), *PRP*, 42; first published in *Europe*, no. 118 (15 October 1932): 302–304. De Jong was general secretary of the International Antimilitarist Bureau in Amsterdam.

48. Friedrich Adler, "Lettre de Fritz Adler à Henri Barbusse," *Monde*, no. 217 (20 July 1932), 13; E.-Paul Graber, "Les Idéalistes entre les mains des manoeuveristes," *La Sentinelle*, no. 168 (22 July 1932), 1.

49. Friedrich Adler, "Un Congrès contre la guerre. Lettre du secrétaire de I.O.S. à Romain Rolland," *La Sentinelle*, no. 164 (18 July 1932): 1; Friedrich Adler, "Le Congrès mondial contre la guerre n'est qu'une manoeuvre communiste dirigée contre les partis socialistes," *Populaire de Paris*, 20 July 1932, 3.

50. Letters from Rolland to Friedrich Adler, 7 July 1932, 16 July 1932, ARR; Rolland, "La Réponse de Romain Rolland," *Monde*, no. 217 (20 July 1932): 13; Barbusse, "Réponse de Henri Barbusse," *Monde*, no. 217 (20 July 1932): 13–14; Rolland, "La Réponse de Romain Rolland au chief socialiste Graber," *L'Humanité*, 4 August 1932, 1; Rolland, "Lettre de Romain Rolland à Paul Graber," *Europe*, 15 September 1932, 151–152. Maurice Thorez used the Amsterdam Congress to attack French Socialist leader Léon Blum and to accuse the Socialists of being agents of imperialism; see Maurice Thorez, "Avec les ouvriers socialistes contre les saboteurs du Congrès," *L'Humanité*, 21 July 1932, 1.

51. Congrès mondial contre la guerre impérialiste, "Bulletin du Congrès," typescript, 1–8, International Institute for Social History, Amsterdam.

52. Romain Rolland, "Déclaration lue à la première séance du congrès mondial de tous les partis contre la guerre," *PRP*, 45, 46; first published in *Europe*, 15 September 1932, 148–151; also in *Monde*, no. 222 (3 September 1932); in Wladimir Martel, *Vers la guerre ou la révolution* (Alençon, 1933), 18–21; in *The World Congress Against War*, ed. American Committee for Struggle Against War (New York, 1933), 11–15; also see Romain Rolland, "La Guerre est entre les mains du peuple ouvrier," *L'Humanité*, 28 August 1932, 1–2.

53. Rolland, "Déclaration lue . . . du congrès mondial," 46.

54. Ibid., 47–48.

55. Ibid., 49.

56. "Manifesto of the World Congress Against War at Amsterdam, August 27–29, 1932," in *The World Congress Against War*, 16–24; first published as "Le Manifeste du congrès d'Amsterdam," *Monde*, no. 223 (September 1932): 4–5; also published in Martel, *Vers la guerre ou la révolution*,

63–69. Martel's book, with introduction by Barbusse, summarized the Amsterdam Congress from the French communist perspective. For the Soviet viewpoint, see the anonymous pamphlet *Voix de l'URSS à Amsterdam* [1932].

57. "Manifesto of the World Congress at Amsterdam," 20, 24.

58. Letters from Madeleine Rolland to Rolland, 28 and 29 August 1932, ARR. For a right-wing perspective on the Amsterdam Congress see *Le Figaro*, 12 September 1932; for the communist perspective, see Gabriel Peri and J. Berlioz, "Acclamé par le congrès mondial, Marcel Cachin expose les méthodes léninistes de lutte contre la guerre," *L'Humanité*, 29 August 1932, 1; for the French pacifist perspective, see Victor Margueritte, "Quelques Observations sur le congrès d'Amsterdam," *Evolution*, no. 81 (October 1932): 614–621; Victor Méric, "Nos Moyens de lutte," *Patrie humaine*, no. 66 (29 April 1933): 1; for the socialist position, see Adolf Strumthal, "La Manifestation communiste d'Amsterdam," *Populaire de Paris*, 4 September 1932, 3; for the Trotskyist, see Léon Trotsky, "Lettre sur le congrès contre la guerre," *Lutte de classe*, no. 39 (15 June 1932): 2–3; Pierre Naville, "Camarades du parti, repoussez le manifeste de confusion adopté par le congrès d'Amsterdam," *La Verité*, 5 September 1932, 1. For the Surrealist view, see André Breton, "La Mobilisation contre la guerre n'est pas la paix" (1933), in Maurice Nadeau, *Histoire du surrealisme* (Paris, 1964), 371–376; and for the Soviet viewpoint, see Maxim Gorky, "To the Delegates of the Antiwar Congress (A Speech That Was Not Delivered)," in Maxim Gorky, *Articles and Pamphlets* (Moscow, 1951), 342–354.

59. Romain Rolland, "Le Congrès mondial d'Amsterdam contre la guerre," *PRP*, 50; this was first published in *Europe*, 15 October 1932, 249–255. Also see Annette Vidal, *Henri Barbusse. Soldat de la paix* (Paris, 1953), 266 n. 1.

60. Rolland, "Le Congrès mondial," *PRP*, 53, 55–56.

61. Ibid., 56–58.

62. Ibid., 58–59.

63. Romain Rolland, "Lettre à Henri Barbusse" (20 December 1932), *PRP*, 61–64.

64. Bureau international du comité mondial de lutte contre la guerre, "Declaration sur la participation des groupements d'action individuelle au mouvement d'Amsterdam," in *PRP*, 64, signed by Henri Barbusse, Marcel Cachin, Willi Münzenberg, J. Chvernik, and H. Stassova.

65. Rolland, "Le Congrès mondial," *PRP*, 60; Carr, *Twilight of the Comintern*, 391–392.

66. Carr, *Twilight of the Comintern*, 392–394; for primary documents on the Amsterdam-Pleyel movement, see *Tracts politiques d'organisations et partis pacifistes divers circa 1930–1939*, Bibliothèque Nationale, Paris, Lb57 16552; anonymous editorial, "Après le congrès d'Amsterdam," *Europe*, 15 September 1932, 1122–1129; Jacques Duclos, "Le Congrès européen antifasciste," *Europe*, 15 June 1933, 803–808; anonymous editorial, "Après le congrès mondial des jeunes," *Europe*, 1 October 1933, 1303–1306; Henri Barbusse, "Une Etape du front unique," *Monde*, no. 264 (24 June 1933): 15–16; *Tracts du comité mondial de lutte contre la guerre impérialiste* (1933), Archives Nationale, Paris, F[17] 13148.

67. Letters from Rolland to Louis Gibarti, 16 September 1933, 17 September 1933; from Rolland to Willi Münzenberg, 26 December 1933; from Münzenberg to Rolland, December 1933; ARR.

68. Rolland, *L'Ame enchantée* (Paris, 1967), 1143–1144, 1248, 1259, 1358; these volumes of the novel cycle were first published as *L'Annonciatrice. La Mort d'un monde*, 2 vols. (Paris, 1933).

69. Rolland, *L'Ame enchantée*, 1152, 1284.

70. Ibid., 1280–1281, 1302, 1305.

71. Ibid., 1009, 1219, 1284, 1300, 1303, 1305.

72. Ibid., 1147–1151.

73. In a letter to Lucien Roth dated 1 December 1933, Romain Rolland revealed that the liberal antifascist Gaetano Salvemini was the prototype for the character Count Bruno Chiarenza (ARR).

74. Rolland, *L'Ame enchantée*, 1217–1221, 1288.

75. Ibid., 1260–1264.

76. Ibid., 1309–1310, 1343.

77. Ibid., 1358–1361; also see Romain Rolland, "Le Combat," *Commune*, no. 1(July 1933): 41–44.

78. Rolland, *L'Ame enchantée*, 1426 –1430, 1448–1453; also see his "Introduction à *L'Icare* de Lauro de Bosis," *Europe*, May–August 1933, 5–15.

79. Rolland, Introduction (1 January 1934), *L'Ame enchantée*, xv–xix.

80. Rolland, *L'Ame enchantée*, 1357–1358, also quoted in *QAC*, lii–lxii. The German Fascists prevented *L'Annonciatrice* from being translated into German; see ibid., lxxix. For three favorable reviews, see Magdeleine Paz, "*L'Annonciatrice* par Romain Rolland," *Monde*, no. 249 (11 March 1933): 10; "Romain Rolland—*L'Annonciatrice*," *Commune*, no. 7–8 (March–April 1934): 819–820; and Christian Sénéchal, *Europe*, no. 35 (15 March 1934): 137–142.

CHAPTER 8

1. Romain Rolland, "Fragments de journal," *Europe*, 1 January 1946, 4 (dated 1 February 1933); ibid., 9–10 (dated March 1933).

2. Ibid., 7 (dated 2 March 1933).

3. Ibid., 7–8 (dated 2 March 1933). Romain Rolland felt that it was extremely important to have non-Jewish writers protest Nazi injustices. This piece was first published as "Contre le fascisme hitlérien," *Europe*, 15 March 1933, 440; also in *QAC*, 199–200; English translation in *I Will Not Rest*, trans. K. S. Shelvankar (New York, [1935]), 291–292.

4. Romain Rolland, "Contre les bourreaux de l'Allemagne" (20 March 1933), *QAC*, 200 (English translation, *I Will Not Rest*, 292).

5. Letters from Rolland to Jean Guéhenno, 2 February 1933, 1 March 1933, *JG-RR*, 255, 258. On 22 May 1933, Rolland urged Guéhenno to commission a rigorous critique of Hitler's *Mein Kampf* (ibid., 270).

6. Rolland, "Fragments de journal" (dated 10 January 1933), 4–5; letter from German consul in Geneva to Rolland, 19 April 1933, in "Fragments de journal," 12.

7. Letter from Rolland to German consul in Geneva, 30 April 1933, in "Fragments de journal," 12. Also see *QAC*, lxxvii, where this letter is dated 20 April 1933.

8. Letter from Rolland to Stefan Zweig, 30 March 1933, "Fragments de journal," 1–11; published as "Lettre à un ami allemand contre l'abdication du parti social-démocrate allemand," *QAC*, 200–201 (*I Will Not Rest*, 292–293).

9. Letter from Rolland to Ingeborg Andreas, 15 May 1932, ARR.

10. Romain Rolland, "Contre l'antisémitisme en Allemagne" (dated 5 April 1933), *QAC*, 201–202 (*I Will Not Rest*, 293).

11. Romain Rolland, "Contre le racisme et l'antisémitisme" (dated 9 April 1933), *QAC*, 202–204 (*I Will Not Rest*, 294–295); originally a letter to Hardo Bruckner.

12. Letter from Rolland to Vladimir Pozner, secretary of the Guild for Emancipation Through Books, 4 May 1933, "Fragments de journal," 13; Rolland, "From Romain Rolland," *Fight Against War and Fascism* 1, no. 10 (August 1934): 14.

13. Rolland, "Fragments de journal," 15; Henri Barbusse, "Un Appel mondial du Comité d'Amsterdam pour le front unique de lutte contre la guerre et son instrument: Le Fascisme," *Front mondial*, no. 4 (April 1933): 2–3.

14. Romain Rolland, "Lettre à la *Koelnische Zeitung*," 14 May 1933, *QAC*, 205 (*I Will Not Rest*, 295–297); first published in *Europe*, 15 May 1933, and *Front mondial*, no. 6 (June 1933): 14.

15. Rolland, "Lettre à la *Koelnische Zeitung*," *QAC*, 206.

16. Ibid., 206–207.

17. Rolland, "Fragments de journal," 15; also see "Auseinanderdersetzing mit Romain Rolland ein Briefwechsel über das neue Deutschland," *Koelnische Zeitung*, 21 May 1933, 1.

18. *Sechs Bekenntnisse zum neuen Deutschland* (Hamburg, 1933); this included a German translation of Romain Rolland's letter to the *Koelnische Zeitung*, 7–9, a reply from the editorial board, and open letters from Rudolf Binding (14–20), E. G. Kolbenheyer, Wilhelm von Scholz, Otto Wirz, and Robert Fabre-Luce.

19. Rolland, "Fragments de journal," 16, 17.

20. Letter from Rolland to the director of the Nietzsche Archive in Weimar, 4 August 1933, "Fragments de journal," 17.

21. Romain Rolland, "Appel à la jeunesse" (17 May 1933), *QAC*, 207–210 (*I Will Not Rest*, 297–299); first published in *Front mondial*, no. 6 (June 1933): 8–9.

22. *Livre brun sur l'incendie du Reichstag et la terreur hitlérienne*, ed. Comité international d'aide aux victimes du fascisme hitlérien (Paris, 1933).

23. *Dimitroff Contra Goering*, ed. Comité international d'aide aux victimes du fascisme hitlérien (Paris, 1934). See also Rolland, "Fragments de journal," 18; letter from Rolland to Guéhenno, 12 July 1934, *JG-RR*, 304.

24. Romain Rolland, "Contre les vrais incendiaires du Reichstag" (4 September 1933), *QAC*, 210–211; ibid., lxxviii (*I Will Not Rest*, 299).

25. Romain Rolland, "Pour Thaelmann," *QAC*, 214–215; first published in *Monde*, 6 July 1934, 11 (*I Will Not Rest*, 302). Also see Rolland's "Appel au peuple d'Allemagne, pour l'acquittement de Dimitrov et de ses compagnons," *QAC*, 211–212; first published in *Monde*, no. 289 (23 December 1933): 3; "Pour Torgler," *QAC*, 213–214, first published in *L'Humanité*, 22

December 1933, and *Dépêche de Toulouse*, 21 December 1933; "Sur Ossietzsky et Kurt Hiller," 17 September 1933, published in the *Times* (London), the *Chicago Daily News*, *The Nation*, and the *New York Times*.

26. Letter from Dimitrov to Rolland, 31 August 1933, cited in Georgi Dimitrov, *Letters from Prison*, ed. Alfred Kurella (London, 1935), 60–61; also in Rolland, "Fragments de journal," 19–20.

27. Paul Vaillant-Couturier, "Qu'est-ce que l'AEAR?" in *Ceux qui ont choisi* (Paris, 1933), 1–4; quote is from Rolland's "Message," ibid., 5.

28. Romain Rolland, "Réponse au questionnaire du comité mondial de la jeunesse contre la guerre et le fascisme," 22 March 1934, ARR; Romain Rolland, "Appel à l'aide des victimes au fascisme autrichien,"*Front mondial*, no. 13 (April 1934): 7; Rolland, "Fragments de journal" (18 August 1933), 18.

29. Rolland, "Fragments de journal," 19.

30. Rolland, *QAC*, lxxix, dated summer 1934.

31. Letter from Rolland to Victor Margueritte, 6 October 1933, "Fragments de journal," 21.

32. Nathanael Greene, *From Versailles to Vichy* (New York, 1970), 69.

33. Romain Rolland, "Appel au peuple de Paris (après l'émeute fasciste du 6 février)," *QAC*, 215; first published in *Littérature internationale*, no. 1 (1934):3 (*I Will Not Rest*, 303).

34. Romain Rolland, "Appel à l'union des travailleurs intellectuels avec le prolétariat," *QAC*, 215–216; written for the sixth day of international solidarity sponsored by the Secours Ouvrier International (*I Will Not Rest*, 303–304).

35. Romain Rolland, "Appel aux jeunes contre le fascisme," *QAC*, 216–218 (*I Will Not Rest*, 304–305), first published in *Tribune des jeunes* (Périgueux), May 1934.

36. Romain Rolland, "La Croix et le faisceau (introduction au livre antifasciste autrichien)" (20 June 1934), *QAC*, 218–222; this first appeared as the preface to *Oesterreich Brandherd, Europas* (Zurich, 1934).

37. Letter from Rolland to Carlo Rosselli, 30 May 1934, ARR.

38. Romain Rolland, "Pour ceux qui meurent dans les prisons de Mussolini. Antonio Gramsci," *QAC*, 223 ("For Those Dying in Mussolini's Jails. Antonio Gramsci," in *I Will Not Rest*, 307–313); first published in *L'Humanité*, 27 October 1934, 3; released as a brochure; translated into German as *Die in den Gefangness sterben* (Zurich, 1934); in Italian as *Quelli che muiono nelle prigioni di Mussolini* (1934). During this period Rolland was honorary president of the Comitato Internazionale di Aiuto ai Carcerati e Deportati Antifascisti Italiani. Also see "Appel de Romain Rolland au Secours rouge international pour l'envoi d'une délégation de contrôle en Italie" (also signed by Barbusse, Einstein, and Langevin), ARR. For more information on the relationship between Romain Rolland and Gramsci, see Alfonso Leonetti, "Romain Rolland et Gramsci," in *Notes sur Gramsci* (Paris, 1974), 209–220; in an extract from Romain Rolland's journal of 28 June 1935, he reported meeting Gramsci's two sons in Moscow, who thanked him for his intercessions for their father. Sandro Nelli, "Romain Rolland et le peuple italien," *L'Humanité*, 20 March 1936, 8, applauded Romain Rolland for his antifascist activities and his help in getting the dying Gramsci released from prison. Romain Rolland's last public statement on Antonio Gramsci was

entitled, "Notre Gramsci n'est pas un mort, ni un vaincu,"*L'Humanité*, 24 May 1937, 3.

39. Rolland, "Pour ceux qui meurent dans les prisons de Mussolini," *QAC*, 223–225.

40. Ibid., 229.

41. Romain Rolland, "Salut à la révolution d'Espagne," *QAC*, 230; first published in *L'Humanité*, 6 November 1934, 1; Rolland, "Declaration de Romain Rolland," *La Verité*, no. 199 (30 March 1934).

42. Romain Rolland, "Le Fascisme est l'ennemi. Il faut le briser" (10 June 1934), *QAC*, 230–235; first published in the Soviet review *Front de la science et de la technique*.

43. Romain Rolland, "Appel au monde pour la défense de la paix en danger," *Vigilance*, no. 29 (15 October 1935): 15; also see Romain Rolland and Jean-Richard Bloch, "Contre les crimes du fascisme italien," *Vigilance*, no. 26 (20 July 1935): 14. *Vigilance* was a bimonthly bulletin of the Committee of Antifascist Action, headed by Paul Rivet, Alain, and Paul Langevin. Also see Nicole Racine-Furlaud, "Le Comité de Vigilance des Intellectuals Antifascistes (1934–1939). Antifascisme et pacifisme," *Mouvement social*, no. 101 (October–December 1977): 87–113. Romain Rolland also signed the manifesto "Réponse aux intellectuels fascistes," *Europe*, no. 153 (15 November 1935): 452–453.

44. Romain Rolland, "Pour la défense du peuple éthiopien," 3 September 1935, ARR.

45. Romain Rolland, "Par la révolution, la paix" (20 March 1935), in *PRP*, 169–171; first published as "La Paix est mortelle pour l'hitlérisme," *Monde*, no. 329 (29 March 1935): 1–2. By May–June 1935 there was a consciousness of intellectual antifascism in France, and Romain Rolland was frequently cited as its prototype. See Louis Dolicet, "Courants antifascistes chez les intellectuels français," *Monde*, no. 336 (16 May 1935): 5; and Henri Barbusse, "Pour une compréhension claire des devoirs à propos de la résolution des intellectuels," ibid., no. 340 (13 June 1935): 1.

46. Romain Rolland, "Le Plus Grand Danger," in *Comment empêcher la guerre?* (Paris, 1936), 7–11. This brochure was published by the World Committee Against War and Fascism in a series called *Stratégie et tactique de lutte contre la guerre et le fascisme*.

47. Louis Aragon, "Une Entrevue avec Romain Rolland, l'ingénieur des âmes," *Cahiers du bolchevisme* 13, no. 5 (15 March 1936): 257–263.

48. Romain Rolland, "Lettre adressé par Romain Rolland aux intellectuels et à la jeunesse bulgare," 12 July 1936, ARR.

49. Claude Estier, *La Gauche hebdomadaire, 1914–1962* (Paris, 1962), 57–74; J.-P. Bernard, *Le Parti communiste français et la question littéraire, 1921–1939* (Grenoble, 1972), 191–198.

50. Romain Rolland, "Pour l'indivisible paix," in *Comment empêcher la guerre?* 12–19; first published in *Vendredi*, no. 12 (24 January 1936): 1; also appeared in *L'Humanité*, 29 January 1936, 4; *Le Barrage*, no. 83 (6 February 1936): 2; *Cahiers du bolchevisme* 13, no. 3–4 (15 February 1936): 212–217; *Cahiers des droits de l'homme*, no. 7 (10 March 1936): 156–159.

51. Rolland, "Pour l'indivisible paix," in *Comment empêcher la guerre?* 14–15.

52. Ibid., 16–19.

53. Romain Rolland, "Lettre à Georges Pioch, 13 April 1933," *PRP*, 85. Pioch was president of the International League of Fighters for Peace.

54. Henri Bouché, "L'Allemagne est-elle prête?" *Vendredi*, no. 13 (31 January 1936): 1–2.

55. Félicien Challaye, "Réponse à Romain Rolland," *Vendredi*, no. 13 (31 January 1936): 4; also in *Le Barrage*, no. 83 (6 February 1936): 1, and *Cahiers des droits de l'homme*, no. 7 (10 March 1936): 159–161. Challaye outlined his strategy and tactics in two brochures, *Pour la paix désarmée même en face de Hitler* (Paris, 1933) and *Pour la paix sans aucune réserve* (Paris, 1935). The pacifist weekly *Le Barrage*, organ of the International League of Fighters for Peace, most consistently advocated the integral pacifist position. See René Gerin, "Les Pontins s'agitent. Notre Position reste inchangée," *Le Barrage*, no. 16 (30 August 1934): 1; Félicien Challaye, "Le Discours de M. Hitler," *Le Barrage*, no. 54 (30 May 1935): 1–2; Félicien Challaye, "Le Conflit italo-éthiopien et les principes de notre ligue," *Le Barrage*, no. 64 (12 September 1935): 1; Félicien Challaye, "Pour un rassemblement universel des pacifistes intégraux," *Le Barrage*, no. 79 (9 January 1936): 1. The Dutch pacifist Barthélemy de Ligt's book, *Pour vaincre sans violence* (Paris, 1933), most coherently argued the Gandhian position, even deployed against Hitler.

56. Challaye, "Réponse à Romain Rolland," 4.

57. Georges Pioch, "Questions à Romain Rolland," *Le Barrage*, no. 82 (30 January 1936): 1, 3; Georges Pioch, "D'un article nécessaire," *Le Barrage*, no. 83 (6 February 1936): 1; L. Cancouet, "A Romain Rolland. Réponse d'un prolétaire," *Le Barrage*, no. 83 (6 February 1936): 3; Sylvain Brousaudier, "A propos de l'article de Romain Rolland," *Le Barrage*, no. 83 (6 February 1936): 3; L. Emery, "Réponse à Romain Rolland," *Feuilles libres de la quinzaine*, no. 9 (10 February 1936): 33–35.

58. See *Salut et fraternité. Alain et Romain Rolland* (Paris, 1969), 63–132. In the period of this debate, Alain wrote "Pour Romain Rolland" (29 January 1936) and "Propos d'Alain" (15 May 1936), arguing that the great and true spirit of Rolland was that of *Jean-Christophe* and *Liluli* (ibid., 119–126); Alain, "La Politique au citoyen. Propos d'Alain," *Feuilles libre de la quinzaine*, no. 10 (25 February 1936): 56.

59. Romain Rolland, "Pour la défense de la paix," *Vendredi*, no. 18 (6 March 1936): 3; also published in *Cahiers des droits de l'homme*, no. 7 (10 March 1936): 160–164; *Commune*, no. 32 (April 1936); text published in *Comment empêcher la guerre?* 20–30. Also see Romain Rolland's letters to André Chamson, 18 February 1936, 25 February 1936 (ARR), for the editorial politics of this piece. He explained his intention to Jean Courregelongue, 3 March 1936 (ARR). Romain Rolland and Jean Guéhenno debated the issues of war and peace versus revolution and antifascism in letters exchanged between January and March 1936; see *JG-RR*, 368–374.

60. Rolland, "Pour la défense de la paix," in *Comment empêcher la guerre?* 28.

61. Ibid., 28–30.

62. Ibid., 28, 30.

63. Victor Basch, "Le Problème de la paix," *Cahiers des droits de l'homme*, no. 7 (10 March 1936): 148–156; Romain Rolland answered in "Une Lettre

de Romain Rolland à la ligue des droits de l'homme," ibid., no. 8 (20 March 1936): 184.

64. Michel Alexandre and L. Emery, "Une Lettre à *Vendredi*," *Vendredi*, no. 23 (3 April 1936): 4; Pierre Cuenat, "Paix indivisible? Oui . . . mais d'abord faites la paix," *Le Barrage*, no. 92 (2 April 1936): 3–4; Pierre Cuenat, "Manifeste pacifiste," *Feuilles libres de la quinzaine*, no. 18 (25 June 1936): 191–192; Pierre Cuenat, "Où est la paix? Pacifisme et révolution," *Vigilance*, no. 36 (28 April 1936): 15.

65. Marc Rivière, "Nous voulons vivre et éspérer. Lettre ouverte à Romain Rolland," *Feuilles libre de la quinzaine*, no. 39 (25 June 1937): 166–167; Félicien Challaye, "Deux pacifismes," *Cahiers des droits de l'homme*, no. 10 (10 April 1936): 225; Félicien Challaye, "Seconde réponse à Romain Rolland," ibid., 225–228; also in *Le Barrage*, no. 90 (19 March 1936): 2. Romain Rolland came under attack by Gérard de Lacaze-Duthiers, "Preface," in Eugen Relgis, *Les Voies de la paix* (Paris, 1936), 9, 11; and by Victor Margueritte, *Le Cadavre maquillé. La S.D.N. (mars–septembre 1936)* (Paris, 1936), 241, 243.

66. Romain Rolland, "La Paix pour tous," *Paix et liberté*, no. 8 (16 March 1936): 1; Rolland, "La Paix que nous voulons," ibid., no. 19 (14 June 1936): 1; and Rolland, "Discours du rassemblement universel de la paix," ibid., no. 24 (19 July 1936): 2. Romain Rolland replied directly to Alain in *Le Peuple allemand accuse. Appel à la conscience du monde* (Paris, 1937), 7–8. He answered Cuenat's criticism in "Une Lettre de Romain Rolland," *Feuilles libres de la quinzaine*, no. 27 (10 December 1936): 336. For further brochures attacking the French integral pacifists from an antifascist and communist perspective, see Francis Jourdain, *Faut-il donner les colonies à Hitler?* (Paris, 1936); Sir Norman Angell, *La Paix et la securité collective* (Paris, 1936); and esp. René Maublanc, *Le Pacifisme et les intellectuels* (Paris, 1936).

67. Rolland, Introduction to *Comment empêcher la guerre?* 6.

68. George Lichtheim, *Marxism in Modern France* (New York, 1966), 44.

69. André Malraux, "Préface," *JG-RR*, 5–13, esp. 7.

70. Ibid., 12.

CHAPTER 9

1. Romain Rolland, "Sur la mort de Lénine," *QAC*, 65 (*I Will Not Rest*, 155), written 1 February 1924 as a letter to W. J. Panski-Solski, Berlin correspondent of *Izvestia*. Also see letter from Rolland to Marcel Martinet, 28 February 1924, ARR.

2. Romain Rolland, "Réponse à une adresse de l'Académie d'état des sciences d'art," 20 October 1925, *QAC*, xxxvii, lxxii (*I Will Not Rest*, 41–42, 78). This was a reply to P. Kogan's "Address to Western European and American Artists"; for the full text, see Jean-Bertrand Barrère, *Romain Rolland par lui-même* (Paris, 1967), 141–142.

3. Letter from Rolland to Léon Bazalgette, 12 March 1925, ARR.

4. Romain Rolland, "M. Romain Rolland prend position," *Clarté*, no. 5 (15 January 1927): 158; Fourrier answered in "Réponse de Marcel Fourrier," ibid., 158.

5. Romain Rolland, "Lettre au *Libertaire* sur 'la répression en Russie' "

(28 May 1927), *QAC*, 79–80 (*I Will Not Rest*, 175–176); first published in *Le Libertaire*, no. 114 (10 June 1927): 2; also published in *Europe*, 15 October 1927, 270–271.

6. Jean Brecot, "Une Enquête du *Libertaire* sur la répression en Russie," *La Vie ouvrière*, no. 419 (17 June 1927).

7. Letter from Anatole Lunacharsky to Rolland, 2 September 1927, *QAC*, 81 (*I Will Not Rest*, 176–177).

8. Letter from Rolland to Anatole Lunacharsky, 23 September 1927, *QAC*, 81–83 (*I Will Not Rest*, 177–178). The Rolland-Lunacharsky exchange was first published in *Europe*, 15 October 1927, 271–272.

9. Romain Rolland, "Réponse à l'invitation adressé par Voks, pour les fêtes du Xe anniversaire de la Révolution d'Octobre" (14 October 1927), *QAC*, 83–84 (*I Will Not Rest*, 178–179); first published in *Nouvelles soviétiques*, and *L'Humanité*, 7 November 1927, 3. See also Romain Rolland, "Salut au plus grand anniversaire de l'histoire sociale," 4 November 1927, *QAC*, 85–86 (*I Will Not Rest*, 179–180); first published in *Vetchernaya-Moskwa*.

10. N. Lazarevitch, "A Romain Rolland," *Le Libertaire*, no. 139 (5 December 1927).

11. Romain Rolland, "Romain Rolland et la Russie," *Le Libertaire*, no. 140 (16 December 1927): 1; see Guido Miglioli, *Le Village soviétique* (Paris, 1927).

12. N. Lazarevitch, "Romain Rolland et la Russie," *Le Libertaire*, no. 141 (23 December 1927): 2.

13. Romain Rolland, "Romain Rolland et la Russie," *Le Libertaire*, no. 141 (23 December 1927): 2; also see letters from Rolland to Amédeé Dunois, 14 October 1927; to Charles Bernard, 14 November 1927; to Edouard Dujardin, 10 January 1928; and to Martinet, 2 February 1928, ARR.

14. Constantin Balmont and Ivan Bounine, "Le Martyre des écrivains russes. A Romain Rolland. Un Appel déséspéré de Constantin Balmont et Ivan Bounine," *L'Avenir*, no. 3592 (12 January 1928): 1–2.

15. Romain Rolland, "Réponse à Constantin Balmont et à Ivan Bounine" (20 January 1928), *QAC*, 86, 95 (*I Will Not Rest*, 180–187); first published in *Europe*, 15 February 1928, 246–252. For Gorky's reflections on this debate, see "Une Lettre de Maxime Gorky à Romain Rolland" (January 1928), *Europe*, 15 March 1928, 430–432.

16. Rolland, "Réponse à Balmont et à Bounine," *QAC*, 88.

17. Ibid., 92–94.

18. Ibid., 88–89.

19. Ibid., 91 n. 1.

20. Ibid., 96.

21. Romain Rolland, *Les Léonides* (Paris, 1928); Rolland, "Préface" (28 October 1927), ibid., 7–15; letter from Rolland to Lucien Roth, 28 November 1928, ARR.

22. On Istrati, see Michel Ragon, *Histoire de la littérature prolétarienne en France* (Paris, 1974), 220.

23. Romain Rolland, "Foreword," in Panaït Istrati, *Kyra Kyralina*, trans. James Whithall (New York, 1926), v; first published as "Un Gorki balkanique," *Europe*, 15 August 1923, 257–259.

24. Letter from Rolland to Panaït Istrati, cited in Istrati, "Preface," *Kyra Kyralina*, ix. Also see letter from Rolland to Istrati, Holy Friday, 1921, *BV*, 175–177.

25. Panaït Istrati, *Vers l'autre flamme* (Paris, 1929), 3 vols.; Victor Serge, *Memoirs of a Revolutionary*, trans. Peter Sedgwick (London, 1963), 254, 278–279.

26. Letter from Rolland to Jean Guéhenno, 9 October 1929, *JG-RR*, 71.

27. Letter from Rolland to Istrati, 8 October 1929, cited in *JG-RR*, 71–72.

28. Letter from Rolland to Guéhenno, 9 October 1929, *JG-RR*, 72. For Romain Rolland's last reflections on the dying and isolated Istrati, see ibid., 256–257, 337–339.

29. Letters from Rolland to Charles Vildrac, 14 December 1928; to Madame Félicien Challaye, 9 March 1929; to Valentin Boulgakov, 11 April 1929, ARR.

30. Romain Rolland, "Lettre à Eugène Relgis sur les devoirs des intellectuels et la confédération internationale du travail intellectuel et manuel" (20 October 1930), *QAC*, 102–111 (*I Will Not Rest*, 199–207). Also see Eugène Relgis, *L'Internationale pacifiste* (Paris, 1929); Julien Benda, *La Trahison des clercs* (Paris, 1927). Benda specifically censured Romain Rolland as a *clerc* who committed treason (*The Treason of the Intellectual*, trans. Richard Aldington [New York, 1969], 76, 80–81, 164, 187, 217 n. 2). For a contextual analysis of Benda, see David L. Schalk, *The Spectrum of Political Engagement* (Princeton, N.J., 1979), 26–48.

31. Rolland, "Lettre à Eugène Relgis," 106.

32. Romain Rolland, "Deux Voix lancent l'appel contre les forces de réaction" (with Theodore Dreiser), *QAC*, 99–101 (*I Will Not Rest*, 195–196); first published in *Monde*, no. 98 (19 April 1930): 3; Rolland, "Que sera votre attitude en cas d'agression contre l'Union soviétique?" *L'Humanité*, 7 July 1930, 4. Also see letters from Rolland to Martinet, 11 July 1930; to Frans Masereel, 27 September 1930, ARR; and to Heinz Haeberlin, 28 May 1930, in Pierre Abraham, ed., *Romain Rolland* (Neuchâtel, 1969), 139–140.

33. Romain Rolland, "Europe, élargis-toi, ou meurs!" (January 1931), *QAC*, 121; first published in *Nouvelle Revue mondiale*, no. 2 (February 1931), and *Paix mondiale*, April–May 1931. Riou replied in "Les Etats-Unis de l'Europe ou les Etat-Unis du monde," *Nouvelle Revue mondiale*, no. 1 (January 1931) and no. 3 (March 1931). See letter from Rolland to Lucien Roth, 6 February 1931, ARR. Also see letter from Rolland to Count Richard Coudenhove-Kalergi, 14 September 1925, cited in Barrère, *Romain Rolland par lui-même*, 165.

34. Rolland, "Europe, élargis-toi, ou meurs!" 120–121 (*I Will Not Rest*, 209–219). Also see letter from Rolland to Charles Baudouin, 31 January 1931, ARR.

35. Romain Rolland, "Lettre à Serge Radine sur le 'materialisme' communiste," *QAC*, 131 (*I Will Not Rest*, 229–230); letter from Rolland to Baudouin, 24 August 1932 (ARR), paraphrasing Lenin, that "a good idealism was worth more than a bad or foolish materialism."

36. Romain Rolland, "Lettre à Fedor Gladkov et à Ilya Selvinsky sur l'individualisme et l'humanisme" (February 1931), *QAC*, 129 (*I Will Not Rest*, 223–225). First published in *Literaturnaya gazeta*; letter from Rolland to Baudouin, 14 March 1931, ARR.

37. Rolland, "Europe, élargis-toi, ou meurs!" 124.

38. Romain Rolland, "Salut à Gorki" (10 May 1931) *QAC*, 134–135 (*I Will Not Rest*, 233–235); first published in *Literaturnaya gazeta*.

39. Rolland, "Salut à Gorki," 134.
40. Ibid., 135.
41. Romain Rolland, "Au premier *oudarnik* de la République universelle du Travail, salut d'un compagnon français" (October 1931), *QAC*, 136 (*I Will Not Rest*, 236–240); first published as a preface to the French edition of Gorky's *Eux et nous* (Paris, 1931), and in *L'Humanité*, 6 December 1931. Letter from Rolland to Roth, 1 October 1931, ARR.
42. Rolland, "Au premier *oudarnik*," 137.
43. Ibid., 140–141; see Jean Perus, *Romain Rolland et Maxime Gorki* (Paris, 1968), 243–283.
44. Rolland, "Au premier *oudarnik*," 142.
45. Romain Rolland, "Adieu au passé" (6 April 1931), *QAC*, 142–154 (*I Will Not Rest*, 243–278); first published in *Europe*, 15 June 1931, 161–202.
46. Rolland, "Adieu au passé," 181, 184–185.
47. Ibid., 187–188.
48. André Breton, *Misère de la poésie* (Paris, 1932), esp. 10–13; English trans. in André Breton, *What Is Surrealism? Selected Writings*, ed. Franklin Rosemont (New York, 1978), 76–82.
49. "Lettre de Romain Rolland aux Surréalistes" (4 February 1932), in Breton, *Misère de la poésie*, 29–30.
50. Romain Rolland, *L'Ame enchantée* (Paris, 1967). This conclusion to the novel cycle, called *L'Annonciatrice*, was first published in 2 vols., each over 300 pages, in December 1933 by Editions Albin Michel; vol. 1 was called *La Mort d'un monde*, vol. 2, *L'Enfantement*. I will cite the definitive edition of 1967. Rolland also published an important introduction, dated 1 January 1934, ibid., vii–xix. The secondary literature on this text is virtually nonexistent. See Christian Sénéchal, review of *L'Ame enchantée*, *Europe*, 15 May 1934, 137–142; and Marie-Louise Coudert, "*L'Ame enchantée*," *Europe*, November–December 1966, 52–57.
51. Rolland, *L'Ame enchantée*, 1094–1097 (English trans., 111–112); this second volume translated into English as *A World in Birth*, trans. Amalia de Alberti (New York, 1934).
52. Rolland, *L'Ame enchantée*, 961 (English trans., 301); this first volume translated into English as *The Death of a World*, trans. Amalia de Alberti (New York, 1933).
53. Rolland, *L'Ame enchantée*, 1141 (*World in Birth*, 175).
54. Rolland, *L'Ame enchantée*, 1141 (*World in Birth*, 175); Paul Nizan coined the phrase "watchdogs" (*Les Chiens de garde* [Paris, 1932]).
55. Rolland, *L'Ame enchantée*, 1043 (*World in Birth*, 44).
56. Rolland, *L'Ame enchantée*, 1094 (*World in Birth*, 110–111).
57. Rolland, *L'Ame enchantée*, 1198 (*World in Birth*, 250).
58. Rolland, *L'Ame enchantée*, 1043 (*World in Birth*, 43); also see letter from Rolland to Bela Illès, 22 September 1932, in *Literaturnaya nasledstvo* (Literary heritage) (Moscow, 1969), 286.
59. Rolland, *L'Ame enchantée*, 909 (*Death of a World*, 229).
60. Rolland, *L'Ame enchantée*, 787–788 (*Death of a World*, 67–68).
61. Rolland, *L'Ame enchantée*, 982 (*Death of a World*, 328).
62. Rolland, *L'Ame enchantée*, 1255 (*World in Birth*, 326).
63. Rolland, *L'Ame enchantée*, 1146 (*World in Birth*, 182).

64. Rolland, *L'Ame enchantée*, 1285 (*World in Birth*, 364).
65. Rolland, *L'Ame enchantée*, 1046 (*World in Birth*, 49).
66. Rolland, *L'Ame enchantée*, 1252 (*World in Birth*, 321).
67. Rolland, *L'Ame enchantée*, 1047, 1259 (*World in Birth*, 50, 317).
68. Rolland, *L'Ame enchantée*, 1151 (*World in Birth*, 188).
69. Rolland, *L'Ame enchantée*, 1047 (*World in Birth*, 49–50).
70. Rolland, *L'Ame enchantée*, 1440–1441 (*World in Birth*, 572–574); also see letter from Rolland to Alfred Kurella, 10 December 1933, in *Literaturnaya nasledstvo*, 299–300.
71. Rolland, *L'Ame enchantée*, 1146 (*World in Birth*, 181).

CHAPTER 10

1. David Caute, *The Fellow Travellers: A Postscript to the Enlightenment* (New York, 1973), 126–135; David Caute, *Communism and the French Intellectuals, 1914–1960* (London, 1964), 102–111; Michael Kelly, *Modern French Marxism* (Baltimore, 1982), 24–48; George Ross, *Workers and Communists in France: From Popular Front to Eurocommunism* (Berkeley, Calif., 1982), 1–18; Jürgen Rühle, *Literature and Revolution: A Critical Study of the Writer and Communism in the Twentieth Century*, trans. Jean Steinberg (London, 1969), 321–326.
2. L. Darnar, "Chez Romain Rolland," *L'Humanité*, 26 May 1933, 1; Ivan Anissimov, "Romain Rolland passe à la Revolution," *La Littérature internationale*, no. 1 (1933): 26–32; Magdeleine Paz, "*L'Annonciatrice* par Romain Rolland," *Monde*, no. 249 (11 March 1933): 10; Lucie River, "De *Jean-Christophe* à *l'Ame enchantée*," *Monde*, no. 283 (4 November 1933): 7; "Romain Rolland à Marcel Cachin," *L'Humanité*, 15 September 1934, 1.
3. Romain Rolland, "Lénine, l'art et l'action," *Compagnons de route. Essais littéraires* (Paris, 1936), 225–236, esp. 230, 233; first published in *Europe*, 15 January 1934, 5–14; translated as "A Great Master of Action," *International Literature*, no. 1 (January 1939): 71–72.
4. Rolland, "Lénine, l'art et l'action," 225–227, 234–236.
5. Karl Radek, "Contemporary World Literature and the Tasks of Proletarian Art," in *Problems of Soviet Literature*, ed. A. Zhdanov (New York, n.d.), 95, 138–139, 145; published in French, *Correspondance internationale*, no. 83–84 (15 September 1934); also see Romain Rolland, *QAC*, xxxix, lxxiii.
6. Romain Rolland, "Panorama," *QAC*, ix–lxxx (translated into English as "Panorama," in *I Will Not Rest*, 15–88); first published in *Europe*, 15 January–15 April 1935, 5–36, 153–175, 305–328.
7. Rolland, "Panorama," lix–lxii, lxxix; see letter from Rolland to René Arcos, 23 October 1934, requesting that Arcos send him a copy of Marx's *Morceaux choisis* and Paul Nizan's "Marx philosophe" (ARR).
8. Rolland, "Panorama," lx, Rolland's emphasis.
9. Ibid., lviii, lix.
10. Ibid., lvii, lix, lxi, lxiii.
11. Ibid., xxxvii–xxxix, xlv, liv–lvii, lix.
12. Ibid., lix, lvii–lviii.
13. Ibid., xxxviii, li.

14. Ibid., xxxviii.
15. André Malraux, cited in Rolland, "Panorama," lxxx; see Jean Lacouture, *André Malraux*, trans. Alan Sheridan (New York, 1975), 163–196.
16. Romain Rolland, "Pour qui écrivez-vous?" *Commune*, no. 9 (May 1934): 779–780; in *QAC*, 237–238 (translated into English as "For Whom Do I Write?" in *I Will Not Rest*, 319–320). Also see Rolland's "Enquête," in *Littérature internationale*, no. 3 (1934): 3–6. Louis Aragon, *Commune*, no. 9 (May 1934): 778.
17. On Barbusse, see Guessler Normand, "Henri Barbusse and His *Monde* (1928–1935)," *Journal of Contemporary History*, Spring 1976, 173–197; Rühle, *Literature and Revolution*, 326–329; Jean-Pierre Bernard, *Le Parti communiste français et la question littéraire, 1921–1939* (Grenoble, 1972), 57–61, 71–77.
18. Letter from Rolland to Henri Barbusse, 28 December 1934, ARR.
19. Victor Serge, *Memoirs of a Revolutionary, 1901–1941*, trans. Peter Sedgwick (London, 1963), 284–322; Herbert Lottman, *The Left Bank: Writers, Artists, and Politics from the Popular Front to the Cold War* (Boston, 1982), 92–96, 111, 48–53; Caute, *Communism and the French Intellectuals*, 110–111, 134–135, 241.
20. Serge, *Memoirs*, 316, 318–319; Frederick J. Harris, *André Gide and Romain Rolland: Two Men Divided* (New Brunswick, N.J., 1973), 150–152.
21. Letter from Rolland to Jean Guéhenno, 24 October 1934, JG-RR, 313–314.
22. Ibid., 314.
23. Romain Rolland, "Lettre de Romain Rolland à un ingénieur Américain," *Regards*, no. 62 (21 March 1935): 3.
24. Ibid.
25. Ibid.
26. See Paul Hollander, *Political Pilgrims: Travels of Western Intellectuals to the Soviet Union, China, and Cuba, 1928–1978* (New York, 1981), 102–176; Sylvia R. Margulies, *The Pilgrimage to Russia: The Soviet Union and the Treatment of Foreigners, 1924–1937* (Madison, Wis., 1968).
27. Romain Rolland, "Un Séjour chez Gorki" (journal extracts, June–July 1935), *Europe*, February–March 1960, 13–30.
28. Ibid., 19–23, 25, 29–30. Also see letter from Rolland to Madeleine Rolland, 26 June 1935, *BV*, 337–339.
29. Romain Rolland, "Romain Rolland au moment de quitter l'U.R.S.S. proclame, dans une lettre à Staline, la nécessité de la défendre," *L'Humanité*, 22 July 1935, 1.
30. Romain Rolland, "Retour de Moscou," *Commune*, no. 26 (October 1935): 129.
31. Ibid., 130.
32. Ibid., 131–132.
33. Ibid., 132–133.
34. Romain Rolland, "Aux calomniateurs!" *L'Humanité*, 23 October 1935, 1.
35. Ibid., 1, 4.
36. Ibid., 4.
37. Romain Rolland, "L'Esprit européen," *Nouvelles littéraires*, no. 684 (23 November 1935): 6; for Benda's rejoinder, see "L'Esprit européen," ibid., no. 685 (30 November 1935): 6.

38. Rolland, "L'Esprit européen," 6.

39. Vladimir Pozner, "A la recherche d'une patrie humaine," *Monde,* no. 341 (20 June 1935): 8.

40. Nicolai Bukharin, "Salut à Romain Rolland," *Commune,* no. 24 (August 1935): 1431–1434. For a sample of communist reactions to Romain Rolland's Soviet trip, see two unsigned pieces, "Romain Rolland en U.R.S.S.," *L'Humanité,* 1 July 1935, 2; "La Jeunesse soviétique rend visite à Romain Rolland," *L'Humanité,* 17 July 1935, 3. Also see René Blech, "*Quinze Ans de combat* et *Par la révolution, la paix,* par Romain Rolland," *Commune,* no. 25 (September 1935): 94–98; Red Soldiers from Lake Tarkal region, "Lettre à Romain Rolland," *Commune,* no. 25 (September 1935): 122–123.

41. Marcel Martinet, "Réponse à Romain Rolland," *Révolution prolétarienne,* no. 195 (25 March 1935): 101–102; also published in *Les Humbles,* no. 5 (May 1935): 16–22.

42. Léon Trotsky, "Romain Rolland remplit sa mission," *Les Humbles,* no. 12 (December 1935): 3–8; translated as "Romain Rolland Executes an Assignment," in *The Writings of Leon Trotsky (1935–1938),* ed. Naomi Allen and George Breitman (New York, 1970), 161–165. For other Trotskyist articles on Rolland and the Soviet Union, see Georges Henein, "Hommage aux inflexibles," *Les Superbes,* no. 5 (May 1936): 3–4; Maurice Parijanine, "Lettre ouverte à Romain Rolland de Maurice Parijanine," *Les Humbles,* no. 9–10 (September–October 1936): 80–82; Marcel Martinet, "Pour les soixante-dix ans de Romain Rolland," *Révolution prolétarienne,* no. 215 (25 January 1936): 21.

43. Romain Rolland, "A Léon Trotsky," *Les Humbles,* no. 5–6 (May–June 1934): 12.

44. Romain Rolland, "Introduction" (October 1935), *Compagnons de route,* 9–16.

45. Louis Aragon, "Une Entrevue avec Romain Rolland, l'ingénieur des âmes," *Cahiers du bolchevisme,* no. 5 (15 March 1936): 257–262; also in *Commune,* no. 3 (May 1936): 1138–1139.

46. Paul Langevin, "Paix d'abord," *L'Humanité,* 3 February 1936, 1–2; also in *L'Université syndicaliste,* February 1936; reprinted in Paul Langevin, *La Pensée et l'action* (Paris, 1964), 274–277; Jean-Richard Bloch, "Nouvelle Rencontre de la France et Romain Rolland," *Commune,* no. 29 (January 1936): 513–520; Louis Aragon, "Romain Rolland ou les trésors de l'expérience," *Regards,* no. 107 (30 January 1936): 3–4.

47. André Malraux, "Trois Discours" and "Réponse aux 64," *Commune,* no. 28 (December 1935): 411; his appeals were a response to a manifesto signed by 64 right-wing intellectuals (*Le Temps,* 4 October 1935), including Charles Maurras, Henri Massis, Alphonse de Chateaubriant, and Drieu la Rochelle.

48. Romain Rolland, "Réponse à une enquête de *Vendémaire* sur 'le declin des idées de liberté et de progrès,' " *Europe,* 15 January 1936, 104–107.

49. Romain Rolland, "Voyage autour de ma chambre," *L'Humanité,* 26 January 1936, 1, 8.

50. See "Hommage à Romain Rolland pour son soixante-dixième anniversaire," *L'Humanité,* 26 January 1936, 8, with tributes from André Gide, Francis Jourdain, René Arcos, Marcel Prenant, Jules Romains, Victor Marguesitte, Paul Rivet, Alain, Luc Durtain, Paul Nizan, Georges Friedmann,

Andrée Viollis, Jean Cassou, André Chamson, Jean Guéhenno, Charles Vildrac, and Jean-Richard Bloch; "Hommage à Romain Rolland," *Commune*, no. 3 (March 1936): 789–801, with tributes from Maxim Gorky, Waldo Frank, Georgi Dimitrov, Stefan Zweig, T. G. Masaryk, E. Benès, Leonid Leonov, Van Min, and revolutionary students of the University of Lisbon. See Jean-Richard Bloch, *Vendredi*, 17 January 1936; Jean Guéhenno, *Europe*, 15 January 1936; Fernand Déprès, *Regards*, no. 4 (31 January 1936); and Waldo Frank, *New Masses*, no. 18 (21 January 1936): 19.

51. André Gide, *Vendredi*, 24 January 1936, later reprinted in *Nouvelle Revue française*, no. 47 (1 March 1936): 437–438.

52. See Marcel Cachin, "Romain Rolland," *L'Humanité*, 30 January 1936, 1–2; Marcel Cachin, "Magnifique Hommage du peuple de Paris à Romain Rolland," *L'Humanité*, 1 February 1936, 1; Marcel Cachin, "Avec Romain Rolland," *L'Humanité*, 2 February 1936, 1. Also see Francis Jourdain, "Le Rôle du mouvement international Amsterdam-Pleyel," *Clarté*, no. 4 (November 1936): 179–181.

53. Romain Rolland, "Pour un théâtre du peuple," *Regards*, no. 116 (2 April 1936): 3.

54. Romain Rolland, "La Grande Unité," *Clarté*, no. 1 (August 1936): 3–5.

55. Letter from Rolland to Léon Blum, 7 February 1936, ARR.

56. Letters from Rolland to Amédée Dunois, 14 February 1936; to Lucien Roth, 27 May 1936, ARR.

57. Letter from Rolland to André Chamson, 20 August 1936, ARR.

58. Romain Rolland, "A l'aide," *Paix et liberté*, no. 30 (1936): 4; Rolland, "Un Message de Romain Rolland," *L'Humanité*, 6 September 1936, 4, and 11 September 1936, 4; also in *Clarté*, no. 2 (September 1936): 67–69.

59. Romain Rolland, "Appel à tous les peuples au secours des victimes d'Espagne," *L'Humanité*, 22 November 1936, English trans. in *International Solidarity with the Spanish Republic, 1936–1939* (Moscow, 1975), 138. For a splendid analysis of the brigades, see Robert A. Rosenstone, *Crusade of the Left: The Lincoln Battalions in the Spanish Civil War* (Lanham, Md., 1980).

60. Romain Rolland, "Au secours des victimes d'Espagne," *Clarté*, no. 5 (December 1936): 227; Rolland, cited in Dolores Ibarruri, *They Shall Not Pass: The Autobiography of La Pasionaria* (New York, 1976), 266.

61. Letter from Rolland to Blum, 3 October 1936, ARR. Blum never replied. For an account of Blum's dilemmas during this period, see Jean Lacouture, *Léon Blum* (Paris, 1977), 259–387.

62. Letters from Rolland to Jean-Richard Bloch, 10 October 1936; to Howard Dunham, 26 January 1937, ARR.

63. "La Culture en danger," *Commune*, no. 40 (December 1936): 424–426, signed by Romain Rolland, André Gide, Jean-Richard Bloch, André Chamson, Louis Aragon; also see "Déclaration des intellectuels républicains au sujet des événements d'Espagne," *Commune*, no. 40 (December 1936): 389–391, signed by Romain Rolland, Paul Langevin, Georges Politzer, André Gide, Paul Nizan, and Henri Lefebvre.

64. Romain Rolland, "Message to the International Congress of Anti-Fascist Writers in Valencia," cited in Ibarruri, *They Shall Not Pass*, 266–267.

65. Romain Rolland, "Message à la comité pour la défense de la culture espagnol," 7 November 1937, ARR; Rolland, "Frente popular," in *France-*

Espagne, no. 1 (1937); Rolland, "La France est-elle une mission?" *Cahiers de la jeunesse,* no. 12 (15 July 1938): 13–16; Rolland, "C'est pour nous que l'Espagne souffre et combat," *L'Avant-garde,* 20 January 1939, 1. Also see André Malraux, "Pour la collaboration des fronts populaires espagnol et français," in *Agir dans la clarté,* Publications du Comité mondial contre la guerre et le fascisme (Paris, 1936), 61.

66. Romain Rolland, "Adieu à Gorki," *Europe,* 15 July 1936, 289–290; also published in *Regards,* no. 128 (25 June 1936): 3. Also see Romain Rolland, "Mon Ami le plus cher," *L'Humanité,* 21 June 1936.

67. Frederick Brown, *Theater and Revolution: The Culture of the French Stage* (New York, 1980), 393–394; Henri Noguères, *Front populaire* (Paris, 1977), 26, 90. On the cultural politics of the French Popular Front, see Elizabeth G. Strebel, "French Social Cinema and the Popular Front," *Journal of Contemporary History* 12, no. 3 (July 1977): 499–519; Pascal Ory, "De 'Ciné-Liberté' à la Marseillaise," *Mouvement social,* no. 91 (April–June 1975): 153–175; Nicole Racine, "L'Association des Ecrivains et Artistes Révolutionnaires (AEAR)," *Mouvement social,* no. 54 (January–March 1966): 29–47.

68. See P. Gsell, "Romain Rolland et le théâtre du peuple," *L'Humanité,* 14 July 1936, 1–2; and reviews by J. Chabannes, *Nouvelles littéraires,* 18 July 1936, 8; P. Unik, *Regards,* 23 July 1936; and M. Savin, *Nouvelle Revue française,* no. 47 (1936): 396–399.

69. Romain Rolland, "Quatorze juillet 1789 et 1936," *Europe,* 15 July 1936, 293–297; also published in *Regards,* no. 130 (9 July 1936): 16–17; republished in *Europe,* no. 533–534 (September–October 1973): 113–116.

70. Ibid.

71. J. E. Flower, *Writers and Politics in Modern France, 1909–1961* (London, 1977); Renee Winegarten, *Writers and Revolution: The Fatal Lure of Action* (New York, 1974), 274–291; Lewis A. Coser, *Men of Ideas: A Sociological View* (New York, 1965), 233–243. For a more balanced account, see Roger Shattuck, "Writers for the Defense of Culture," *Partisan Review* 51, no. 3 (1984): 393–416.

72. See W. H. Auden, "September 1, 1939," cited in Samuel Hynes, *The Auden Generation: Literature and Politics in England in the 1930s* (New York, 1977), 382; George Orwell, *Homage to Catalonia* (New York, 1952), 181, 46, 65, 145, 149, 159; Raymond Aron, *The Opium of the Intellectuals,* trans. Terence Kilmartin (New York, 1957), 265–324.

73. Letter from Rolland to Bloch, 15 February 1936, ARR.

CHAPTER 11

1. Daniel R. Brower, *The New Jacobins: The French Communist Party and the Popular Front* (Ithaca, N.Y., 1968); Fernando Claudin, *The Communist Movement from Comintern to Cominform,* trans. Brian Pearce (New York, 1975), 1:166–242; Jacques Fauvet, *Histoire du parti communiste français* (Paris, 1964), 1:152–268; Jacques Danos and Marcel Gibelin, *Juin 1936,* 2 vols. (Paris, 1952; reprint 1972); George Ross, *Workers and Communists in France: From Popular Front to Eurocommunism* (Berkeley, Calif., 1982), 1–11; Georges Lefranc, *Histoire du front populaire* (Paris, 1965); Daniel Guérin,

Front populaire, révolution manquée (Paris, 1963; reprint 1970); Jean Gacon, "1934–1938: Le Front populaire en France comme mouvement populaire," *Cahiers d'histoire de l'Institut Maurice Thorez*, no. 5 (October–November 1973): 44–56; Annie Kriegel, "Front populaire," *Mouvement social*, no. 54 (January–March 1966).

2. Ronald Tiersky, *French Communism, 1920–1972* (New York, 1974), 54–95; Michelle Perrot and Annie Kriegel, *Le Socialisme français et le pouvoir* (Paris, 1966); George Lichtheim, *Marxism in Modern France* (New York, 1966), 34–68; Nicole Racine and Louis Bodin, *Le Parti communiste français pendant l'entre-deux-guerres* (Paris, 1972), 205–262.

3. Letter from Rolland to Maurice Thorez, 12 July 1936, published as "Une Lettre de Romain Rolland," *Cahiers du bolchevisme*, no. 12–13 (25 July 1936): 879; Maurice Thorez, *Fils du peuple* (Paris, 1937).

4. Letters from Rolland to Sergei Dinamov, 1 October 1935, in *Literaturna nasledstvo* (Literary heritage) (Moscow, 1969), 324–325; to Alfred Kurella, 14 February 1936, ibid., 326; to Jean-Richard Bloch, 10 October 1936, ARR.

5. Letters from Rolland to Jean Guéhenno, 24 March 1936, 2 April 1936, 31 December 1936, *JG-RR* 373–374, 376, 378.

6. André Gide, *Retour de l'U.R.S.S.* (Paris, 1936); André Gide, "Avant-propos du *Retour de l'U.R.S.S.*," *Vendredi*, 6 November 1936; Claude Naville, *André Gide et le communisme* (Paris, 1936); Jean Guéhenno, "Lettre ouverte à André Gide," *Vendredi*, 17 December 1937; Jean Guéhenno, "Réponse à André Gide," *Vendredi*, 24 December 1937; Georges Friedmann, "Gide et l'U.R.S.S.," *Europe*, 15 January 1937, 5–29. For a full discussion, see Frederick J. Harris, *André Gide and Romain Rolland: Two Men Divided* (New Brunswick, N.J., 1973), 110–165.

7. Romain Rolland, "L'U.R.S.S. en a vu bien d'autres. Une Lettre de Romain Rolland à propos du livre d'André Gide," *L'Humanité*, 18 January 1937, 1; English trans. in Harris, *André Gide and Romain Rolland*, 154–155.

8. Rolland, "L'U.R.S.S. en a vu bien d'autres," 1.

9. Ibid.; also see letters from Rolland to Lucien Roth, 31 December 1936; to Georges Friedmann, 4 January 1937; conversation with Louis Aragon, 29 June 1937, ARR; letter from Rolland to Guéhenno, 29 December 1937, *JG-RR* 380–381.

10. André Gide, *Retouches à mon retour de l'U.R.S.S.* (Paris, 1937; reprint 1978), 95, 146; also see André Gide, *Littérature engagée* (Paris, 1950).

11. Romain Rolland, "Romain Rolland, Largo Caballero, La Pasionaria saluent l'U.R.S.S., la grande patrie du socialisme," *L'Humanité*, 25 January 1937, 4.

12. Romain Rolland, "L'Adresse de Romain Rolland à la conference nationale du parti communiste," *L'Humanité*, 25 January 1937, 6.

13. Letters from Henri Guilbeaux to Rolland, 17 February 1936, 3 September 1936, 22 September 1936, ARR.

14. Henri Guilbeaux, *La Fin des Soviets* (Paris, 1937), 27–48.

15. Letter from Rolland to Guilbeaux, 4 May 1937, ARR; see Lucien Roth's review of Guilbeaux's *La Fin des Soviets* in *Feuilles libres de la quinzaine*, no. 40 (10 July 1937): 186; letter from Rolland to Roth, 18 September 1937, ARR.

16. Romain Rolland, "Brief an einen Australier," *Die neue Weltbühne* 33,

no. 7 (11 February 1937): 219; Rolland, "La Grand Voix de Romain Rolland appelle à l'aide pour sauver de la hache Rembts et Stamm," *L'Humanité*, 12 June 1937, 3; Rolland, "Un Appel de Romain Rolland. Sauvez de la hache les otages allemands de la paix," *L'Humanité*, 11 October 1937, 3, also published in N. Marceau, *Cinq Ans de dictature hitlérienne* (Paris, 1938), 31–32.

17. Romain Rolland, "Romain Rolland salue de IXe Congrès du parti communiste français," *L'Humanité*, 25 December 1937, 1.

18. Georges Sadoul, "Maîtres de la culture. *Compagnons de route* par Romain Rolland," *L'Humanité*, 11 December 1937, 8.

19. I have followed accounts of the trials in Roy A. Medvedev, *Let History Judge: The Origins and Consequences of Stalinism*, trans. Colleen Taylor (New York, 1972), 152–239; Robert Conquest, *The Great Terror: Stalin's Purge of the Thirties* (New York, 1968); Isaac Deutscher, *Stalin: A Political Biography* (New York, 1967), 345–385, 414–460.

20. Letter from Rolland to Liliane Fearn, 14 October 1936, ARR; Romain Rolland had made a similar accusation about the role of revolutionary anarchists and Trotskyists in Spain; see letter to Bloch, 15 February 1936, ARR.

21. Letter from Rolland to Count Michel Karolyi, 12 February 1937, ARR; also see *Le Procès du centre antisoviétique trotskiste* (Paris, 1936). Letter from Rolland to Jean Courregelongue, 18 March 1937, ARR; in a journal extract dated 27 January 1937, Romain Rolland stated that he was unconvinced by Pierre Dominique's characterization of Stalin as un-Leninist, Bonapartist, imperialist, and militarist (ARR).

22. Letter from Rolland to Karolyi, 12 February 1937, ARR.

23. Ibid.

24. Letter from Rolland to Madeleine Rolland, 4 August 1937, *BV*, 353.

25. Letter from Rolland to Karolyi, 12 February 1937, ARR.

26. Letter from Rolland to Georgi Dimitrov, 29 December 1937, sent via Maurice Thorez, ARR.

27. Ibid; letter from Rolland to Thorez, 10 February 1938, ARR.

28. Letter from Hermann Hesse to Rolland, 3 March 1938, *HH-RR*, 163–164.

29. Letter from Rolland to Hesse, 5 March 1938, *HH-RR*, 165.

30. Letters from Rolland to Bloch, 3 March 1938; from Rolland to Friedmann, 7 March 1938, ARR.

31. Letter from Rolland to Courregelongue, 15 November 1937, ARR.

32. Letter from Rolland to Toshihiko Katayama, 8 December 1937, *BV*, 354–355.

33. Romain Rolland, "La Mission de la France dans le monde. Un Appel de Romain Rolland," *L'Humanité*, 31 March 1938, 1.

34. Letter from Rolland to Léon Moussinac, 27 April 1938, ARR.

35. Romain Rolland, "Télégramme à Daladier et à Chamberlain," in Jean Giono, "Précisions," *Cahiers du contadour*, no. 7 (November 1938): 4, dated early September 1938, and also signed by Paul Langevin and Francis Jourdain; reprinted in Jean Giono, *Précisions* (Paris, 1939), 8–9.

36. Alain, Jean Giono, Victor Margueritte, "Télégramme à Daladier et à Chamberlain," reprinted in Giono's *Précisions*, 9–10. Curiously, Romain Rolland, Alain, and Giono had together signed an antiwar protest: "Contre

la guerre, Romain Rolland au côté des instituteurs," *L'Oeuvre*, 1 October 1938, cited in Giono, *Précisions*, 6. In a letter written to Guillaume Boniface, 3 September 1937, Romain Rolland strongly objected to Giono's pacifism, seeing it as a "puerility unworthy of a literary man. Let him not imagine that their shepherd's crook will disarm the threatening and degrading fascisms" (ARR).

37. Romain Rolland, "La 'Paix' de Munich est une capitulation dégradante," *L'Humanité*, 14 October 1938, 1.

38. Letter from Rolland to Francis Vogarde, 23 September 1938, ARR; also see letter from Rolland to Naoum Aronson, 5 December 1938, *BV* 357–358.

39. Romain Rolland, "Deuil sur l'Europe," *Europe*, no. 49 (15 April 1939): 433–434; reprinted in *Europe*, no. 533–534 (September–October 1973): 169–170. Also see his address to the National Congress of the Amsterdam-Pleyel movement, 11–13 November 1938, published in *L'Humanité*, 13 November 1938. See also Romain Rolland, "Appel. Du 15 au 22 janvier semaine nationale de solidarité. Un Appel de Romain Rolland," *L'Humanité*, 14 January 1939, 3.

40. Letters from Rolland to Thorez, 28 November 1938, and 20 March 1939, ARR.

41. Romain Rolland, "Préface" (October 1938), *Robespierre* (Paris, 1939), 7; parts of *Robespierre* were published in *Europe*, February–March 1939, 145–162, 289–298; in *International Literature*, no. 7 (July 1939): 3–8; and in *Commune* (January–April 1939): 1–14, 506, 633.

42. Romain Rolland, "La Parole est à l'histoire" (1 January 1939), *Robespierre*, 312; also see "Félicitations de Romain Rolland après la création du *Robespierre* à la radio," *L'Humanité*, 16 August 1939; Rolland, "Préface," in N. Marceau, *L'Allemagne et la Révolution française* (Paris, 1939), 9–15.

43. Rolland, "Préface," *Robespierre*, 8.

44. Rolland, *Robespierre*, 286–287. On the influence of Rousseau on Robespierre, see Romain Rolland, "Jean-Jacques Rousseau," introduction to *The Living Thoughts of Rousseau*, ed. Romain Rolland (London, 1939), 1–2, 24.

45. Rolland, "La Parole est à l'histoire," 315–317; Rolland, *Robespierre*, 286.

46. Rolland, *Robespierre*, 63, 88.

47. Ibid., 180, 300, 258.

48. Ibid., 162; also see Rolland, "Préface," *Robespierre*, 8.

49. Walter Laqueur and George L. Mosse, eds., *The Left-Wing Intellectuals Between the Wars, 1919–1939* (New York, 1966); also see Jürgen Rühle, *Literature and Revolution: A Critical Study of the Writer and Communism in the Twentieth Century*, trans. Jean Steinberg (London, 1969).

50. Richard Crossman, ed., *The God That Failed* (New York, 1950), 1–10; David Caute, *The Fellow Travellers: A Postscript to the Enlightenment* (New York, 1973), 250–266; Paul Hollander, *Political Pilgrims: Travels of Western Intellectuals to the Soviet Union, China, and Cuba* (New York, 1981), 70–176, 400–437; Irving Howe, "Intellectuals, Dissent, and Bureaucrats," *Dissent*, Summer 1984, 303–308.

51. Romain Rolland, "Nécessité de la révolution," *Europe*, 15 July 1939, 289–302.

52. Ibid.
53. Ibid.
54. Letter from Rolland to Jean Cassou, 30 August 1939, ARR.
55. Ibid.
56. Ibid.
57. Ibid.
58. Letter from Rolland to Friedmann, 19 September 1939, ARR.
59. Romain Rolland, "Lettre adressé par Romain Rolland au président Daladier" (3 September 1939), *Le Temps*, 19 September 1939.
60. Romain Rolland, "Adresse de Romain Rolland à la jeunesse française," *L'Avant-garde*, 20 January 1939, 1; letter from Rolland to Charles Baudouin, 15 September 1939, ARR; "Deux Heures avec Romain Rolland au pays de *Colas Breugnon*," *L'Avant-garde*, 16 June 1939, 1, 5.
61. Letters from Rolland to Clara Beerli, 29 January 1939; to Baudouin, 10 January 1940; to Georges Duhamel, 7 November 1939, ARR.
62. Letter from Rolland to Bloch, 20 November 1939, ARR.

CONCLUSION

1. Letter from Rolland to Helen F. Farrere, 3 June 1940, *BV*, 366. On the Vichy regime, see Robert O. Paxton, *Vichy France: Old Guard and New Order* (New York, 1972); Jean-Pierre Azéma, *De Munich à la libération, 1938–1944* (Paris, 1979); Michael Marrus and Robert O. Paxton, *Vichy France and the Jews* (New York, 1982).
2. Letter from Rolland to Jean-Richard Bloch, 8 November 1944, *BV* 380. See also Marcel Doisy, *Romain Rolland, 1866–1944* (Brussels, 1945), 87–91; William T. Starr, *Romain Rolland: One Against All* (The Hague, 1971), 245–248; D. A. Prater, *European of Yesterday: A Biography of Stefan Zweig* (London, 1972), 286–341.
3. Letters from Rolland to Farrere, 3 June 1940; to Bloch, 8 November 1944, *BV*, 366, 381; Marie Romain Rolland, "Préface," *Lettres de Romain Rolland à un combattant de la Résistance* (Paris, 1947), unpaginated.
4. Letter from Rolland to Jean Guéhenno, 2 January 1939, *JG-RR*, 386.
5. Romain Rolland, *Beethoven. Les Grandes Epoques créatrices* and *La Neuvième Symphonie* (Paris, 1943); Romain Rolland, *Les Derniers Quatuors* (Paris, 1943).
6. Romain Rolland, *Péguy*, 2 vols. (Paris, 1945). Letter from Rolland to Guéhenno, 31 December 1942, *JG-RR*, 400–401; letter from Rolland to Madeleine Rolland, 8 May 1943, *BV*, 375.
7. Marie Romain Rolland, "Préface"; *Journal officiel*, 21 February 1941.
8. Letter from Rolland to Guéhenno, 1 January 1941, *JG-RR*, 389.
9. See "Note biographique," in *Lettres de Romain Rolland à un combattant de la Résistance* (Paris, 1947); H. R. Kedward, *Resistance in Vichy France* (London, 1978).
10. Letter from Rolland to Eli Walach, 1 March 1940, in *Lettres de Romain Rolland à un combattant de la Résistance*. For a good discussion of the reaction of French intellectuals to the Resistance, see James D. Wilkinson, *The Intellectual Resistance in Europe* (Cambridge, Mass., 1981), 25–77.
11. Letters from Rolland to André George, 7 January 1942, *BV*, 370–371; to Guéhenno, 4 January 1942, *JG-RR*, 395–396.

12. Letter from Rolland to M. and Mme. R. Mercier, 7 December 1944, *BV*, 382.

13. Romain Rolland, "Message de Romain Rolland lu pour lui en son absence à la Sorbonne à une séance solennelle de commémoration des intellectuels victimes de l'occupation," 9 December 1944, first published as "France et Liberté," *Nouvelles littéraires*, 5 April 1945; cited in Doisy, *Romain Rolland*, 203–204. Also see "Un Message de Romain Rolland aux *Lettres françaises*," in *Lettres françaises*, 16 September 1944, where he signed an appeal of the Comité National des Ecrivains.

14. See Doisy, *Romain Rolland*, 89–90.

15. See *Lettres françaises*, 6 January 1945; this episode is discussed in Otis Fellows and John Pappas, "Requiescant in Pace: Bergson, Péguy, Rolland," *French-American Review* 5, no. 2 (Fall 1982): 217–233.

16. Romain Rolland, "Le Testament de Romain Rolland," cited in Doisy, *Romain Rolland*, 205.

Bibliography

For a complete bibliography of Rolland's published writings see:

William T. Starr. *A Critical Bibliography of the Published Writings of Romain Rolland*. Evanston, Ill., 1950.

M. N. Vaksmakher, A. V. Paievskaya, E. L. Galperina. *Romain Rolland, Index bio-bibliographique*. Moscow, 1959.

WORKS BY ROMAIN ROLLAND

I. Novels

Jean-Christophe (1904–1912). Edition définitive. Paris, 1966.
Colas Breugnon, bonhomme vit encore (1919). Paris, 1969.
Clérambault. Histoire d'une conscience libre pendant la guerre (1920). Geneva, 1971.
Pierre et Luce (1920). Geneva, 1971.
L'Ame enchantée (1922–1933). Paris, 1967.

II. Theater

Les Tragédies de la foi: Saint-Louis (1897), *Aërt* (1898), *Le Triomphe de la raison* (1899). Paris, 1913.
Les Vaincus (1897). Paris, 1922.
Le Théâtre de la Révolution: Le 14 juillet (1902), *Danton* (1900), *Les Loups* (1898). Paris, 1909.
Le Théâtre du peuple. Paris, 1903.
Le Temps viendra. Paris, 1903.
La Montespan. Paris, 1904.
Les Trois Amoureuses. Paris, 1906.
Liluli. Paris, 1919.
Le Jeu de l'amour et de la mort. Paris, 1925.
Pâques fleuries. Paris, 1926.
Les Léonides. Paris, 1928.
Robespierre. Paris, 1939.

III. Biographies

François Millet. London, 1902.
Beethoven. Paris, 1903.
Vie de Michel-Ange. Paris, 1906.
Haendel. Paris, 1910.
Vie de Tolstoï. Paris, 1911.
Empédocle d'Agrigente et l'âge de la haine. Paris, 1918.
Mahatma Gandhi. Paris, 1924.
Beethoven. Les Grandes Epoques créatrices. 7 vols. 1928–1945. Paris, 1966.
Essai sur la mystique et l'action de l'Inde. 1. *La Vie de Ramakrishna*. Paris, 1929.
    2. *La Vie de Vivekananda et l'évangile universel*. 2 vols. Paris, 1930.
Péguy. 2 vols. Paris, 1944.

IV. Essays

"La Décadence de la peinture italienne au XVIᵉ siècle." Thesis, University of Paris, 1895.
Les Origines du théâtre lyrique moderne. Histoire de l'opera en Europe avant Lully et Scarlatti. Paris, 1895.
Paris als musikstadt. Berlin, 1905.
Musiciens d'aujourd'hui. Paris, 1908.
Musiciens d'autrefois. Paris, 1908.
Au-dessus de la mêlée. Paris, 1915. Republished in *L'Esprit libre*. Geneva, 1971.
Les Précurseurs. Paris, 1919. Republished in *L'Esprit libre*. Geneva, 1971.
Voyage musical au pays du passé. Paris, 1919.
La Révolte des machines, ou La Pensée déchaînée. Paris, 1921.
Ceux qui meurent dans les prisons de Mussolini. Paris, 1934.
Quinze Ans de combat. Paris, 1935.
Par la révolution, la paix. Paris, 1935.
Compagnons de route. Essais littéraires. Paris, 1936.
Comment empêcher la guerre? Paris, 1936.
Valmy. Paris, 1938.
Les Pages immortelles de J.-J. Rousseau. New York, 1939.
Le Voyage intérieur (Songe d'une vie). Paris, 1942.
Le Périple. Paris, 1946.
Lettres de Romain Rolland à un combattant de la Résistance. Paris, 1947.
Souvenirs de jeunesse (1866–1900). Paris, 1947.
"Gabriel d'Annunzio et La Duse." *Les Oeuvres libres*, no. 20, 1947.
Inde. Journal 1915–1943. Paris, 1951.
Journal des années de guerre. Paris, 1952.
Mémoires. Paris, 1956.

V. Correspondence

Cahiers Romain Rolland

Cahier 1. *Choix de lettres à Malwida von Meysenbug.* Paris, 1948.

Cahier 2. *Correspondance entre Louis Gillet et Romain Rolland.* Paris, 1949.

Cahier 3. *Richard Strauss et Romain Rolland. Correspondance et fragments du Journal.* Paris, 1951.

Cahier 4. *Le Cloître de la rue d'Ulm. Journal de Romain Rolland à l'Ecole Normale (1886–1889).* Paris, 1952.

Cahier 5. *Cette Ame ardente. Choix de lettres d'André Suarès à Romain Rolland (1887–1891).* Paris, 1954.

Cahier 6. *Printemps Romain. Choix de lettres de Romain Rolland à sa mère (1889–1890).* Paris, 1954.

Cahier 7. *Une Amitié française. Correspondance entre Charles Péguy et Romain Rolland.* Paris, 1955.

Cahier 8. *Retour au Palais Farnèse. Choix de lettres de Romain Rolland à sa mère (1890–1891).* Paris, 1956.

Cahier 9. *De la décadence de la peinture italienne au XVIᵉ siècle. Thèse latine de Romain Rolland.* Paris, 1957.

Cahier 10. *Chère Sofia. Choix de lettres de Romain Rolland à Sofia Bertolini Guerrieri-Gonzaga (1901–1908).* Paris, 1959.

Cahier 11. *Chère Sofia. Choix de lettres de Romain Rolland à Sofia Bertolini Guerrieri-Gonzaga (1909–1932).* Paris, 1960.

Cahier 12. *Rabindranath Tagore et Romain Rolland. Lettres et autres écrits.* Paris, 1961.

Cahier 13. *Ces Jours lointains. Alphonse Séché et Romain Rolland. Lettres et autres écrits.* Paris, 1962.

Cahier 14. *Fraülein Else. Lettres de Romain Rolland à Elsa Wolff.* Paris, 1964.

Cahier 15. *Deux Hommes se rencontrent. Correspondance entre Jean-Richard Bloch et Romain Rolland (1910–1918).* Paris, 1964.

Cahier 16. *Romain Rolland et le mouvement florentin de "la Voce." Correspondance et fragments du Journal.* Edited by Henri Giordan. Paris, 1966.

Cahier 17. *Un Beau Visage à tous sens. Choix de lettres de Romain Rolland (1866–1944).* Paris, 1967.

Cahier 18. *Salut et fraternité. Alain et Romain Rolland.* Paris, 1969.

Cahier 19. *Gandhi et Romain Rolland. Correspondance, extraits du Journal et textes divers.* Paris, 1969.

Cahier 20. *Je commence à devenir dangereux. Choix de lettres de Romain Rolland à sa mère (1914–1916).* Paris, 1971.

Cahier 21. *D'une rive à l'autre. Hermann Hesse et Romain Rolland. Correspondance, fragments du Journal et textes divers.* Paris, 1972.

Cahier 22. *Pour l'honneur de l'esprit. Correspondance entre Charles Péguy et Romain Rolland (1898–1914).* Paris, 1973.

Cahier 23. *L'Indépendance de l'esprit. Correspondance entre Jean Guéhenno et Romain Rolland.* Paris, 1975.

Cahier 24. *Monsieur le Comte. Romain Rolland et Léon Tolstoy textes.* Paris, 1981.

Other Published Correspondence

De Jean-Christophe à Colas Breugnon. Pages de Journal. Paris, 1946.
Hermann Hesse–Romain Rolland Briefe. Zurich, 1955.
Jean-Christophe et Armel. Correspondance de Romain Rolland et de Jean Bodin. Lyons, 1955.
Romain Rolland—Lugné Poe, correspondance (1894–1901). Edited by Jacques Robichez. Paris, 1957.
Richard Strauss and Romain Rolland, Correspondence. Edited by Rollo Meyers. Berkeley, California, 1968.
Bon Voisinage. Edmond Privat et Romain Rolland. Edited by Pierre Hirsch. Neuchâtel, 1977.
Correspondance Panaït Istrati–Romain Rolland (1919–1935). Cahiers Panaït Istrati. Valence, 1987.

Unpublished Letters and Manuscripts Consulted

Archives Romain Rolland, Bibliothèque Nationale, Paris.

WORKS ON ROMAIN ROLLAND

Georges Anquetil. *Essai sur Romain Rolland. La Beauté de son oeuvre et ses erreurs.* Paris, 1918.
René Arcos. *Romain Rolland.* Paris, 1948.
V. E. Balakhonov. *Romain Rolland, 1914–1924.* Leningrad, 1958.
Jean-Bertrand Barrère. *Romain Rolland par lui-même.* Paris, 1955.
———. *Romain Rolland, l'âme et l'art.* Paris, 1966.
Charles Baudouin. *Romain Rolland calomnié.* Paris, 1918.
Jean Bonnerot. *Romain Rolland. Sa Vie, son oeuvre.* Paris, 1921.
René Cheval. *Romain Rolland, l'Allemagne et la guerre.* Paris, 1963.
Paul Colin. *La Vertu d'héroïsme et Romain Rolland.* Brussels, 1918.
Ernst Robert Curtius. *Die literarischen Wegbereiter des neuen Frankreich.* Potsdam, 1918.
Maurice Descotes. *Romain Rolland.* Paris, 1948.
Marcel Doisy. *Romain Rolland (1866–1944).* Brussels, 1945.
R. Dvorak. *Das Ethische und das Aesthetische bei Romain Rolland.* Bottrop, 1933.
M. Elder. *Deux Essais: Romain Rolland–Octave Mirbeau.* Paris, 1916.
Pierre Grappin. *Le Bund neues Vaterland (1914–1916), ses rapports avec R. Rolland.* Lyons and Paris, 1952.
Otto Grautoff. *Romain Rolland.* Frankfort am Main, 1914.
H. Hatzfeld. *Paul Claudel und Romain Rolland.* Munich, 1921.

Werner Ilberg. *Traum und Tat. Romain Rolland in seinem Verhältnis zu Deutschland und zur Sowjet Union.* Halle, 1950.

———. *Der schwere Weg. Leben und Werk Romain Rollands.* Schwerin, 1953.

Pierre-Jean Jouve. *Romain Rolland vivant (1914–1919).* Paris, 1920.

Zofia Karczewska-Markiewicz. *Teatr Romain Rollanda.* Warsaw, 1955.

Marcelle Kempf. *Romain Rolland et l'Allemagne.* Paris, 1962.

Josef Kopal. *Romain Rolland.* Prague, 1964.

B. Krakowski. *La Psychologie des peuples allemand et juif dans les romans de Romain Rolland.* Toulouse, 1931.

Miriam Krampf. *La Conception de la vie héroïque dans l'oeuvre de Romain Rolland.* Paris, 1956.

Walter Küchler. *Romain Rolland, Henri Barbusse, Fritz von Unruh.* Würzburg, 1920.

Joseph Kvapil. *Romain Rolland—Son Itinéraire, sa place dans la littérature générale.* Prague, 1967.

———. *Romain Rolland et les amis d'Europe.* Prague, 1971.

Fr. Laichter. *Romain Rolland et Charles Péguy.* Prague, 1956.

Eugen Lerch. *Romain Rolland und die Erneuerung der Gesinnung.* Munich, 1926.

Arthur R. Lévy. *L'Idéalisme de Romain Rolland.* Paris, 1942.

M. Lob. *Un Grand Bourguignon, un grand européen.* Auxerre, 1928.

Harold March. *Romain Rolland.* New York, 1971.

Maurice Martin du Gard. *Feux tournants.* Paris, 1925.

Marcel Martinet. *Pages choisies de Romain Rolland.* Paris, 1921.

Henri Massis. *M. Romain Rolland ou le dilettantisme de la foi.* Paris, 1913.

———. *Romain Rolland contre la France.* Paris, 1915.

Jean Maxe. "Le Bolchevisme littéraire. 'L'Idole, l'européen,' Romain Rolland." *Cahiers de l'anti-France.* Paris, 1922.

W. Michel. *Essays über Gustav Landauer, Romain Rolland. . . .* Hanover, 1920.

T. Motyleva. *Tvorcestvo Romena Rollana.* Moscow, 1959.

Jean Perus. *Romain Rolland et Maxime Gorki.* Paris, 1968.

Jacques Robichez. *Romain Rolland.* Paris, 1961.

Alphonse Séché. *Romain Rolland, l'humble vie héroïque.* Paris, 1912.

Paul Seippel. *Romain Rolland, l'homme et l'oeuvre.* Paris, 1913.

Christian Sénéchal. *Les Grands Courants de la littérature française contemporaine.* Paris, 1934.

———. *Romain Rolland.* Paris, 1933.

S. Södermann. *Romain Rolland.* Stockholm, 1916.

Paul Souday. *Les Livres du temps.* 3 vols. Paris, 1913–1930.

William T. Starr. *Romain Rolland and a World at War.* Evanston, Ill., 1956.

———. *Romain Rolland: One Against All.* The Hague, 1971.

R. A. Wilson. *The Pre-War Biographies of Romain Rolland and Their Place in His Work and the Period.* London, 1939.

J. Ziegler. *Romain Rolland im "Jean-Christophe" über Juden und Judentum.* Vienna, 1918.

Stefan Zweig. *Romain Rolland, der Mann und das Werk.* Frankfurt, 1920.

———. *The World of Yesterday.* Lincoln, Neb., 1964.

SPECIAL STUDIES, ANTHOLOGIES, ARTICLES

Maxim Gorky, Georges Duhamel, and Stefan Zweig, eds. *Liber Amicorum Romain Rolland*. Zurich, 1926.

Der Romain Rolland Almanach zum 60. Frankfort am Main, 1926.

"Le 60ᵉ Anniversaire de Romain Rolland." *Europe*, February 1926.

"Romain Rolland." *Europe*, January–February 1955.

"Gorki." *Europe*, February–March 1960.

"Romain Rolland." *Europe*, November–December 1965.

Romain Rolland. Sa Vie, son oeuvre, 1866–1944. Archives de France. Paris, 1966.

Pierre Abraham, ed. *Romain Rolland*. Neuchâtel, 1969.

Bulletin de l'Association des amis du fonds Romain Rolland. Edited by Marie Romain Rolland. Paris, 1946–1984.

Index

Action Française, 38, 173, 187, 192, 199, 255; and assassination of Jaurès, 226; and assault on Blum, 259; and Orientalism, 117
Adler, Alfred, 277
Adler, Friedrich, 163, 164
Adler, Valy, 277
Aesthetics, 24, 86, 106, 222, 226
Alain, 280, 339n.43
Alexandre, Michel, 201
Algeria, 113
L'Ame enchantée (Rolland), 105, 344n.50; antifascism in, 147, 170–176, 201–202, 227, 246; anti-imperialism in, 173; Cartesian rationalism in, 228; fellow traveling in, 227–228, 230–235; and Gandhism, 173, 176, 234; individualism in, 170, 174, 230, 234; and Italian fascism, 234; justifiable violence in, 173; Leninism in, 173, 234; Marxist analysis of fascism in, 171, 175; and Marxist culture in France, 230–233; as mirror of Rolland's politics, 170, 172, 173; mysticism in, 227; as novel of engagement, 172, 173; pre–Popular Front politics in, 174–176; portrait of Mussolini in, 171–172; praised by communist writers, 237, 239; pro-Sovietism in, 173, 201–202, 230–235, 282; and social revolution, 234; worker-intellectual alliance in, 232, 235
Amendola, Giovanni, 136, 148, 149–150, 183
Amsterdam-Pleyel movement, 110, 158, 162, 164, 166, 181, 234; and anticapitalism, 162, 164, 169; and antifascism, 159, 165, 166, 168, 169, 170, 181, 187, 192, 202, 237; and anti-imperialism, 159, 160, 162, 164, 165, 166, 169; and antiwar activity, 159, 160, 161, 162, 166; and Comintern, 158, 162, 163, 168; and communism, 161, 162–164, 167, 170, 335nn.56, 58;

and French Communist Party, 159, 168, 169, 334n.50, 335n.56; and intellectuals, 160, 163, 164, 166–167, 192; leftist schisms in, 162–164; manifesto of, 165–167, 180; and pacifism, 161, 163–168, 170; and Popular Front, 158, 159, 162, 181, 187, 258; and pro-Sovietism, 237; and right wing, 335n.58; Rolland's declaration to, 164–165; and Serge, 245; and socialism, 161, 162–164, 166, 334n.50; Soviet control over, 163, 168–169; and Surrealism, 335n.58; as umbrella organization, 161; workers represented in, 163, 164
Anarchism: and Amsterdam-Pleyel movement, 161; and anti-Sovietism, 207–208, 210, 215–217, 274; and communism, 80, 90, 95; and engagement, 4; French, 104, 207–208; and Gandhism, 126; German, 184; martyrs of, 67; and pacifism, 115, 159, 197; and Rolland-Barbusse debate, 95, 98, 104, 108; Russian, 207; and Spanish Civil War, 351n.20
Andrews, C. F., 129
Angell, Norman, 47, 104
Annamites, 156, 157
Anticommunism: and anarchism, 202–208, 210, 215, 216, 274; and anti-Semitism, 280–281; and Gestapo's collusion with anti-Soviet left, 274; and liberal antifascism, 151, 153; and Machiavellianism, 230; and Nazism, 184, 185–186; and "Red Imperialism," 165–166; and Russian emigrés, 211
Antifascism, 6, 110, 135, 137, 147, 203–204; in L'Ame enchantée, 147, 170–176, 227, 234, 246; and Amsterdam-Pleyel movement, 154, 165, 166, 168, 169, 170, 181; and anticommunism, 151, 153; and anti-imperialism, 153, 155, 157, 159, 165; and antinationalism, 183; and anti-Semitism, 180–181; and

361

Yagoda, G. G., 244, 277
Young India (periodical), 119, 121, 129, 132
Yugoslavia, 171

Zangwill, Israel, 47
Zeldin, Theodore, 3
Zinoviev, G. E., 210, 254, 274
Zionism, 251
Zola, Emile, 4, 46, 297
Zweig, Stefan, 39, 60, 87, 104, 293

Compositor:	Huron Valley Graphics
Printer:	Maple-Vail Book Mfg. Group
Binder:	Maple-Vail Book Mfg. Group
Text:	10/13 Palatino
Display:	Palatino